Microfinance and China's Regional Development

Wen Xiao • Jiadong Pan • Wenwu Xie

Microfinance and China's Regional Development

The Case of Luqiao

Translated by Liang Cai, Fei Long, and Xing Zhao

palgrave
macmillan

Wen Xiao
Zhejiang University
Hangzhou, Zhejiang, China

Jiadong Pan
Zhejiang Institution of Administration
Hangzhou, Zhejiang, China

Wenwu Xie
Zhejiang University
Hangzhou, Zhejiang, China

Translated by
Liang Cai
Ningbo Tech University
Ningbo, Zhejiang, China

Fei Long
Changshu Institute of Technology
Changshu, Jiangsu, China

Xing Zhao
China Agricultural University
Beijing, China

The publication is sponsored by 2020 National Social Science Foundation (Translation Project of the Chinese Humanities and Social Sciences Academic Boutique), NO. 20WJYB003

ISBN 978-981-99-1959-8 ISBN 978-981-99-1960-4 (eBook)
https://doi.org/10.1007/978-981-99-1960-4

This Palgrave Macmillan imprint is published by the registered company Springer Nature Singapore Pte Ltd.
The registered company address is: 152 Beach Road, #21-01/04 Gateway East, Singapore 189721, Singapore

Preface

Over the past three decades of reform and opening up, China has risen to the world's second largest economy. In this process, millions of micro and small enterprises (MSEs) are largely credited for the rapid development of China's economy. According to the *National Report on the Development of Micro and Small Enterprises* released by the State Administration for Industry and Commerce, by the end of 2013, there were 11,694,870 MSEs in China, accounting for 76.57% of the total number of enterprises. If 44.3629 million individual industrial and commercial households were considered as micro-enterprises, MSEs then accounted for 94.15% of the market entities registered for industry and commerce. MSEs and individual businesses generated more than 60% of China's GDP, 75% of job opportunities, and more than half of China's export and tax revenues. In Zhejiang Province, for example, MSEs, with a workforce of more than 11 million, created more than half of the province's job openings, and 56.3% of its total industrial output. In recent years, however, MSEs get caught up in various internal and external difficulties. Due to China's economic slowdown, structural adjustment, and international economic downturn, MSEs' development has been severely affected. They fall victim to the crowding-out effect from large enterprises; especially against the backdrop of macroeconomic depression, all kinds of social resources tend to favor medium-sized and large enterprises. MSEs, with the workforce of more than 11 million, created more than half of the province's job openings, and 56.3% of its total industrial output. In recent years, however, MSEs get caught up in various internal and external difficulties. The fact that increasing amounts of social resources are distributed in favor of developed enterprises further erodes into MSEs' living space. In the process of development, MSEs still faced the crowding out effect of large enterprises, especially under the background of the depression of the macroeconomic environment. All kinds of social resources tended to favor medium-sized and large enterprises. The distribution of social resources also favored developed enterprises, which further squeezed MSEs' living space. Therefore, it is of strategic significance for the nation's economic and social development to offer quality financial services for MSEs and promote their healthy development to do a good job of financial services for MSEs because this is related to the overall economic and social development and has important strategic significance for the nation. However, there still exists a gap between the development of micro and small finance (MSF) and MSEs' financial services demands, which obviously does not match their great contribution to the national economy.

In recent years, China's MSF has witnessed some growth but is still lacking. Ideal microfinance needs to make financial support accessible to MSEs as well as urban and rural disadvantaged populations. The microcredit balance of the relatively larger 12 national joint-stock commercial banks, city commercial banks, and rural commercial banks, however, accounts for only 22% of the national banking loan balance. It is time for more resources to be distributed to serve entities with real financial needs. However, the rising costs of financing are partially responsible for the bottlenecks to MSEs' development. From the perspective of financial inclusion, financial institutions have not tapped the potential of the market fully. For a long time, small and medium-sized enterprises (SMEs) have been struggling with financing, with access to loans accounting for a mere 10% of the nation's total bank loan amount. SMEs, regardless of their industries, the life cycles of the industries, location environments, extension stages of the industrial value chain, asset scales, etc., are widely hit with financing difficulties; granted, they may face varying degrees of such difficulties, that is, the varying degrees of their "hematopoietic function". Looking into the origin of the issue, we can sum up the financing difficulties of SMEs in three major questions: "Who faces the difficulties?" "What are the difficulties?" and "Why are there such difficulties?"

Question 1: "Who face the difficulties?" To sum up, SMEs face the challenge of "3-3-3" structural financing. The top one-third SMEs are not short of money; they "never borrow money from banks", but rather draw upon abundant corporate funds to make private loans for quick returns. The middle one-third barely gets financing but usually with short term loans and seldom long-term loans. The bottom one-third have difficulty obtaining financing, even though they are in need. Such enterprises are usually unable to achieve "leveraged development" under the existing banking credit system due to light assets, no collateral, no guarantee, and unstable future cash flow. Meanwhile, they are denied access to development funds through direct financing channels owing to some entrepreneurial factors, such as unstable business models and lack of innovation, low market share and narrow market channels, slow product updates, and high imitability at the research development stage, great technical or managerial personnel mobility.

Question 2: "What are the difficulties?" Why is the financing difficulty of SMEs particularly prominent at present? What are the direct causes of their financing difficulty? First, changes in the internal and external economic environment lead to setbacks in their real operations and increased financing needs. Following the 2008 financial crisis, a large number of SMEs are facing deteriorating production and sales environments, brought about by the sluggish international economy and medium-high growth of the domestic economy. In addition, the rising costs of raw materials and labor further narrow their profit margin. Second, insufficient credits and over-high guarantee costs push their loan interest rates even further. The bottom one-third of SMEs share the characteristics of a higher asset-liability ratio, smaller assets, a larger proportion of intangible assets. But to acquire credit funds they need to enhance their credit level, so these enterprises of a low credit level have to pay a 2–3 points fee to a guarantee agency to get the much-needed credit funds, which undoubtedly incurs an extra burden on these companies already trapped in financing troubles. Third, the existing credit evaluation system of banks greatly limits the financing space of SMEs. Due to the lack of a mature and perfect evaluation system, most banks currently evaluate the credit qualifications of enterprises by "whether they have business dealings with small loan companies". More often than not, because they have financing relations with small loan companies, SMEs are regarded by banks as having poor financial conditions, and hence excluded from financing investigations. Fourthly, the widespread "loan transfer" and "loan withdrawal" in the capital market deal fatal blows to SMEs (loan withdrawal refers to the act of a bank lending to an enterprise but withdrawing the loan before the due time stipulated in the agreement because the bank thinks that corporate business runs into problems). Governments, industry associations, and organizations have tried to pull SMEs through their fund shortage phases by setting up "on-lending" funds. But on-lending funds can bring great risks because after the on-lent funds help the SME make repayments, banks must lend new money to reimburse the on-lending funds, otherwise, the on-lending fund provider will become the creditor of the SME, thus preventing the on-lending funds from their continuous operation. Fifth, the congenital defects of SMEs' irregular operations cause banks to be cautious about their financing. Most of the one-third of SMEs at the bottom suffer from imperfect financial systems and high employee mobility. Some of them even do not have clear financial statements. This strong information asymmetry leads to some banks' decreased loan willingness. At the same time, due to their imperfect operations and unstable business models, they can win no favor from medium and long-term VC or PE equity capital.

Question 3: "Why are there such difficulties?" SMEs' financing difficulty has long been a global challenge, but why is it so prominent in China? What are the underlying reasons? This is the third question of this book: What are the causes of the Chinese SMEs' financing difficulty? From the perspective of the evolution of China's financial system, financial development and innovation have been distorted by a long-time financial repression environment, while the development of the real economy has created a strong demand for sound financial systems in the process of continuous market segments and industry segments, and uninterrupted industrial transformation and upgrading. On the one hand, financial systems are suppressed; on the other hand, there are strong demands for financial institutions or systems, which eventually leads to the mismatch between the supply and demand of effective financial institutions/systems. Specifically, the structures of the banking industry, of the capital market, and the financial functions and operations do not match the financing needs of SMEs. In short, the fundamental cause of SMEs' financing difficulty lies in the lack of financial system innovation.

However, Luqiao District of Taizhou City, Zhejiang Province, has made extraordinary achievements in the development of MSF. In the past twenty years, through effective platform construction, close communication, and win-win cooperation, local financial institutions were supported and promoted to optimize financing services, enrich financing products, and improve financing systems for SMEs, realizing good cooperation between the regional financial institutions and the local enterprises and making Luqiao a national model of providing good financial services to MSEs. The Private economy in Luqiao was developed, with many SMEs encountering capital bottlenecks in their development. However, through the close cooperation of the Luqiao District government, banks and SMEs, the financing difficulties of SMEs in and Luqiao District have been effectively alleviated, and the development of MSF has enjoyed a good momentum. Luqiao has also established a cross-Straits micro and small financial service cooperation experimental zone, which effectively drew on the advanced experience of Taiwan and actively attracts Taiwan investments to solve the shortage of funds for SMEs.

The development of MSF in Luqiao District presents the following three major characteristics: First, Luqiao District is the pilot area of national private urban commercial banks. It now boasts three corporate banks—Taizhou Bank, Tailong Commercial Bank, Luqiao Rural Cooperative Bank, of which Taizhou Bank and Tailong Commercial Bank are two private local city commercial banks. As the only county-level district in China to have these financial resources, Luqiao has become a "vanguard" in the development of private city commercial banks in the country. Second, Luqiao District is a model of financial services providers to MSEs in China. Taizhou Bank, Tailong Commercial Bank, and Luqiao Rural Cooperative Bank persist in forging themselves as "partner banks to SMEs" and "growth partners to MSEs," focus on serving MSEs, self-employed entrepreneurs, family firms and farmers, and have set up a "simple, convenient and fast" brand of high-quality financial services in the country. Third, MSF has become the pillar industry of Luqiao District. In 2012, the financial industry contributed 11.1% of the total output value of Luqiao District, and paid taxes of RMB 1.25 billion, accounting for 22.3% of the total fiscal and tax revenues of the District. MSF has become one of the four golden business cards of Luqiao, which takes the development of MSF as an opportunity to actively build the District into "the capital of micro and small financial services in China".

This book focuses on the "innovative development of MSF", taking Luqiao District, Taizhou as a sample to extract and promote advanced experiences of the regional innovative development of MSF. Based on the theoretical research of MSF, this book analyzes the history and current situation of the development of MSF in Luqiao District and focuses on the *Three Positionings, Five Characteristics, and Three Models* of the innovative development of MSF in Luqiao to explore and summarize the connotations of MSF samples. Then, it analyzes the experiences and path of facilitating MSEs' development from five perspectives: the innovative development of small and medium-sized banks, the innovative development of non-bank financial institutions, the role of private capital, local government policies, and cross-strait cooperation. Finally, based on the research conclusions, the book envisions the future of the innovative development of MSF in Luqiao. This book is divided into five parts with a total of twelve chapters as follows.

The first part, Chap. 1, is a theoretical overview of the development of MSF. It combs the existing researches on MSF and lays theoretical support for the development of MSF in Luqiao District. First, it reviews the definitions and characteristics of MSF and pays full attention to the current hot topic of inclusive finance. Secondly, it reviews the research on the development of MSF and the current difficulties encountered in its innovative development. Thirdly, this part examines current academic theories on innovations and development of MSF and the relief of MSEs' financing difficulties.

The second part, with three chapters, is mainly a comprehensive review and analysis of the origin, historical background, and current development of MSF in Luqiao District.

Chapter 2 is about the historical changes of MSF in Luqiao District. It explores the development of MSF from the perspectives of the humanistic environment, economic development, and cultural changes in Luqiao. Firstly, this part investigates the backgrounds of the development of MSF, including humanistic, economic, cultural, regional backgrounds, etc. Secondly, it probes into the origin of the development of MSF in Luqiao. Thirdly, it highlights the foundation of MSF development in Luqiao. Finally, it divides the development of MSF in Luqiao into several historical stages and analyzes the development status and characteristics of each stage.

Chapter 3 makes a comprehensive and systematic review of the current situation and achievements of the development of MSF in the area. Firstly, it combs the current situation of the development of MSF in Luqiao. Secondly, it describes Luqiao's brilliant achievements in the process of developing MSF. Thirdly, it focuses on the positive impact of MSF on the development of Luqiao's real economy. Finally, it builds an evaluation system and selects Wenling in Taizhou, Yiwu in Jinhua, Yinzhou in Ningbo, and Lucheng in Wenzhou, the districts at the same administrative level, to evaluate the development of MSF.

Chapter 4 is about the Luqiao Model of MSF development. Based on the analysis of the current situation of MSF in Luqiao, this chapter digs deeper into the development of MSF in Luqiao and outlines a mature "Luqiao Model". Firstly, it analyzes the Three Positionings of the development of MSF in Luqiao. Secondly, it extracts Five Characteristics of the development of MSF in Luqiao from the aspects of business paradigms and coverage. Finally, it focuses on the three unique models of innovative development of MSF in Luqiao.

The third part studies the innovative development of MSF in Luqiao from five perspectives: the innovative development of small and medium-sized banks, the innovative development of non-bank financial institutions, the role of private capital, local government policies, and cross-strait cooperation. As the "top priority" of the book, this part is composed of five chapters.

Chapter 5 is about how small and medium-sized banks promote the innovative development of MSF in Luqiao. It elaborates the significance of innovative development of local small and medium-sized banks for the development of MSF. encountered in its innovative development. Thirdly, this part reviews current academic theories on innovations and development of MSF and the relief of MSEs' financing difficulties, the development of MSF from the theoretical perspective. Finally, through typical cases, it showcases how the innovation and development of small and medium-sized banks helps highlight the distinctiveness of Luqiao's MSF.

Chapter 6 is about how non-bank financial institutions promote the innovation of MSF in Luqiao. It examines the significance of innovative development of local non-bank small and medium-sized financial institutions for the development of MSF. Firstly, it explores the paths of non-bank financial institutions helping the development of MSF from the theoretical perspective. Secondly, it analyzes the development status of non-bank financial institutions and how they help with MSF innovation. Finally, through typical cases, it showcases how the innovation and development of non-bank financial institutions helps highlight the specialization of Luqiao's MSF.

Chapter 7 is about how private capital activates the innovative development of MSF in Luqiao. It scrutinizes the significance of reasonable guidance and utilization of local private capital for the development of MSF. Firstly, it explores the mechanism of rational utilization of private capital to help the development of MSF from the theoretical perspective. Secondly, it analyzes the "incorporation" of private capital and the current situation of private capital promoting the development of MSF in Luqiao. Finally, through typical cases, it showcases how private capital plays a "financing agent" role in helping highlight the highlights of MSF in Luqiao.

Chapter 8 is about how the Luqiao government promotes the innovative development of MSF. It studies the significance of local government guarantee for the development of MSF. Firstly, it explores the important role of government guarantee in the development of MSF from the theoretical perspective. Secondly, it analyzes the status quo of how the government's conducts and policies support the development of MSF. Finally, through typical cases, it showcases how the government's powerful guarantees provide powerful support for the innovative development of Luqiao's MSF.

Chapter 9 explains Luqiao's practice of cooperative innovation of MSF across the Taiwan Straits. This part, with its focus on the Cross-strait Micro and Small Finance Cooperation Innovation Pilot Zone, studies the practical experiences of cross-strait cooperation in promoting the development of local MSF. Firstly, it discusses the innovation mode of MSF cooperation between Luqiao and Taiwan. Secondly, a case study of the Cross-strait Micro and Small Finance Cooperation Innovation Pilot Zone is conducted to analyze how cross-strait cooperation promotes the innovative development of MSF. Finally, it puts forward a long-term plan for the development of the Cross-strait Micro and Small Finance Cooperation Innovation Pilot Zone.

The fourth part is about countermeasures. Based on the research conclusions, this part puts forward inspirations of Luqiao's MSF innovation, and extracts and promotes the advanced experiences of Luqiao's MSF development. Firstly, it proposes the "Luqiao secrets" of the innovative development of MSF and summarizes the characteristic practices and innovative experiences of MSF. Secondly, it detects the "Luqiao difficulties" of the innovation and development of MSF. Finally, it concludes the "Luqiao inspirations" of the innovation and development of MSF.

The fifth part mainly collates the news reports and innovative products of the innovative development of MSF in Luqiao to provide a practical reference for all parts of the country. It is divided into two chapters, with Chap. 11 being a chronology of the development of Luqiao's MSF, and Chap. 12 covering news reports and innovative products.

The innovations of this book can be summarized as the following three aspects:

First, a unique research perspective., with MSF in Luqiao taken as a sample. MSEs' financing difficulty, a long-standing problem, is not only a hot topic in academic research but also a key issue that the government pays attention to. A lot of research on MSF has been done, especially on its innovation modes and countermeasures, but few of such researches paid attention to the development of MSF in Luqiao. With the development of its private economy, Luqiao has constantly improved micro and small financial services and explored the development path of MSF with Luqiao characteristics, to ensure MSEs' healthy growth. The experiences obtained thus are worth promoting across the country.

Second, new research methods, with *dots*, *lines*, and *planes* woven together. The present research, based in Luqiao, digs into its local data, innovative services, and policy support to the development of MSF, by adhering to the research method of weaving *dots*, *lines*, and *planes* into one. The method of *dots* involves the analysis of typical cases of innovation and development of small and medium-sized financial institutions in Luqiao, that is, the typical cases of local small and medium-sized banks and non-bank financial institutions. The method of *Lines* involves, by constructing a corresponding evaluation system, evaluating the development level of MSF in Luqiao, and connecting the dots of and conducting a comparative analysis of the parallel districts such as Wenling in Taizhou, Yiwu in Jinhua, Yinzhou in Ningbo, and Lucheng in Wenzhou. The method of *planes* involves a comprehensive exploitation of the advanced experiences of innovation and development of MSF in Luqiao from the dimensions of enterprises, industries, financial institutions, and governments.

Third, novel research conclusions—from secrets to success to experience-based inspirations. Based on the exploration of the innovative development of Luqiao's MSF, this book delves into the root causes for the success of Luqiao's MSF development, grasps the "secrets to success", and proposes the "three inspirations". Meanwhile, given common problems encountered in the development of MSF, this book discusses the "six difficulties" in the development of MSF in the light of Luqiao's local experiences.

Zhejiang, China Wen Xiao
Zhejiang, China Jiadong Pan
Zhejiang, China Wenwu Xie

Contents

List of Figures

List of Tables

PART I

Theories

The right to credit is a human right. That is, everyone should have access to financial services. Only when everyone has the opportunity to enjoy financial services can everyone have the opportunity to participate in the development of the economy, can the common prosperity of the society be realized, and can a harmonious society and a harmonious world be established.

—Yunus the Nobel Peace Prize winner

CHAPTER 1

A Theoretical Review of Micro and Small Finance Development

The healthy development of micro and small enterprises (MSEs) is an important driving force for the sustainable development of a country because they play an important role in increasing employment opportunities, invigorating the market, and promoting scientific and technological innovation. With its status rising in China's economic composition, micro and small finance (MSF) has become the most dynamic part of China's financial system. There is a bulk of research on MSF at home and abroad, which offers different interpretations about its positioning, the difficulties, and its developmental measures, etc.

1.1 Features of Micro and Small Finance and Inclusive Finance

Definitions and Characteristics of MSF

Liu (2012) defines MSF, with precise figures, as a loan business whose target customers possess assets worth between RMB 10 million and 50 million, and each receives a credit extension of less than RMB 5 million. However, the current academic community generally believes that MSF is not only about micro and small loans. Liu and Tang (2010) point out that MSF refers generally to financial institutions' financing of MSEs, organizations, systems, economic units, and economic acts. Li

W. Xiao et al., *Microfinance and China's Regional Development*,
https://doi.org/10.1007/978-981-99-1960-4_1

(2012) points out that MSF is providing MSEs or low-income groups with small amounts of sustainable financial products or services. Such services include not only giving loans, but also equity, capital, savings, insurance, and other value-added services. The wide range of MSF institutions falls into the following five major categories—commercial banks, credit cooperative unions, non-profit organizations, NBFIs, and rural banks.

Since the 1970s, the micro and small economy has undergone profound changes, which comprehensively involve service clientele, business entities, and business modes, and greatly expanded the development space for MSF. Such changes have exhibited the following characteristics:

First, the clientele of MSF services keeps expanding. Traditionally, when it comes to the clientele, one would think of poor people, and the services include subsidy giving and governmental spending. But now the situation has changed. The clientele is mainly individuals or small enterprises who cannot obtain financial services through formal channels (Li Yang, 2012). MSEs have become the most important service clientele of MSF. How to define an MSE is not only related to its positioning and development in the financial market but also affects the preferences of national fiscal policies and the overall operation of the macro economy. According to *The Micro-enterprise For Self-Reliance Act*, a law enacted by the USA Congress in 2000, and *Micro-enterprise Enhancement* signed by President George W. Bush in 2003, micro-businesses include companies that employ no more than 10 people, or are run or owned by people living in poverty. The World Bank defines micro-enterprises as those with employees less than 10, total assets worth less than $1 million, and annual sales of less than $1 million. Enterprises with employees of 11 to 50, total assets between US $1 million and $3 million, and annual sales between US $1 million and $3 million are defined as small enterprises. In China, according to *Classification Standards for SMEs* stipulated by the Ministry of Industry and Information Technology, National Bureau of Statistics, National Development and Reform Commission, and Ministry of Finance in June 2011, SMEs are divided into three types: micro, small and medium-sized enterprises. The specific classification standards, as listed in Table 1.1, take into account the indexes such as the number of employees, operation revenue, total assets, etc. based on an overall consideration of 16 sectors.

Second, the products of MSF keep increasing. In the past, the products were mainly micro and small loans. After decades of development, they

Table 1.1 Classification standards for MSEs

Sectors	*Standards for small enterprises*	*Standards for micro enterprises*
Farming, forestry, animal husbandry and fishing	Operation revenue RMB 0.5–5 million	Operation revenue below RMB 0.5 million
Industry	Employees 20–300 and operation revenue RMB 3–20 million	Employees below 20 or operation revenue below RMB 3 million
Construction	Operation revenue RMB 3–60 million and total assets RMB 3–50 million	Operation revenue below RMB 3 million or total assets below RMB 3 million
Wholesale	Employees 5–20 and operation revenue RMB 10–50 million	Employees below 5 or operation revenue below RMB 10 million
Retail	Employees 10–50 and operation revenue RMB 1–5 million	Employees below 10 or operation revenue below RMB 1 million
Transportation	Employees 20–300 and operation revenue RMB 2–30 million	Employees below 20 or operation revenue below RMB 2 million
Warehousing	Employees 20–100 and operation revenue RMB 1–10 million	Employees below 20 or operation revenue below RMB 1 million
Postal	Employees 20–300 and operation revenue RMB 1–20 million	Employees below 20 or operation revenue below RMB 1 million
Lodging	Employees 10–100 and operation revenue RMB 1–20 million	Employees below 10 or operation revenue below RMB 1 million
Catering	Employees 10–100 and operation revenue RMB 1–20 million	Employees below 10 or operation revenue below RMB 1 million
Information transmission	Employees 10–100 and operation revenue RMB 1–10 million	Employees below 10 or operation revenue below RMB 1 million
Software and information technology services	Employees 10–100 and operation revenue RMB 0.5–10 million	Employees below 10 or operation revenue below RMB 0.5 million
Real estate development and operation	Operation revenue RMB 1–10 million and total assets RMB 20–50 million	Operation revenue below RMB 1 million or total assets below RMB 20 million
Property management	Employees 100–300 and operation revenue RMB 5–10 million	Employees below 100 or operation revenue below RMB 5 million
Leasing and commerce services	Employees 10–100 and total assets RMB 1–80 million	Employees below 10 or total assets below RMB 1 million
Other unlisted sectors	Employees 10–100	Employees below 10

have covered various financing items such as loans, guarantees, and insurance, and credit technology and financing modes have been constantly innovated. Li (2012) points out that MSF covers more than micro and small loans. Zhang, et al. (2013) find from their research on financial products for small enterprises in China's banking industry that financial products launched by commercial banks are actively innovating in terms of length of maturity and limit of loans, and the banks have developed signature products for specific sectors. In addition, many financial products combine the functions of "financing, business, and social interaction" into one, providing diverse services to MSEs. Li (2013) analyzes the financial products provided to MSEs by joint-stock commercial banks as represented by China Minsheng Bank and China Merchants Bank. Li believes the unique business modes of the two banks are the pilots for the industry. The enhanced service version 2.0 of Minsheng Bank no longer limits its services to small loans to MSEs but also provides settlement and household wealth management services. Merchants Bank's *"All Business in One Card"* provides MSEs with comprehensive financial services, including deposit settlement, transfer and remittance, salary agency, wealth management, and value-added financial services such as business travel booking, discounts, etc. Furthermore, besides credit technology innovation, new types of financing for MSEs are constantly being put into practice. Zhang (2012) analyzes Quanzhou City's supply chain financing model from the perspective of industrial clusters, which effectively solved SMEs' financing difficulty. Luo (2011) probes into the development and practice of SMEs' reciprocal guarantee financing with a case study of Yuchang, Shandong Province.

Third, the business entities of MSF keep diversifying. In addition to state-owned commercial banks and joint-stock commercial banks, small and medium-sized financial institutions such as urban commercial banks, rural credit cooperatives, rural banks, and small loan companies are playing an important role in solving the financing difficulties of MSEs. When discussing the concept of MSF, Liu and Tang (2010) point out that micro and small financial institutions include formal micro and small financial organizations, such as rural credit cooperatives, rural commercial banks, rural postal savings institutions, rural banks, small loan companies, mutual funds unions, agricultural insurance institutions, etc. and informal MSF organizations such as rural cooperative foundations, economic service departments, financial service departments, private banks, etc. Small and medium-sized financial institutions are natural partners to private SMEs (Chen Shixing, 2007), and at present, whether theoretically or in practice, the development of small and medium-sized financial institutions is being actively encouraged. In his exploration of effective measures for the development of MSF, Ba (2012) proposes appropriately extending financial market access and encouraging the development of such micro and small financial institutions as small loan companies, to achieve a sustainable development model for micro and small financial institutions.

Inclusive Finance

The term *inclusive finance* was derived from the concept of the *inclusive financial system*, introduced by the United Nations in the International Year of Micro-credit 2005, which means a financial system that effectively and comprehensively serves all social classes and groups, especially the poor and the low-income population. In 2005, the United Nations invited many experts to draft a blue book on setting up an inclusive financial system based on online surveys, expert interviews, and seminars and held a global conference to launch the system in Geneva in May 2005. The blue book describes the future of inclusive finance as such: Every developing country should build a sustainable financial system, supported by policies, legislation, and regulations, which provides its people with the right products and services.

An inclusive financial system should embody the following connotations: First, inclusive finance is an ideology. Professor Yunus, 2006 Nobel Peace Prize winner and president of Grameen Bank in Bangladesh, said that the right to credit is a human right; that is, everyone should have access to financial services. Access to financial services for everyone is crucial, as it enables widespread participation in economic development, fosters the achievement of common prosperity within society, and contributes to the establishment of a harmonious world. Second, the path to inclusive finance involves innovating the financial system, including system innovation, institutional innovation, and product innovation. Third, the main task of inclusive finance is to provide opportunities to the vast number of middle and low-income communities and even poor people outside the traditional or formal financial system and to make financial services accessible to the poor, low-income population, and micro enterprises.

International practices of inclusive finance include welfarism microfinance, institutionalism small loans, and other models. Welfarism microfinance features small loans with the nature of relief and poverty alleviation. It is not market-oriented and does not aim at sustainable development. A typical representative is the Grameen Bank (GB), which provides financial services mainly to poor farmers, especially women. Its backbone is farmers' mutual assistance panels, with the characteristics of "mutual help, mutual supervision, and mutual insurance". Institutionalism small loans emphasize institution building, market orientation, and sustainable development, with a typical representative being Unit Desa of Bank Rakyat Indonesia (BRI-UD). Unit Desa, established by Bank Rakyat Indonesia operated independently and administered regional people's banks, base-level banks, and village banks. As the primary operating unit, a village bank conducts independent accounting, determines its loan scale, term, and mortgage by itself, and implements the issuance and recovery of loans. Under the category of *Other Models*, there is the famous village bank model in Latin America. The model is supported by the overall credit of a village, and small loans are provided within the scope of the village. It operates like this: members of a village bank, usually composed of 30–50 members (over 95% of whom are poor women), independently decide deposit and loan rates, which are generally higher than those of commercial banks. A borrower's deposit must be higher than 20% of the loan he or she wants to borrow. The deposit is mandatory, and the size of the deposit determines the size of the next loan. At present, the village-banking model is put into practice in 3000 places in 25 countries. In addition, there is the Novaliches development organization model, a typical cooperative model, in the Philippines. It is a non-governmental organization established with the approval of the Philippine Agricultural Cooperation and Development Council. It accumulates funds mainly through attracting deposits and providing services and lends money to its members only. Under this model, after acquiring a certain amount of initial capital, organizers apply to relevant government departments for approval of registration. Then they recruit members by attracting deposits and collecting membership fees, elect the loan review committee and other divisions, and provide members with a series of services such as capital credit.

At present, international financial inclusion displays three major tendencies: The first is about the sustainability of micro-credit. The focus is shifting from micro-credit to microfinance, that is, a shift from a single credit service to the provision of more financial services to the public. The second is about the institutionalism of micro-credit. The focus is shifting from welfarism to institutionalism, that is, a shift of international microfinance institutions from poverty alleviation agents to commercial enterprises. The third is about the diversification of financial services provided by micro-credit. An international consensus is emerging as to the principles of regulating microfinance (industry)—distinguishing between prudential and non-prudential regulation and gradually loosening up regulation on microfinance interest rates.

China's Practices of Inclusive Finance

In recent years, China's inclusive finance has developed rapidly, especially in 2013, when explosive growth was witnessed in internet finance. Micro and small financial enterprises have "become internetized" in succession, seeking business innovation and exploring cooperative modes on the internet. In addition, since the establishment of the China (Shanghai) Pilot Free Trade Zone, financial institutions have frequently sought strategic layouts to provide financial services of the whole industrial chain to MSEs in the zone. These new practices have attracted the attention of the Communist Party of China (CPC) Central Committee and other sectors of society.

After the concept of inclusive finance was introduced in China in 2005, the Central Bank promptly promoted the piloting of commercial small loan companies in five counties in Shanxi, Shaanxi, Inner Mongolia, Sichuan, and Guizhou provinces. On June 19, 2012, former Chinese President Hu Jintao remarked at the G20 Summit in Mexico: "Inclusive finance is essentially an issue concerning development. We hope all countries will strengthen communication and cooperation, improve the level of consumer protection, and jointly build a financial system that benefits all countries and their people, to ensure that people in all countries, especially those in developing countries, enjoy modern, safe and convenient financial services." This is the first time that a Chinese leader officially addressed inclusive finance in public. On November 12, 2013, the third Plenary Session of the 18th CPC Central Committee approved the "Decision of the Central Committee of the Communist Party of China on Some Major Issues Concerning Comprehensively Continuing the Reform", which formally proposes "developing inclusive finance, encouraging financial innovation, and enriching financial market layers and products" (Article 12, Part III) (Table 1.2).

Table 1.2 An overview of China's inclusive financial system

Micro-credit	Institutions	Agricultural Development Bank of China, state-owned commercial banks, joint-stock commercial banks, rural credit cooperatives, postal savings banks, village banks, loan companies, small loan companies, small re-loan companies
	Businesses	Traditional small credit loan, co-guarantee loan, core enterprise guarantee loan, small amount guarantee loan, intellectual property pledge, receivables pledge, movable property pledge, equity pledge, land contract management right mortgage, collective forest right mortgage, agricultural science and technology patent mortgage, industrial chain financing, commercial circle financing, enterprise group financing
Insurance		Systems of policy-based agricultural insurance, commercial agricultural insurance, and agricultural reinsurance
Direct financing		In 2004 and 2009, the SME Board market and the ChiNext market were respectively launched. In May 2012, the Shenzhen Stock Exchange announced the "Pilot Programs of SMEs' Private Placement Bonds". On January 16, 2013, the national SMEs share transfer system operation, agricultural industry investment funds and agriculture-related enterprises were listed.
Others		Internet finance, private-capital-founded micro and small financial institutions.

As can be seen from the above table, currently micro-credit is still the main body of inclusive finance in China, but the number of financial institutions continues to increase, and financial products are constantly diversifying. Direct financing is developing rapidly, along with the formation of a multi-level capital market. Insurance lags behind other financial sectors but is starting to pace up. Internet finance begins to emerge as a major power. Private banks and other financial institutions initiated by private capital will appear onstage in large numbers.

1.2 Theoretical Review of the Development Dilemmas of Micro and Small Finance

MSEs witnessed rapid development in their early stages when a series of national supportive policies were introduced, but now they are faced with a huge shortage of capital supply in their development phase, and financing difficulties have become the biggest obstacle for them to enter a higher development stage. Ba (2012) mentions that China's financial reform has made great progress, especially in their financial services to large enterprises, but commercial banks have become cautious in their providing micro and small financial services due to the decline of both economic growth and MSEs' profitability and made no obvious response to financial departments' incentive policies. MSEs' financing difficulty, as a global challenge, attracts extensive academic research worldwide. Macmillan (1931) first raised the financing difficulty of small enterprises, which is termed as "Macmillan Gap" due to *the Macmillan Report*.

"Macmillan Gap"

Macmillan Gap refers to the huge capital deficiency caused by the shortage of financial resources for modern SMEs, especially in long-term financing. The UK Business Finance Council is the first to use the concept and put it in its government reports. To cope with the economic crisis in 1929, the British government appointed a committee led by Sir Macmillan to investigate the commercial and financial industries. In 1931 Macmillan submitted a report pointing out that in the financial system, despite providing guarantees, SMEs still had difficulties in raising necessary long-term capital. He also found that if its asset worth was less than 250,000 pounds (equivalent to today's 4 million pounds), a small business would encounter financing difficulty. The investigation found that the main reason for this phenomenon was the government, out of policy considerations, made the benchmark interest rate set by the central bank lower than the market equilibrium interest rate. As a result, a large number of SMEs closed down due to the huge capital allocation gap. Macmillan suggested that the government take a series of measures to survive the crisis. Hence, people refer to the financing barriers SMEs face in the financial system as the "Macmillan Gap". Once put forward, the term immediately attracted the attention of western governments and theorists. Since the birth of *the Macmillan Report*, a large number of survey reports on SMEs' development organized by the World Bank, such as *Small Firms: the Bolton Report* (1971), *Small Firms (Wilson Report)* (1979) and *Aston Business School Report* (1991), have confirmed the widespread financing gap of SMEs in many countries.

Macmillan Gap is essentially a market failure in the financial system. The so-called "market failure" refers to the phenomenon that in countries implementing a market economy, the market is unable to function properly in some fields or some problems occur so that resource allocation cannot reach Pareto Optimality. Seen from its characteristics and causes, firstly, Macmillan Gap is a state of "Pareto improvement". In a market with an emphasis on economic efficiency, the flow of capital should be directed by the demand of the market, and the market can timely attain the match between capital supply and demand. However, in the case of Macmillan Gap, SMEs, as capital demanders, do not effectively have the funds allocated into their hands due to the existence of financing barriers. Supply and demand is not coordinated and Pareto Optimality is not realized. Therefore, seen from its performance, Macmillan Gap is a kind of "market failure". Secondly, the core cause of the Macmillan Gap is that in the financial system, market forces cannot allocate capital to SMEs, i.e., the market is impotent here. Why is that? Under a market economy, financial institutions as economic entities are in pursuit of the maximization of their interest. On the other hand, the financial and management systems of SMEs are not well-developed, so it is difficult for them to obtain credit. With SMEs' weak guarantee ability, low-quality collateral, small but frequent single loans, and complex financing procedures, financial institutions hold that financing to SMEs involves high risks—great costs but low profits. They are more willing to deal with large enterprises with ample capital rather than provide funds to SMEs. As a result, it is difficult for SMEs to obtain sufficient funds from general financial institutions. Furthermore, SMEs are not well known. Even if they issue stocks and bonds, they are difficult to be listed. There are great obstacles for them to finance through the financial market. Thus, in the financial system, whether in direct financing or in indirect financing, market forces have not played an effective role in SMEs' financing. Thirdly, in the case of the Macmillan Gap, the underlying reasons why market forces do not play an effective role lie in the monopoly of large banks, insufficient information that banks have on SMEs, information asymmetry between banks and SMEs, and higher transaction costs. All these evidences demonstrate that Macmillan Gap is a market failure.

In China, research on the financing difficulties of SMEs started relatively late. In the 1990s, Chinese academia began to probe into the financing difficulties of small enterprises and contributed a series of monographs and literature on the financing of SMEs. At the present stage, research on the development predicaments of MSF in China focuses on MSEs' indirect financing predicament, direct financing predicament, private financial predicament, and credit system predicament.

Research on Indirect Financing Dilemma

Indirect financing here refers to the financing mode in which the funds of scattered entities are pooled together by financial intermediaries such as banks and then lent to the demanders by way of credit—mainly deposits and loans. According to the statistics, more than half of the total financing of SMEs in China is obtained through commercial bank credit, with short-term and small-amount loans, mainly used to meet temporary working capital needs.

Fan and Zhang (2007), focusing on asymmetric information and credit rationing, analyze the indirect financing gap of SMEs in China, and find that in recent years, as banks and financial institutions put emphasis on money safety and stability in credit activities, they tend to provide loans to large enterprises but implement credit rationing on SMEs under the same risk levels, which puts SMEs in financing difficulties. Wang and Zhao (2009) make a SWOT analysis on the indirect financing of SMEs and point out that China's SMEs face a large gap in short-term loans, and long-term loans are even more scarce. For 81% of SMEs, their working capital in a year can only meet part of their needs. Such indirect financing difficulties of SMEs are mainly caused by the following three aspects: lack of collateral, information asymmetry, and lack of credit guarantee. Yuan and Zhou (2010) analyze ownership discrimination in indirect financing of SMEs of different types of ownership in China from 2000 to 2006 and find in their empirical research that ownership discrimination of non-public SMEs in indirect financing was widespread. Lu (2012) analyzes the current situation and characteristics of indirect financing of SMEs in China and points out that financial institutions are reluctant to lend money to SMEs. The general principle of state-owned commercial banks is to give priority to guaranteeing large state-owned enterprises over SMEs. According to statistics, 60.5% of SMEs do not receive long-term loans of 1 to 3 years. Secondly, because loans to SMEs have the characteristics of high financing cost, small scale, high frequency, and weak credit guarantee, the operating and administrative costs of banks will increase. So banks often raise the interest rates of loans to SMEs. Compared with large and medium-sized state-owned enterprises, SMEs cannot enjoy preferential interest rates when borrowing. They even have to pay floating interest rates, which are much higher than those of large and medium-sized state-owned enterprises. Xing and Liang (2013) find that at present, loans to small enterprises account for about one-third of all loans from financial institutions. In other words, SMEs, which account for 99% of the total number of enterprises, share about only 30% of the total credit. SMEs' difficulty in getting loans is still a severe problem.

Research on Direct Financing Dilemma

Direct financing refers to financial behaviors in which suppliers and demanders of funds form a direct relationship of equity and debt through certain financial instruments (equity or debt). Direct financing includes equity financing and bond financing.

In terms of equity financing, enterprise stock listing financing is strictly restricted, because the capital market in China is still in the stage of development. Since most SMEs are at the start-up stage or the growth stage, it is difficult for them to arrive at the threshold of listing (Xing Lecheng & Wei Qian, 2011). And the main board market was designed to serve large and medium-sized state-owned enterprises, which excluded SMEs. By the end of September 2012, there were a total of 1437 listed enterprises in the main board market (953 in Shanghai and 484 in Shenzhen), which were large and medium-sized enterprises (Xing Lecheng & Liang Yongxian, 2013). Deng Qiwei (2011) points out in his analysis of the SME equity financing problem in China that the second board market in our country is still not well developed. Although in 2004 and 2009, the SME Board and the ChiNext markets were launched respectively, China's capital market system is not yet complete. To be particular, the threshold for SMEs to be listed is too high, with only a very limited number of SMEs meeting the listing requirements. Many SMEs find the strict supervision and management and information system unbearable, especially when the listing requirements of pegging a company's management level, profitability, and financing quota to its net assets make a large number of SMEs in rapid development difficult to get listed, shutting a lot of promising SMEs out of the capital market. Xing and Liang (2013) find through statistics that by the end of September 2012, there were only a total of 698 enterprises listed on the SME Board and 354 enterprises listed on the ChiNext market.

Bond financing is another channel of direct financing. There are many different kinds of bonds, but corporate bonds SMEs are allowed to issue are few, because the *Company Law* and the *Securities Law* of China have made very clear and harsh provisions on the company issuing bonds, which limits SMEs' bond financing channels, so the bond market is virtually closed to SMEs. To effectively alleviate the financing difficulties of SMEs, under the promotion of the People's Bank of China, the Association of Dealers issued the *Guidance on Collective Notes for Small and Medium-sized Non-Financial Enterprises in the Inter-Bank Bond Market*, and officially launched collective notes for SMEs. In 2011, the regional pooling and optimization debt-financing model was launched to promote product development through institutional innovation and to facilitate direct debt financing for more SMEs (Xing Lecheng & Liang Yongxian, 2013). However, there are still many problems. Jin Dan and Zhang Guoliang (2009) point out, when researching collective bonds of SMEs, that the main problems of collective bonds at present are guarantee difficulty, sparse trading after listing, and high entry threshold.

Research on Private Finance Dilemma

Private or informal finance is defined by the World Bank as financial activities that are not controlled by the central bank or regulatory authorities. It is a general term for financial activities carried out outside the national financial system in China. The main forms include Market Angels, private free lending, Rotating Savings and Credit Associations (ROSCAs), unions, rural cooperative foundations, microfinance, and private banks.

The research group with the Finance School of the Central University of Finance and Economics conducted surveys on SME financing in China in 2005 and 2011 respectively, which demonstrate that in 2005 more than 30% of SMEs nationwide chose informal financing, and the proportion increased by 10% in 2011. Also in 2011, a survey conducted by the All-China Federation of Industry and Commerce on the financing of private enterprises in the country showed that more than 90 percent of private SMEs could not get loans from banks, and nearly 62.3 percent of all private and family enterprises financed themselves through private loans. Shu, Zhang, and Yang (2011) find in a recent random sampling survey of SMEs in Wenzhou that it was difficult for SMEs to get formal financial support in the early stage of development, so they mainly relied on private funds. It can be seen that private finance plays an important role in the financing process of MSEs. However, at present, informal finance still has a series of institutional defects, including illegal financing, the legitimacy of private finance, and other issues. Deng (2004) points out that rural private finance is a "double-edged sword", with both positive and negative effects, among which usury exploitation, economic disputes, financial frauds, and latent financial risks are the major ones. Li, Wei, et al. (2013), based on the analysis of the problems existing in rural private finance, point out that at present the private financial interest rates are out of control. In addition, it is easy for private finance to breed illegal financial acts, such as individuals or organizations' illegal pooling of public deposits, loaning at unreasonably high-interest rates, and opening illegal underground banks, which may disrupt the financial market of the country. Xiong and Pan (2013) probe into the legal supervision plight of private finance and point out that China has yet to grant private finance the proper legal status. Only part of civil lending, urban credit cooperatives, rural credit cooperatives, agricultural banks and agricultural cooperative banks, microfinance, and pawn shops are taken as legal in our financial laws. In addition, when specific dealings of private finance are concerned, relevant laws, departmental regulations, and administrative rules offer only simple provisions, or they are low in legal effect, being superficial and not systematic.

Research on the Credit System Dilemma

A credit system includes credit rating and credit guarantee. Credit rating refers to a process in which an independent third party evaluates, through its technical advantages and professional experience, the credit risk scale of economic entities and financial tools, and produces expert ratings by making use of simple and clear symbols (such as AAA, BB, etc.). A Credit guarantee is a guarantee provided by a lawfully established guarantee agency to an enterprise (the debtor) according to a contract signed between the enterprise and a bank (the creditor) for a financing purpose, under which the guarantee agency shall repay the creditor the debtor's liability on condition that the debtor could not repay its debt so that the creditor's rights should be guaranteed.

In terms of credit rating, research mainly focused on the low participation of MSEs in credit rating, the difficulty in obtaining corporate information, and the lack of authority in rating. Zhang Ming (2008) finds based on his analysis of SMEs' credit rating realities that in credit rating SMEs' information is difficult to acquire. SMEs generally do not disclose their basic information, financial and financing information, etc. To obtain such information from public channels is more difficult; usually, it is only possible when the credit reference system is utilized. According to Liu Jice (2011), China's credit rating authorities' responsibilities are not clear at present. The National Development and Reform Commission, People's Bank of China, China Banking Regulatory Commission, China Securities Regulatory Commission, and China Insurance Regulatory Commission have all authorized rating qualifications of rating agencies in their respective regulatory areas. The market lacks unified management, and rating authority needs to be further improved. Pan Jingrong (2013) points out that SMEs' participation in a credit rating is not high in China. Most SMEs believe that credit rating is optional and regard it only as an honor, rather than as an objective and real reflection of their credit strength.

As to credit guarantees, research mainly focused on risk dispersion mechanisms, sources of compensation funds of guarantee institutions, and so on. Zhou and Luo (2011) analyze the institutional defects of the credit guarantee system for SMEs in China and point out that the supply mechanism of credit guarantee funds in China is unstable, and guarantee institutions lack effective risk dispersion and control mechanisms. Wang et al. (2011) point out that credit risk is the main risk SME credit guarantee agencies are facing. In a credit guarantee process for SMEs, banks/credit guarantee agencies and SMEs form a commission—agency relationship. SMEs as financing agents know very well of the actual investments and risks of the financed funds, while institutions providing credit guarantee to them know little of such information. At the same time, because credit guarantee agencies provide a guarantee in SMEs' financing and bear most of the risks, banks have no incentive to investigate the operation and reputation of these enterprises before lending, or they simply lower their judgment standards. Therefore, in guarantee rendering, there is serious information asymmetry between banks, SMEs, and credit guarantee agencies.

1.3 Theoretical Rationale of the Development Dilemmas of Micro and Small Finance

Since the 1960s, many scholars at home and abroad have begun to conduct theoretical and empirical research on the causes of MSEs' financing difficulties and have produced a series of mature classical theories. This section reviews and sorts out important literature on MSEs' financing theories. The main theories are credit rationing, information asymmetry, small bank advantage, ownership discrimination, and scale discrimination.

"Credit Rationing" Theories

Credit rationing refers to a typical phenomenon in the credit market, that is, (1) Among all the loan applications, only a part are granted, while the rest are not, even if they pay a higher price (interest rate); (2) The demand of a loan applicant is only partially approved, while the rest is rejected (Yang Zaibin & Kuangxia, 2003). Under a market economy, the financing difficulties of SMEs come mostly from the first type of credit rationing (Wang Xiao & Zhang Jie, 2003).

According to the traditional economic theory, it is the interest rate mechanism that controls the credit market. When the demand for loans is greater than the supply, interest rates go up. When the demand for loans is smaller than the supply, interest rates go down. When the market supply and the demand are equal, the interest rate is the only equilibrium rate, which clears the market and realizes the optimal allocation of credit resources. Only when there is the interference of external factors such as price control in the credit market, will the relationship between the supply and the demand become unequal, which is a temporary and unbalanced state. However, credit rationing is so abundant and so frequent in the credit market that it cannot be regarded simply as temporary. The earliest modern study of credit rationing theory was done by Roosa in the 1950s. In *The Financial Availability Doctrine* published in 1951, Roosa et al. proposed the Credit Availability Doctrine, emphasizing that credit rationing is a long-term disequilibrium caused by some institutional constraints (such as interest rate ceilings). After Roosa, some economists began to explore the causes of credit rationing, and as a result, the micro basis of credit rationing theory was gradually established. In the 1960s, the debate on the causes of credit rationing was mainly centered around market inadequacies. The representative figure was D. Hodgman, who argues in his article *Credit Risk and Credit Rationing* that banks face a group of borrowers with fixed income distribution. No matter how interest rates change, there is always a ceiling on the supply of credit. When the demand of borrowers exceeds the limit, credit rationing occurs. Since the late 1970s, the development of information economics provided a new opportunity for the development of credit rationing theories. Stiglitz and Weiss (1981) include information asymmetry in their credit rationing theory and point out that adverse selection and moral hazard caused by information asymmetry between banks and enterprises force banks, as rational entities, to implement credit rationing. Banks would rather reject some borrowers' applications at relatively low rates, that is, credit rationing, than approve all borrowers' applications at high rates. Therefore, the loan supply of banks is not necessarily a monotonously increasing function of the loan interest rate. Even under a competitive equilibrium, credit rationing may occur, and it can appear as a long-term equilibrium. Therefore, credit rationing caused by information asymmetry between banks and enterprises is an important cause of SMEs' financing difficulties.

Many domestic scholars also use credit rationing to explain the cause of MSEs' financing difficulties. Yang (2002) argues that private enterprises need to pay a non-interest cost in their application for a loan, which produces an adverse selection effect for banks. If a private enterprise needs to pay a high non-interest cost, then only risky private enterprises would venture to apply for such loans. As a result, high non-interest costs would increase the probability that it is difficult for state-owned banks to recover loans, which would lead the banks to implement credit rationing to private enterprises. Yang and Kuang (2003) use credit rationing to analyze the endogenous institutional source of state-owned commercial banks' credit rationing to SMEs. Because of the defects of China's financing system, state-owned commercial banks' credit rationing to SMEs could not be avoided even under the guidance of external policies. This rationing, to a large extent, is caused by the rationality of commercial banks, reflecting the outcome of commercial banks' enterprise operation. Wang and Zhang (2003) use a theoretical model of endogenous collateral and firm size to analyze the problems of bank credit rationing and SME loans. They find that in the process of credit rationing, banks excluded those SMEs and some high-risk enterprises whose asset size was smaller than the critical collateral value required by the banks. Chen and Zheng (2006), based on credit rationing theory and with China's current realities taken into consideration, designed a bank credit decision model incorporating factors such as collateral value, mortgage settlement transaction cost and bank reviewing cost, and concluded: In a non-competitive credit market with information asymmetry, credit rationing is the result of banks' rationality; SMEs are in a disadvantageous position in bank credit rationing and have difficulty in obtaining financing from banks. Su et al. (2011) explain the reasons for the financing difficulties of SMEs through a model based on credit rationing and point out that relational loans are a solution to the controversies surrounding credit rationing.

"Information Asymmetry" Theories

Scholars generally agree that MSEs' financing difficulties are caused by information asymmetry. Asymmetric information is a situation in which one party of a transaction or a contract possesses more information than the other. It can be divided in terms of time: when it occurs before the parties sign the contract, it is called an ex-ante asymmetry; when it occurs after the parties sign the contract, it is called an ex-post asymmetry. Game models focusing on ex-ante asymmetry are called adverse selection, while game models focusing on ex-post asymmetry are referred to as moral hazard.

Adverse selection refers to an inconsistency in business and risk management caused by information asymmetry between a capital supplier and a demander. In a lending market of information asymmetry, a bank cannot fathom investment risks in SMEs, so they raise interest rates, which would drive some SMEs of low risk and good credit out of the lending market. Those who remain in the market are the ones who are willing to pay high-interest rates, those with high risks but low repayment capabilities, so the average risk of banks' lending goes up. A moral hazard refers to the behavior that after a contract is signed, due to information asymmetry, one party of the contract makes the other party suffer losses by taking actions that are advantageous to itself without being discovered by the other. Due to information asymmetry between borrowers and lenders, borrowers always tend to choose self-serving but high-risk business strategies after obtaining loans, thus causing losses to lenders.

In the borrowing-lending relationship between MSEs and banks, the latter do not know about the former's financial status and credit records. Adverse selection and moral hazard caused by such information asymmetry make commercial banks, which pursue a unity of profitability, liquidity, and security of funds, cautious about the financing needs of MSEs, even inclined to ignore the legitimate demands for loans from a healthy segment of SMEs. There are many kinds of researches on the relationship between information asymmetry and MSEs' financing difficulties in China. Lin and Li (2001) point out that when internal funds cannot meet SMEs' capital needs, they must resort to external financing. In the case of information asymmetry, SMEs' financing choices are closely related to whether they can solve the problem of information asymmetry. Li (2001) mentions the serious information asymmetry between banks and enterprises and the relatively high moral hazard when analyzing the causes of financing difficulties for SMEs. Li (2002) points out that the vast majority of SMEs have their capital needs satisfied through indirect financing (mainly bank loans). China's banking industry is highly concentrated, and SMEs' small loan scale, serious information asymmetry and insufficient fixed assets combined leave big banks with "high cost, difficult mortgaging, big risk" when they lend to SMEs. According to Wang and Chu (2002), the information asymmetry between financing parties often leads to SMEs' financing dilemma of adverse selection and moral hazard when obtaining debt funds. Guo and Liu (2002), through research and analysis of cases in Wenzhou, point out that SMEs have a large demand for private finance, that there is a long-term interactive relationship between the private financial system and the development of SMEs, and that the development of private capital market can help alleviate the information asymmetry in the financing of SMEs. According to Lin and Sun (2005), SMEs usually do not provide transparent information or sufficient guarantee or mortgage, so it is difficult for formal financial institutions to effectively overcome the problem of adverse selection caused by information asymmetry, while informal finance has advantages in collecting "soft information" about

SMEs. Li and Cheng (2005) established an analytical mechanism for information asymmetry and SME financing, and believe that adverse selection and moral hazard caused by information asymmetry directly affect financing costs, financing structure, and financing behavior of SMEs. Yi and Zhang (2007) believe that due to information asymmetry, China's commercial banks often classify borrowing enterprises according to some simple and easily accessible information, which leads to the concentration of credit resources in the dominant market, while the vulnerable market is subject to credit constraints.

"Small Bank Advantage" Theories

The "Small Bank Advantage" theory was developed based on a negative correlation between bank size and SME loans. It holds that large financial institutions are generally more willing to provide loans to large enterprises. On the other hand, small financial institutions are more willing to provide loans to SMEs (Berger & Udell, 1995; Peek & Rosengren, 1998; Jayaratne & Strahan, 1996). Cole, Goldberg and White (1999) study small business loans of large commercial banks and find that a small business loan carried out by a large commercial bank is more based on financial indicators. Relatively, small banks pay more attention to the previous relationship with small businesses. Berger (1998) makes an empirical study based on the financing data of small businesses in the United States, which indicate that small business loans gradually decrease with the merger of large commercial banks, while small business loans increase after the merger of small banks. Strahan and Weston (1998) explain the above phenomenon as such: at the beginning of a merger, the risk-resistant ability of small banks is enhanced due to the diversified business structure, so that they can provide more loans to small businesses. However, with further expansion of small banks, the management becomes more complicated, and the capital capacity is enhanced. A greater willingness to lend to large companies leads to a further reduction in the share of small business loans. Berger and DeYoung (2001) analyze the data of China and conclude that the complex organizational structure and long decision-making chain of large commercial banks lead to a lower control efficiency of the headquarters over branches, which makes it impossible to effectively carry out financial businesses with SMEs by implementing relational loans.

Theories of "Ownership Discrimination" and "Scale Discrimination"

The theory of ownership discrimination holds that China's financial system discriminates against the non-public economies in terms of mechanism and institutional design, resulting in financing difficulties for SMEs which dominantly belong to the private economy. An external environment for the growth of the endogenous financial system is in great need (Zhang Jie, 2000). Yi (2000) believes that banks are predisposed to lending to large enterprises and discriminating against SMEs. Li and Yang (2001) believe that institutional and structural barriers peculiar to a transition economy are also important factors affecting the financing of SMEs. Yuan and Zhou (2010) analyze ownership discrimination in the indirect financing of SMEs of different ownership types in China from 2000 to 2006, and find in their empirical research that ownership discrimination in indirect financing of non-public SMEs is widespread. Zhang and Wang (2002) believe that the main reason for the financing difficulties of SMEs is the widespread scale discrimination in the market economy, not exactly ownership discrimination in the transition economy. Collateral and firm size are incorporated into the endogenous decision variables. It is found that scale discrimination is widespread in credit rationing. Zhang and Wu (2009) conduct a study on SMEs in the counties of southern Jiangsu Province and find that SMEs are more inclined to borrow from small banks and large banks pay more attention to such indexes as firm size.

Other Theories

Domestic scholars also try to explain MSEs' financing difficulties from the perspective of the insufficient development of small and medium-sized financial institutions. Lin and Li (2001) believe that China's large commercial banks occupy too many financial resources, while small and medium-sized financial institutions lag behind. Such a serious mismatch between bank formation and corporate formation inevitably leads to financing difficulties for SMEs in China. Li (2002) analyzes the relationship between the market structure of banks and the financing of SMEs under information asymmetry and concludes that currently based on a highly monopolized banking industry and an economy with relatively excessive capital, an introduction of small and medium-sized financial institutions will help ease the financing difficulties of SMEs and increase the overall social welfare. In addition, many researchers start with MSEs themselves. Wang (2011), after analyzing the internal causes of the financing difficulties of SMEs, points out that SMEs are lacking in self-owned capital strength, firm size, mortgaged assets, and internal management (especially financial management). As is known to all, MSEs' small size, development instability, and weak bargaining power constitute barriers to their production and operation and leave these enterprises in "short but urgent" financing demands, which contradicts the conventionally slow loan approval process of commercial banks and adds to MSEs' financing costs and risks (Wang Weifang, 2012).

1.4 Cournot Model for the Development Dilemma of MSF

Bank loans are the most important source of funds for enterprises. However, due to imperfect credit reference systems of micro, small, and medium-sized enterprises and their shortage of collateral, banks are more inclined to give loans to large enterprises, so loans given to micro, small, and medium-sized enterprises take up only a small proportion. In this case, small and medium-sized banks, especially small and medium-sized city commercial banks, play an important role in providing loans to micro, small, and medium enterprises. Because of their small scale, these banks are in a disadvantageous position in competing with large banks to serve large customers. Therefore, small and medium-sized banks, especially local small and medium-sized city commercial banks, tend to target SMEs as their customers. At the same time, small and medium-sized banks, rooted in local towns/cities, have a solid grasp of the economic development of the town/city and the credit statuses of the enterprises to reduce lending risks. The rise and development of small and medium-sized banks is not only a good supplement to the financing of micro, small, and medium enterprises, but also plays an important role in regulating the credit market and improving the financial market. This section will establish, based on Cournot Competition, an SME credit market model with different operating costs and information costs, and analyzes the impact of financial institutions' costs and loan market competition on market interest rates and capital allocation, illustrating the impact of the development of small and medium-sized banks on the credit market.

Suppose there are n SMEs in a loan market. Because there are a large number of enterprises, a single enterprise has little bargaining power in the loan market, i.e. it is assumed to be a passive recipient of the loan interest rate. Every business faces the same demand curve for loans. The curve of an enterprise tilts to the lower right, that is, the loan demand of an enterprise is inversely proportional to the loan interest rate. Suppose the loan demand of enterprise i is as follows:

$$l_i = a_i - b_i r_i$$

In the equation l_i is the loan demand of enterprise i, r_i is the loan interest rate, and b_i is the interest rate elasticity of the loan, or the sensitivity of the enterprise's loan size to the interest rate.

Let us continue to assume that every enterprise in the market shares homogeneity in loan demands, that is, the same interest rate elasticity for loans expressed as $a_i = a$, $b_i = b$, $i \in (1, 2, \cdots, n)$. Since it is assumed that each enterprise has accepted the interest rate of the market, the market demand function can be obtained by summation based on symmetry as follows:

$$l = a - br$$

where l is the total demand in the loan market, r is the market interest rate, and b is the interest rate elasticity of the loan.

Monopolistic Lending of Large State-Owned Banks

Suppose that all the funds in the market are supplied by a large state-owned bank, then the profit function of the bank is

$$\pi_m = l_m \left(\frac{a - l_m}{b} \right) - l_m r_d - l_m c_m$$

where l_m is the loan size and r_d is the market deposit interest rate. Since the deposit interest rate in China is under the regulation of financial authorities, let us assume r_d to be a constant and c_m the unit operating cost of the monopolistic large state-owned bank, and the first order condition of profit maximization is $\frac{\partial \pi_m}{\partial l_m} = 0$, then

$$l_m = \frac{a - br_d - bc_m}{2}$$

$$r_m = \frac{a + br_d + bc_m}{2b}$$

$$\pi_m = \frac{1}{b}\left(\frac{a - br_d - bc_m}{2}\right)^2$$

Competitive Lending by Large Oligopolistic State-Owned Banks

Suppose that all the funds in the market are supplied by two large state-owned banks, they run into the same market interest rate and operating cost, hence Cournot competition between them. Then the profit function of bank i is

$$\pi_i = l_i\left(\frac{a - l}{b}\right) - l_i r_d - l_i c_i, i \in (1,2)$$

where l is the total supply of market funds, l_i is the loan size of bank i, r_d is the deposit interest rate in the market, and c_i, which is assumed the same, is the unit operating cost of the two large banks respectively. The reaction functions of the two banks can be obtained under the first-order condition of profit maximization as follows:

$$\frac{\partial \pi_1}{\partial l_1} = \frac{a - 2l_1 - l_2}{b} - r_d - c_i = 0 \text{ and } \frac{\partial \pi_2}{\partial l_2} = \frac{a - 2l_2 - l_1}{b} - r_d - c_i = 0.$$

A Cournot equilibrium can also be obtained:

$$l_1 = l_2 = \frac{a - br_d - bc_i}{3}$$

$$r = \frac{a + 2br_d + 2bc_i}{3b}$$

$$\pi_i = \frac{1}{b}\left(\frac{a - br_d - bc_i}{3}\right)^2.$$

Now let us make some brief discussions on the above two types of markets with varying degrees of competition by large state-owned banks. First, if we assume that the unit cost of a large bank that monopolizes the lending market is the same as in the Cournot Competition market, then the total amount of money lent in the Cournot Competition market is greater than the amount lent in the market monopolized by a single bank, and the interest rate in the latter lending market is greater than that of the former lending market. Let's make a simple proof.

For the total capital, $l_1 + l_2 = \frac{a - br_d - bc_i}{3} > \frac{a - br_d - bc_m}{2} = l_m$

For the market interest rate, $r_m = \frac{a + br_d + bc_m}{2b} > \frac{a + 2br_d + 2bc_i}{3b}$.Q.E.D.

This result can be understood more generally as follows: Compared with a loan market monopolized by state-owned banks, a market with a higher level of competition has a larger capacity and a lower interest rate. In the current capital lending market for SMEs, between the interest rate and the amount of funds, the latter is perhaps more important in many cases and plays a critical role in the survival and development of SMEs. The conclusion of the above Cournot model is obvious—a reduction of the interest rate leads to a relative increase in the total amount of capital.

Second, the profits of large state-owned banks fall, and the overall social welfare rises. We can make a comparison of the profits of large state-owned banks in the two cases. If the unit cost is assumed to be the same, then

$$\pi_1 + \pi_2 = \frac{2}{b}\left(\frac{a - br_d - bc_i}{3}\right)^2 < \frac{1}{b}\left(\frac{a - br_d - bc_m}{2}\right)^2 = \pi_m.$$

So if there is a Cournot equilibrium, their profits become lower. It is concluded that a competitive capital market plays a certain role in restraining large state-owned banks in China from acquiring excessive profits and an optimal allocation of social resources can be achieved. If we measure overall social welfare from the perspective of total economic surplus, we can also find that Cournot competition brings fewer deadweight losses than a monopoly market does.

What follows is an investigation of a loan market with small and medium-sized banks on the basis that large state-owned banks run in a Cournot competition model.

Small and Medium-sized Banks' Entry into the Loan Market

Suppose a small and medium-sized bank enters a market where two large oligopolistic state-owned banks run under a Cournot competition model. Compared with the large state-owned bank, the small and medium-sized bank enjoys the advantages of more flexible operation and smaller information costs. Therefore, it has relatively lower unit operating costs in the lending market and is more competitive. Suppose that the unit operating cost of the small and medium-sized bank $c_s < c_i$, its capital supply is l_s, and other hypotheses remain the same, then its profit function can be put as follows:

$$\pi_s = l_s\left(\frac{a-l}{b}\right) - l_s r_d - l_s c_s.$$

The first order condition of profit maximization can be obtained as

$$\frac{\partial \pi_s}{\partial l_s} = \frac{a - 2l_s - l_1 - l_2}{b} - r_d - c_s = 0.$$

In this case, the form of the profit function of large state-owned banks does not change, and the response function can be

$$\frac{\partial \pi_1}{\partial l_1} = \frac{a - 2l_1 - l_2 - l_s}{b} - r_d - c_i = 0 \text{ and } \frac{\partial \pi_2}{\partial l_2} = \frac{a - 2l_2 - l_1 - l_s}{b} - r_d - c_i = 0.$$

The Cournot equilibrium is solved simultaneously as

$$l_1 = l_2 = \frac{(a - br_d - bc_i) + bc_s - bc_i}{4}$$

$$l_s = \frac{(a - br_d - bc_i) + 3bc_i - 3bc_s}{4}$$

$$r = \frac{a + 3br_d + 2bc_i + bc_s}{4b}.$$

Based on the above results, what can be further proved is that, as long as the unit cost of the small and medium-sized bank's lending is smaller than that of large state-owned banks in the lending market where the two types of banks co-exist, either because of transaction cost or information advantage, the overall capital supply, or the market capacity, will expand, and the borrowing rates will fall, from which SMEs can benefit.

Participation in Competition by Multiple Small and Medium-sized Banks

Assuming that in the Cournot competition model with two large oligopolistic state-owned banks, more than one (the number is *k*) small and medium-sized banks enter the lending market, and they have the same cost function, then competition among financial institutions in the loan market is stronger. Suppose the capital supply of each small and medium-sized bank is l_s^i, the cost function is $c_s^i = c_s^*, i \in (1, 2, \cdots, k)$, and $c_s^i < c_i$ when compared with large state-owned banks With other conditions the same as in case 3, the profit function of each small and medium-sized bank can be put as

$$\pi_s^i = l_s^i \left(\frac{a - l}{b} \right) - l_s^i r_d - l_s^i c_s^i$$

The first order condition of profit maximization can be obtained as

$$\frac{\partial \pi_s^i}{\partial l_s^i} = \frac{a - 2l_s^i - l_s^{i-} - l_1 - l_2}{b} - r_d - c_s^i = 0$$

where $l_s^{i-} = \sum_{i=1}^{k} l_s^i - l_s^i$.

Because small and medium-sized banks are assumed homogeneous, the following can be obtained based on equilibrium symmetry

$$\frac{\partial \pi_s^i}{\partial l_s^i} = \frac{a-(k+1)l_s^i - l_1 - l_2}{b} - r_d - c_s^* = 0.$$

Similarly, the response function of large state-owned banks is

$$\frac{\partial \pi_1}{\partial l_1} = \frac{a-2l_1 - l_2 - kl_s^i}{b} - r_d - c_i = 0 \text{ and } \frac{\partial \pi_2}{\partial l_2} = \frac{a-2l_2 - l_1 - kl_s^i}{b} - r_d - c_i = 0.$$

The Cournot equilibrium is solved simultaneously

$$l_1 = l_2 = \frac{a - br_d - (k+1)bc_i + kbc_s^*}{k+3}$$

$$l_s^i = \frac{a - br_d + 2bc_i - 3bc_s^*}{k+3}$$

$$r = \frac{a + (k+2)br_d + 2kbc_i + kbc_s^*}{(k+3)b}.$$

The above is a discussion of introducing *k* small and medium-sized banks into a loan market where large oligopolistic state-owned banks compete under the Cournot model, from which we can make two conclusions. First, compared with when there is only one small and medium-sized bank in the lending market (where large oligopolistic state-owned banks compete under the Cournot model), it can be proved that the total volume of market funds increases when there are *k* small and medium-sized banks in the market. The market share held by large state-owned banks decreases while that of small and medium-sized banks increases. In addition, interest rates, or the cost of borrowing for SMEs to invest, are further reduced, which will create favorable conditions for SMEs' short-term financing and long-term development. Second, under the homogeneity hypothesis, it can be proved that with the growth of the number of small and medium-sized banks *k*, or the increase of market competition, the total volume of loans by small and medium-sized banks will increase, while loan interest rates will decrease.

To summarize, generally speaking, with the institutionalization and generalization of market access, competition in the lending market, whether between large state-owned banks (case 2), or between small and medium-sized banks themselves, or between large state-owned banks and small and medium-sized banks (case 3 and case 4), intensifies. Consequently, to a certain extent, the capacity of the capital market will expand, and the price of money used will decrease. It is conducive to alleviating the capital gap of SMEs and to improving their development environment. Furthermore, it also plays a role in breaking monopolies, and improving the efficiency and structure of the entire financial market.

1.5 Non-bank Financial Institutions and Micro-finance

According to classical financial theories, a developed and effective financial system plays a vital role in the healthy development of the national economy. The positive effect of financial development on economic growth stems from the special function of the financial system, which can effectively allocate and optimize resources to make productive investments by different economic entities of better liquidity. Considerable theoretical literature has demonstrated that an increase in the number of financial institutions significantly reduces frictional costs and information costs, which in turn affects savings rates, investment decisions, and technological innovation. Many other studies employ different models and techniques to explore the relationship between financial development and economic growth, and the results show that a well-functioning and fully effective financial system has a positive effect on economic growth.

Many early studies defined the development of the banking system or the development of the capital market as financial development and used the development degree of the banking system/the capital market as an indicator of financial development. A large number of rapidly rising non-bank financial institutions (NBFIs), a crucial subset of the financial system, did not get enough recognition for their contributions to economic development for a long time. The relationship between NBFIs and economic development had not been fully tested until the twenty-first century when the contributions of NBFIs to economic growth are being paid attention to.

Most of the researches on NBFIs see them as variables of endogenous growth models and proceed to judge their impacts on the real economy. One of the more famous models is Stiglitz's, improved from Solow's. According to Stiglitz, there is information asymmetry in the financial market, causing adverse selection and moral hazard from time to time. The financial system can only convert part of the savings into investments, and this conversion renders cost. The more advanced the financial system is, the lower the conversion cost is. Earlier studies on NBFIs regarded banking institutions and NBFIs as two variables to measure the level of financial development:

$$\Lambda F(\Psi,\Lambda)......F_{\Psi}^{'} > 0, F_{\Lambda}^{'} > 0$$

where Ψ and Λ represent banking institutions and NBFIs respectively, and F is the financial development index—the derivatives of F with respect to Ψ and Λ are bigger than 0, indicating that when the number of banking institutions or NBFIs increases, the financial development index increases and the financial system functions become more refined. In a sound financial system, the cost of converting savings into investment is lower, and the degree of converting savings into investment is higher. The next step is to bring the financial development level index into the growth model.

Suppose that only capital *(K)* and labor *(L)* are used in production, and the output is registered as *(Y)*. Suppose that the production function conforms to the C-D function, then economic growth can be expressed by a total production function:

$$Y_t = AK_t^{\alpha} L_t^{\beta}$$

where Y_t represents the medium output of a time t, K_t the capital stock, L_t the number of labor force, A the technical conditions of the time t, and α and β respectively the output elasticity of capital and labor. In the model, α and β are assumed to be two constants, with $0 < \alpha < 1$ and $0 < \beta < 1$, so the principle of diminishing marginal productivity is satisfied.

Suppose that the production function is homogeneous, and both sides of the labor force are divided by the number of labor, then the relationship between the output per capita and the capital per capita can be obtained as

$$\frac{Y_t}{L_t} = A\left(\frac{K_t}{L_t}\right)^{\alpha}.$$

Using lowercase letters *y* and *k* to represent the averages, we can obtain:

$$y_t = Ak_t^a$$

In this function, under the condition that production technology and output elasticity remain unchanged, the per capita output level is a function of per capita capital quantity. The derivatives of both sides of the above equation can be obtained:

$$g_y = g_A + ag_k.$$

It can be seen that the average output level is equal to the growth of technological progress plus the multiplication of the growth of capital by the elasticity of capital output. At the equilibrium state, assuming that the marginal production efficiency is diminishing, then the elasticity of capital output is infinitely close to 0. Therefore, at the equilibrium state, the growth of per capita output is equal to technological progress.

Now let's consider the generation process of capital. We use the following formula to tell the formation process and agglomeration process of capital. The per capita capital accumulation equation can be expressed as:

$$\overline{k} = sF(\Psi,\Lambda)y - (n+\delta)k$$

where k is the differential of per capita capital stock with respect to time, that is, the change of per capita capital; s is the savings rate; n is the population growth; the model assumes that population growth is linear, and δ is the depreciation of assets. The equation states that the change in the per capita capital stock is equal to the portion of output used for savings multiplied by the savings conversion rate and then minus the portion used to compensate for capital depreciation and then minus the decline in capital due to population growth. $F(\Psi, \Lambda)$ can reflect the financial development of a country. F is affected by the number of NBFIs, and the marginal impact is positive. $y_t = Ak_t^a$ and $\overline{k} = sF(\Psi,\Lambda)y - (n+\delta)k$ form differential equations, by which per capita capital stock and per capita output at equilibrium can be obtained as follows:

$$k^* = \{sF(\Psi,\Lambda)A/(n+\delta)\}^{1/(1-a)}$$

$$y^* = \{sF(\Psi,\Lambda)A/(n+\delta)\}^{a/(1-a)}$$

The above equation provides answers to the core problems of economic growth and financial development. When the number of NBFIs increases, both the per capita capital stock and per capita output in the equilibrium state will increase.

This model is based on the equilibrium of the labor market, the capital market and the product market—the equilibrium of the product market guarantees that the output is equal to the sum total of savings and consumption, the equilibrium of the financial market guarantees that savings are converted into investment, and the stability of the labor market guarantees that the population is equal to the labor. But in reality, it is hard to meet the above conditions. The markets are usually in a disequilibrium state. Take the financial market as an example. As a result of the existence of information asymmetry, friction costs and information costs stay high. When there are abundant NBFIs, F will increase, and friction costs will be reduced to raise the level of social welfare and to improve the per capita capital and per capita output. The essential function of NBFIs is to reduce friction and information costs in the process of investment and financing. Their role in the financial system exhibits the characteristics of a quadratic function. When their operation costs are lower than the friction and information costs they bring, the increase of their quantity can improve social welfare. Conversely, when their operation costs are higher than the friction and information costs they bring, their quantity should be reduced. In view of the above, there should exist an optimal number for NBFIs. Let's set it as Λ^*. When the number of NBFIs is Λ^*, social welfare rises to an optimal state. A second order analysis between $k^* = \{sF(\Psi, \Lambda)A/(n + \delta)\}^{1/(1-a)}$ and $y^* = \{sF(\Psi, \Lambda)A/(n + \delta)\}^{a/(1-a)}$ shows that there is an optimal relation between the number of NBFIs and the number of financial institutions, which is to be elaborated as follows:

Firstly, there is a positive relationship between the number of NBFIs and the efficiency of the financial system. With the increase of financial institutions, the contribution of financial institutions to the system efficiency shows a decreasing tendency, formulated as:

$$F_{\Lambda}^{'} > 0 \ldots F_{\Lambda\Lambda}^{''} < 0$$

When the efficiency of the financial system is maximized, social welfare is maximized. When optimal social welfare exists, it must meet the following requirements:

$$F_{\Lambda\Lambda}^{''} \text{ " } F_{\Psi\Psi}^{''} > F_{\Psi\Lambda}^{''}{}^{2}$$

The above equation can turn into:

$$\frac{F_{\Lambda\Lambda}^{''}}{F_{\Psi\Lambda}^{''}} \bullet \frac{F_{\Psi\Psi}^{''}}{F_{\Psi\Lambda}^{''}} > 1$$

It can be seen that efficiency attenuation caused by the expansion of banks or NBFIs is larger than the impact of NBFIs on banks. In this case, the society shares optimal welfare. In other words, if the share of increasing one unit of bank capital is used to increase NBFIs and the efficiency obtained is higher than that obtained by increasing the share of the unit of bank capital, then optimal welfare exists. According to this interpretation, NBFIs are beneficial supplements to banks. Non-bank institutions have cost advantages in some areas and can obtain the information required by banks at a smaller cost in the process of investment and financing. If banks "outsource" this function, both parties will benefit.

1.6 Theoretical Research on the Development Strategies of MSF

At present, research on the policies addressing MSE financing difficulties keeps on emerging in large numbers. Different scholars cut into the arena from different perspectives. Based on a literature review, this section combs through and generalizes past research and does a policy summary from the angles of government support, the financial system, enterprises, and new financing patterns.

Policy Research Based on Government Support

Due to credit rationing, information asymmetry, and other problems, MSEs have difficulty in financing. To solve the problem of financing market failure, it is necessary to make use of the "visible hand" of the government. The government support system means that the government, to make up for the defects of the market operation mechanism, makes use of macro-control means to directly or indirectly engage in policy support in specific business fields, to create financing opportunities for SMEs and alleviate their financing difficulties. At present, from the perspective of government support, research on policy proposals for solving MSEs' financing difficulties is generally carried out as follows:

First, construct and improve the legal system for MSEs financing. Liu (2011) argues that although our country has promulgated the *SME Promotion Law of the People's Republic of China* and constructed related policy systems, these are not enough to create sufficient financing for SMEs. The State shall also establish and improve the *SME Development Act*, *SME Assistance Act*, *SME Technology Innovation Act*, and other related laws and regulations to protect the interests of SMEs. In addition to regulating and supporting SMEs' development, a series of legal systems for credit guarantee, direct financing and the legalization of private finance are also focuses in the theoretical circle. Liang (2005) points out that the guarantee trading legal systems which suit the development of the market economy should be built, the *Guarantee Law* be improved, and chattel mortgage guarantee systems introduced, expanding the scope of the movable collateral, allowing accounts receivable and inventory as collateral, setting up guarantee on ordinary creditor's rights, and introducing floating guarantee systems, to enhance the capacity of SME financing. Yang and Yin (2003) point out that relevant laws should be revised and improved to activate private lending and expand the financing scope for SMEs. Xiong and Pan (2013) emphasize that private finance should be given legal status in their discussion of the legal supervision of private finance.

Second, build and improve the government supervision system of MSEs. The government supervision system refers to the section the government sets up especially for the management of small and medium-sized businesses, such as the Small Business Administration of the United States, the Small and Medium Business Hub of the United Kingdom, the Small and Medium Business Administration of France, the Small and Medium Enterprise Agency of Japan, and its branches. Liang (2005), in his proposals for improving the financing environment of SMEs, suggests that a ministry-level unit should be set up to serve SMEs, with branches stationed in different places, These branches should be relatively independent of the government so that they can effectively exercise their authority in supervising the support of other government departments to SMEs. Such management agencies can provide economic, and policy advice, technical support, education and training for SMEs to strengthen their competitiveness. According to a survey, the government service most needed by SMEs in the financing process is information service (Yi Guoqing, 2001).

Third, build and improve the credit guarantee system for MSEs. The responsibility of policy-based credit guarantee institutions is to implement the government's policies to support SMEs and eliminate the obstacles of lack of mortgages or collateral when SMEs apply for commercial finance to improve their financing capacity (Li Juan, 2006). Qian Lijiao (2013) points out that government departments can encourage banks, guarantee institutions, and insured enterprises to establish risk-sharing mechanisms through financial subsidies, policy guidance, and other means to jointly bear risks. Governments at all levels should increase input and expand the scale advantages of guarantee institutions, to enhance their business development ability and risk resistance ability. In addition, a financially limited compensation mechanism can also be established. Every year, the government can allocate a certain proportion of funds to compensate policy-based guarantee institutions for their losses caused by invested guarantee funds. Wang (2011) points out that the government can set up a re-guarantee fund in the fiscal budget to improve the security and stability of guarantee institutions in operation and help them effectively spare risks.

Fourth, build and improve the financial support system for MSEs. The financial support system refers to government departments providing financial assistance to MSEs to relieve their disadvantageous position in the market economy, generally by means of tax incentives, fiscal subsidies, and government procurement. Yin (2011) stresses the need to strengthen the understanding of the functions of government procurement and, under the same conditions, determine a certain proportion of or give priority to the purchase of goods, constructions, and services from SMEs. In terms of fiscal subsidies, appropriate subsidies should be provided for the training and wage costs of SMEs' new employees, and subsidies should be provided for the expenditure of scientific research and development projects with fruitful results. Li in his study on fiscal policy support for SME financing, mentions that tax incentives for SMEs should be strengthened, unreasonable administrative fees be abolished, and fiscal subsidies such as employment subsidies, R&D subsidies, export subsidies, and venture investment subsidies for SMEs be increased.

Policy Research Based on the Financial System

First, actively encourage and develop small and medium-sized financial institutions and support MSEs' development. Banerjee et al. (1994) puts forward a long-term interaction hypothesis, believing that small and medium-sized financial institutions are generally regional enterprises, and long-term cooperation with local SMEs greatly reduces the degree of information asymmetry, so they are willing to provide services. However, large financial institutions lack this advantage. In consideration of risk aversion, they are more inclined to provide loans to large enterprises, but unwilling to provide loans to SMEs with asymmetric information. Therefore, the establishment of small and medium-sized financial institutions can help solve the financing difficulties of SMEs. Strahan and Weston (1998) also believe that small and medium-sized financial institutions have obvious comparative advantages in financing SMEs. Lin and Li (2001) point out that the cost and efficiency of financial services provided by different financial institutions to enterprises of different sizes are different. In the period of the planned economy, China established a highly centralized financial system dominated by large banks. Large financial institutions were inherently not suitable for serving SMEs, which inevitably led to financing difficulties for SMEs in China. Developing and perfecting small and medium-sized financial institutions is the fundamental way to solve SMEs' financing difficulties in China. Gao (2008) explains the "small bank advantage" of small and medium-sized financial institutions in financing SMEs and believes that small and medium-sized financial institutions are the best option for SME financing. Xing and Liang (2013) believe that small financial institutions play a very important role in solving SME financing. Whether it is Grameen Bank in Bangladesh or community banks in western countries, this holds true. The development of small financial institutions in China is lagging behind, which is the fundamental cause of SMEs' financing difficulties. We must vigorously develop community banks, rural banks, and other small financial institutions.

Second, actively innovate the financing system of commercial banks to support MSEs' development. At present and for a long time in the future, commercial bank financing is still the main external financing channel for SMEs, so we must make institutional changes to the loaning concepts and objects of commercial banks. Liang (2011) believes that banks can ease credit conditions through mortgage guarantee innovation and facilitate SME financing. Banks can transform the traditional fixed asset mortgage lending into comprehensive loan examination, which adds a financing channel for SMEs, especially those with good operating conditions and credit. Comprehensive loan examination means that not only are fixed assets used as collateral, but also previous taxes, export records, production and sales records, intellectual property rights of enterprises, and market share of products can be used as credit collateral for a loan application. Xing and Liang (2013) put forward four constructive suggestions for innovating the financing system of commercial banks: policy easing, targeted leniency, differentiated treatment, and new varieties. Policy easing refers to exempting business tax on SME credit businesses and reducing their income tax. Tax relief should be used to write off bad loans of SMEs, and a floating interest rate for loans to SMEs should be implemented to ensure that bank lending is tilted toward SMEs. Targeted leniency means the SME credit scale involves a targeted easing. That is, when they supervise the credit scale of banks and financial institutions, regulatory authorities should encourage the institutions to increase credit input to SMEs, and the scale is not counted in the total monitored scale or the loan-to-deposit ratio. Differentiated treatment is a differentiated supervision in which the risk tolerance of loans to SMEs can increase and the SMEs' non-performing loan ratio can be raised to more than 3%. New varieties mean that institutionally commercial banks are allowed to conduct credit technology innovation and develop more loan varieties suitable for SMEs. They can design credit products such as loans pledged by a warehouse receipt, by intellectual property rights, by management rights of shops, by accounts receivable, and so on according to the needs of the SMEs of different industries, different sizes, and different life cycles.

Third, open up direct financing channels for micro and small businesses to support their development. At present, with banks' reluctance to lend, it is increasingly important to open up direct financing channels for SMEs. Tang (2003), when discussing the difficulties and countermeasures of SMEs' direct financing, proposes that the fundamental way to develop SMEs' direct financing lies in the establishment of a multi-level capital market system, which refers to an open network-like capital market combination of the domestic main board market, the second board market, the over-the-counter market and the bond market suiting the SMEs of different sizes, different ownership structures, and different industry characteristics. Zhang (2009) analyzes the direct financing difficulties of SMEs from the perspective of a high listing threshold and difficulties in bond financing. He believes that a multi-level financing system with stock financing as the main body should be established, which includes financing from the domestic Shanghai and Shenzhen main board markets, financing from overseas second board markets like Hong Kong GEM, and actively creating China's second board markets, to serve SME financing. In addition, the bond market access threshold should be lowered to allow some SMEs with strong growth, great market potential, and high credit ratings to issue corporate bonds within the policy scope. Wang and Ma (2010), in an examination of the current situation of SME direct financing in our country, find that the existing SME direct financing market provides financing services only to high-growth high-tech SMEs, so there exist defects of a high threshold and a single trading system. As few SMEs can obtain loans through the direct financing market, it is necessary to lower the listing threshold of China's current direct financing market, accelerate the development of national unified over-the-counter market and legal private equity funds, so as to benefit more SMEs.

Fourth, improve the private financial system for MSEs to support their development. Private financing, as the main source of financial support for SMEs, plays an important role in SME financing. But the existing civil financial supports to SMEs lag far behind SMEs' financial demands. Therefore, the institutional guarantees should be provided to SME civil financing so that it can be innovated and make greater contributions to providing financial support for the development of small and medium enterprises. Yu and Li (2007) find through their case study in Hangzhou that there exists a strong symbiosis relationship between civil finance and SMEs. To create a good financial ecological environment, relevant laws should be formulated to protect the legitimate rights and interests of creditors and debtors, and to restrict too high interest rates in the civil financial market to avoid the spread of financial risks. The supervision of various forms of private finance should be strengthened to regulate its development and restrain adverse factors. Gradually, private financial organizations with a certain scale can transform into community banks or cooperative financial organizations to drive and stimulate the orderly development of private finance. Hai (2011) fully affirms the important position of private finance in providing financial support to SMEs. To deal with the illegal operation of private finance and other problems, he emphasizes that relevant laws and regulations should be formulated to further guide the standardized operation of private finance. For example, civil financing management rules, informal lending management rules and regulations, and other laws and regulations should be made to specify the rights and obligations of both parties, modes of transaction, conditions, and terms of contracts, interest rates, taxes, liabilities for breach of contract, etc. to regulate lending activities and avoid problems such as illegal fund-raising. In addition, civil finance should be allowed and encouraged to hold shares of formal financial institutions. For instance, civil finance can, according to their strengths and circumstances, acquire shares of city commercial banks, regional small and medium-sized commercial banks, rural credit cooperatives, regional investment companies, investment funds, venture capital funds, etc., which can improve the services of formal financial institutions and provide more financial support for SMEs.

Policy Research Based on New Financing Modes

At present, due to the imperfect financial system and financial market in China, MSEs are faced with financing difficulties in their development. To apply for loans from banks or to issue corporate bonds or stocks are means of financing commonly employed by large state-owned enterprises, but they are a nightmare experience for MSEs. How to innovate MSE financing to meet the capital requirements of domestic MSEs at different stages of development is an urgent issue for enterprise management and relevant government departments. It is also an important theme for academia.

First, innovation of the industrial chain financing modes: in an industrial cluster there are usually some core large enterprises whose upstream and downstream SMEs in large numbers assume the roles of suppliers and distributors. By making use of these core enterprises' strengths and credibility, banks and other financial institutions can provide comprehensive financial services to multiple upstream and downstream enterprises to promote stability and smooth circulation of these chains. Gou et al. (2009) carry out tentative research on the main factors restricting China's industrial chain financing, based on combing the intrinsic relations in the industry cluster—credit chain—financing chain and doing comparative analyses between the three basic modes of industry chain financing (accounts receivable, confirming storage, and transportation and warehousing financing). Zhang (2012) analyzes Jinjiang-made shoes and clothing industry chain financing in Quanzhou City, Fujian from the perspective of an SME industrial cluster. She points out that the industry chain financing model incorporates each link, including core enterprises, upstream suppliers, and downstream distributors, into one and effectively solves the problem of information asymmetry. She argues in this model,

SMEs, core enterprises, banks and logistics enterprises have established a mutually beneficial and complementary industrial chain financial platform and achieved a "multi-party win-win" cooperation.

Second, group loan financing mode innovation: the mode involves joint and several liability debts, as compared with individual independent loans, issued for urban and rural low-income classes and SMEs based on groups formed out of self-choice. A group loan has the following characteristics: first, compared with an individual loan, a group loan is used for the advantage of membership mutual insurance, which an individual loan does not have; second, the core feature of a group loan is the joint and liabilities guarantee, which ensures that members can fulfill their debts on time; third, such a group is generally formed spontaneously by SMEs based on mutual understanding and trust. Feng (2012) researches and discusses the current development situation of SMEs in China, the mechanism of group loans for SMEs, and the feasibility of their application in SME cluster zones. He finds that group loans, as a financial innovation, have great application value in solving the difficulty of SMEs obtaining loans.

Third, mutual guarantee loan financing mode innovation: small and medium-sized businesses in an industrial cluster pool their money, based on mutual trust, mutual benefit, and membership, to voluntarily form mutual funds and to set up mutual guarantee companies, which provide guarantee for SMEs in the cluster when they apply for a loan from a bank, and each year do a credit audit of the member enterprises. Wang (2008) believes after theoretical and game analyses that SMEs in an industrial cluster can form stable mutual guarantee associations (companies), which serve as the center of the cluster financing platform and help realize, under the existing market conditions, SMEs' direct financing through securitized assets and indirect financing from financial institutions through guarantee, alleviating the financing difficulty of SMEs in the cluster.

Fourth, SME collective bill financing mode innovation: the mode involves a debt financing tool jointly issued in the inter-bank bond market by two (or above) to ten (ten included) small and medium-sized non-financial enterprises with legal person status, under the rule of "unified product design, unified bill name, unified credit increase, and unified issuance registration", and agreed on to repay the capital and the interest in a certain period. It is an innovative financial product launched by the People's Bank of China and the National Association of Financial Market Institutional Investors in November 2009 to facilitate SME financing.

Liu et al. (2010) take collective bills of "agriculture, rural areas, and rural residents" SMEs in Shouguang City, Shandong province as an example and conclude its institutional innovations and breakthroughs. They hold that it is a unique way of financing, achieving a series of breakthroughs in SME financing—transitioning from loans to bonds, from one place to nationwide, from random individuals to groups, from assets mortgage to credit increase. In terms of financing scale, term, cost, and incentive, it has imposed a comprehensive effect that differs from traditional credit financing and serves as a reference for improving SME financing.

Policy Research Based on the Enterprise Itself

In addition to external factors such as financial systems and policy environment, the overall quality of MSEs also plays an important role in the development of MSF. At present, many theoretical researchers are committed to improving MSEs' credit records and financial management. Shen (2009) points out that improving their quality is an important way for SMEs to get out of the financing difficulty. He believes that SMEs should establish a sound internal management system as soon as possible, boldly absorb the SME business strategies and management experiences in developed countries, innovate their management systems, break through the traditional family management pattern, and establish a modern enterprise system. Meanwhile, they should accelerate knowledge and technology updates and enhance their development potential.

Li (2012) bases her analysis of SME financing on SMEs themselves. She believes that SMEs should first perfect their financial systems, improve information credibility and transparency, including a sound system of internal financial management to ensure that their financial statements data are factual and reliable, and formulate their data under the normative requirements of bank lending. Secondly, they should strengthen their financial management personnel construction by hiring or training professional financial managers. At the same time, the majority of SMEs should strengthen credit awareness, improve credit rating, and actively participate in credit rating and governmental crediting system construction. Bao (2013) puts forward some countermeasures to SME financing from the perspective of enterprise strategy. To survive in fierce competition and win their places in the market, SMEs must not stick to the old pattern of lacking management strategies and making quick money in whatever trade they find suitable. They should make in-depth analyses of business competition and careful evaluations of the strengths of their existing and potential competitors, then position themselves accordingly in the market and choose the trades which accentuate their development advantages. In addition, SMEs should carry out production cooperation among themselves, and form SME cluster organizations where they can adopt the mode of supply chain financing or the mode of enterprise joint and several guarantee liability loans to allocate funds and alleviate their financing difficulties.

1.7 Summary

A review of the above researches and theories helps highlight the related fields and aspects instrumental to this book, especially the development and evolution of the theories of MSF. It can be seen from the existing studies that scholars are more focused on large and medium-sized commercial banks than on small financial institutions, especially rural MSF. In addition, when discussing the development countermeasures of MSF, the vast majority of studies propose actively encouraging and developing small and medium-sized financial institutions, but fail to offer an in-depth exploration of how to establish and what to establish. Most of the discussions are superficial and generalized. The author of this book believes that the future trends of MSF research will be as follows. First, research on small and medium-sized financial institutions is still a hot topic. Since inclusive finance aims to establish a set of effective and comprehensive financial systems which provide services to all social classes and groups, especially the poor and low-income populations, micro-credit and small financial institutions are essential for this purpose. Second, research based on new varieties of financial products and financing mode innovation is still important. In the short term, problems such as banks' reluctance to lend and the lack of easy access to direct financing channels cannot be fundamentally solved, so the innovation of financing modes calls for urgent attention to provide an impetus for MSE financing. Third, research on the measures of financial system reforms will lay more emphasis on the exploration of private capital and other financing channels. Specifically, how reasonable policies are formulated to nurture and supervise private capital, and how private capital can lend support to MSF, are the issues that are worth domestic scholars' attention.

References

Stiglitz, J. E. & Weiss, A. Credit Rationing in Markets with Imperfect Information [J]. *The American Economic Review*, 1981.3.

Li Jidong. Development of Financial Services for Micro and Small Enterprises in the "Era of Big Data" [J]. *Chinese & Foreign Entrepreneurs*, 2013.10.

Yin Danli. On China's Present Financial Policy Supporting Small and Medium Enterprises Financing [J]. *Journal of Central University of Finance & Economics*, 2011.8.

Ba Shusong. Focusing on the Development of Micro and Small Finance in the Next Financial Reform [J]. *Focus*, 2012.6.

Liu Wenfang. On Solutions to Chinese SMEs' Financing Difficulty [J]. *Money China (Academic)*, 2011.5.

Yu Qun'e & Li Aixi. Empirical Analysis of the Co-existence of Private Finance and SMEs—Hangzhou Case [J]. *Journal of Financial Research*, 2007.12.

Liang Jun. Research on Financing Difficulties of SMEs in China [J]. *Reform and Opening*, 2011.7.

Li Hui. Analysis of Financing Problems Based on SMEs [J]. *Social Sciences Review*, 2012.2.

Zhang Baoshan. Zhang Xiaoni. & Dang Shan. Comparative Research on Financial Product Innovation of Small Business in Chinese Commercial Banks [J]. *South China Finance*, 2013.3.

Liang Bing. A Survey Report on the Development and Financing of Chinese SMEs [J]. *Journal of Financial Research*, 2005.5.

Wang Ning. Analysis of the Causes and Countermeasures of Financing Difficulties of Chinese SMEs [J]. *China Market*, 2011.7.

Shen Yong. Research on the Current Situation and Countermeasures of Chinese SMEs Financing [J]. *Contemporary Economics*, 2009.8.

Zhang Zuoqing. On Direct Financing of SMEs in China [J]. *Financial Perspectives Journal*, 2009.11.

Li Yang. Micro and Small Finance Is Not Just Micro and Small Loans [N]. *China Economic Herald*, 2012.6.

Liu Xingsai. Electronic Banking Application for Micro and Small Financial Business [J]. *International Finance*, 2012.10.

Wang Xiaojie. Relying on Mutual Guarantee Association (Company) to Solve Financing Problems of In-cluster SMEs [J]. *Statistics & Decision*, 2008.7.

Gao Minghua. On the Development of Small and Medium-sized Financial Institutions and the Financing of SMEs again [J]. *Financial Theory & Practice*, 2008.10.

Chen Shixing. On Development Motivation, Model and Countermeasure of Small and Medium-sized Financial Institutions in Zhejiang [J]. *Zhejiang Academic Journal*, 2007.5.

Li Dawu. On Causes and Countermeasures of SME Financing Difficulty [J]. *Journal of Financial Research*, 2001.10.

Li Juan. On Government Support Systems and Financing Difficulties of SMEs [J]. *Special Zone Economy*, 2006.2.

Luo Xia. On Mutual Guarantee Financing Mode of SMEs—A Case Study of Yucheng City, Shandong Province [J]. *Productivity Research*, 2011.8.

Liu Yunzhao. Yang Jinzhu. & Liu Zhongbo. Institutional Innovation and Breakthrough of Collection Bills in SMEs: A Case Study of Shouguang [J]. *Journal of Financial Development Research*, 2010.1.

Hai Ming. On Private Finance's Support to SMEs and Its Innovation [J]. *Theory Monthly*, 2011.2.

Bao Nuoming. On the Causes and Countermeasures to Financing Difficulties of SMEs—Analysis of Their Own Factors [J]. *Knowledge Economy*, 2013.7.

Xing Lecheng. & Liang Yongxian. On SMEs' Predicament and Way Out of Financing Difficulty [J]. *Journal of Jinan University (Social Sciences)*, 2013.2.

Yang Linrui. & Yin Liangpei. A Legal Perspective of SME Financing Difficulty [J]. *China Legal Science*, 2003.3.

Feng Zhangwei. On Group Loan Financing of SMEs [J]. *Journal of Jilin Financial Research*, 2012.5.

Tang Decai. Problems and Countermeasures of Direct Financing of SMEs [J]. *Modern Management Science*, 2003.10.

Yuan Cheng. & Zhou Peiqi. Ownership Discrimination in Indirect Financing of SMEs in China: Empirical Evidence from Double Difference Estimation [J]. *South China Finance*, 2010.12.

Fan Wangbang. & Zhang Meili. Economic Analysis of Asymmetric Information, Credit Rationing and Indirect Financing Gap of SMEs [J]. *Journal of Northwest University (Philosophy and Social Sciences)*, 2007.3.

Wang Yue. & Zhao Qingguo. SWOT Analysis and Countermeasures of Indirect Financing of SMEs [J]. *Modern Economics*, 2009.10.

Lu Gaoxiang. On Indirect Financing of SMEs [J]. *Co-operative Economy & Science*, 2012.3.

Guo Bin. & Liu Manlu. Private Finance and SME Development: An Empirical Analysis of Wenzhou [J]. *Economic Research Journal*, 2002.10.

Deng Dacai. Demand-induced Institutional Change and Institutionalization of Rural Folk Finance [J]. *The Journal of Humanities*, 2004.5.

Xiong Jinguang. & Pan Liqin. The Legal Supervision of Chinese Folk Finance [J]. *Journal of Chongqing University*, 2013.1.

Wang Xiao. & Zhang Jie. Bank Credit Rationing and SMEs Borrowing: A Theoretical Model of Endogenous Collateral and Firm Size [J]. *Economic Research Journal*, 2003.7.

Li Wei. & Cheng Jinhua. On the Feasibility of SME Financing Based on Information Asymmetry [J]. *The Journal of World Economy*, 2005.1.

Liu Lun, Tang Ruolan. Analysis of the dual transition path of China's credit market after reform and opening up[J]. *Finance Theory and Teaching*, 2010(1): 7–12.
Zhang Yanting. The Study of Financing Mode for Small and Medium Enterprises' in Quanzhou Based on Industry Cluster[D]. Huaqiao University, 2012.
Deng Qiwei. Analysis on the Problems and Countermeasures of Equity Financing for Small and Medium-sized Enterprises in China[J]. *China Business & Trade*, 2011(24): 115–116.
Zhang Ming. Research on Credit Rating for Small and Medium-sized Enterprises[J]. *Wuhan Finance Monthly*, 2008(2): 25–27.
Liu Jice. Credit Rating for Small and Medium-sized Enterprises: Issues and Suggestions[J]. *Credit Reference*, 2011, 29(1): 58–59.
Pan Jingrong. External Credit Rating for Small and Medium-sized Enterprises: Problems and Countermeasures [J]. *Northern Finance Journal*, 2013(4): 55–56.
Zhou Junxia & Luo Jun. Institutional Defects in Credit Guarantee System for Small and Medium-sized Enterprises and its Development Strategies[J]. *Enterprise Economy*, 2011(1): 29–31.
Wang Xiaojun, Liu Kai, et al. Risk and Control in Credit Guarantee for Small and Medium-sized Enterprises[J]. *Journal of Socialist Theory Guide*, 2011(6): 91–94.
Yang Zaibin & Kuangxia. An Analysis of the Endogenous Institutional Roots of State-owned Commercial Banks in Credit Rationing Behavior for Small and Medium-sized Enterprises[J]. *Finance and Trade Research*, 2003, 14(1): 26–32.
Yang Tianyu. A Study on the Institutional Barrier of China's Non-SOEs' Direct Financing[J]. *Economic Management Journal*, 2002, 28(20): 75–79.
Chen Xihua & Zheng Xiaohu. Credit Rationing: A Realistic Choice for Banks' Credit Decisions for Small and Medium-sized Enterprises during the Transition Period[J]. *Productivity Research*, 2006(8): 55–57.
Su Jun, He Jia, et al. Re-discussion of GEM and SMEs Financing-On the Basis of Lucas Paradox Consideration[J]. *Securities Market Herald*, 2011(6): 9–13.
Lin Yifu & Li Yongjun. Promoting the Growth of Medium and Small-sized Enterprises through the Development of Medium and Small-sized Financial Institutions[J]. *Economic Research Journal*, 2001(1): 10–18.
Li Zhiyun. Banking Structure and the Small-Medium Enterprise Financing [J]. *Economic Research Journal*, 2002(6): 38–45.
Wang Xuanyu & Chu Xiaoping. Studies of Private Enterprise Corporate Governance Structure Evolution Model[J]. *Economic Science*, 2002(3): 89–93.
Lin Yifu & Sun Xifang. Information, Informal Finance and SME Financing[J]. *Economic Research Journal*, 2005, 40(7): 35–44.
Yi Xingjian & Zhang Dechang. Asymmetric Information, Simple Classification, Credit Constraints, and Credit Concentration Coexist – A New Approach to Explaining the Incoordination of Credit Resource Allocation in China[J]. *Finance & Trade Economics*, 2007(11): 15–23.

Berger A N, Udell G F. Relationship lending and lines of credit in small firm finance[J]. *Journal of Business*, 1995: 351–381.

Peek J, Rosengren E S. Bank consolidation and small business lending: It's not just bank size that matters[J]. *Journal of Banking & Finance*, 1998, 22(6–8): 799–819.

Jayaratne J, Strahan P E. The finance-growth nexus: Evidence from bank branch deregulation[J]. *The Quarterly Journal of Economics*, 1996, 111(3): 639–670.

Cole R A, Goldberg L G, White L J. Cookie-cutter versus character: The micro structure of small business lending by large and small banks, in business Access to Capital and Credit, edited by JL Blanton, A[C]//William, and SLW Rhine, A Federal Reserve System Research Conference. 1999: 362–389.

Berger A N. The efficiency effects of bank mergers and acquisition: A preliminary look at the 1990s data[M]. Bank Mergers & Acquisitions. Boston, MA: Springer US, 1998: 79–111.

Strahan P E, Weston J P. Small business lending and the changing structure of the banking industry[J]. *Journal of Banking & Finance*, 1998, 22(6–8): 821–845.

Berger A N, DeYoung R. The effects of geographic expansion on bank efficiency[J]. *Journal of Financial Services Research*, 2001, 19: 163–184.

Zhang Jie. Financial Difficulties and Financing Sequences of Private Economy[J]. *Economic Research Journal*, 2000(4): 3–10.

Yi Gang. Why should we adhere to the prudent principle of monetary policy?[J]. *International Economic Review*, 2000(1): 47–48.

Li Yang & Yang Siqun. Small and Medium-sized Enterprises Financing and Banking[M]. Shanghai: Shanghai University of Finance and Economics Press, 2001: 8.

Wang Xiao & Zhang Jie. On the Bank Credit Rationing and Loan of Small and Medium-sized Enterprises[J]. *Economic Research Journal*, 2003(7): 68–75.

Zhang Longyao & Wu Tingting. Bank Scale and Bank Enterprise Financing-Empirical Study on Small and Mediumsized Enterprises in Southern Jiangsu[J]. *Economic Theory and Business Management*, 2009(8): 51–55.

Wang Weifang. Loan Difficulties of China's Small & Micro -Enterprises and the Countermeasures[J]. *Academic Exploration*, 2012(6): 92–94

Yi Guoqing. Research on the Government Management and Policy Support System for Small and Medium-sized Enterprises[D]. Hubei: Zhongnan University of Economics and Law, 2001.

Qian Lijiao. Research on the Current Situation, Problems, and Countermeasures of the Development of Credit Guarantee Industry for Small and Medium-sized Enterprises in China[J]. *Times Finance*, 2013(2): 108–114.

Banerjee P, Chandy J A, Gupta M, et al. The PARADIGM Compiler for Distributed-memory Message Passing Multicomputers[C]//Proceedings of the First International Workshop on Parallel Processing. Bangalore India, 1994: 322–330.

Wang Shumei, Ma Xue, et al. Analysis on the Development of Direct Financing Market for Small and Medium sized Enterprises in China[J]. *China Collective Economy*, 2010(10): 107–108.

Gou Wenfeng, Wang Jinfeng, et al. Exploration of Supply Chain Financing for Small and Medium Enterprises from the Perspective of Industrial Clusters[J]. *Development Research*, 2009(10): 71–73.

Xing Lecheng, Wei Qian, Wang Kai. Small and Medium-sized Enterprise Investment and Financing Companies: A New Way to Solve the Financing Difficulties for Small and Medium-sized Enterprises[J]. *Shandong Social Science*, 2011(1): 88–94.

Jin Dan, Zhang Guoliang. Reflections on Developing Collective Bonds for Small and Medium-sized Enterprises [J]. *Academic Journal of Zhongzhou*, 2009(5): 47–49.

Lin Shule, Zhang Shaqi, Yang Fengsu. Financing and Informal Finance of Small and Medium-sized Enterprises in the Post Financial Crisis Era: Empirical Evidence based on Private Enterprises in Wenzhou [J]. *Research of Finance and Accounting*, 2011(4): 59–61.

Li Yan, Wei Xiang. Research on the Current Situation and Countermeasures of Rural Private Finance in China [J]. *Journal of Anhui Agricultural Sciences*, 2011(3): 37–39.

PART II

Realities

We hold that diligence, honesty, boldness, and initiative are roads and bridges leading to business successes under the sun.

—Luqiao (meaning road and bridge) spirit

CHAPTER 2

The Historical Changes of Microfinance in Luqiao District

In China's transition from a planned financial system to a market one, there is a gradual process for the market to act as a fundamental resource allocator and provide institutional supply. The state-owned financial enterprises, which are the main market players, can only provide the institutional supply of some specific businesses before they become the self-developing and self-restraining "economic person", while the basic financial system, operation mechanism, and management system need to be provided by the government. However, microfinance in Luqiao shows different characteristics due to its unique development background and foundation. The evolution of microfinance in Luqiao District has gone through three periods, namely, the pilot stage from 1988 to 2001, the development stage from 2002 to 2010, and the rapid development stage of cooperation between securities and banks from 2011 to the present.

2.1 Development Background of Microfinance in Luqiao

Luqiao Folk Customs: From Wu-Yue Culture to Yangtze River Delta Civilization

Luqiao, formerly known as "Xin'an", was affiliated with Lingshan Township, and then to Huijie in Qin Dynasty (222 AD). Under the regnal title of Jianwu in the Eastern Han Dynasty (25–36 AD), it was affiliated

W. Xiao et al., *Microfinance and China's Regional Development*,
https://doi.org/10.1007/978-981-99-1960-4_2

with Zhang'an County (later changed to Linhai County). In the second year of the Shangyuan title of Emperor Tang Gaozong (675 AD), Luqiao was affiliated with Yongning County which was separated from Linhai County and later changed to Huangyan County in the first year of the Tianshou title during the rule of Emperess Wu Zetian (690 AD). Since then, Luqiao remained affiliated with Huangyan County. However, in 1994, approved by the State Council, Taizhou was restructured as a city, and Luqiao was separated from Huangyan to become a prefecture-level city district, and then one of the urban areas of Taizhou. Its total area is 274 square kilometers, with a total population of 616,600 people (according to the Sixth National Census in 2010). Luqiao District has jurisdiction over 6 streets and 4 towns: Lunan Street, Luqiao Street, Lubei Street, Luoyang Street, Tongyu Street, Fengjiang Street, Xinqiao Town, Hengjie Town, Jinqing Town, and Pengjie Town, with the District People's Government stationed in Guanlin Village, Lubei Street. Luqiao District is among the first national model regions of the strong intellectual property counties project and the first pilot counties of provincial private financing management innovation.

Luqiao, once called Xin'an before the Northern Song Dynasty, got its present name in the Southern Song Dynasty. Legend has it that Zhao Gou, Emperor Gaozong of the Southern Song Dynasty, was chased by enemy soldiers and sailed to the mouth of the Jiaojiang River on the lunar New Year's Day of the fourth year of the regnal title Jianyan (1130 AD). With the enemy at his tail at sea, Zhao Gou disembarked at Sanjiangkou at night eight days later. Then, he entered Bailongao Village by way of Shanxialang Village and stayed overnight at the Zhusha Temple (later renamed the Yinju Temple). Later, the Emperor and his subjects went over Baishi Ridge and entered the Luqiao area. They got drenched in the heavy rain and sought shelter in Butou Hall. But once they were out of the shelter, the Emperor's horse was ridden to exhaustion and fell. He was extremely anxious, and only managed to escape by having his men build makeshift bridges under the guidance of a local old man. Relieved, Zhao Gou asked about the name of the place. The local official immediately seized the opportunity to say, "Please name this place, Your Majesty!". Zhao thought for a while and said, "Here the roads are bridges and the bridges are roads, so call it 'Luqiao (meaning "Roads and Bridges")'." Hence, the name "Luqiao" was coined.

Luqiao District, located in the coastal area of southeastern Zhejiang Province and at the foot of the mountains, has been a prime location for coastal traffic since ancient times. Luqiao civilization revolves around the five mountains in the district—Lingshan Mountain, Fenjiangmeiyu Mountain, Renfeng Mountain, Gonghe Mountain, and Zulang Mountain, offering a glimpse into the living conditions of the ancestors who lived in the mountains. Although its geography makes land transportation difficult, the region "has long enjoyed the traditions of short hair, tattooed foreheads, dyed black teeth, divination with copper drums and chicken bones, nesting, great crafts with boats and water battles, etc." As a result, waterway traffic is very developed, exposing the ancestors of Luqiao to the culture of the Central Plains at an early stage. In the whole Taizhou area, these ancestors' degree of enlightenment in Luqiao District came in first. The ancestors are mainly of "Ouyue origin", according to the States and Languages: Yue (one chapter of the book which gives an account of the history of the State of Yue during the Warring States Period): "The area under Lord Goujian's reign was a hundred miles wide, with Juwu (now Zhuji City) at the south, Yu'er (now Chongde County, Tongxiang City) at the north, Yin (now Ningbo City) at the east, and Gumie (now Longyou County) at the west. " Since Lord Goujian of Yue annexed the State of Wu in 475 B.C., Luqiao was officially under the jurisdiction of the State of Yue. Industry and commerce in Luqiao gradually prospered at the end of the Qing Dynasty and the Republic of China, but as early as the Wu-Yue period, there was a prototype of industry and commerce. The Wu-Yue ancestors were skilled at rice cultivation and smelting, developed mulberry farming and sericulture, and traded cloth and grains in the bazaar, sprouting primitive industry and commerce.

Luqiao, with Linhai City in the north, Haimen District in the east, the County Center in the west, and Zeguo Town in the south, is at the intersection between Huang and Wen counties, and thus the main traffic and communications route connecting the north and south of Taizhou. As for land transportation, Luqiao is an indispensable section of the Huang Yan—Zeguo—Luqiao—Jiaojiang highway, especially playing an important role in connecting the southern region of Taizhou. Throughout its history, Luqiao witnessed both its prosperity and decline because of water. During the reign of Qian Liu (907–932 A.D.), King of Wu Yue in the Five Dynasties and Ten Kingdoms era, the Official River was dug in the Huangyan area. Luqiao District (then called Lingshan Mountain Township), located in the golden middle section of the longest southward official riverway, enjoyed the benefits of irrigation and convenient transportation. However, due to its coastal geography, the district suffered from Japanese piracy during the Ming Dynasty; its people were displaced, and the fishing industry and sea-bound commerce were forcibly interrupted. It was not until the imperial government eliminated Japanese pirates that the people were able to return to their hometown. Taizhou City, which Luqiao is a part of, enjoys a long coastline and excellent harbors and has traditionally been a maritime gateway for foreign interactions. As early as 230 A.D., Sun Quan, the King of Eastern Wu, dispatched his generals Wei Wen and Zhuge Zhi to operate and govern Yizhou (now Taiwan) with an army of more than 20,000 soldiers from Taizhou (now Zhang'an county on the northern shore of Haimen port in the downtown), marking the beginning of the mainland's exercise of jurisdiction over Taiwan. At present, there are 21 ports of various sizes in Taizhou, mainly consisting of three bays and three harbors, namely, Haimen Port in Taizhou Bay, Jiantiao Port in Sanmen Bay, and Damaiyu Port in Yueqing Bay. Haimen port, located downtown and with a history of more than 1000 years, witnessed Japanese merchant ships sailing in and out of the port during the reign of Emperor Song Lizong in the Southern Song Dynasty. Since the nineteenth century, it has become an important maritime trade port along the southeast coast of China.

Yue Culture, in the process of blending with the China Central Plains Culture over generations, gradually transformed from a penchant for "gallantry and valiancy" to an aesthetic pursuit of "genteel spirit and scholarly temperament". After the Southern Song Dynasty, the pursuit of refinement and elegance in Yue Culture became increasingly obvious. The sprouting of modern industry and commerce gradually led to the emergence of "Shanghai-school culture" and "extravagant ethos". Now, against the backdrop of the development of the Yangtze River Delta civilization, Locals in Luqiao, even all the Zhejiangese, project the social ethos of inclusiveness and diversity, resourcefulness and wisdom. The life attitude of pragmatism and truthfulness and relentless pursuit of trailblazing and innovation are gradually becoming synonymous with the Yangtze River Delta civilization.

However, the prosperity of the Luqiao industry and commerce mainly appeared in the Qing Dynasty. This period saw the emergence of the earliest commercial organization in Luqiao District—the chamber of commerce, followed by the development of trade associations in the late Qing Dynasty. The development of its industry and commerce benefits from the local characteristics of abundant materials and products, shaped by convenient land and sea transportation and superior climate and environment.

Its deep-rooted business traditions can date back to as early as the years under the reign of Emperor Guangxu in the Qing Dynasty, when the chamber of commerce, called the Merchant-operated Zhejiang Railroad Company, was established. During the Republic of China, township chambers of commerce were established in various places, mainly to provide merchants with public services such as arbitrating commercial disputes, issuing certificates, and facilitating the transportation of goods. While providing the services, these chambers of commerce also started to establish trade associations, the famous ones being those dealing in western medicine, cigarettes, and kerosene, formed by the Nanzha Temple Luqiao Chamber of Commerce. In 1929, the Nationalist Party Government promulgated The Industrial and Commercial Trade Association Law, organizing more than seven(later changed into more than five) industrial and commercial enterprises in the same region into a trade association. According to The Annals of Huangyan County in the Republic of China, there were at least 50 trade associations in Luqiao District, dealing in a wide variety of goods and services such as delicacies from South China, delicacies from North China, general merchandise, fruits, sugar, wine, tobacco, sauce, mountain goods, oil, meat, fresh fish, caramel, vegetables, grains, tea, cotton, silk, cotton yarn, coarse cloth, wool fabrics, shoes, straw hats, silk threads, gauze, jute fiber, cotton, timber, mat grass, knitting, secondhand clothes, dyeing, automobiles, steamships, civilian ships, masoning, carpentry, paper, pewter, iron, copper, hardware and electric materials, kerosene, oil candles, copper and tinware, porcelain and pottery, board and charcoal, coal, library supplies, traditional medicine, western medicine, photography, tax banking, pawn business, private banking, etc. It was also during this period that the trend of cooperative management emerged in Luqiao District (also known as Huangyan County at that time), with rural production cooperatives and rural credit cooperatives being established. By the end of 1947, 28 township cooperatives, 11 general cooperatives, 9 insurance cooperatives, and 1 county union were established in Huangyan Country. However, the establishment of cooperatives was all about practical results, so they dissolved automatically at the end of the cooperation.

After the founding of New China, along with the national land reform and the big wave of economic restructuring, the production relations in Luqiao District also underwent a big adjustment. In urban areas, alongside state-owned commercial cooperatives, grass-roots commercial supply and marketing cooperatives as well as production, supply, and marketing cooperatives of the handicraft industry were simultaneously established. In rural areas, rural production mutual aid groups were vigorously developed to bring all forces into play to revitalize the economy. In 1953, along with the socialist "One Industrialization and Three Transformations", the economy of Luqiao District completed the transformation from private ownership to a socialist public ownership economy.

Reform and opening up brought opportunities to its private economy and market-oriented development. With the active support of the masses, individual delivery on the combination of responsibilities, rights, and benefits of agricultural production was first attained in rural areas, changing the scenario that people's communes invoked and allocated all resources in a unified manner and all residents "ate from the same pot". By the end of 1982, the responsibility system of contracting output quotas to households was fully implemented in Luqiao. In terms of industrial production, the state-owned and collective enterprises which failed to operate were phased out, and completed the joint-stock reform, the property rights structure of township enterprises was reformed, and gradually a modern enterprise system was established. The reform of cooperative shares adopted in Luqiao also released the great advantages of institutional mechanisms and drove great enthusiasm toward private entrepreneurship. In the early 1980s, Luqiao District took the lead in establishing a professional wholesale market in the country. Since the 1990s, it has been leading the country in the manufacturing of daily necessities with a unique daily necessities mall. What is worth mentioning is the development of its commerce in this period. In 1982, the Luqiao Town Office of Industry and Commerce Management and the Office of Finance and Taxation took the lead in setting up the Luqiao Small Commodity Wholesale Market together in Yongyue Village, which became an important force to promote the development of its commerce. Since then, concentrated small commodity markets such as Luqiao Old Steel Market, Luqiao Non-staple Foodstuffs Market, China Daily Necessities Mall, Luqiao Architectural Decorations Mall, and Luqiao Electronic and Electrical Appliances Market sprung up. The emergence of these markets not only drove the market transformation of the economy but also laid a solid foundation for the development of the private economy in Luqiao, stimulating its future economic development. The industrial and trade interaction between the specialized markets (especially those of means of production) and the manufacturing industry promoted the manufacturing industry cluster and the service market cluster of its regional economy, as well as the vertical organic integration of the industrial chain, leading to a mechanism of efficient labor division and cooperation. The development of the private economy, characterized by that of specialized markets, was the source of vitality of its economy. By the end of 2012, there was a total of 35 specialized markets with an annual turnover of RMB 40.363 billion yuan(approximately USD 5.5 billion), accounting for 31.17% of the trading volume in the city, with 9 markets exceeding 1 billion yuan. There were nearly 45,000 registered business units in the whole district, with registered capital of RMB 26 billion yuan and a workforce of over 130,000. Wholesale and retail volumes accounted for 22.73% of its overall GDP, generating RMB 677 million yuan in taxes. The development of specialized markets not only effectively solved its employment and entrepreneurship but also brought great wealth effect to society. According to statistics, in 2012, individual savings deposits in financial institutions reached RMB 39.15 billion yuan(approximately USD 5.357 billion), about RMB 87,500 yuan per capita(approximately USD 12,020). The total retail consumption of the whole society reached RMB 23.223 billion yuan(approximately USD 3.19 billion). The per capita disposable income in urban areas was RMB 40,700 yuan (approximately USD 5591 and 6751 yuan higher than the city's average level). Furthermore, every hundred urban households had 62 cars.

Private Capital: The Diesel Engine of Private Economy

The early financing industry in Luqiao District mainly took the form of "pawn shops", "banks" and "parties", all of which were private-capital-funded organizations. In ancient times, there was only the pawn industry, so it was the leader of all industries. In the Republic of China, there were dozens of pawn shops in Luqiao District (called Huangyan County at that time), among which Taisheng Pawn Shop in Chengguan Town and Daheng Pawn Shop in Luqiao District were the larger ones, with a longer history and the capitals of more than ten thousand silver coins (the currency then) each. The pawn industry mainly provided capital appropriation and transfer for ordinary folks, local authorities, and small-business owners. "Banks" in Luqiao arose in the late Qing dynasty and the early Republic of China and flourished before the founding of P.R.C. Initially, they were officially approved by the local authorities. Later with lots of privately organized banks, there were two types of "banks": those in the light and those in the shadow, the latter of which were called "underground banks or hawala shops". Compared with pawn shops, banks were more formal, with floating interest rates on deposits and loans and a relatively large loan amount, so they tended to serve industry and commerce. In 1933, there were already 7 banks in Luqiao District. Compared to pawn shops and banks, "parties" were more able to reflect the characteristics of Luqiao credit organizations. This type of economic activity took no fixed form; only when someone needed a large amount of money, his friends, relatives, family, and neighbors who were good friends and financially well-off were invited to participate in a "party". The size of the party depended on the amount of money needed and the number of people that could be invited. Since there was no specific coercive binding, its members borrowed and lent money solely out of trust among them, and the "party" became an important symbol of good a credit relationship among the locals.

Luqiao Bank was established as a branch of Zhejiang Local Bank in April 1940 and renamed Luqiao Office of Zhejiang Bank in 1947. Luqiao Office of the Bank of China was established in May 1944. After Luqiao operated as a district, banks began to operate independently. In 1995, there were 4 state-owned commercial banks in Luqiao District: Taizhou Luqiao District Sub-branch of Industrial and Commercial Bank of China (ICBC), Taizhou Luqiao District Sub-branch of Agricultural Bank of China (ABC), Taizhou Luqiao District Sub-branch of China Construction Bank (CCB), and Taizhou Luqiao District Sub-branch of Bank of China(BOC). There was one cooperative bank Taizhou Luqiao District Rural Credit Cooperative Union, two private financial institutions: Luqiao Yinzuo City Credit Union and Tailong City Credit Union, and others including Agricultural Development Bank of China, Taizhou Luqiao District Sub-branch of Industrial Bank, Taizhou Luqiao District Sub-branch of Bank of Communications, Taizhou Luqiao District Sub-branch of Shanghai Pudong Development Bank, etc.

Before the reform and opening up, Taizhou City, where Luqiao District is located, received little governmental investment as a coastal defense front. According to statistics, from 1949 to 1978, the accumulated investment from the government was only RMB 460 million yuan(approximately USD 64.44 million). Its economy, especially its industrial economy, was quite backward, with its economic aggregate and strength ranking second last among the 11 cities and prefectures in Zhejiang province. Since the reform and opening up, its people have seized the opportunity to accelerate the development of the local economy and society by relying on self-accumulation and self-investment in the absence of big national investment and special policies. Take the period between 1986 and 2002 as an example, the city witnessed a total of RMB 154.3 billion yuan(approximately USD 21.29) of fixed assets investment, among which only RMB 29.3 billion yuan(approximately USD 4.04 billion) came from government budgets, bank loans, and foreign investment. And the remaining RMB 125 billion yuan(approximately USD 17.25 billion), accounting for 81% of the total, was pooled by its people.

2.2 Origin and Development of Microfinance in Luqiao

The financing difficulty faced by small and medium-sized enterprises is a global problem. Foreign scholars have studied various aspects such as the characteristics and contributions of the development of MSEs and the impediments to financial services for MSEs. Since the 1970s, the micro-economy has grown rapidly. It has undergone profound changes in the operation concept, main body, and operation mode, and gradually become the most active part of the national economy, thus providing space for the development of microfinance and opportunities for its reform.

The Rise and Risks of Private Lending in Luqiao

The civil mutual aid association (*BiaoHui* in Chinese, literally meaning the Bidding Meeting, a Chinese version of ROSCA, Rotating Savings and Credit Association), consists of an initiator (called *HuiTou* in Chinese, literally meaning the Head of the Bidding Meeting) and some members (called *HuiJiao* in Chinese, literally meaning the Feet of the Bidding Meeting, mainly the initiator's relatives and friends) who are invited by the initiator to participate. The meeting is held at the appointed time, and each time a specified amount of money is collected and given to one person at a time in rotations to be used for mutual assistance. The user pays a certain amount of interests. Each member can only get the money once, while the head of the bidding meeting, as the organizer, has the priority to use the first money without interest. And *DaoHui*, literally meaning the inversion of the bidding meeting, means that one (or more) of the participants get the money and then run away, no longer paying the balance, so the rest will not get back the money that they paid at the beginning. As an informal form of finance, *BiaoHui* is widely used in Jiangsu, Zhejiang,

Fujian, and Guangdong provinces. It is especially popular among families with unstable incomes and few savings, and those who need to spend large amounts of money due to big events in their life (such as illness, death, business start-up, marriage, large education expenses, etc.). Before 2009, although there were cases of the inversion of the bidding meeting in the southeast coast of China, with some exerting large impacts in Yueqing (1986) and Cangnan County (2005) in Zhejiang, and Fu'an, Fujian Province(2004), the impacts were limited to the vicinity, and there was a certain time interval and not much correlation between the cases. However, since 2009, the southeast coast of China (Longyan, Ningde, and Fuzhou, Fujian Province, and Taizhou, Zhejiang Province) has witnessed a series of incidents of "the inversion of civil bidding meetings".

In the early 1980s, under the institutional constraints of state-owned commercial banks dominating the market, small and medium-sized private enterprises in Taizhou were unable to obtain credit support and had to turn to the informal financial sector, which led to the flourishing of private financing such as *fund-raising*, *parties* and *bidding meetings*. These unregulated forms of informal financing seriously undermine financial order. It was during this period when Luqiao Yinzuo Financial Services Agency (the precursor of Taizhou Commercial Bank) was founded. The weakening of the informal financial "boom" proved to be strongly correlated with the establishment and growth of Yinzuo Financial Services Agency and later Tailong Commercial Bank. Small legal person financial institutions in Taizhou meet the financing needs of small and medium-sized enterprises which account for more than 96% of all enterprises in Taizhou.

Establishment and Improvement of Microfinance Order

Small-sized legal person financial institutions with clear property rights, flexible operating mechanisms, and market orientation can take advantage of the inextricable ties with local human and geographical resources to minimize transaction costs and credit risks. By supporting the credit of small and medium-sized enterprises, these financial institutions support the most dynamic productive sector and play a role in optimizing the allocation of financial resources. They have introduced competition into the monopolized financial system of state-owned commercial banks, prompting the latter to accelerate the pace of reform. For example, in Luqiao District in 1996, the deposits of Taizhou Commercial Bank (then called

Yinzuo City Credit Union) accounted for 27.4% of the total deposit balance of financial institutions in the district and its loans occupied 25.7% of the total loan balance, while the figures for Tailong City Credit Union reached 15% and 14.6% respectively, all the ratios being higher than those of any local state-owned commercial bank. And both city credit unions had lower non-performing assets ratios than state-owned commercial banks. So market-oriented small legal person financial institutions with private capital holding and clear property rights are in line with the economic characteristics of Taizhou.

The development of the Luqiao industry, commerce, and agriculture has driven the construction of the financial system. Since the late 1980s, several pawn shops have emerged in Luqiao. And at the beginning of the twenty-first century, these shops began to show signs of flourishing. Although they can provide temporary financing for small and medium-sized enterprises, they cannot provide sustainable financial services for these enterprises. The dual drive of the private economy and agricultural economy promotes the transformation and upgrading of the financial industry and service industry in Luqiao District. Since the first state-owned commercial bank, Taizhou Luqiao Sub-branch of Agricultural Bank of China, was officially established in 1995, a modern financial system with state-owned banks as the main body, supplemented by cooperative banks and foundations, and integrating private financial institutions, has been established in Luqiao. The famous Taizhou Bank and Zhejiang Tailong Bank, two large private financial institutions, were established in this period. During the "Tenth Five-Year Plan" period, Luqiao District focused on the construction of financial institutions to support the development of the private economy. Three local legal person banks—Taizhou Bank, Tailong Bank, and Luqiao District Rural Cooperative Bank conducted the joint-stock reform, which became an important step in the development of microfinance.

In June 1988, approved by the China Banking Regulatory Commission, Chen Xiaojun and his partners co-founded Luqiao Yinzuo Financial Services Agency, which is the first private financial institution in China since the reform and opening up. In 1995, it became a real bank—Luqiao City Credit Union. In November 1998, it was renamed Taizhou Yinzuo City Credit Union. And in March 2002, Luqiao City Credit Union, by uniting 8 other credit unions, divesting non-performing assets, and absorbing private small and medium-sized enterprises' shares, transformed into Taizhou City Commercial Bank, with a registered capital of RMB

300 million *yuan*, with the head office located in Luqiao, becoming the first city commercial bank in Luqiao to provide financial services to small and medium-sized enterprises. In August 2009, the "2009 China Commercial Bank Competitiveness Evaluation Report", initiated by *The Banker* with the participation of the Institute of Finance of the Chinese Academy of Social Sciences, was released in Beijing. And Taizhou City Commercial Bank was awarded "Third in the Competitiveness of Large City Commercial Banks" and "the Most Profitable City Commercial Bank". In September 2010, it increased its registered capital and shares and was officially renamed Taizhou Bank.

In June 1993, Tailong City Credit Union was established by Wang Jun and his partners. In August 2006, it was transformed into Zhejiang Tailong Commercial Bank through shareholding reform, with its headquarters in Luqiao, becoming a micro and small financial services bank with exclusively private capital. In 2008, the bank set up branches in Hangzhou and Ningbo, and sub-branches in Wenling, Taizhou, Yuhuan, Taizhou, and Qingtian, Lishui. In 2009, Premier Wen Jiabao met twice with its chairman and praised it as "a very well-run bank, the Yunus of China".

Luqiao Rural Cooperative Bank is also a microfinance services bank. The establishment of these three banks pioneered the development of microfinance, and also mapped out the basic pattern of microfinance development in Luqiao District. During the "Eleventh Five-Year Plan" period, the People's Government of Luqiao District lent further support to the local growth of the three banks, and vigorously introduced domestic commercial banks into Luqiao. At the same time, the local capital market was actively developed, and enterprises were encouraged to raise funds through the stock and fund markets and the property rights trading market. In addition, in terms of NBFIs, the government supported the construction of a multi-channel, multi-level, multiform insurance service system, encouraged the establishment of branches of securities, leasing, fund management, trust and investment companies, etc., and strove to create an environment where banking and NBFIs, indirect and direct financing markets jointly developed, to provide further financing services for enterprises, especially small and medium-sized enterprises. By the end of 2012, 15 banking financial institutions, 25 insurance institutions, 3 securities institutions, 3 micro-credit companies, 6 financing guarantee companies, and 4 pawn shops were established in Luqiao. These financial institutions have played an important role in promoting Luqiao District as a regional financial industry supermarket with strong influence and a sub-center of Taizhou finance, as well as providing an important guarantee for the local SMEs' development.

2.3 Foundation for the Development of Microfinance in Luqiao

As one of the first regions in China to develop a private economy, Luqiao offers a model for the development of small and medium-sized enterprises and microfinance. The emergence and development of microfinance in Luqiao is the result of the deepening of the national economic market in a situation when the financial deepening of the traditional state-owned financial system couldn't advance substantially. Luqiao is located in the middle of the Wenhuang Plain, the most densely populated area in Taizhou known for the tradition of trading and doing business. As early as the Song Dynasty, there was "no street without a market, no lane without a peddler, no household without a merchant". After the reform and opening up, due to the lack of government investments in central and southern Zhejiang and the internal demand for expected profits, small and medium-sized enterprises, mainly specializing in processing industries, developed rapidly, and various specialized markets were established. By the early 1990s, a large economic system dominated by the private economy had been steadily developing in Luqiao District. According to statistics, as of 2011, the output value of the private economy accounted for 95% of Taizhou's GDP, and more than 85% of the fiscal revenue comes from the private economy. The number of small and medium-sized enterprises, the main body of the private economy, reached 99% of the total number of enterprises in the city, which drove the growth of a series of economic indicators such as employment, import and export, and fiscal revenue in Taizhou.

The development of the private economy has directly driven the rapid accumulation of private capital and provided the necessary economic support for the shareholding reform of commercial banks in Taizhou, especially in Luqiao. Three local legal person banks that carry out the innovative development of microfinance in Luqiao—Taizhou Bank, Zhejiang Tailong Commercial Bank, and Luqiao Rural Cooperative Bank, are all private capital-holding banking institutions.

Taizhou Bank was established in March 2002, formerly known as Luqiao Yinzuo City Credit Union, which then transformed into "Taizhou

City Commercial Bank" by uniting 8 other credit unions, divesting non-performing assets, and attracting private SMEs as shareholders. In 2010, Taizhou City Commercial Bank increased its registered capital and shares and officially changed its name to Taizhou Bank. In terms of shareholding ratio, 92% of its shares are held by social legal persons, and the ratio of state-owned shareholding is only 5%, making it the first non-state-owned city commercial bank in China. Since its shareholding reform, Taizhou Bank has continuously innovated to help MSEs develop, and its services cover the entire market of Luqiao District by setting up sub-branches and business outlets. In addition, through the establishment of village banks and the implementation of cross-regional services, Taizhou Bank has also extended its microfinance business to the whole country. Like Taizhou Bank, Zhejiang Tailong Bank was transformed through the shareholding reform of the Longcheng City Credit Union. Since its registration in 2006, the Employee Shareholders Association of Taizhou Tailong City Credit Union has been the largest shareholder with 19.52% of the shares (as of the end of 2011). Besides, social legal persons and individual shareholdings are still the main body of Tailong Bank shareholding. Luqiao Rural Cooperative Bank, the first rural cooperative bank in Taizhou, was established in March 2005, and mainly serves the financial needs of Luqiao District and other regions of Taizhou. Like the other two banks, its main shareholders are local private small and medium-sized enterprises.

On the other hand, the development of the private economy promotes the expansion of the market for microfinance and guarantees the commercial sustainability of microfinance. After years of cultivation and development, an industrial system, with the modern service industry and manufacturing industry as the main body and the interactive development of industry and trade, has been established in Luqiao. Its distinctive characteristics as a regional modern trade center, logistics center, financial center, and exhibition center begin to come into the spotlight. There are 20 markets with the trade volume of above RMB 100 million *yuan* (approximately USD 13.91 million), including 10 markets with a trade volume of above RMB 1 billion *yuan* (approximately USD 139.17 million), ranking among the "Top 10 Commodity Trading Market Counties/Cities/Districts in Zhejiang Province". Luqiao China Commodity Mall and Taizhou Electronic Digital City have jumped into the ranks of "China's Top 100 Commodity Markets". As the base of the advanced manufacturing industry in the Yangtze River Delta, now there are five leading industries in Luqiao: automobiles, motorcycles, and their spare parts; mechanical and electrical products; metal resources recycling; injection and molding; and new building materials. Luqiao is an important industrial base for private automobile manufacturing and metal resources recycling in China, and enjoys many reputations such as "the Capital of Plant Protection and Cleaning Machinery in China" and "the Hometown of Injection and Moulding". Most of these industries are organized in the form of small and medium-sized enterprises or individual private enterprises, so there is a huge gap in capital needs. It can be said that the demand for microfinance services will continue to exist in Luqiao District and even the whole of Taizhou City. Take the three microfinance services banks in Luqiao as an example. By the end of 2012, the total deposits in the three banks exceeded RMB 100 billion *yuan* (approximately USD 13.92 billion), and their total loans reached nearly RMB 74 billion *yuan* (approximately USD 10.3 billion). Among them, the total deposits in Taizhou Bank by the end of 2012 were RMB 57.913 billion *yuan* (approximately USD 8.06 billion), the total loans were RMB 36.876 billion *yuan* (approximately USD 5.13 billion), the non-performing loan ratio was less than or equal to 0.43%, and the net profit was 1.532 billion *yuan* (approximately USD 0.21 billion). At the end of 2011, the total deposits of Zhejiang Tailong Bank were RMB 38.688 billion *yuan* (approximately USD 5.38 billion) and the total loans were RMB 28.105 billion *yuan* (approximately USD 3.91 billion), the non-performing loan ratio was less than or equal to 0.51%, and the net profit was RMB 772 million *yuan* (approximately USD 107 million). Luqiao Rural Cooperative Bank has a deposit balance of 12.72 billion *yuan* (approximately USD 1.77 billion), a loan balance of 9.38 billion *yuan* (approximately USD 1.31 billion), a non-performing loan ratio of 1.18%, and a profit of 370 million *yuan* (approximately USD 51.49 million). And these indicators are better than those of the sub-branches and business outlets of the four major state-owned banks over the same period, and the operating efficiency of these three banks shows the trend of gradual optimization. In addition, as of the end of June 2013, the ratio of their MSE loans (including individual business loans) to all the loans was as high as 70%, much higher than that of the financial institutions of similar levels in Zhejiang Province and even the whole country.

The rapid development of the private economy in Luqiao is the inherent impetus for the emergence of private finance, and also the inexhaustible source to ensure the sustainable development of private finance. This interactive adjustment and development between SMEs and microfinance has become a unique "Taizhou model".

2.4 Development Stages of Luqiao Microfinance

Stage I: Piloting Microfinance (1988–2001)

The horizontal comparison of China's reform process shows that there has been a relatively developed private financial sector in Taizhou since the end of the 1980s. As a form of financial organization that is different from state-owned formal finance in terms of property rights structure and operation, private finance has grown with difficulty under the double pressure of government control and the monopoly advantage of state-owned finance, but it has shown a strong motivation to develop and play a unique functional role in regional economic development. Since the 1990s, the state-owned joint-stock banks under Taizhou's jurisdiction have become the national key microfinance pilot banks within their systems, accumulating a wealth of experience that were drawn from around the world. As early as 1999, the Taizhou Branch of ICBC took the lead in introducing loan management measures for SMEs, which became a model of the credit business for small enterprises in the ICBC system. At present, 7 state-owned and joint stock banks under Taizhou's jurisdiction have been designated by their head offices, and 3 of such banks are designated by the provincial-level banks to be pilot microfinance banks. So Taizhou has become a key pilot area for major banks. The microfinance business of state-owned commercial banks in Taizhou has become a useful reference for the development of microfinance in Luqiao District.

The financial institutions have laid a solid foundation for the development of micro and small financial services in Luqiao. Founded in 1988, Luqiao Yinzuo City Credit Union is a joint-stock private financial institution with a rapid growth rate. In a little more than ten years, it became become the largest city credit union in Zhejiang Province, and its non-performing assets ratio remained below 1%. Before the formation of Taizhou Commercial Bank, its deposit balance had reached RMB 261.7 billion *yuan* (approximately USD 36.4 billion), with the ratio of non-performing assets being only 0.172%, and the annual profit-generating capacity of more than RMB 30 million *yuan* (approximately USD 4.17 million). Now Taizhou Commercial Bank is headquartered in Luqiao, Taizhou, with a registered capital of RMB 300 million *yuan* (approximately USD 41.75 million). As of July 2003, it opened 46 business institutions with more than 750 employees.

Tailong City Credit Union, established in June 1993 and with investors all being local private enterprises and individuals, is a local joint-stock financial institution with clear property rights. Since its establishment, it has achieved rapid development and excellent business performance. By June 2002, its registered capital expanded from 1 million *yuan* (approximately USD 139,100) to 27.5 million *yuan* (approximately USD 3.82 million), with net assets of nearly 50 million *yuan* (approximately USD 6.96 million) and 350 employees, and an organizational structure based on the operation of 10 branches had been formed. In terms of financial business volume, Taizhou's private financial institutions have grown into an important force in the local financial industry. By June 2003, Taizhou Commercial Bank's deposit and loan balances had reached RMB 611.8 billion *yuan* (approximately USD 85.14 billion) and RMB 481.5 billion *yuan* (approximately USD 67.01 billion) respectively, while Tailong City Credit Union's deposit and loan balances had reached RMB 291.7 billion *yuan* (approximately USD 40.6 billion) and RMB 1.7 billion *yuan* (approximately USD 0.24 billion). Locally speaking, private finance is in a position to compete with local branches of state-owned banks in terms of scale and strength.

Taizhou Luqiao Rural Credit Cooperative is also an important part of the development of the microfinance industry in Luqiao. Since its establishment, it has been providing financial services for agricultural, farmers', and rural economic development by pooling rural idle funds. Following national laws and financial policies, it organizes and regulates rural funds, supports agricultural production, comprehensive rural development, various forms of a cooperative economy and its members' family economy, and restricts and combats loan sharks. Therefore, it facilitates the financing of agriculture and of small and medium-sized enterprises in Luqiao District.

Stage II: Development of Microfinance (2002–2010)

Since the beginning of the twenty-first century, Luqiao's private finance has gradually expanded along with the development of its private economy. At present, there are two major private financial institutions, namely Taizhou Commercial Bank and Taizhou Tailong City Credit Union. Both of them have achieved a certain degree of development in the scale of deposits and loans, business outlets, and the amounts of equity capital, and enjoy high social visibility and good public reputation. Founded in

March 2002, Taizhou City Commercial Bank was originally formed by divesting non-performing assets from Taizhou Yinzuo City Credit Union and 7 other credit unions in Taizhou City and then absorbing shares from 10 private enterprises. Among them, Yinzuo City Credit Union had a larger scale and higher asset quality before the formation of the commercial bank. Taizhou Commercial Bank was the product of mergers and acquisitions based on Yinzuo City Credit Union. After its establishment, Tailong Bank forged ahead and explored SMEs' credit services and risk control techniques in practice. It concluded a small business financial services model featuring "three qualities (clients' morality, products, and pledges), and three forms(water and electricity bill forms, and customs declaration form)" and achieving "three low-costs" for small business financing—low-cost information acquisition before financing, low-cost monitoring and management during financing, and low-cost default penalty after financing. This model provides a Chinese solution to the international "Macmillan Gap" of small business financing difficulties. The unique and nationally appropriate business model has enabled Tailong Bank to win a blue ocean in the small business financial services market, achieving the mutual interplay and harmony between sustainable corporate development and social responsibility. In August 2010, the Publicity Department of the CPC Central Committee ranked Tailong Bank as a specialty bank to transform the economic development mode and serve small enterprises. Since then, it has been officially listed as a representative bank providing small capital financing to SMEs.

When it comes to business performance, these two private financial institutions are generally better than local state-owned banks in terms of non-performing loan ratio and profitability. When it comes to the market positioning of financial services, such institutions as these two mainly provide financing services for local individual entrepreneurs, small and medium-sized private enterprises, etc. Except for a small portion dedicated to urban infrastructure and public utilities, the vast majority of their loans are invested in private economic sectors, mainly small and medium-sized enterprises. When it comes to service functions, they are now engaged in the traditional deposit and loan businesses and have started to venture into the business areas of bank cards and bill financing. For example, Taizhou Commercial Bank issued its bank card—the Datang Card after its establishment and joined the national UnionPay network.

In addition to these two banks, Luqiao Rural Cooperative Bank was officially opened on March 18, 2005, becoming the first rural cooperative bank established in Taizhou. At present, the bank, with the most business outlets in the Luqiao area, offers the largest support for agriculture and ordinary folks easiest access to services. Since its establishment, it actively launched new platforms and businesses such as the "Small Agricultural Loan Center" and "Luqiao Banking Access", which lent strong support to the development of more than 50,000 rural households and more than 3000 SMEs in the region. By the first quarter of 2013, the bank's deposit balance reached 15.06 billion *yuan* (approximately USD 2.096 billion), accounting for 21.8% of that of all the financial institutions in the district, up 2.3 percentage points compared with at the beginning of the year, and the deposit scale ranked first in the region. The balance of various loans reached 10.02 billion *yuan*(approximately USD 1.39 billion), an increase of 650 million *yuan* (approximately USD 90.46 million) or 6.9% over the beginning of the year. Among them, the balance of agriculture-related loans reached 8.53 billion *yuan* (approximately USD 1.19 billion), an increase of 790 million *yuan* (approximately USD 109.9 million) or 10.2% over the beginning of the year; the balance of loans to micro and small businesses reached 8.92 billion *yuan* (approximately USD 1.24 billion), an increase of 620 million *yuan* (approximately USD 86.28 million) or 7.5% over the beginning of the year. In a word, the establishment of Luqiao Rural Cooperative Bank has provided strong financial support for the local economic construction.

After the establishment of the three banks, the basic framework of microfinance construction in Luqiao District has been formed. These banks have absorbed scattered private capital and introduced various types of loans that conform to the characteristics of SME financing, innovate risk management models and internal institutional construction. In nutshell, they have set up a new model for the construction of MSF banks in China.

Stage III: Rapid Development of Government-Bank Cooperation (2011–present)

Since the establishment of the three local legal person banks, the Luqiao District government has provided a lot of support. In recent years, MSEs have experienced some difficulties with corporate development, especially with financing guarantees, and the provincial government has required the construction of "SME financial services centers" and "private wealth management centers" Accordingly, the district government has taken the initiative to bring its experiences obtained through the pioneering efforts of the three local legal person banks into line with the financial reform practices in Wenzhou, vigorously implemented the construction of the financial ecological environment, striving to build a "micro and small financial services innovation demonstration area", alleviating the SME financing difficulties, and promoting the transformation and healthy development of the economy. Meanwhile, the order of business operation has been regulated, and financial risks have been timely resolved. In brief, with the gradually increased credit awareness of the whole society and continued optimization of the credit and investment environment, Luqiao has become one of the best regions in providing MSE financial services and developing microfinance institutions in the country.

First, the district government has explored the servicing system of the microfinance industry and effectively promoted the integration between microfinance and the real economy. Based on industry clusters and specialized markets in Luqiao, the leading enterprises in the industry have led the establishment of small loan companies targeted at various trades. At the same time, these enterprises MSEs and merchants within the clusters, shaping a new micro and small financial industrialized mutual aid mode, specific to the microfinancing industry, between large/strong enterprises and small/weak enterprises. In 2012, these small loan companies in the district distributed more than 1200 loans, with a cumulative lending amount of nearly 1 billion *yuan* (approximately USD 0.14 billion). Hence, it is a unique model of microfinance services.

Second, the government has promoted MSEs' development by setting up innovation incentive mechanisms and directly realizing government-bank-enterprise cooperation. First, the "Microfinancing Innovation Awards" have been established to encourage various financial institutions to develop a variety of financial products and services such as microloans, green credit, letter of credit financing, and science and technology finance, tailored to the MSEs' needs. The government has further improved the incentive mechanisms, strengthened the classification and assessment of local financial institutions, and increased the proportion of loans to MSEs. In 2012, the government provided a total of nearly 30 million *yuan* (approximately USD 4.17 million) as innovation incentive funds. Second, it has encouraged and supported financial institutions in their use of credit leverage, further promoted such financial products as "Green Financing" in cooperation with the United Nations Environment Programme, and the medium and long-term fixed assets credit in Sino-German financial cooperation, and steered MSEs to improve their equipment and strengthen their technological transformation and innovation by exploring and carrying out direct financing leasing of equipment. In 2012, the program "Green Financing" in Luqiao granted loans with a total of nearly 66 million *yuan* (approximately USD 9.19 million), effectively alleviating the capital needs of regional environmental protection and energy-saving enterprises. Financial institutions are encouraged to use such financial instruments as merger and acquisition loans and venture capital for industrial mergers, acquisitions, and restructuring. Local banks are supported to innovate SMEs' loan repayment with working capital by launching such products as interest-paying revolving loans and weekly special-purpose loans. Last, a microfinance talent training base is constructed. The government has strengthened the training of local banking talents and encouraged individuals and social organizations to carry out the training of microfinance talents, to build a training base for MSE credit technology targeted at the national needs, and to enhance the agglomeration and radiation of Luqiao finance. For example, Tailong Finance School and Yinzuo Finance Training School have received governmental support in their development by obtaining social training licenses to train more microfinance professionals.

Third, the district government has actively created a unified government-supervised private financing regulation center, focusing on forming a win-win situation for multiple parties through a voluntary registration of fund lenders, sustainable commercial development of private financing regulation center, and increase in MSE financing channels. It guides the orderly integration of private funds into the existing financial system so that private capital is docked on banking businesses through the launching of entrusted loans in its cooperation with private financial institutions. In addition, microfinance in Luqiao is actively expanding the sources of funds by issuing financial bonds and directional bonds and bringing in strategic investors, who have provided some experience, to the industry in terms of its business development and management. For example, the government actively strove for and made full use of relevant policies to encourage and support private banks to issue special-purpose financial bonds; it guided all kinds of private capital to participate in the new establishment and development of microfinance institutions; it encouraged private capital to participate in the equity capital increase of local legal person banks, and in the microfinance services institutions such as rural banks (community banks), financial guarantee companies, and private capital management companies. Lastly, the government, by exploring various ways for private capital to dock on small loan companies, has strengthened cooperation with specialized private equity institutions to set up small loan funds with the participation of private capital, and to place targeted investment in the equity of microfinance companies so that small loan companies can solve the problems of insufficient capital and low financing leverage.

Fourth, the district government has strengthened financial credit risk control and created a healthy financial credit environment. To begin with, it has initiated the enterprise credit project. The construction of the project began in 2002; the Luqiao Credit Construction Leading Team, along with the Luqiao Credit Information Network, was set up in 2008, concluding the construction of the social credit system. The government also actively promotes cooperation between relevant departments including the court, public security, industry and commerce, and taxes departments. It has implemented classified handling of the enterprises with the rupture risk of capital and guarantee chains, to achieve "three ensurings": one, ensuring enterprise development on condition that banks are required not to delay loans to or withdraw in advance loans to enterprises with good asset quality and product market but affected by the guarantee chain; two, ensuring creditors' (such as banks') interests to avoid the worsening situation when it comes to enterprises with sales stagnation and insolvency; three, ensuring the prevention of "debt evasion" on condition that public security departments are required to pay close attention to the business owners with the motive to flee. At the same time, financial fraud and other illegal financial acts are severely and vigorously combated, and illegal private financial activities such as illegal fund-raising and underground banking are firmly banned. Also, 20 million *yuan* (approximately USD 2.78 million) of emergency transfer special-purpose funds are set up in the fiscal budget to help growing enterprises solve the temporary turnover of repayment and enhance short-term security; 20 million *yuan* (approximately USD 2.78 million) of emergency loan risk funds are set up to help the MSEs that encounter tight budgets and other emergencies in the course of production and operation. For every designated emergency loan which shows signs of risks, the finance department shall compensate local financial institutions at the standard of no less than 10% of the loan amount. Finally, the government has piloted provincial small loan guarantee insurance in earnest—the finance department has established a risk compensation mechanism that grants 30% of the premium as a subsidy to the policyholder and 50% in compensation to insurance institutions for the part exceeding 150% of the current year's premium, strengthening insurance institutions' responsibilities for guarantee insurance on loan principals and interests.

2.5 Summary

In general, each step of the financial system changes in China originates from the top-down mandatory governmental supplies rather than the bottom-up induced institutional demands of micro-entities. Moreover, the government-led mandatory institutional changes only start from satisfying the utility maximization of institutional suppliers and fail to reflect and meet the requirements of those in need of financial services, which leads to the oversupply of the ineffective financial system and the under-supply of the effective financial system, and even a relatively serious non-equilibrium of China's financial system due to financial system changes seriously lagging behind economic system changes. First, the government pushes for mandatory financial reforms. Given the goal adjustments and dynamic process of the stages in the financial system changes over the 30 years of the reform and opening up in China, the timing and sequencing, speed, pause, and restart of these changes are completely subject to the capabilities and preferences of government entities. Each stage of these changes is a manifestation of a specific goal set by the government at a specific stage of economic development, so the reform mentality and policies formulated by the government have always been the main driving force for China's financial system changes. Second, China has taken an incremental approach to financial reform. China has established step-by-step, stage-by-stage, part-to-whole financial reform goals, by adopting the same "incremental reform" approach as that of its economic reform in terms of financial system changes. Being a process of "incremental reform" followed by "cumulative reform", this encouraged the rapid development of new financial institutions outside public sectors first and then the reform of the ownership of state-owned financial institutions. In addition, the reform of the financial organization structure emphasized continuation instead of working from scratch, and financial changes have been steadily promoted under the government's regulation, with the financial order being rectified and financial macro-control strengthened throughout the market-oriented financial reform. Third, financial reform lags behind economic development. On the premise that China has gradually relaxed its direct control over financial resources, the financial system has not been transformed in a timely and effective manner though; the changes of the financial system lag behind the changes of its associated investment and financing systems and the enterprise property rights system. In terms of timing and sequencing, the changes in China's financial system lag behind economic system changes. In practice, the main manifestation of this lag is that the former depends on and is attached to the macroeconomic system reform, and financial system innovation is "imitative" of and compatible with the path of the latter.

However, in the case of Luqiao, Taizhou, there is a huge amount of private capital in the local economy, which has a strong inner urge to be transformed into financial capital. The current financial system hinders this transformation, so private capital has to exist in various forms between the cracks of the system. During China's economic and financial development, the traditional financial system, dominated by state-owned banks, did play an important role in the early stage of China's economic development by pooling limited resources to develop important industrial fields. However, with advancing marketization, private SMEs continue to grow and have become the most productive part of economic development. Naturally, there is an increasing demand for microfinance supply; the accumulation of private capital has also laid an important economic foundation for the emergence of microfinance. The development of microfinance as represented in Luqiao, Taizhou has proved: Microfinance institutions, when providing financing services to enterprises, can effectively safeguard the sustainable development of microfinance in Luqiao, due to the positive ecological environment of private economic development, as well as these institutions' information advantages, effective repayment mechanisms, more flexible interest rates and loan terms, greater financing speed, lower loan costs, and higher service levels.

In places like Luqiao, Taizhou with a developed private economy, the growth of the private economy, especially that of the private industrial economy, coincides with that of the local economy. As the birthplace of the shareholding cooperative economy, Taizhou is one of the most active areas of the private economy in China, and home to the first joint stock cooperative enterprise with a business registry and the first policy supporting the development of joint stock cooperative enterprises in the country. The private economy—led development model, which is described by economists as the "grassroots" economy, has created a prosperous regional economy, and this prosperous market economy has greatly stimulated the continuous innovation of the financial industry, especially that of microfinance businesses. With microfinance developing and the economy growing in Luqiao, the continuous increase of the residents' income and the rising demand for financial services in the economic sector will in turn stimulate the development of the local financial industry and will continue to deepen the financial reform.

References

Garmaise, M. Informed Investors and the Financing of Entrepreneurial Projects, *Stanford University Working Paper*, 1997.

Berger, A. N. & Udell, G. F. The Economics of Small Business Finance: the Role of Private Equity and Debt Markets in the Financial Growth Cycle[J], *Journal of Banking and Finance*, 1998, 22: 613–673.

Berger, A. N. & Udell, G. F. Small Business Credit Available and Relationship Lending: the Importance of Bank Organizational Structure[J], *Economic Journal*, 2002, 112(447):32–54.

Zhang Jie. SMEs' Relational Borrowing and Banks' Organizational Structure [J]. *Economic Research Journal*, 2002(6): 32–54.

Guo Bin & Liu, Manlu. Private Finance and Development of SMEs: an Empirical Analysis of Wenzhou [J]. *Economic Research Journal*, 2002(10): 40–46.

Shi Jinchuan. Financial Deepening and Development of "Private Finance"—an Observation from the Perspective of Regional Economy [J]. *Zhejiang Social Sciences*, 2002(13): 32–33.

Zhang Jie. Financial Predicament and Financing Order of Private Economy [J]. *Economic Research Journal*, 2000(4): 77–80.

Fan Gang. Overcoming Credit Downturn and Reforming the Banking System [J]. *Economic Research Journal*, 1999(1): 3–8.

Chen Huiling. The Formation and Innovation of Financing Difficulty of SMEs [J]. *Productivity Research*, 2009(3): 213–216.

Chen Xiaoling & Zhou Baosheng. Accelerating the Development of Small and Medium-sized Financial Institutions and Expand Financing for SMEs [J]. *Modern Management Science*, 2005(8): 105–106.

Ba Shusong. Focusing on the Development of Micro and Small Finance in the Next Financial Reform [J]. *Development Research*, 2012 (6): 4–6.

Cai Ningwei. Misunderstandings and Development Measures of Small and Microfinance [J]. *Financial Management and Research: Journal of Hangzhou Finance Research Institute*, 2013 (4): 45–48.

Chen Weibin. Cooperation between Government, Bank and Enterprise Is an Effective Way to Solve the SME Loan Difficulty [J]. *Development Research*, 2007 (8): 29–31.

Chen Yuan. Development and Countermeasures of Small and Microfinance in Chinese Joint-stock Commercial Banks—Based on a Case Study of China Citic Bank. *A Master's Thesis of Zhejiang University*, 2013(6).

Chen Yihong. On the Supply Chain Finance Model of Micro and Small Enterprises—Micro and Small Finance Service Model of City Commercial Banks [J]. *Journal of Chongqing University of Posts and Telecommunications (social sciences)*, 2012a, 24(5): 107–112.

Chen Yihong. Developing Micro and Small Finance Based on Industry and Supply Chain Finance—On Micro and Small Finance Service Mode of Urban Commercial Banks [J]. *West Forum on Economy and Management*, 2012b, 23(3): 61–65.

Fan Lulin, Zhou Yiping & Li Shijie. Private Financing and the Development of Micro and Small Enterprises—an Empirical Analysis Based on the Financing of 300 Micro and Small Enterprises in Taizhou, Zhejiang Province [J]. *Economic Vision*, 2013 (18).

Fu Qingxi. Taizhou (Zhejiang) Supporting Micro and Small Businesses: Efforts from the Government and the Banks [N]. *China Economic Herald*, April, 2013.

Huang Jun & Guo Yichen. New Trends in the Micro and Small Financial Market [J]. *The Banker*, 2013 (12).

Li Junlong. On Positive Effects and Risk Response of Rural Banks Controlled by Private Capital [J]. *Research of Finance and Accounting*, 2013 (2): 76–77.

Lin Li. The Development of Small and Microfinance Business of Wells Fargo Bank—from the Perspective of Financial Function View [J]. *Review of Investment Studies*, 2012, 31(11): 20–32.

Li Yang. Micro and Small Finance Is Not just Micro and Small Loans [J]. *Prospects for China's Financial Reform and Development*, 2012(6).

Liu Kegu. Building China's Grassroots Financial System, Promoting Grassroots Economic Development and Urban and Rural Employment—also on the Cracking of Financing Difficulties for Small Enterprises in China [J]. *Management World*, 2009, 11: 001.

Mo Zhili & Shao Danping. Financing Limitation and Channel Expansion of Private Enterprises—a Case Study of Luqiao District, Taizhou City [J]. *Journal of Hubei University of Economics (Humanities and Social Sciences)*, 2005, 2(5): 50–52.

Pan Jianhua. How Can Local Financial Institutions Boost the Development of Micro and Small Enterprises [J]. *Policy Outlook*, 2012 (10): 41–43.

Yang Fenglai & Huang Yonghang. Corporate Governance Structure, Information Asymmetry and SME Financing [J]. *Journal of Financial Research*, 2006(5): 159–166.

Fang Fang & Ding Mingxing. Strategic Financing Dilemma and Optimal Financing Strategy of SMEs [J]. *Economic Theory and Business Management*, 2006(8): 44–49.

Luo Danyang & Yin Xingshan. On Informal Financing of SMEs [J]. *Journal of Financial Research*, 2006(4): 142–150.
Lin Yifu & Sun Xifang. Information, Informal Finance and SME Financing [J]. *Economic Research Journal*, 2005(7): 35–44.
Tian Xiaoxia. A Review of Theories and Empirical Research on Small Business Financing [J]. *Economic Research Journal*, 2004(5): 107–116.
Wang Xiao & Zhang Jie. Bank Credit Rationing and SME Borrowing: a Theoretical Model of Endogenous Collateral and Firm Size. *Economic Research Journal*, 2003(6): 68–75.
Hu Xiaoping, et al. Life Cycle, Profits Expectations and Financing Difficulties of SMEs [J]. *Economy Forum*, 2003(16): 24–26.

CHAPTER 3

The Development of Micro and Small Finance in Luqiao

Over the past two decades and more, Luqiao district has been building platforms, conducting close exchanges and win-win cooperation to support and promote local financial institutions in improving financing services, diversifying financing products, and strengthening the financing system for micro and small businesses. As a result, regional financial institutions and enterprises cooperate closely with each other, making Luqiao a national model for providing financial services to micro and small businesses. The private economy thrives in the district with numerous SMEs. They might be financially trapped in the pursuit of development. However, with the joint efforts of the district government, banks, and enterprises, the financing difficulties of SMEs in Luqiao have been effectively alleviated, and small and microfinance maintains a good momentum of growth.

3.1 The Status Quo of Micro and Small Finance in China

SMEs need to address information asymmetry to overcome financing difficulties. However, information asymmetry naturally exists in China's financial system in the process of transforming from savings to investment, and SMEs are relatively not good at disclosing their information. Whether the supply of financial services goes well with SMEs and their diversified financial needs is the core to providing better access to financing for SMEs.

W. Xiao et al., *Microfinance and China's Regional Development*,
https://doi.org/10.1007/978-981-99-1960-4_3

There are four mismatches in the development of small and microfinance in China: first, a mismatch between the banking structure and the financing needs of SMEs; Second, the mismatch between capital market structure and SMEs' financing needs; Third, mismatch between financial structure and the financing needs of SMEs; Fourth, mismatch between the structure of the financial sector and the financing needs of SMEs.

Mismatch Between the Banking Structure and the Financing Needs of SMEs

Small and medium-sized banks have comparative advantages in serving SMEs, while large banks have comparative advantages in serving large enterprises. In the real economy, we have both large-scale, standardized production and small-scale, customized production. We must build an appropriate banking structure based on market demand and mechanism design. Financing difficulties are fundamentally caused by a banking structure with state-owned commercial banks as the main player. It means they are the main provider of credit, but hold discrimination against SMEs and there aren't enough other financing channels. The financial industry is developing in this direction: financing services are increasingly comprehensive, and financial institutions are becoming more niche and specialized. On the whole, the industry is increasingly diverging: first, commercial banks are mainly engaged in short-term loans, and financial institutions engaged in financing for medium-and-long-term fixed assets. Second, industrial funds are engaged in industrial investment (including venture funds) and investment funds in securities. Third, large financial institutions provide huge loans to large enterprises and small and medium-sized financial institutions provide micro loans to SMEs (Fig. 3.1 and Table 3.1).

First is credit discrimination. During the progressive reform of China's economic system, to ensure the steady growth of the state-owned sector, most financial resources were allocated to state-owned enterprises, thus creating a favorable reform environment. However, SMEs were inadequately financed by the state financial system in the process. In addition, state-owned commercial banks falsely believed that assets of state-owned banks and enterprises belong to the country, thus, giving loans to state-owned enterprises should be taken for granted, even if there are significant credit risks. However, the majority of SMEs are private enterprises, and their assets were believed to have nothing to do with those of the banks. If the loans cannot be recovered, there will be a major liability crisis. As a

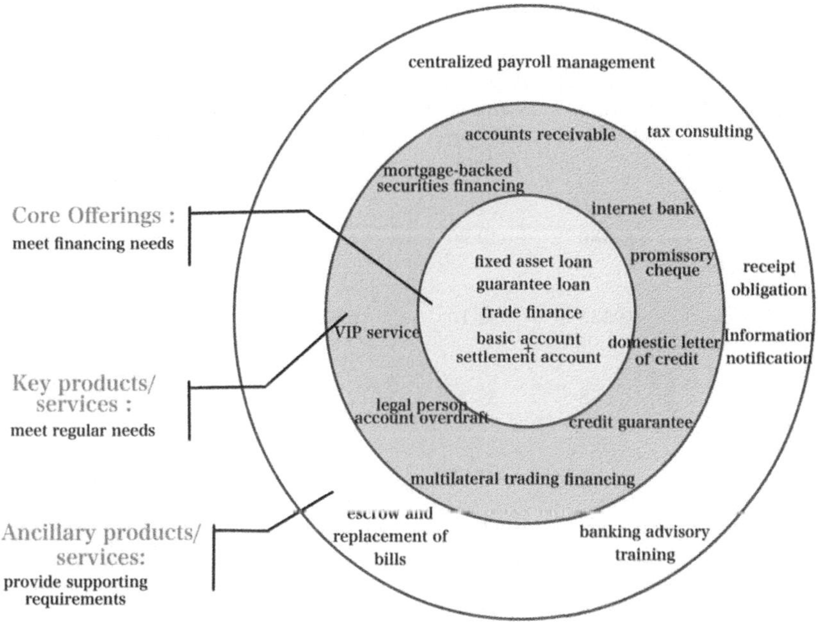

Fig. 3.1 Financing needs of SMEs

result, state-owned banks are particularly cautious, if not reluctant, when it comes to lending to SMEs. What these commercial banks have done naturally impacts the financing of SMEs: First, township or rural banks have more deposits than loans, and have to abide by strict credit authorization systems, thus finding it difficult to issue loans. They also apply stringent requirements for businesses to take out loans, clean up small individual borrowers, and control the number of new applicants, depleting sources of financing for SMEs. Second, although these banks have put in place the mechanism that lowers loan risks, the corresponding mechanism that provides incentives has yet been established. Especially when it comes to the existing property rights system, the absence of property rights owners of state-owned commercial banks discouraged lower-level banks to support SMEs. Third, the write-off of non-performing and bad debts is treated differently according to ownership. The government endorses state-owned large enterprises without limits by subsidizing for the losses and bankruptcy of state-owned enterprises, but the bad debts of SMEs are

Table 3.1 The proportion of micro and small business loans and personal business loans of different types of banks in China in 2012 (%)

Banking category	*Average assets (RMB 100 million)*	*Proportion of SMB loans to enterprise loans*	*Proportion of SMB loans to assets*	*Proportion of personal business loans to assets*	*Proportion of SMB loans and personal business loans to assets*
Large-scale commercial bank	115880	19.90	6.84	1.85	8.69
Joint-stock commercial bank	19533	22.10	6.98	4.17	11.15
City commercial bank	858	39.72	12.91	3.38	16.29
Rural bank	4	87.88	32.67	31.28	63.90

Source: Based on the relevant data of CBRC (China Banking and Insurance Regulatory Commission)

Note: (1) The data of average assets of rural banks are recorded by June 2012, all the others by the end of 2012; (2) Micro and small enterprises are divided according to the Notice on Printing and Distributing the Standards for Small and Medium-sized Enterprises by the Ministry of Industry and Information, the National Bureau of Statistics, the National Development and Reform Commission, and the Ministry of Finance; (3) Personal business loans include loans from individual businesses and those from micro and small business owners

not considered eligible for a write-off. This worryingly discourages and frightens state-owned commercial banks from developing SME credit businesses. Fourth, the credit application process at state-owned commercial banks is protracted and complicated, while SMEs need flexible money and quick turnover, increasing the cost of management and single transaction.

Second, the development of small and medium-sized financial institutions lags. By the end of August 2012, China had 147 urban commercial banks, 212 rural commercial banks, 190 rural cooperative banks, and 635 rural and township banks. The structure of China's current banking system: the central bank is the core, and the four state-owned commercial banks are the main players. After the system reform of these banks, they started focusing on bulk wholesale business without paying much attention to the needs of SMEs. Local financial institutions became local state-owned enterprises following reform, but failed to live up to their role as supporter of financing SMEs. China's small and medium-sized financial institutions are faced with a serious shortage, and also encounter many obstacles to further development. At present, financial institutions below the county level are mainly branches of the four state-owned banks, city commercial banks, and rural credit cooperatives. The four banks have cut down on their branches below the county level to varying degrees or disabled their right to provide loans. There are just over 100 city commercial banks in over 100 cities, and they are problematic. There is a large number of rural credit cooperatives, but they are unable to meet the financing needs of SMEs as these cooperatives suffer losses and prominent risks. At the same time, local small and medium-sized banks don't regard SMEs as their target clients. Instead, they prefer competing with big banks for big customers and reducing their financing support for SMEs.

Third, policy banks struggle to finance SMEs. According to Article 15 of China's Law on the Promotion of SMEs, state policy financial institutions shall provide financial services to SMEs in various forms within their business scope. But China's current policy on the financial sector means it is difficult to implement the article. Take China Development Bank for example; its main task is to support policy projects and supporting construction projects, including the construction of large and medium-sized infrastructure, basic industries, pillar industries, and technical upgrades. The main task of the Export-Import Bank of China is to provide policy-based financial support for the expansion of China's capital exports, such as mechanical and electrical products and complete equipment. The main task of the Agricultural Development Bank of China is to raise agriculture policy funds to facilitate economic development in agriculture and rural areas. It is fair to say that supporting SME financing is not the main task of the three policy banks.

Banks dominate the financing market and they are still the preferred financing channel for SMEs. China's financial system is characterized by a double-track system. To be specific, efforts were made to firstly vigorously develop joint-stock commercial banks in addition to state-owned ones, and secondly, commercialize state-owned banks by making them compete against each other, to establish a modern commercial bank system. Due to the stable government reform and the preference for a state-owned system, reforming state-owned financial banks has given them a strong monopoly. From the point of institutional supply, the government-led institutional reform has produced supply excess, that is, in contrast to the shortage of private financial system supply. According to the ownership

Table 3.2 Total assets of banks (Unit: RMB 100 million Yuan)

Bank type	*2007*	*2008*	*2009*	*2010*	*2011*
Policy bank	42781	56454	69456	76521	93133
Large-scale commercial bank	285000	325751	407998	468943	536336
Joint-stock commercial bank	72742	88337	118181	149037	183794
City commercial bank	33405	41320	56800	78526	99845
Rural commercial bank	6097	9291	18661	27670	42527
Rural cooperative bank	6460	10033	12791	15002	14025
Urban credit cooperative	1312	804	272	22	30
Rural credit cooperative	43434	52113	54945	63911	72047
New rural financial institutions and postal savings bank	17687	22163	27045	35101	43536

Note: (1) Policy Banks include the China Development Bank, the Export-Import Bank of China, and the Agricultural Development Bank of China; (2) Large Commercial Banks include the Industrial and Commercial Bank of China (ICBC), Agricultural Bank of China, Bank of China, China Construction Bank, and Bank of Communications; (3) Joint-stock commercial Banks include China CITIC Bank, China Everbright Bank, Huaxia Bank, Guangdong Development Bank (CGB), Shenzhen Development Bank, China Merchants Bank, Shanghai Pudong Development Bank, Industrial Bank, China Minsheng Bank, Evergrowing Bank, China Zheshang Bank and China Bohai Bank; (4) New rural financial institutions include rural banks, loan companies and rural capital mutual societies

structure of the financial organization system in Table 3.2, most financial institutions have public financial property rights, and the proportion of private financial property rights in the financial organization system is very small.

Generally speaking, large banks, due to their size, number, and business scope, are more likely to lend under the market-based transaction to carry out business efficiently and control risks effectively. Given whether to issue credit is decided by only a few and it entails a protracted approval procedure, loan issuance from big banks is generally a slow process. Large banks find it suitable to provide credit services for large enterprises. Small banks, with fewer branches, smaller assets, and fewer business types, are more likely to lend based on relationships. Different from their larger counterparts in terms of decision-making and approval process, small banks generally issue loans very quickly. Private small and medium-sized lenders can acquire information easily, as they understand how local SMEs operate, their project prospects and credit level at a low cost, which is the easiest way to overcome high transaction costs because of information asymmetry. Private financial institutions find it easier to do SME financing. Statistics on small business loans in the United States show that with the

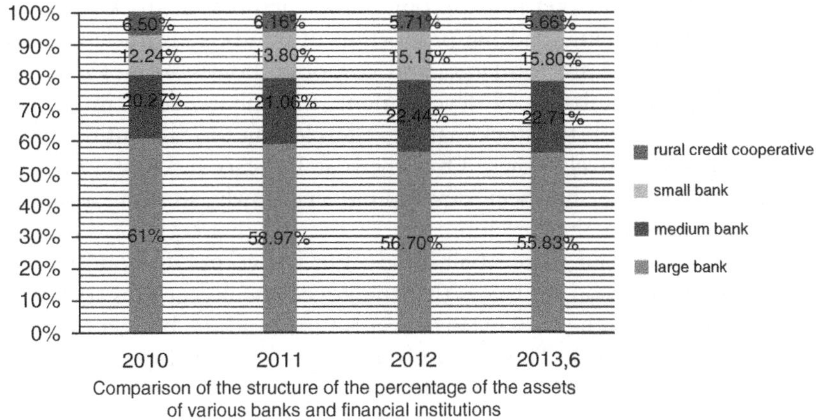

Fig. 3.2 Comparison of the structure of the percentage of the assets of various banks and financial institutions

expansion of assets, the proportion of small business loans to bank assets and the proportion of small and medium business loans to bank loans are gradually decreasing. And China's SME loan statistics share similarities. Statistics show that with the gradual increase in asset size, the proportion of SMEs loans in enterprise loans of all kinds of banks decreased gradually in 2012: the proportion of rural banks, city commercial banks, joint-stock commercial banks and large commercial banks was 87.88%, 39.72%, 22.1%, and 19.9% respectively. At the same time, the proportion of SMEs and personal business loans in assets has gradually decreased: the proportion of rural banks, city commercial banks, joint-stock commercial banks, and large commercial banks is 63.9%, 16.29%, 11.15%, and 8.69% respectively (Fig. 3.2).

Mismatch Between Capital Market Structure and SMEs Financing Needs

A Multi-level capital market structure does not take shape in direct financing. We have different kinds of capital markets, including the main board market and the second board market, the stock market and the private equity market, the equity market and the debt market, the exchange trading, and the over-the-counter trading. They provide loans for SMEs with different characteristics and financial needs.

China's capital market is inappropriately structured, as stock plays too big a part in financing, and the proportion of bonds is insufficient. Also, government bonds are too large, and corporate bonds are not enough. Specifically, such unbalanced development is mainly reflected in the following aspects: First, the stock market is developing too fast but the bond market grows relatively slowly. Over the past 10 years and more, the corporate bond market has been developing very slowly, showing a serious mismatch between the developments of the two markets. Government bonds took the main share of all bonds, but the corporate bond market lags. The main reason for this is that the government regulates corporate bonds, meaning higher risk means lower return. And the budget of credit funds has limitations. This not only hampers the development of the corporate bond market but also harms the interests of creditors. A slow-growing corporate bond market is a barrier to direct investment; limitations on credit increase the risk of bank operation and damage the interests of depositors. Second, treasury bonds and policy financial bonds dominate the bond market, while corporate bonds shrink. Since state bonds started to be issued in 1981, China's bond market has experienced rapid development. In 1993, to keep economic and financial order, China began cleaning up the bond market, cracking down on unruly, illegal fund-raising, and blocking ways of issuing other financial bonds, corporate bonds, and state-invested corporate bonds. In 1995, policy financial bonds were developed, which led to the rapid expansion of financial bonds, making both government bonds and policy financial bonds dominate the bond market. Third, the securities market is unbalanced. The second board market has not yet been established, so it is difficult for SMEs and high-tech enterprises to finance through the capital market. The securities trading market is unitary, and the over-the-counter securities trading market needs to be improved, which is not conducive to the circulation of securities.

A diversified, complementary financial organization system, made possible through financial system reform, not only conforms to market rules but also strengthens the financial competition mechanisms and improves efficiency. However, this organizational structure is still far from appropriate. In 2011, indirect financing reached 54,794.6669 billion yuan, 94.25 times that of direct financing, which was 581.419 billion yuan. This means that the vast majority of assets are owned by financial institutions engaged in indirect financing, in other words, by large state-owned commercial banks. The financial organization system presents an oligopoly pattern.

The financial organization system is monopolized by commercial banks, which are monopolized by state-owned commercial banks. Indirect finance is too strong and direct finance is too weak.

With the gradual development of China's new financing system, direct financing has become the main financing approach for many SMEs, including fund-raising, stock, debt, private lending, and so on. Due to the immaturity of China's capital market, SMEs lack direct financing means, and major problems exist in the market structure. A lack of different levels of financing suitable for various types of SMEs affects their development. To be specific: (1) The single-level securities market, due to access restrictions, has not opened a direct financing channel for SMEs. They cannot use existing capital markets for financing, which seriously affects their development. (2) The single-level capital market mainly provides funds for the restructuring of large state-owned enterprises, while there is yet a channel connecting the supply and demand sides in the private equity capital market. (3) The long-term bill market is underdeveloped, if not developed at all. (4) For a long time, the development of the corporate bond market has been slow, the role of the bond market has been ignored, and the cultivation of the bond market has not been taken as an important means of private enterprise financing. (5) Private financing plays an important role in the development of SMEs. However, China has a discriminatory policy to private financing, as it provides no legal protection, and this kind of financing is ill-regulated and risk-prone. All these factors make private financing difficult to be provided in the market despite its low cost.

Mismatch Between Financial Structure and the Financing Needs of SMEs

Apart from financing, SMEs also have needs for value-added services, thus requiring comprehensive financial functions. In recent years, China Banking Regulatory Commission (CBRC) has implemented some measures to deliver services for small businesses: First, establish professional mechanisms in financial services. In 2005, CBRC urged banks to establish six institutions providing financial services for small businesses under market principles and commercial operation. They, including interest rate risk pricing, independent accounting, efficient approval, incentives and restraints, professional training, and default information notification, have laid a foundation for the sustainable development of small business finance. Second, create a favorable institutional environment of financial services for small businesses. Considering the accountability and assessment system for non-performing assets of banks and the due diligence requirements for credit granting of small businesses cannot fully meet their needs, the CBRC has issued documents with a complete regulatory framework such as *Guideline on Due Diligence in Credit Granting of Small Enterprises by Commercial Banks.* Together with other departments, CBRC introduced interim measures for the management of financing guarantee companies, which fundamentally created an institutional environment for promoting the sustainable development of financial services for small businesses. Third, ensure a priority credit policy for small businesses. Promote the industrial upgrading of small enterprises, and address imbalanced financial resources distribution among regions. Fourth, build a credit guarantee system for small enterprises. After more than ten years of development, the small business credit guarantee industry has begun to take shape. Rules for prudential regulation and operation in the guarantee industry have been defined, and market access for guarantee institutions has been strict. At the same time, CBRC continues to promote cooperation between financing guarantee institutions and banks, encouraging risks and benefits sharing among small enterprises, financing guarantee institutions, and banks. Sixth, formulate differentiated financial regulatory policies for small businesses. At the end of May 2011, to implement guidelines on further promoting the development of SMEs, and improving financing for SMEs, CBRC issued a Notice on Supporting Commercial Banks to Improve Financial Services for Small Businesses, with a series of differentiated regulatory policy measures from the aspects of market access and off-site regulation indicators. In addition, CBRC works closely with ministries and departments. In 2009, CBRC and the Ministry of Science and Technology issued the Guidelines on Increasing Credit Support for Small and Medium-sized Tech Firms. In 2010, CBRC, together with the People's Bank of China, the Securities Regulatory Commission, and the Insurance Regulatory Commission, issued the Guidelines on Improving Financial Services for SMEs. In 2011, the CBRC, together with the Ministry of Commerce, issued the Guidelines on Supporting the Development of Financing in Business Districts.

However, there are several problems when it comes to innovation in the products and services of major banks. First, the financial products of commercial banks are seriously homogenized. The financial products of many SMEs are simply a copy from large banks. They slightly modify loan terms, amount of credit, and guarantee mode, before providing them to small businesses. As you can see, SMEs' financial products on the market are largely identical in functions, although product names are different. Second, the approval system of large and medium-sized banks for SME financing is too harsh and complicated. On the one hand, large and medium-sized banks have too high requirements for SMEs, be it mortgage or credit guarantee. At the same time, some state-owned enterprises or large projects took out a significant portion of loans provided by large and medium-sized banks, making it even more difficult for SMEs to finance; On the other hand, large and medium-sized banks have complicated approval procedures for SME financing. SMEs usually need a small amount of capital in a short time. The complicated approval procedures force SMEs to give up loans from state banks and instead turn to private lenders. According to the person in charge of the Taizhou Branch of ICBC, it takes about three months to approve the application by an SME, which is a long time for the enterprise that is in urgent need of funds to solve its development crisis. Third, the financing market for SMEs is huge, but the financial industry needs to be more competitive. Based on field investigation of the project team, state-owned commercial banks, joint-stock banks, and local banks are positive towards loans to SMEs, especially small and micro loans. However, the biggest concern for these banks is not occupying the market, but they still have much room for improvement in terms of financing services and product innovation. In addition, a big challenge is to have enough manpower to do deals with a large number of enterprises. If the banking industry plans to adjust its previous strategy by targeting SMEs, it needs to improve its products, management, and technology, among others.

At present, financial services provided by banking financial institutions to SMEs are problematic in the following areas. First, in terms of market positioning, some banks, especially a few small and medium-sized banks, and rural financial institutions lack a clear position in the market; Second, in terms of mechanism and institution, some banks' credit approval procedures do not meet the needs of small businesses; Third, in terms of incentives, some banks have not formulated the assessment, promotion and accountability-exempt system for clerks that do small business loans; Fourth, concerning risk control, some banks' internal control system and risk management measures can not adapt to such financial services.

Mismatch Between the Structure of the Financial Sector and the Financing Needs of SMEs

With the advancement of science and technology, the social division of labor is becoming increasingly sophisticated. The socialization, virtualization, networking, and electronization of social and economic activities require diversified financial services. Although some achievements have been made in the development of China's financial market in recent years, there is still no substantial improvement in reducing heavy reliance on banks for private financing, or in diluting bank risks. Therefore, it is necessary to diversify financial service providers. First, financial services for SMEs in the service industry are underdeveloped and insufficient. At present, one of the difficulties in meeting the financing needs of SMEs is the lack of development of all kinds of non-banking financial institutions, which leads to information asymmetry and inefficient financing. In addition to developing the banking, securities, and insurance sectors, a more efficient financial environment needs to be created for them to thrive, such as scientific and technological achievements appraisal institutions, science and technology guarantee agencies, pawn companies, financial consultancy, insurance intermediary institutions, third-party payment institutions, and credit enhancement institutions. New types of financial entities such as enterprise annuity, asset management, wealth management, private equity funds, and financing guarantee companies need to be well-quipped to provide better financing services to SMEs. Second, a defective credit investigation system leads to a bad financing environment for SMEs. Establishing a credit system involves information collection, processing, evaluation, and usage. China has established a basic database of business credit, but this does not include most SMEs. On the one hand, some ill-behaved SMEs do not want to provide true information, but more importantly, SMEs' credit information is collected by different departments, such as industry and commerce, public security, customs, and tax departments. Due to a lack of coordination and a sharing mechanism between departments, SMEs' credit information is difficult to be integrated. At present, China has not put in place regulations on the establishment and optimization of specific evaluation standards, the credit system is not playing its due role. From the perspective of credit rating, independent credit rating agency is not credible enough, which is undoubtedly a problem, but from the perspective of banks, when they receive applications for loans, each bank has its independent credit rating system and a different rating standard. An enterprise rated as Grade A in one bank could be rated as Grade B in another. Institutions that govern SMEs are yet established, and the information disclosure mechanism is dysfunctional. At present, the credit evaluation system for SMEs in China has not been established. It is difficult to regulate them, and for enterprises to be investigated and punished for their bad behaviors, which will easily lead to the deterioration of credit. Both large enterprises and SMEs have huge differences in their development. The crunchy credit investigation system makes well-developed SMEs face the same financing difficulty as bad-performing ones, which is not good for market competition. Third, the credit guarantee system is not perfect, and there is a lack of a favorable bank credit environment. It is difficult for SMEs to obtain loans by solely relying on their credit, and credit problems are prevalent among SMEs. Establishing a credit system and improving credit guarantee help with indirect financing for SMEs. At present, the risk-sharing mechanism between banks and guarantee institutions is not sound. Without a clear risks sharing mechanism, banks have no incentives to perform the duty of loan review and management, and after loan risks appear, the bank also has no incentives to recover. In that case, the rights and responsibilities between banks and guarantee agencies are unequal, thus increasing the operating costs of the latter, and even if they gain profits from the loans, they cannot compare with returns on ordinary investment. As a result, many guarantee companies withdraw from the market, and the whole guarantee industry gradually shrinks. SMEs find it more difficult to finance. From the perspective of the guarantee system, on the one hand, the guarantee system of SMEs lacks a funds compensation mechanism, so relying solely on the guarantee is unsustainable; on the other hand, due to a lack of risk disperse mechanism, when SMEs are over-indebted, guarantee agencies need to repay the bank funds with interests, taking 100% of risks (Fig. 3.3).

3.2 Brilliant Achievements in the Development of Luqiao Micro and Small Finance

The small and microfinance in Luqiao District came into being in response to financial reform mandated by the central government, starting from solving financing difficulties of SMEs in Luqiao District. On July 5, 2013, The State Council issued the Guidelines on Financial Support for Economic Restructuring and Upgrading, which gave comprehensive instructions on micro and small financial services and promoted financial

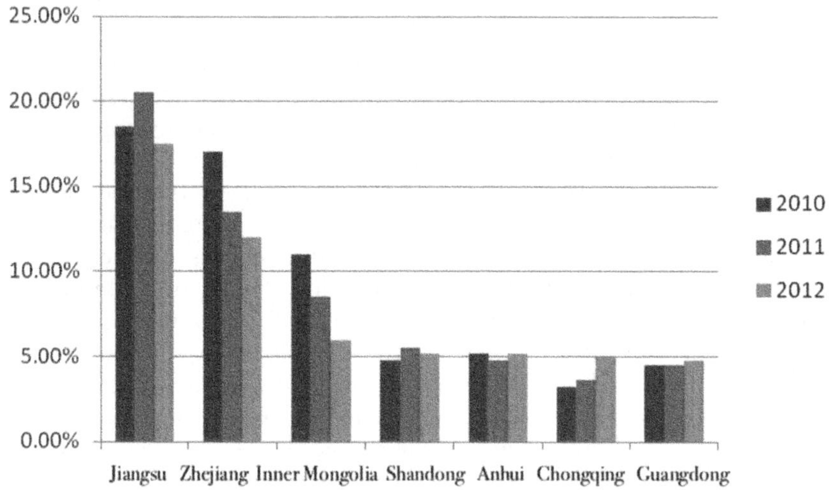

Fig. 3.3 Top seven provinces (autonomous regions and municipalities) with the percentage of small, medium, and micro-loans to bank loans. (Data source: China Industrial Bank internal research report)

support for micro and small enterprises. Micro and small businesses are new forces driving the economy, playing a very important role in keeping steady growth, providing employment, promoting innovation, invigorating markets, and meeting the needs of the people. Strengthening financial services for micro and small businesses is instrumental in supporting the real economy, stabilizing employment and encouraging entrepreneurship. It bears on overall economic and social development and is of great strategic significance.

The development of small and microfinance in Luqiao District is obviously at the forefront of China. In 2012, Taizhou municipal government issued the Five-year Plan for Financial Development, aiming to build a city of featured small finances with nationwide influences, a private finance demonstration zone, a small business financial service demonstration zone, and a financial innovation experimental zone. The city will focus on Luqiao District and then replicate best practices in other districts, cities, and provinces.

At present, three local corporate banks in Luqiao District, Taizhou set up their headquarters in Nanguan Avenue, Luqiao District, and its surrounding areas. Taizhou Bank has 15 branches in Luqiao District, 9 branches in Jiaojiang District and Huangyan District respectively, 8 branches in Wenling, 3 branches in Yuhuan County, 5 branches in Linhai, 3 branches in Tiantai County, and 1 branch in Xianju County, with a total of 53 branches and 1 head office in Taizhou. The number of branches in Taizhou exceeds that set up by other cities. Talon Bank has 25 branches in Taizhou and a total of 67 branches in the surrounding cities of Ningbo, Hangzhou, Suzhou, Shanghai, Jinhua, Quzhou, Lishui, Jiaxing, and Huzhou. The headquarters and all 14 branches of Luqiao Rural Cooperative Bank are located in the Taizhou downtown area. It has also become Taizhou's first cross-regional cooperative bank with a branch in Taizhou Development Zone. After more than two years of preparation, the Development Zone branch of Luqiao Rural Cooperative Bank was approved by the China Banking Regulatory Commission (CBRC) for trans-regional operation in September 2012. A rural cooperative bank often has difficult access to markets in other districts when it intends to operate across regions. It is for example required to have an asset size of more than 10 billion yuan. As early as 2012, the assets of Luqiao Rural Cooperative Bank reached 15 billion yuan. There are 25 banks and 48 financial institutions in Taizhou Development Zone, and the competition is very fierce. Most deposits from the Luqiao Rural Cooperative Bank Development Zone Branch come from a large number of households. It can win over people as business contacts and develop personal financial services, including consumer finance, personal finance, and financial management. In general, the three banks provide services in ever wider-ranging areas, with Taizhou at the center. Tailong Bank took the lead in trying to expand its services to wider Zhejiang province and Shanghai. To break down the capital and geographical restrictions of local corporate financial institutions under market competition, the three banks in Luqiao District are seeking to deliver cross-regional services.

On November 19, 2012, the first cross-strait Seminar on Small and Microfinance Development was held in Luqiao District. It was closely followed by the Central and Provincial Taiwan Affairs Offices and attended by nearly 400 well-known scholars and financial professionals from both sides of the Straits. The seminar brought in best practices of micro and small financial services from Taiwan and boosted innovation efforts of micro and small financial services in Luqiao. In order to create a favorable environment for the development of small and microfinance, the government is building a financial talent-training base. Efforts are made to step up training local banking personnel, encourage the private sector to carry out relevant training programs, build credit technology training bases for micro and small enterprises nationwide, and improve the agglomeration and radiation function of Luqiao finance. For example, support is provided for the further development of Talon College and Ginza College by encouraging them to obtain private training licenses, to train more professionals. To provide more ways of small and micro-financing, the district government encourages SMEs to file for IPO. The listing of enterprises is itself a breakthrough for industrial transformation and upgrading, which encourages more businesses to go listing, to make full use of the SMEs board, the Growth Enterprise Market, and the international market for direct financing. At the same time, the government has been working with the Provincial Stock Exchange Center for Unlisted Companies (OTC Market), to encourage SMEs to list on the OTC market to realize the circulation of shares and create conditions for listing and financing. In 2012, Zhejiang Yilida Ventilator Co., Ltd., was listed on the Shenzhen Small and Medium-sized Board with a fund-raising of RMB270 million. Ten enterprises including Golden Dragon Electric and Green Field Machinery are now making pre-listing preparations. Second, the government makes efforts to promote bond financing. The district finance has set up special funds to encourage enterprises, especially those to be listed, to issue bonds such as privately raised bonds, short-term financing bonds, and medium-term bills. At the same time, the government cooperates with securities brokers to establish a quick, easy bond-issuing service platform for enterprises. Third, the government accelerates the development of equity financing. To establish district-level industrial and venture capital funds, it takes the lead in providing the fund and steers all kinds of private capital to support industrial upgrading and the development of SMEs in Luqiao. The fund is raised by strong enterprises in the area and well-known private equity institutions from the province and beyond, and organized in a limited partnership. At the same time, the government pushes capital outside of the district to come back in the form of private equity and venture capital. By the end of 2012, the district had attracted more than 2 billion yuan.

Over the years, the government of Luqiao District has made remarkable achievements in the reform, innovation, and practice of small and microfinance by focusing on serving the real economy and exploring the innovative reform of small and microfinance. Till now, it has created a distinctive and widely influential Luqiao Experience and it has become a brand of financial support for SMEs in China. By the end of March 2012, loans for SMEs (including individual businesses) in Taizhou accounted for 46.9% of total loans, and 75.7% of the loans were issued by the three city commercial banks. More than 94% of the clients took out an average single loan of only about 500,000 yuan (Table 3.3).

On November 29, 2013, the second Cross-Straits Small and Microfinance Development Forum was held in Luqiao District. The forum attracted more than 300 participants from academia, finance, business, and other communities across the Straits. The theme of the forum, "Serving SMEs, Innovative Development", has been a complete success as it had good organization, rich content, in-depth exchanges, and remarkable results.

First, Taizhou Financial Service Credit Information Center was inaugurated. It draws on the experience of Taiwan joint credit center and other credit systems and platforms by integrating information from financial institutions, industries, commerce, taxation, quality control, environmental protection, public security, and courts, to provide comprehensive credit information to financial institutions, government departments, and the

Table 3.3 Deposits and loans of financial institutions in Luqiao district

Date	*Deposit balance (RMB 100 million)*	*Loan balance (RMB 100 million)*	*Loan-Deposit ratio*	*Non-performing loans ratio*
1995	19.10	12.98	67.92%	
1996	26.59	17.02	64.00%	
1997	37.30	21.81	58.47%	
1998	52.81	28.80	54.53%	
1999	72.45	41.31	57.01%	
2000	91.36	54.55	59.71%	
2001	109.73	63.79	58.14%	
2002	140.72	96.79	68.78%	
2003	179.68	128.54	71.54%	
2004	204.33	148.04	72.45%	
2005	251.25	185.08	73.66%	
2006	302.38	238.30	78.81%	
2007	345.62	286.76	82.97%	
2008	397.77	328.84	82.67%	
2009	450.81	417.81	92.68%	
2010	539.42	494.52	91.68%	
2011	588.61	576.38	97.9%	0.88%
2012	642.89	612.30	95.2%	0.93%

society. It helps not only address information asymmetry but also guard against financial risks. Moreover, it is of great significance to make financial services serve the real economy and innovate in social management. The establishment of the Taizhou Financial Service Credit Information Center also lays a foundation for the city to introduce a series of innovative measures of financial services for SMEs. Second, the Taizhou Micro and Small Enterprises Credit Guarantee Fund Operation Center was launched, thanks to the best practices of the Taiwan SMEs credit guarantee fund. The Taizhou credit guarantee fund is mainly supported by the municipal and district governments, with donations from city commercial banks, rural cooperative financial institutions, and others. Non-profit corporation funds provide financing guarantees for SMEs, establishing a risk-sharing system for the three parties of the government, financial institutions, and enterprises, solving SMEs' financing guarantee and mortgage difficulties. Third, institutions across the Straits signed relevant cooperation agreements. Taizhou Banking Association and Taiwan Financial Research Institute agree to utilize their respective resources to promote cooperation in various types of training and investigation, including mutual visits of practitioners and joint holding of forums and seminars. Taizhou University and three universities in Taiwan are working closely on, say, allowing students majoring in finance to do research or take courses in the partnership university, making professor exchanges in the field of finance, and jointly holding academic lectures and other activities. Taizhou Luqiao Rural Cooperative Bank and these universities in Taiwan have agreed to conduct internship cooperation for students majoring in finance. These will deepen cross-strait financial exchanges and cooperation. Fourth, the Zhejiang Cross-Straits (Luqiao, Taizhou) Small, and Microfinance Cooperative Innovation Experimental Zone was officially approved. The pilot zone will promote the exchanges and cooperation on financial services between micro and small enterprises across the Straits. It will work on the cross-straits establishment of offices, investment attraction, and business cooperation between banking and financial institutions; It will promote the introduction and cooperation of other financial (intermediary) institutions across the Straits; It will participate in the establishment of micro and small enterprises financing guarantee system and financing guidance system, to help enterprises in Luqiao enter Taiwan's capital market. In 3 to 5 years, efforts will be made to build Luqiao District into a micro and small financial service pilot zone, innovation zone, and demonstration zone with Zhejiang province as the core and services covering both sides of the Taiwan Straits. Our goal is to put in place a micro and small business financial service system with active innovation, quick services, complete institutions, a developed market, and appropriate regulation, to promote sound and rapid economic development.

3.3 The Role of Micro and Small Finance in the Real Economy

Goldsmith (1969) proposed the definition of financial development from the perspective of financial structure, namely the development and change of financial structure, which is generally called financial deepening. As a tool to fill the loopholes in the financing system of SMEs, small and microfinance is itself an adjustment made by financial institutions to adapt to economic development. The emergence of small and microfinance is conducive to the effective use of savings funds in areas where SMEs develop and flourish, and promote the growth of productive investment. Before the idea of small and microfinance was raised, private capital usually went to the real estate, stock, futures, and bond markets, precious metals, art, and other fields, and some of them entered the real economy in the form of private lending.

From the perspective of endogenous growth of financial development, economic growth is always the result of capital accumulation and technological innovation. Therefore, the deepening of the financial system is bound to ultimately promote economic development through these two approaches. Endogenous financial development theorists represented by King and Levine (1993) and Stieglitz (1997) believe that the complexity and friction in the process of economic development contribute to the emergence of financial markets and financial services. The improvement of the structure and function of the financial market reduces the cost of capital transactions, thus reducing the savings rate and the price of capital, improving the efficiency of capital use, promoting the accumulation of capital and the occurrence of technological innovation, and further ensure sustainable development of the economy.

In general, small and microfinance mainly plays the roles of gathering savings, facilitating credit, optimizing resource allocation, and ultimately promoting economic growth through capital accumulation and technological innovation.

The private economy thrives in Zhejiang, particularly in Taizhou. As the cradle of China's stock cooperative economy, private enterprises account for more than 90% of all in the city, and they help drive Taizhou's economic development. Over the years, the private economy has contributed more than 90% of the city's GDP, more than 70% of fiscal revenue, and created about 80% of jobs, of which, the contribution of more than 100,000 micro and small enterprises cannot be underestimated. As the most densely populated district in Taizhou, Luqiao is the first development area for the private sector in China and has adopted a market-based approach. By 2012, the number of all kinds of private enterprises in Luqiao District has been close to tens of thousands. The number of all kinds of markets has reached nearly 100, and 99% of the businesses are micro, small and medium enterprises. These SMEs contribute 80% of Luqiao District GDP and created 40% of jobs, and are the most active part of regional economic development.

Vertically, Luqiao's economy used to be driven by agriculture with limited resources and a weak economic foundation. It is now growing thanks to its industrial cluster with the gradual transformation and upgrading of specialized markets. Over the course of eight years, from 1994 to 2011, the GDP of Luqiao District experienced remarkable growth, soaring from 2.67 billion yuan to 36.715 billion yuan, an increase of nearly 14 times. This significant development demonstrates the district's accelerating pace of progress. Local fiscal revenue also increased 32 times from 85 million yuan to 2.881 billion yuan, with an average annual growth rate of 23 percent. SMEs are the major contributor to such a growth rate.

Horizontally, in 2011, Luqiao created 13% of Taizhou's GDP and 14% of total fiscal revenue with 7% of its population and 2.9% of the land, among which, the major economic indicators such as GDP, fiscal revenue, gross industrial output and total retail sales of consumer goods took the lead in Taizhou.

The development of financial services for SMEs in Luqiao District has received a lot of attention in recent years, and relevant policies and measures have been followed through. By the end of November 2013, there had been 15 banking institutions, 4 small loan companies, 1 new financial service company (private loan transferring company), 6 financing guarantee companies, 25 insurance institutions, and 5 securities institutions in Luqiao District. Meanwhile, the three major local SME financing banks in Luqiao, namely, Taizhou Bank, Talon Bank, and Luqiao Rural Cooperative Bank, offered loans worth 100 billion yuan to more than 200,000 SMEs. These clients accounted for more than 90% of their total customers, and loans they provided to SMEs took up 80% of all they issued. The development of private financial institutions shows that small and medium-sized financial institutions are an effective form of financial organization to support the development of SMEs and play a positive role in promoting the development of a regional economy.

First, we will innovatively adopt new standards for credit rating and guarantee for SMEs, lower the threshold for loans to SMEs, and provide them with better access to loans in keeping with local realities. SMEs are of small size, do not have much collateral and do not reveal information effectively. These constitute the biggest obstacles to SME financing. To overcome information asymmetry, small and microfinance innovates boldly by coming up with a new credit evaluation model. For example, Luqiao Talon Bank gave up on the traditional credit model of simply relying on collateral, an adopted a new credit evaluation standard judged by their water & electricity usage, customs declaration, business owner's virtue, business products, and collateral. Taizhou Bank adopts a special client-manager system to obtain comprehensive information on micro and small enterprises through surveys and face-to-face communication. Client managers account for 40% of all employees of the bank, which is adequate to meet the needs of the information survey. Given SMEs have few fixed assets and struggle to pay for the mortgages, local banks come up with new ways of guaranteeing. The implementation of multiple joint guarantees, credit guarantees, moral guarantee, and others, combined with stock pledges, inventory warehouse receipts, store lease pledge, and right pledge credit products, provides an innovative guarantees. Apart from reducing bank risks, it makes SMEs' guarantees easier. With many stakeholders involved in the guarantee, they can supervise each other on guarantee repayment, thus effectively helping solve the problem of SME loan difficulty. In addition, several banks delegate the approval power, simplify the process of credit approval, and enable SMEs to get loans quickly.

To reduce the pressure on SMEs, some small and microfinance providers have also introduced preferential policies on loan fee reduction. For example, Taizhou Bank launched a service in 2012 that exempted 42 service fees, covering almost all RMB settlement services, as well as some other commonly used services. For example, the bank exempted fees on inter-bank cash transfers, deposits and withdrawals of the small payment system, online banking, mobile banking, bank draft, and so on. It has directly reduced costs of micro and small enterprises, agriculture, rural areas, farmers, and others. In the case of online inter-bank remittance, it used to charge 5 yuan for a 10,000 yuan cash transfer, 10 yuan for an amount between 10,000 to 100,000 yuan, and 0.002% of the total with a maximum of 200 yuan for more than 1 million. After the service was provided, cash transfer is all free of charge despite the amount. This saves a significant amount of money for SMEs that need to make regular online payments.

Second, the government and state-owned commercial banks work together to make good use of savings funds and private capital, reduce loan costs and risks, and accelerate the flow of capital to SMEs with great potential. In recent years, the Luqiao government has been running platforms to boost the development of the financial industry, to encourage state-owned and city commercial banks to work together using their complementary strengths and shared resources. Through money lending and business cooperation, deposits in state-owned commercial bank savings will be used by private financial institutions to SMEs with huge financing needs. This is a win-win mechanism for bank-enterprise cooperation. Such cooperation has brought down the costs of city commercial banks that provide micro and small financial services. At the same time, it has also improved the benefits of state-owned commercial banks and reduced the risks of their regional branches. In addition, regulating small and microfinance squeezes the development space of private finance and further reduces lending risks. At present, private finance in Luqiao includes direct lending, private fund-raising, mutual financing, and so on. It is often not regulated, and provides loans when regulated credit funds are unable to offer. In this case, the government of Luqiao District, with the help of Taizhou Bank, Zhejiang Talon Bank, and Luqiao Rural Cooperative Bank, squeezed the space of unregulated finance through the high satisfaction rate of credit demand and controlled the risk of private lending. The three local banks in Luqiao also made full use of the central bank's policy of relaxing the deposit interest rate and raised it by 10%. This gave these banks a competitive edge against unregulated financing and attracted a large number of private funds. According to statistics, by the end of 2012, the balance of deposits in these local banks reached 24.881 billion yuan, accounting for 66.49% of the deposits of urban and rural residents in Luqiao.

Third, we closely follow national industrial policies, support and promote green loans, and facilitate regional industrial upgrading. As the intermediary of gathering and providing capital factors, banks support the development of specific industries through the targeted investment of capital. Small and microfinance, which is positioned to serve SMEs, agriculture, rural areas, and farmers, and private businesses, plays an important role in facilitating the transformation and upgrading of SMEs. In response to national industrial policies, Taizhou Bank proposed green & energy-saving loans to help with their transformation and upgrading. The green & energy-saving loan by Taizhou Bank was raised in the innovative loan project on climate finance, jointly initiated by the United Nations Environment Program, Germany's Environmental Protection Agency, and the Frankfurt Institute. It is designed for those in the industrial sector to save energy and reduce emissions, improve energy efficiency, and update and eliminate outdated production capacity. It plays an important role in promoting the transformation and upgrading of SMEs in energy conservation, efficiency improvement, and greenhouse gas emissions reduction. At present, many enterprises are under pressure to upgrade as a result of environmental campaigns. Their small size and large capital shortage make them less motivated for technological transformation. Taizhou Bank cooperated with the Luqiao government in providing green & energy-saving loans for SMEs. These businesses, with assets below 5 million yuan, are given a loan between 50000 yuan to 5 million yuan, and they need to pay the loans between 3 months to 3 years after receiving them. Such loans help businesses purchase energy-saving equipment, improve production technology, and enhance competitiveness by reducing energy costs. In terms of repayment, SMEs have many options, including equal installment, one-time repayment, or flexible repayment, depending on their conditions. From the beginning of December 2011 to the end of October 2013, Taizhou Bank issued a total of 176 green & energy-saving loans, with the amount of 100.4436 million yuan. It is estimated that under the same output, 25,500 tons of carbon dioxide emissions can be reduced annually, and 33.83 million kilowatts of electricity can be saved. What Luqiao has done in small and microfinance is crucial for the development of intensive and innovative local SMEs.

Fourth, the bank has set up a fund to support business startups and a special fund for the elderly and the disabled to promote coordinated economic and social development. In addition to benefiting SMEs, steering funds to SMEs, and promoting their transformation and upgrading, small and microfinance providers themselves are also part of local enterprises. They play an important role in promoting the coordinated development of society and economy. In 2011, the Quzhou Branch of Zhejiang Talon Bank set up charity relief funds of The Red Cross for public welfare. In

August of the same year, Talon Bank, together with Taizhou Municipal Bureau of Human Resources and Social Security, Bureau of Finance, Taizhou central sub-branch of the People's Bank, and Talon Commercial Bank launched the Talon Startup Loans Project, providing business loans for individuals, businesses, startups and legal persons. In 2012, Luqiao Rural Cooperative Bank donated 10 million RMB to set up the Charity Fund for Extremely Poor Farmers, which aims to subsidize the life of extremely poor farmers. These special loans and funds play a significant role in facilitating local consumption, providing employment and boosting regional innovation capacity, and drive the social and economic development of the region and beyond.

In general, such an innovative financial model can meet the loan needs of SMEs in the region, steer funds to businesses, make good of savings and restrain unregulated lending. Green financial products enable the financial field to go green, driving the transformation and upgrading of micro and small enterprises, and promoting the development of SMEs and local financial systems. The development and transformation of SMEs is also a manifestation of the healthy, fast, and sustainable economic development of the Luqiao District. In addition, micro-finance also helps boost local consumption and employment, further pushing the district to grow sustainably. It is worth noting that while developing small and microfinance to support economic development, we should also pay attention to the research on the cost and risk control of small and microfinance and establish a benign business model.

3.4 Evaluation of the Development of Micro and Small Finance in Luqiao

Design of Evaluation System for the Development of Small and Microfinance

Setting up the indices for the innovative development of small and microfinance is a systematic project, which is essential to the evaluation of how small and microfinance has developed. As financial institutions in various regions increase their support for micro and small enterprises, and small and microfinance is becoming more innovative, the evaluation will be adjusted and improved in due time.

Basic Principles of the Evaluation System for the Development of Small and Microfinance

To establish a scientific, standardized, and feasible evaluation system for the development of small and microfinance, it is necessary to take the scientific outlook on development as the guideline to fully reflect its development. Therefore, we adhere to the following principles when establishing the evaluation system:

First, scientific. The design should be based on the scientific outlook on development. Select a series of indicators that can best measure and reflect the development and trend of small and microfinance, and build an evaluation index system that can accurately reflect its development based on scientific research and sufficient demonstration.

Second, directive. Through the evaluation and dynamic monitoring of the development of small and microfinance, the index system can timely find deficiencies, to point the right direction for the development of small and microfinance in terms of planning, policy, and management.

Third, comprehensive. The indicators can comprehensively describe the development, cover features of the development of small and microfinance, and accurately reflect the connotation of the development of small and microfinance.

Fourth, comparable. Full consideration should be given to the availability, measurability, practicability, and operability of data, combining value index and physical index, and measuring according to the relative amount of the index to maintain its comparability and continuity. At the same time, the dynamic comparison of different periods should be considered to ensure the best performances.

Fifth, operable. Indicators should be quantifiable and supported by long-term statistical data to avoid uncertainties such as subjectivity. The indicators included in the system should have clear concepts and can be measured or calculated in practice to facilitate quantitative analysis with an emphasis on operability. At the same time, the index system should be as concise as possible. When several indices can all reflect certain content, the most representative index should be selected to avoid repetition.

Basic Framework and Indices Establishment for the Evaluation of Small and Microfinance

The indices include 3 level-one indicators of supply, demand, and policy, and 13 level-two indicators (Table 3.4 for specific indicators). The

Table 3.4 The development indices of small and microfinance

Level-one indicators	*Domain*	*Number*	*Indicators*	*Unit*
Supply	banking institution	1	Number of local people	individual
		2	Registered capital of corporate bank	100 million
		3	The proportion of micro and small business loans of corporate banks	%
	private capital	4	Registered capital of small loan companies	100 million
		5	Total private capital	100 million
Demand	Financing efficiency	6	Small and microfinance loan balance	100 million
		7	Average loan amount to micro and small businesses	10 thousand
	Enterprise development	8	number of increased micro and small businesses	individual
		9	Financing satisfaction of micro and small enterprises	%
Policy	Policy supply	10	Number of policies introduced	individual
		11	Government guarantees	%
	service level	12	Enterprise satisfaction evaluation	%
		13	Self-evaluation of government satisfaction	%

indicators are based on the supply and demand of small and microfinance and the level of government services, which is the foundation of the development of small and microfinance.

An Explanation for the Development of Small and Microfinance

In terms of supply, financial institutions are an important way and basic guarantee of financing for micro and small enterprises, especially for growing local city commercial banks. Therefore, this book uses the three indicators of local commercial banks, registered capital, and the proportion of loans to micro and small businesses to measure how local city commercial banks can provide better financing for micro and small businesses. That is how their contribution to the development of local small and microfinance is gauged. At the same time, the accumulation of local private capital is a supplement to the financing efforts. In particular, small loan companies established by private capital have become an important choice for micro and small businesses to get quick money. Therefore, this book evaluates the contribution of private capital to the financing of micro and small enterprises using the two indicators of the total amount of private capital and the registered capital of small loan companies.

In terms of demand, how small and microfinance develops is reflected in the financing efficiency and development level of micro and small enterprises. Accordingly, this book selects the two indicators of the balance of small and microfinance loans and the average amount of micro and small business loans to measure the financing efficiency for micro and small businesses, to illustrate whether the efficiency has increased in the development of local small and microfinance. At the same time, this book uses the number of newly increased micro and small businesses in a year and their financing satisfaction to measure the development of local micro and small businesses, thereby indirectly illustrating how local small and microfinance develops.

In terms of policy, small and microfinance has always been the priority of what the government does, so it has introduced a host of policies to ensure its development, and to provide government services to ensure the financing of micro and small enterprises. In policy supply, the government generally introduces supporting policies and guarantee policies to facilitate financing efforts. Therefore, this book selects two indicators, the number of policies and government guarantee, to measure the contribution of policy supply to the development of small and microfinance. Meanwhile, this book selects corporate satisfaction evaluation and government satisfaction self-evaluation to measure how good government services are, to more objectively evaluate the role of the government in the development of local small and microfinance.

Specific Indicators Establishment

This book establishes relatively comprehensive and systematic indices to evaluate the development of the regional small and microfinance but due to the limited data availability, this book just compares the other 4 regions—Wenling of Taizhou, Lucheng of Wenzhou, Yinzhou, Ningbo, and Yiwu of Jinhua—with Luqiao of Taizhou, ensuring more objective evaluation. These regions have a well-developed private economy with booming city commercial banks. Wenling is home to Mintai Commercial Bank, Lucheng to Wenzhou Bank, Yinzhou to Yinzhou Bank, and Yiwu to Chouzhou Commercial Bank. At the same time, this book simplifies the above evaluation indices. In terms of supply, this book measures the contribution of city commercial banks to the development of local small and microfinance by counting the number of regional city commercial banks and the credit products of commercial banks. Since it is difficult to count private capital, this book uses the number of local micro-loan companies to measure the role of private capital in financing micro and small businesses. In terms of demand, since more than 90% of the businesses in these regions are micro and small enterprises, it is difficult to collect data on relatively micro indicators such as loan balance and the average amount of loans. This book uses the proportion of micro and small enterprises to all businesses as a way of measuring the demand for local small and microfinance. In terms of policy, on the one hand, we searched for supporting policies for small and microfinance published on the Internet; on the other hand, we had telephone interviews with officers involved in finance in these regions to learn about how local governments see small and microfinance, and then gave corresponding scores. On this basis, we assign a certain proportion to the above six indicators depending on how important they are and calculate the scores of the development of small and microfinance in the five regions. The results are shown in Table 3.5.

As can be seen from Table 3.5, Luqiao tops the list, which shows that small and microfinance in Luqiao is best developed. However, it is not difficult to find that there is not a big gap in the development level between Yiwu of Jinhua and Luqiao. Two reasons: First, although there are two commercial banks in Luqiao, and only one in Yiwu, the two banks in Luqiao have similar product designs, but they are not innovative enough to produce new products. While with only one city commercial bank in Yiwu, there is no competition at all and it is not eager to innovate; Second, microfinance companies in Yiwu outnumber those in Luqiao. There are seven micro-loan companies in Yiwu, such as Lanswe Micro-loan Company, and Xinguang Micro-loan Company, but there are only four in Luqiao. This is because the Yiwu economy is dominated by commodities, making its private economy more vibrant than that of Luqiao. In that case, it has a rich source of private capital, so it naturally provides fertile ground for microfinance companies to develop in terms of both demand and supply.

Table 3.5 Evaluation of the development of small and microfinance in five regions

	Number of city commercial banks (weight: 0.35)	*Quantity of credit products of city commercial banks (weight: 0.1)*	*Small loan company (weight: 0.1)*	*Number of micro and small financial policies in the past two years (weight: 0.2)*	*Share of micro and small enterprises in enterprises (weight: 0.15)*	*Government officials evaluate local small and microfinance development (weight: 0.1)*	*score*
Luqiao Taizhou	2	12	4	6	0.968	1	3.75
WenlingTaizhou	1	8	5	0	0.95	1	1.89
Luchen Wenzhou	1	11	4	1	0.95	1	2.29
Yinzho Ningbo	1	6	2	3	0.87	1	1.98
Yiwu Jinhua	1	18	7	1	0.96	1	3.29

3.5 Summary

The financial industry cannot develop without a solid foundation of the real economy. The vigorous development of Luqiao's small and microfinance is also due to its solid real economy. A lackluster real economy means weak small and microfinance. Therefore, we should attach importance to the development of the real economy, regard it as the most fundamental strategic goal, and increase tech capabilities and economic competitiveness, from the perspectives of both macroeconomic regulation and micro-economic management. The real economy should be supported by strong high-tech industries and advanced manufacturing. To develop the real economy, we should not only make full use of existing economic resources but also develop and absorb external resources, to provide favorable market conditions for the development of the real economy. On the other hand, the financial industry's support of the real economy is very important. How should the financial industry better serve the real economy? First, we must bear in mind that the financial sector should serve the real economy and ensure that capital is invested in it. A growing real economy has promoted the development of the financial industry and built a platform for its vigorous development. With a solid real economy, the financial sector has thrived and prospered. When the real economy is in need, the financial industry should spare no effort to serve the real economy and inject vitality into it. While serving the real economy, the financial industry can promote its development thanks to a thriving real economy. Secondly, we should improve the financial market and prevent financial risks, strengthen business innovation, and establish a communication mechanism. Finance and the real economy are mutually reinforcing. Without either of them, the economy will decline. Only when the financial industry and the real economy closely cooperate, China's economy can develop steadily and healthily.

Finance and economy go hand in hand. The banking industry in Luqiao District is deeply engaged in the local market and attaches great importance to financial services for micro and small enterprises. Its services have always been distinctive and at the forefront of the country. While China as a whole has encountered difficulties for small and microfinance, Luqiao District of Taizhou city has prepared well for a development path of small and microfinance. On the one hand, the number of financial institutions steadily increased, and financial organizations and market systems gradually improved. The growth of the small and microfinance industry in

Luqiao has contributed to the diversified development of financial institutions, made the financial system steady, ensured the orderly development of the financial sector, provided more financing opportunities for industrial and commercial enterprises, and promoted local financial deepening. On the other hand, the district has witnessed growing financial services and rising business scale. Private financial institutions such as Taizhou Bank and Talon Bank in Luqiao focus on providing financial services for private SMEs. That is how they survive and thrive in the financial market.

From the experience of Luqiao District, the impact of small and micro-finance on the real economy is also substantial. Many financial institutions pay closer attention to micro and small businesses, accelerate strategic transformation, and are committed to providing them with a full range of financial services. Small and micro-financing is becoming better and has achieved considerable economic and social benefits. The financing environment has also greatly improved and the local economy booms. The expansion of private financial institutions in Luqiao enables SMEs and individuals to enjoy financial services, providing more sources of financing, and businesses no longer need to mix savings and investments. Conversely, the development of small and medium-sized economies also provides more ways for the investment of private capital, which in turn facilitates the development of small and microfinance.

References

Peng Zhi. Research on the Interaction between Financial Institutions, Financial Environment and Financial Functions—A Case Study of the Change of Australian Financial System [D]. Liaoning University, 2012.

Shao Zhibao. Difficulties and Breakthroughs in Micro Finance Practice in China [J]. *Financiers' Forum*, 2013(12): 24–26.

Tao Kaihui. Creating a Favorable Financial Service Environment and Providing "Service Samples"—Taizhou Financial Industry Innovative Lending to the Development of Micro and Small Enterprises [N]. *Taizhou Daily*, 2013–11.

Wu Jiangtao. Research on Financial Services of Micro and Small Enterprises in Commercial Banks [D]. Jiangxi University of Finance and Economics. 2012.

Xu Renbiao, Accelerating the Transformation and Upgrading of Traditional Industry is the Inevitable Road to the New Industrialization of Luqiao [N]. *China Economic Times*, 2013–2014.

Xia Xiaoyi. Micro and Small Services: from Strategy to Tactics [J]. *Chinese Financier*, 2013 (010): 63–64.

Xiao Zongfu. Innovative Practice of Small and Microfinance in Taizhou [J]. *China Finance*, 2013 (14): 82–83.
Xi Zunxia. Research on the Development Path of Small and Microfinance from the Perspective of National Strategy—Based on Financial Function Perspective and SEM Model [J]. *Zhejiang Finance*, 2013 (8): 13–17.
Yan Gujun & Wen Yuechun. Private Finance and Economic Development in Economic Transition: An Empirical Analysis based on Taizhou [J]. *Financial Research Journal*, 2005 (7): 182–191.
Zhou Lin. Research on Local Government Innovation and Private Economy Development Mechanism—Taking Taizhou Phenomenon as an Example (1978–2007) [D]. Fujian Normal University. 2008.
Zhang Jianhua. Promoting Reform and Innovation in Small and Microfinance Through Leading Roles [J]. *Financial Micro Review*, 2012(9): 4–9.
Zheng Miliang. Three industries in Taizhou Luqiao District are Major Players in County Development [N]. *China Economic Times*, 2008–7.
Zheng Minqiang. Financial Innovation Related to the Life of Thousands of Micro and Small Enterprises [J]. *Zhejiang Today*, 2012 (17): 33–33.
Zhang Xiaoyan. Study on Financial Industry Agglomeration and its Influence on Regional Economic Growth [D]. Shandong University. 2012
Lin Yifu & Li Yongjun. The Causes and Solutions of Financing Difficulties of Small and Medium-sized Enterprises [J]. *Science and Technology Today*, 2004(3): 27–28.
Lin Yifu & Li Yongjun. Development of Small and Medium Financial Institutions and financing of Small and Medium Enterprises [J]. *Economic Research Journal*, 2001(10): 10–18.
Lu Jiashi. Alleviating the Financing Difficulties of Small and Medium-sized Enterprises Based on Supply Chain Finance [D]. Fudan University, 2012.

CHAPTER 4

The Luqiao Model of Microfinance Development

With a highly developed private economy, Luqiao District has been persistently improving its micro financial services and exploring a path for developing microfinance with Luqiao characteristics to ensure the healthy growth of Micro and Small enterprises (MSEs). Luqiao's experience in developing microfinance is worth promoting to the whole country. Based on the analysis of the current status of microfinance in Luqiao, this chapter thoroughly explores the development of microfinance here and outlines the mature "Luqiao Model". First, an analysis of the three orientations in its development is provided; Secondly, its five characteristics from business form and coverage are presented. Lastly, its three unique innovation modes are discussed.

4.1 Development Orientations of Luqiao Microfinance

Committing to Serving SMEs Principally and Realizing the Financial Function of Supporting SMEs

Microfinance refers to financial activities that provide micro, small and medium-sized enterprises and middle or low-income people with sustainable microfinance products and services. By definition, it is a common feature of microfinance to serve SMEs principally. However, compared

W. Xiao et al., *Microfinance and China's Regional Development*, https://doi.org/10.1007/978-981-99-1960-4_4

with large commercial banks in many areas that develop microfinance, the three municipal commercial banks in Luqiao District are more professional and dedicated to the supply of microfinance. First of all, in terms of market positioning of financial services, private financial institutions such as Zhejiang Tailong Commercial Bank mainly provide financing services to local individually-owned industrial and commercial businesses, small and medium-sized private enterprises, etc. Except for a small percentage of loans supplied to urban infrastructure and public utilities, the vast majority of the loans of the two institutions are supplied to the SMEs in the private economic sector. Instead of a branch business, it is the main business of these three banks to supply microfinance loans and credit. Take the Bank of Taizhou as an example. Since its inception, the Bank of Taizhou has consistently taken "a partner bank of SMEs" as its market positioning, adopted the distinctive "community bank" operation model, and "thoroughly cultivated" the micro financial market. By the end of November 2013, the Bank of Taizhou had 106,900 clients with outstanding loans, with an average loan of 492,900 yuan per client. Among them, the number of SMEs with loans less than 1 million Yuan accounted for 91.04%, and the number of loans accounted for 44.05%, which constituted a high proportion of the number and amount of bank loans in Taizhou. Besides the Bank of Taizhou, the microfinance supply services of the other two banks account for about 90% of all their services respectively.

As for the realization of service functions, the microfinance in Luqiao District is mainly engaged in traditional deposit and loan business and has become involved in other business fields such as bank card and bill financing, etc. From the scale of deposits and loans of several banks, the source of deposit funds is mainly private capital, and the target of loans is set to SMEs, realizing a reasonable allocation of private capital. In terms of deposit and loan charges, banks have also adopted various methods to reduce the transaction costs of SMEs to better serve them. For example, since 2011, Luqiao Rural Cooperative Bank has implemented a "twelve-level interest rate" mechanism, providing products with different loan interest rates for different SMEs in order to meet the real needs for the development of SMEs. In addition, in the process of serving SMEs, the microfinance sector also attaches importance to collecting information about the SMEs' customer groups. By analyzing the data, the financing characteristics of SMEs can be further defined, and more accurate product pricing can be done. In short, the development of microfinance in Luqiao District focuses on providing financial services to SMEs, and on realizing effectively various functions of microfinance.

Focusing on Serving Local Clients and Seeking Cross-regional Development

The 12th Five-year Plan of Taizhou's Financial Industry Development points out that in the next two years, Taizhou will build its "one city three districts" into a national model with distinctive characteristics, namely, building itself into a "two small" financial city with national influence, a private financial pilot zone, a small business financial service demonstration zone, and an innovative financial pilot zone. As a pioneering district for the development of microfinance in Taizhou, the strategic deployment of Luqiao District in the next two years is bound to be the focused and thorough development of the local region, supplemented by exploring the potential of cross-regional services. Moreover, the purpose of the development of trans-regional services will mainly be to disperse the risks of financial services in the region and to realize the advantages of financial resource mobilization in multiple regions.

The business outlets of micro financial service institutions in Luqiao also show the characteristics of basing in Luqiao, radiating to Taizhou and the surrounding urban areas. The Luqiao District government proposed in the *12th Five-Year Plan of Luqiao's Service Industry* the goal to develop Luqiao into a "micro financial services center of China" with leading experiences in "SME financial service coverage rate, SME financial service satisfaction rate, the proportion of the added value of micro financial services, the quality and quantity of domestic micro financial service, and the service system and credit environment of local micro financial institutions. To break through the capital and geographical restrictions of local corporate financial institutions in the competitive market environment, the three municipal commercial banks in Taizhou are also seeking cross-regional services. For example, as a regional financial institution, Luqiao Rural Cooperative Bank passed the CBRC's standard for trans-regional operation in 2012 and set up a branch in Taizhou Jiaojiang Development Zone. In the following two years, the Bank successively set up 13 sub-branches in the Jiaojiang District and Huangyan District of Taizhou city, realizing cross-regional cooperation in three sections of Taizhou. In the future, it may break through the boundaries of Taizhou and realize more extensive cross-regional cooperation services.

Adhering to Independent Decision-making of Private Capital and Introducing Strategic Investors to Optimize the Shareholding Structure

The process of breaking the state-owned monopoly of micro financial service institutions in Luqiao District is attributed to the market-oriented operation policy of local financial institutions formulated by the Luqiao District Government. The policy stipulates: local governments do not control the shares of local financial institutions, and these institutions have market-based operation autonomy. As of the end of 2011, private capital accounted for 42% and 54% of the total equity of joint-stock commercial banks and city commercial banks respectively. However, the proportion of private capital in the three local incorporated banks in Luqiao District reached 95% to 100%, much higher than the national average.

Microfinance with private capital holding has inherent advantages. First of all, with the continuous advance of China's marketization process, the level of national economic development is constantly improved, and the scale of private capital is continuously growing. Statistics from the Chinese Academy of Social Sciences in 2011 showed that the total amount of private capital in China reached 30 trillion yuan in 2012, and the private capital in Zhejiang Province alone reached one trillion yuan. However, the lack of effective investment channels for a large amount of private capital, coupled with unsound investment policies and strict restrictions on the investment field, resulted in a large amount of private capital flowing into the speculative market. In recent years, from the rampant speculation of private capital in all parts of the country to the crazy fund-raising chaos of underground banks, these are the abnormal manifestation of huge amounts of private capital seeking a way out. The development of microfinance provides a good channel for private capital investment. It can not only effectively guide the private capital into legal and normalized channels to realize its power to support the development of the real economy but also include the private capital into the effective jurisdiction of the regulatory authorities, to maintain the stability of the financial order and financial markets. Secondly, the private capital "originates and develops in the private sector". It itself is a product of the private economy and therefore has a deep understanding of the characteristics and mode of the private economic capital demand. In the process of innovations of micro financial products and services, the private capital can give full play to the power of "grassroots", which have bolder innovation and reform power and richer reform wisdom than state-owned capital and play an important role in enabling microfinance to support the private economy. Finally, private capital holds shares in microfinance, and microfinance in turn supports the development of the private economy, which can form a positive cycle of the economy—finance—economic development and provide a good environmental guarantee for microfinance to realize its business sustainability. The investment of private capital in microfinance can also improve the status quo of state holding in the financial system and disperse certain capital monopoly risks.

Of course, the risks of private capital holdings cannot be ignored. This is mainly reflected in the uncontrollability of private capital and the nature of "profit-seeking". In case of mismanagement or policy changes, private capital may stop or even withdraw funding quickly, causing instability in the development of financial institutions and great risks. Therefore, it is necessary to set strict market access standards and introduce strategic investors to diversify risks. Under the active guidance of the government of Luqiao District, the banks have introduced strategic investors and dispersed the management decision-making power to play the role of diversifying and dispersing risks. For example, the Bank of Taizhou actively introduced China Merchants Bank, Ping An Trust, Ping An Life Insurance, and other strategic investors, which not only enriched the shareholding structure, but also provided the opportunity to gain internal management and risk control experience through cooperation with large commercial banks with rich development experience. Second, the local industrial structure is relatively homogenous and microfinance focusing on providing loan services for local SMEs may be affected by systemic risks. The so-called "eggs should not be put in one basket" means that the banks in Luqiao District should not only focus on the services of local SMEs but also expand their business to other provinces and cities appropriately to reduce the systemic risk of a singular industrial institution.

After years of practice, the three local corporate financial institutions developed a set of equity structure systems suitable for their strategic direction through a process of testing. The speed and efficiency of the transformation of private funds into industrial capital have injected a large number of funds into the development of private SMEs, which has provided effective financing channels for SMEs.

4.2 Characteristics of Luqiao Microfinance Development

Since the beginning of its development, microfinance in Luqiao District has been advancing along the path of providing high-quality financing services for SMEs. Luqiao microfinance is different from other areas in terms of economic foundation, asset scale, development orientation, and development strategy. In terms of serving SMEs, Luqiao District has developed an innovative financial system suitable for the financing characteristics of SMEs in Luqiao District by innovating financial products and businesses, exploring new financing guarantee methods, and risk control management. Under the positive encouragement of Luqiao District, microfinance introduces strategic investors, optimizes the equity structure and governance system, and promotes the diversified integration of financial institutions. At the same time, Luqiao actively facilitates exchanges and debates on the development of microfinance and promotes joint research on it between industry, university, and research, resulting in a unique advantage in its development.

Diverse Formats and Wide Coverage

At present, there are 34 banking financial institutions in Taizhou, nearly half of which have local legal persons and private capital as the main body. Among them, the number of micro-loans accounts for 99% of the total number of enterprise loans. By the end of 2012, the balance of local and foreign currency deposits and loans in Luqiao District reached 64.3 billion yuan and 61.2 billion yuan respectively, with a loan-to-deposit ratio of 95.2%. Meanwhile, there are 15 banking financial institutions, 25 insurance institutions, 3 securities institutions, 4 microfinance companies, 6 financing guarantee companies, 4 pawn shops and 3 listed companies in Luqiao District of Taizhou City now. In particular, there are three banks with local legal persons, among which the two private city commercial banks—the Bank of Taizhou and Zhejiang Tailong Commercial Bank, focus on relieving the financing difficulties of SMEs, with the balance of SME loans accounting for 49% of all loans.

Continuous Innovation and Development of Service

Compared with Wenzhou, Taizhou has a larger amount of SMEs in wider fields. To develop micro financial services compatible with local economic development characteristics, it is necessary to distinguish it from the comprehensive volume reform carried out in Wenzhou's financial sector, and pay more attention to the innovation of service in supporting SME finance. Therefore, in the process of developing microfinance, Luqiao District paid more attention to the innovation of products and mechanisms and provided more personalized and diversified services.

To solve the problem of information asymmetry between SMEs and banks, the three local financial institutions took the lead in implementing a characteristic customer manager service. Through household surveys, face-to-face communication, and other channels, comprehensive information on SMEs was obtained in an all-around way, and a full-way service including before, during, and after a loan which was approved could be timely offered. Since its establishment in 1993, Zhejiang Tailong Commercial Bank has accumulated more than 100,000 loan customers in its nearly 20 years of development, and the average loan volume of each client is 500,000. Corporate financial institutions in Luqiao District, such as Zhejiang Tailong Commercial Bank, are faced with a large number of SME customers in a wide coverage of fields, and the credit status of customers varies widely, which requires a large amount of labor input. In line with a large number of clients and low profit, the number of customer managers of Tailong Bank accounts for a significantly high proportion, and the labor cost accounts for about 65% of the total cost, while the labor cost of large state-owned commercial banks only accounts for 30%. The Bank arranged a large number of customer managers to investigate the credit status of SMEs more comprehensively. In addition, it also innovatively adopted a method of "three tables and three products" to determine a loan recipient, which, to a certain extent, is a valuable experience accumulated in the development process of Luqiao microfinance.

Taking financial innovation as the premise of development, the three local legal person financial institutions have adapted to the changing market environment and the ever-growing customer needs, vigorously expanded financial service products, and effectively improved their level of financial services. Take Taizhou's "self-help loan" as an example. A business owner can sign a contract of maximum loan amount with the bank, and check and ratify the maximum loan amount and term. Within the amount limit of the loan, channels such as bank counter, online banking, and telephone banking can be used by the client to determine the amount, term, and interest rate of every sub-loan. The feature of this loan is self-service, and the funds can be repeatedly withdrawn after initial use, fully meeting SMEs' capital needs featuring "short-term, small-amount, frequency, and urgency". The "green energy saving loan" jointly launched with the government of Luqiao District complies with the new national policy background of national economic restructuring and environmental protection. It can meet the needs of SMEs that do not have enough capital for equipment renewal or green transformation.

Innovative policies for reducing or exempting service fees and tiered interest rate policies to minimize the cost of loans to SMEs were introduced. The Bank of Taizhou has been implementing a "free banking" service since 2011, reducing and exempting 42 service fees in the service process, effectively reducing the burden of SMEs that frequently use such services. Luqiao Rural Cooperative Bank launched the "321" tiered interest rate discount policy. Adopting the principle of "one client one policy", a model was set up, which divides the interest rate pricing into "12 tiers" according to an enterprise's actual operation status, business cooperation dependency, analysis of the specific loan, and other indexes. An SME's loan acquisition cost is then determined by the model, which is an important improvement for well-run SMEs.

Scientific Risk Control

The strict control of credit risk is the lifeline of local banks. Microfinance serves SMEs with high operational risks. In addition, there is no experience to follow in operation methods, management models, or the process of product innovation, so the risk level is higher. To control risks, the three local financial institutions in Luqiao District explored and formed a set of effective credit procedures and systems. Examples include innovative guarantee systems in which multiple people jointly undertake the guarantee, and "originator is responsible" deposit accountability systems [i.e., credit officers are permanently responsible for every loan made until it is recovered], and the deposit accumulation system [that is, the amount of deposited funding of a client is directly related to the amount and terms of a loan and its interest rate. This control mechanism helps banks acquire information on the cash liquidity, financial structure, solvency of the enterprise.], differentiated interest rate pricing system, etc. All these measures have reduced the risks of micro financial operations.

Faced with the incomplete financial statements of most SMEs and their inability to provide effective collateral, the three banks adopted various ways to prevent the emergence of credit risks. For example, in addition to the empirical method of "three tables and three products", Zhejiang Tailong Commercial Bank innovatively introduced a multi-person guarantee, which reduces the possibility of credit risk occurrence through a joint guarantee of customers' relatives and friends as well as upstream and downstream customers and can minimize the bank's loss even if a risk occurs.

In addition to innovative guarantees, a comprehensive risk prevention system is also necessary. The risk prevention system of Zhejiang Tailong Commercial Bank focuses on the systematic management of human resources. For account managers who follow up on customer information of SMEs, the model of linking performance assessment with service quality is adopted. Every customer is in contact with an account manager. If credit risks occur, the information obtained by the account manager can be queried to see if there are any falsifications and omissions, to achieve accountability of all personnel; For customer managers with good service quality, corresponding incentives are given. On the other hand, the Bank of Taizhou formulates a series of regulations including a basic risk-management system, security measures management, crisis response plans for payment and settlement system, anti-money laundering management, electronic banking risk management, "Datang Card" anti-cash out measures and abnormal transaction management, etc., forming a complete system of preventing safety risk, network risk, ethics risk and credit risk.

Furthermore, through cooperation with the government, the three banks used fiscal leverage to sign loan projects with SMEs, which also plays a positive role in obtaining financial security and reducing bank risks. The introduction of strategic investors is also an important risk prevention mechanism to reduce bank decision-making mistakes.

Consistent Support from Local Governments

The private economy in Luqiao District is developed, and the financing need of SMEs is in great demand. The government of Luqiao District promotes the development of local microfinance and solves the financing difficulties of SMEs through supportive policies. First, they set up a microfinance development strategy in a scientific way, focusing on strengthening the construction of the 5 aspects of "SME financial service coverage", "SME financial service satisfaction rate", "proportion of the added value of micro financial services", "quantity and quality of local micro financial institutions", and "local micro financial service system and credit environment" to promote the regional brand into the "Capital of micro financial services in China". Second, they build platforms, focus on innovation, serve real entities, and strive to do a good job of government promotion. The government tries to build a district-level financial development platform and set clear goals of building six district-level platforms—a demonstration platform for microfinance, an interactive platform for microfinance and private capital, and a research and development exchange platform for microfinance. The government actively promotes financial institutions to innovate products, and promotes financial institutions to pay attention to SMEs, increases credit supply, innovates financial products, and serves the real economy through the assessment of financial institutions' performance in supporting economic development and the allocation of fiscal deposits. Third, they give full play to strengths, perfect mechanisms, stabilize the financial sector, and work hard in a guidance role. They give full play to the advantages of private finance, encourage and guide the orderly integration of abundant private capital into the existing financial system, connect private capital with banking services, and strengthen the interaction between private finance and SMEs. They improve the mechanism of cooperation between government and banks, between banks, and between banks and enterprises. The government and banks jointly set up businesses such as "energy saving loans for SMEs" and "e-commerce credit for online banking", and guide private financial institutions and state-owned commercial banks to complement each other with advantages and share resources to promote the surplus funds from state-owned commercial banks to flow to the disadvantaged SMEs through the "capillary" of private financial institutions.

Take the development of small-loan companies as an example. Luqiao District actively strove for a bigger pilot quota, developed and expanded the team of microfinance companies, implemented all the supporting policies on the provincial, municipal, and district levels, and constantly strengthened supervision to guide their compliance operation.

First, striving for a bigger pilot quota, integrating overall planning and deployment, and seeking a catfish effect of "1+1 > 2." Given the developed market economy and large amount of SMEs in Luqiao District, the market for small loans is big. At the same time, the natural advantages for developing microfinance companies lie in the abundant private capital and active private financing. Since the commencement of the piloting, Luqiao District has applied to the Taizhou Finance Office for a bigger pilot quota of small-sum loan companies, established the resource pool of potential small-sum loan company clients, and carefully selected the leading enterprises with standardized management, ethical operations, and strong business strength as the main initiators of small-sum loans. At the same time as the application to be a pilot district, the Luqiang District persisted in making sound planning, actively yet prudently expanded coverage for the pilot program under the premise of adapting to the market demand, gradually expanding to central towns, with the third microfinance company being located in the provincial-central town of Jinqing, and avoided the phenomenon of excessive competition between microfinance companies when they rush in and fight for business.

Second, actively implementing policies, vigorously supporting, and striving for a multiplication effect of "1+1>1." To encourage the development of microfinance companies, Luqiao District implements corresponding supporting policies issued by the province and the city in tax reduction, financial subsidies, and small loan risk compensation. In 2010, district finance provided the two companies with a tax subsidy of 1.819 million yuan and a small loan risk compensation of 550,000 yuan. In 2011, the tax subsidy was 1.943 million yuan, and the risk compensation of small loans was 7.029 million yuan (part of the risk compensation of small loans in 2010 was subsidized in 2011). In 2012, the support funds of microfinance companies will also be released, which is expected to reach more than 8 million yuan. Taizhou City matches the Luqiao District's tax return to the microfinance companies as subsidies. Luqiao District also supports microfinance companies to establish more offices and increase the capital and enlarge stock shares. The District Finance gives a one-off subsidy of 200,000 yuan to new microfinance companies with a registered capital of 200 million yuan or more. For existing microfinance companies that expand the scale of loans and increase registered capital to reach 300 million yuan or more, the district government will give a one-off subsidy of 150,000 yuan. The implementation of supporting policies can better stimulate the enthusiasm for the development of microfinance companies, and further guide microfinance companies to adhere to the target of "supporting agriculture" and "supporting small businesses".

Third, improving the supervision system, guiding compliance management, and realizing a "1 ÷ 1 = 0" South Wind effect. Compliance management is an important cornerstone for the long-term and healthy development of small-loan companies. Microfinance companies are engaged in high-risk businesses that banking financial institutions avoid, so they are prone to the impulse of "high yield to cover high risk" while ignoring business compliance. Therefore, since the piloting began, Luqiao District has been improving supervision and service measures, clarifying the cooperation responsibilities of finance, industry and commerce, audit, and other departments, striving to establish a supervision mechanism with long-term effects, and strengthening the business guidance for small-loan companies based on strict entry threshold of small-loan companies. Luqiao has also guided and regulated the operation of small-loan companies, and improved their risk prevention and control awareness and operational standards through the comprehensive use of on-site and off-site inspections, other regulatory means, and policy supports. At the same time, the Office of Finance, Administration of Industry and Commerce, Bureau of Finance, People's Bank of China and China Banking Regulatory Commission, and other relevant departments are organized to conduct regular and random inspections, and assessment of microfinance companies and guide them to operate in compliance. At the end of each year, small-loan companies are required to be audited by a third party. At present, the three small-loan companies in Luqiao District are all well-run. Among them, Yufeng Small-loan Company has been awarded "A+ Outstanding Small-loan Company of Zhejiang Province" for four consecutive years (only 7 received this award in the province). In addition, Jiuding Microfinance Company has been awarded "A+ Excellent Small-loan Company of Zhejiang Province" in 2010 and 2011, and "A+ Excellent Small-Loan Company of Zhejiang Province" in 2012.

Development Advantages of Local Enterprises

Luqiao, which has led the development of the specialized market in Zhejiang and even the whole country, has a large number of SMEs, and is known for "no street without a market, no alley without a peddler, no household without someone in business". At present, Luqiao has 82 registered markets of various types and 35,714 registered individual businesses, including 8204 in the secondary industry and 27443 in the tertiary industry. The group of private financial institutions composed of the Bank of Taizhou, Zhejiang Tailong Commercial Bank, and Luqiao Rural Cooperative Bank supports the development of these SMEs through service concept innovation, forming a mutually supportive and beneficial relationship between private commercial banks and SMEs.

The economic development of Luqiao District first benefited from the development of the commercial and trade industry. It once had a brilliant history of "buying from the whole country and selling to the whole country". In recent years, the process of industrialization and urbanization is speeding up, and the dismantling of scrap metal and automobile manufacturing industry show a rapid growth trend. In 2013, the GDP of Luqiao District reached 42.84 billion yuan, with a year-on-year growth of 8.3%. The growth rate was the first among the three districts and the third in the city, which was 0.4 percentage points higher than the average level of the city. The added value of the primary industry was 1.101 billion yuan, down 0.8%; The added value of the secondary industry reached 20.188 billion yuan, up by 7.9%, among which the added value of industry reached 18.478 billion yuan, up by 8.0%; the added value of the tertiary industry was 21.55 billion yuan, up 9.1%.

In the aspect of ownership, the private economy dominates, and the proportion of the state-owned and collective economies is very low. The private economy is composed of a commercial economy, joint-stock cooperative economy, and so on. Its characteristics are "privately funded, privately run, and privately owned". At present, Luqiao District has formed a huge private economic system with leading industries such as motorcycle and accessories, mold and plastic products, air conditioner and refrigeration accessories, and agricultural machinery. It is an important business center of Taizhou city and even southeast Zhejiang Province.

Therefore, the good ecological environment for the development of enterprises in Luqiao District provides good soil for the development of microfinance in Luqiao District.

4.3 Development Models of Microfinance in Luqiao District

The *"12th Five-Year Financial Industry Development Plan" of Zhejiang Province* points out that, through the construction of " SME financial center" and "private investment management center", Taizhou and other regions shall focus on building themselves into cities with a financial feature and on cultivating several financial innovation demonstration counties (cities, districts). These policies provide opportunities for Taizhou's financial industry to strengthen its features and develop unique models of microfinance. In the development process of Luqiao District in recent years, it has established characteristic microfinance development models with three city commercial banks as the core and various integrated financial institutions. Industrial clusters and specialized markets initiate micro financial services for SMEs and merchants in the industry that encourages more developed businesses to help the small and underdeveloped businesses; another model is the government, banking sector, and enterprises cooperating under the government's supportive policies.

The Institution Agglomeration Model of Microfinance Development

Industrial agglomeration refers to an industrial phenomenon in which relevant enterprises and institutions in a geographical region in a specific industry are connected due to commonality and complementarity, thus forming a strong and sustained competitive advantage. As a kind of industrial economy, financial-industry agglomeration refers to a special industrial spatial structure in which a country's financial resources, financial institutions, domestic and foreign financial enterprises, and other institutions with headquarters function gather in a specific area and maintain close ties with the headquarters of such financial institutions in other regions.

Responding to the *"12th Five-Year Plan" for the Service Industry in Luqiao District*, Luqiao District has now formed a Luqiao Financial Headquarters Hub with Nangong Road and its surrounding area, where the headquarters of the Bank of Taizhou and Tailong Bank areas are situated, as the core and the Taizhou Central Road and the surrounding area as the development zone. With a total land area of 6.69 hectares and a total construction area of 226,700 square meters, a regional bank headquarters building and a headquarters support center were established. At the same time, regional branches were established through the introduction of joint-stock commercial banks, securities companies, insurance institutions, and other financial institutions.

The industrial agglomeration of financial institutions brings knowledge spillover and facilitates various institutions with external benefits. On the one hand, the financial industry cluster can enable the sharing of excellent innovation experience and knowledge between institutions in the cluster, and improve the innovation ability of regional microfinance. On the other hand, due to the existence of an information externality, newly stationed financial enterprises can learn from the production and management experience of financial institutions in the cluster, which is conducive to the improvement of the overall operational efficiency and level of financial institutions in the region. Regional financial industry agglomeration's advantages also lie in bringing financial rent and in effectively promoting the development of a regional economy. And industrial agglomeration and radiation effect can spread financial resources from the core regions to their surrounding areas, stimulating the economic growth of the surrounding areas by encouraging technological progress, increasing capital accumulation, and promoting the transformation of savings into investment. At present, stationed in the core industrial cluster area in Luqiao District, the core financial development area for SMEs financing, are mainly urban commercial banks and related institutions that mainly provide financing services for SMEs. Among them, there are similarities in business objectives and differences in business models among the three urban commercial banks. They can learn from each other and benefit from each other's innovation achievements to achieve common progress in innovation and development. At the same time, the introduction of relatively mature large and medium-sized state-owned commercial banks and cross-regional cooperation financial pilot zones can help these newly developed urban commercial banks learn advanced management and risk control experience, and develop a new model suitable for the development of microfinance based on the traditional financial industry. The introduction of securities companies and insurance institutions, based on banking financial institutions, introduces diverse financial operation subjects, which not only facilitates the financing services of SMEs but also promotes the exchanges and cooperation between different types of financial service institutions to a certain extent. The microfinance cluster in Luqiao District also promotes the compliance, standardization, and mass production of small and micro-credit based on adopting and innovating the microfinance service model of private banks by introducing the credit technology training base for SMEs nationwide, to improve the agglomeration and radiation function of Luqiao Finance.

Finally, the industrial agglomeration of financial institutions results in the formation of a regional financial center, which is in line with the plan of Zhejiang Province and Taizhou Municipal government to build Luqiao District into a "micro financial service center".

The Micro Financial Service Model of Large-scale/Developed Businesses Helping Small/Underdeveloped Businesses in Industrial Clusters

Luqiao District of Taizhou City Commodity Mall and Small Commodity Wholesale Market are models of the domestic specialized market. In June 1982, the merchants in Luqiao District set up the first small commodity wholesale market, steel market, and roasted seeds and nuts market in China. Under the cultivation of the Industrial and Commercial Bureau, the commodity markets represented by bearings, hardware, and furniture appeared successively. At this time, the Luqiao specialized market cluster has been preliminarily established. Since the reform and opening up, under the leadership of the Industrial and Commercial Bureau, Luqiao District has developed a specialized market with three major groups—daily necessities, production materials, and agricultural by-products, forming a harmonious and unified "markets-city commensalism". After the establishment of Luqiao District, a variety of economic entities have been introduced to set up markets and enterprise groups, and modern enterprise systems were introduced to guide the traditional specialized market in the direction of specialization, modernization, and enterprise. In the decades of development, Luqiao District has made full use of local advantages to develop the private economy. At present, it has formed an industrial system with the modern service industry and manufacturing industry as the main body and interactive development of industry and trade. It has become an advanced manufacturing base and a regional trade center in Taizhou and formed a characteristic industrial cluster to develop the economy.

The development of industry clusters in Luqiao District has spawned the development of microfinance. Many micro financial service institutions in Luqiao District, such as small loan companies, are jointly initiated by a number of the core enterprises in the industry cluster. These enterprises already have upstream and downstream business associations or they supply the same products, thus having a lot of business contacts and communication already. The establishment of micro financial institutions is also to serve the various enterprises in the industries. Through the capital agglomeration function of micro financial institutions, an asset pool within the industry is formed. Enterprises with surplus funds can inject capital into micro financial institutions through investment. Enterprises that are temporarily short of funds can replenish funds through financing from these micro financial institutions. As SMEs within the industry clusters have business transactions with one another and know about their business situations very well, there is an important trust relationship. The cluster micro financial service model developed under the background of the industry clusters in Luqiao District has great interactive advantages.

The specialized development and industrial market agglomeration of the private economy is also of great significance for commercial banks to overcome the two difficulties of cost and risk in financing SMEs. It is often difficult to control the costs and risks of providing financial services to scattered SMEs. In the regions with industry clusters, on the one hand, microfinance providers can focus on the core enterprises in the cluster industry and develop clients at both ends of the supply and marketing chain, thus reducing the cost of providing loans to these SMEs. On the other hand, the cluster of SMEs also provides a good environment for the service innovation of microfinance, such as the development of new financial products of the multi-person guaranteed loans. Using the upstream and downstream enterprises in the industry cluster chain to provide a guarantee, such as accounts receivable guarantee financing, inventory guarantee financing, advance payment financing, and other structural financing models, can efficiently solve the capital needs in the process of internal procurement within the industry and can provide financial support for the cluster development of SMEs.

The Micro Financial Service Model of Government Supporting, Banks Leading and Government, Bank, and Enterprise Cooperating

It is far from enough to rely solely on the independent development of microfinance to solve the problem of loan difficulties for SMEs. It also requires active guidance and policy assistance from the government. With the proposition of the "Twelfth Five-Year Development Plan for the Financial Industry" and the "Suggestions for Accelerating the Development of the Financial Industry", many preferential policies in land use, taxation, human resources, etc. have been implemented. More than 30 million yuan of the supportive funds has been allocated. The Luqiao government has been actively promoting the development of the financial industry into a pillar industry of economic development of the Luqiao District.

At present, the Luqiao District government has played its guiding role in facilitating the cooperation of micro financial institutions and SMEs in three aspects. The first is to use fiscal leverage to inject financial funds into microfinance institutions to enable their cooperation with competent SMEs in financing. Local commercial banks and local SMEs share common interests. The development of SMEs cannot be separated from the support of microfinance. The survival and development of microfinance also depend on the support of enterprises and the local economy. The purpose of exploring micro financial services is to mobilize capital factors to invest in the real economy through the financial intermediation function and to promote financial services to the real economy for the development of the real economy. To this end, the government of Luqiao District has continuously improved the cooperation negotiation system between banks and enterprises, and actively held bank-enterprise business matching events to promote mutual understanding and financing docking between various financial institutions and SMEs to promote cooperative projects between banks and enterprises. The government of Luqiao District also encourages financial institutions to carry out a series of activities to "help enterprises solve their problems and promote the development of the real economy." For example, Tailong Bank launched campaigns of "visiting a thousand households and enterprises" and "visiting ten thousand households in a hundred days". Through field visits, enterprises with operation difficulties were identified, credit support was increased, and a more preferential interest rate policy was implemented to help such SMEs get out of difficulties.

Second, through government guidance, government funding supports the micro financial service institutions to set up innovative loan products to boost the industrial transformation and upgrading of SMEs. By assessing the performance of financial institutions in supporting economic development and allocating financial deposits, the government of Luqiao District promotes financial institutions to increase credit supply and innovate financial products to further serve the real economy. For example, the Bank of Taizhou introduced the Climate Finance Innovation Funding (CFIF) program of the United Nations Environment Programme, for which the government allocated 2 million yuan a year as special funds to support the Bank to launch the "Green Energy Saving Loan", which provides preferential interest rates for SMEs to update energy-saving equipment, improve the production process and realize upgrading of industrial structure for energy saving and efficiency improvement. The micro and small business loan project "SG Tairongyi", jointly launched by Tailong Bank in cooperation with Chinese and German government finance, focuses on supporting the financing needs of SMEs for equipment procurement and technical transformation, and on helping SMEs accelerate the structural adjustment of fixed assets. The Rural Cooperative Bank of Luqiao District launched the "Universal Credit Loan" to further serve the rural market, advocate the concept of "family credit", and focus on alleviating the difficulty of ordinary people's loan guarantee problem.

Third, through the establishment of market change monitor mechanisms, the government tries to help microfinance build a risk control mechanism, innovate the design of microfinance products, and reduce the risk of providing loans to SMEs.

In 2013, the Luqiao District government introduced the Specification on Preventing Financial Risks and Promote Healthy Development of the Economy to standardize and help the risk control of SMEs from the following aspects: fully recognize the importance of funds safety, strengthen the awareness of risk prevention, standardize enterprise external guarantees, clarify the bottom line of risk prevention, strengthen enterprise financial management, prevent enterprises from leaving the real economy, create diverse financing innovation, increase the financing channels of enterprises, strengthen the construction of a culture of integrity, and optimize the development environment of enterprises. Luqiao government has successively established a special team for the prevention of financial risk and standardization of business order and a team for leading the crackdown on illegal fund-raising, organized the Office of Finance, Economic and Information Office, Administration of Industry and Commerce Commission, Bureau of Commerce, Public Security Bureau, the court and other relevant departments on time to master relevant information, and established a monthly information update system to get timely information on funding difficulties of enterprises, illegal fund-raising cases and other related developments, and actively prevented the emergence of a capital supply problem and other situations. In addition, the Luqiao District government has also set up 20 million yuan of government emergency special funds for the transfer of loans to SMEs with capital turnover difficulties timely to prevent financial institutions from further loan pressure and to alleviate the risk of capital supply for financial institutions to serve SMEs.

4.4 Summary

Compared with the central government's supply-led institutional innovation in Wenzhou financial reform, Pearl River Delta financial reform, Quanzhou financial reform, and Shanghai Free Trade Zone reform, the Luqiao Model of microfinance shows more characteristics of demand-induced institutional innovation. Luqiao District has a developed private economy and many SMEs, which also encounter a financing bottleneck in the process of development. However, through the collaboration of the government, banks, and enterprises in Luqiao District, the financing difficulties of SMEs there have been effectively alleviated, and the development momentum of microfinance is strong. From China's current experience in promoting the innovation of enterprise financing guarantee system, the financial system reforms at the national level, including the Wenzhou financial reform, the Pearl River Delta financial reform, and the Quanzhou financial reform, lack strength and the pace is slow. The main reasons are the various risks brought by a mismatch between the regional economic environment and the regional financial environment, which leads to the concerns of governments at all levels in the introduction and implementation of policies. On the contrary, the bottom-up process of the SMEs financing system innovation in the Luqiao District of Taizhou city has achieved very good results, which brings a valuable research example for the innovation of the microfinance systems.

Based on the characteristics and development model of the "Luqiao Example" of microfinance, it can be concluded that in the future financial system innovation and development, the reform experience at the national and local levels should be positively summarized, and the diffusion system innovation led by local government should be adhered to. In this process of adaptation, the intervention of the local government will meet the institutional needs of micro subjects in the financial system and the implementation of market financial policies will accelerate. From the perspective of the relationship between the government and the market, it is advisable for the government to appear as an intermediary. Therefore, in the financing ecology of the collaboration of "government, enterprise, and finance", the main responsibility of local governments is to provide a platform to eliminate information asymmetry. In the process of bank lending, the most critical dilemma is the information asymmetry between banks and enterprises. Local governments can organize and provide a platform for information openness in the process of bank credit issuance, thus eliminating the problem of information asymmetry, because they have mastered the business relationship between the upstream and downstream of enterprises as well as the background and experience of the controller of enterprises. On the one hand, this can improve the information receipt level of banks. On the other hand, it can also give enterprises more autonomy and realize information exchange between the two sides, which is conducive to the expansion of SMEs' financing in industrial clusters.

With the development of the national economy, the number of SMEs is increasing, which has increasingly become the main force in promoting rapid economic growth. Therefore, it has become the focus of local governments to relieve the financing difficulties of SMEs. Local governments should focus on the main line of financial services for local economic development, firmly grasp new opportunities of the transformation of the economic development model, and carry out solid, effective, and innovative work from the three aspects of "financing supply platform", "government credit enhancement platform" and "risk prevention platform".

First, build powerful financing supply platforms to enhance financing security for the whole society. Local governments should encourage the continuous development of locally incorporated banks to become bigger and stronger and provide facilities to serve the development of banks. In addition, they should actively introduce more financial institutions, vigorously develop new financial organizations, actively introduce all kinds of banks, insurance, and other financial institutions to set up local branches, and promote the establishment of local microfinance companies and other new local financial organizations to play the role of "financial capillary". Furthermore, they should actively promote the direct financing of enterprises, vigorously support the listing of SMEs, and increase the cultivation of backup enterprises.

Second, make sure government credit enhancement platforms can effectively solve the problem of "two shortages" of enterprises. To begin with, actively learn from advanced experience and participate in the construction of a non-profit SME credit guarantee fund with government input and bank participation. Then, explore the establishment of standard private financing centers under unified government supervision. By establishing a registration and filing system for the supply and demand of private funds, the transaction process can be standardized, credit joint liability and verification services provided, and a unified, orderly, and standardized local private financing platform formed. Thirdly, explore the establishment of a local non-bank credit sharing system, collect the credit information of local enterprises for query from the financial institutions, and improve the information level of regional credit system construction.

Third, work hard on risk prevention platforms to maintain the stability of microfinance. Firstly, explore the possibility of establishing local counseling centers to help standardize micro, small, and medium-sized enterprises financing process and documents, change SMEs' deficiencies of not having financial statements and no accounting, and guide SMEs to finance under regulation. Secondly, explore the establishment of private emergency-to-lending funds, and guide private capital to set up service companies specializing in emergency turnover of due loans for enterprises to realize seamless renewal of maturing loans for enterprises. Thirdly, further strengthen financial risk prevention and early warning mechanisms, strengthen the dynamic monitoring of key industries, key areas, key enterprises, prevent and resolve financial risks, and strengthen the analysis and judgment of emerging problems, crack down on illegal financial activities, and guard against systemic and regional financial risks.

References

Peterson, M. A. & Rajan, R. G. The Benefits of Lending Relationships Evidence from Small Business Data [J]. *Journal of Finance*, 1994, 49(1): 3–37.

Strahan, P. & Weaton, J. Small Business Lending and the Changing Structure of Banking Industry [J]. *Journal of Banking and Finance*, 1998(22): 821–845.

Charles B. Wendel & Matthew Harvey, SME Credit Scoring: Key Initiative, Opportunities and Issues [J]. *Access Finance*, 2006(10): 35–41.

William D. Bradford & Chao Chen, Creating Government Financing Programs for Small and Sized Enterprises in China: Theory and Practice [J]. *China &World Economy*, 2004: 145–153.

Ottati, G. D. Social Concentration and Local Development: The Case of Industrial Districts [J]. *European Planning Studies*, 2002, 10(4): 613–673.

Ruan Jianqin & Zhang Xiaobo. Finance and Cluster-Based Industrial Development in China [J]. *Economic Development and Cultural Change*, 2009, 58(1): 143–164.

Fang Junxiong. Ownership, Institutional Environment and Capital Allocation [J]. *Economic Research Journal*, 2007(12): 82–92.

Wang Shuguang & Deng Yiting. A Study of the Expanding Mechanism, Transition Path and Future Evolution of Informal Finance [J]. *Journal of Financial Research*, 2007(6): 69–79.

Yan Lurong, Lai Yongwen, Zhang Bin, et al. On the Financing Guarantee System for Small-and-Medium-Sized Enterprises [J]. *Journal of Financial Research*, 2007(10): 152–165.

Guo Baoming. Credit-rating: Rational Choice for Alleviating Small and Medium-sized Enterprises Financing [J]. *Journal of Financial Research*, 2007(8): 79–87.

Wang Sen. Growth of Small and Medium-sized Enterprises: Financing, System and Strategic Choice [J]. *Finance & Trade Economics*, 2007(3): 103–105.

Xie Qinghe. On Developing Credit Guarantees System of Chinese Small and Medium-sized Enterprises [J]. *On Economic Problems*, 2007(2): 71–73.

Zhao Guoxin. Review on Research of Effect Evaluation of Foreign Financial Support Policy for SMEs [J]. *Economist*, 2007(2): 116–121.

Li Zhihui & Li Meng. Analysis of Development Financial Support (DFS) of Small and Medium-sized Enterprises [J]. *Nankai Economic Studies*, 2007(1): 68–80.

Gao Langeng & Wang Xiaozhong. The Logical and Puzzles in the Evolution of China's Financial Institution [J]. *Journal of Financial Research*, 2006(6): 170–178.

PART III

Innovations

Luqiao should base itself on the practical basis of the developed services of micro and small financial enterprises and the institutional advantages of private finance, promote the second take-off of the financial industry, and provide financial support for the development of the real economy.

—Zheng Minqiang

CHAPTER 5

Small and Medium-Sized Banks Contributing to the Innovative Development of Luqiao's Microfinance

Small and medium-sized banks (SMBs) enjoy advantages in providing information services to small and medium-sized enterprises (SMEs), which elaborates the relations between credit loans for SMEs and bank scale and structure. On the one hand, SMBs are too frequently unable to run large loan projects due to their limited scale, so they have no choice but to serve principally SMEs. On the other hand, SMBs, like SMEs, are so located to understand well the credit and operation status of SMEs, thus effectively reducing the impact of information asymmetry and greatly mitigating loan risks. Therefore, SMBs are more willing to provide financing services to SMEs than large banks are. Many SMBs, including the Bank of Taizhou, Zhejiang Tailong Commercial Bank, and Luqiao Rural Cooperative Bank, focus on micro and small enterprises (MSEs) in Luqiao District, Taizhou City, and have become models of efficient microfinance development.

5.1 Luqiao's SMB Models Focusing on Microfinance Development

Three local corporate banks, the Bank of Taizhou, Zhejiang Tailong Commercial Bank, and Luqiao Rural Cooperative Bank, have effectively solved the following problems: investment difficulties massive private capital met and financing difficulties large quantities of SMEs encountered. Take the first three quarters of 2012 as an example. Loans less than one

W. Xiao et al., *Microfinance and China's Regional Development*,
https://doi.org/10.1007/978-981-99-1960-4_5

million yuan from these three banks to SMEs accounted for 38.10%, 48.94%, and 56.65% respectively. SME clients with a loan of less than one million yuan accounted for 91.41%, 85.42%, and 89.74% respectively. Loan balances per enterprise were only 483,700 yuan, 626,800 yuan, and 280,000 yuan respectively, as shown in Figs. 5.1 and 5.2.

The Bank of Taizhou

The Bank of Taizhou has unceasingly satisfied the financial needs of the market segment of SMEs and now provides convenience-store-like financial services. It has been focusing on SMEs. Till late July 2013, there were nearly 100,000 borrowers with a loan balance to the Bank. The loan amount per borrower was 509,900 yuan, and the loans offered to SMEs accounted for 87.97%. The borrowers with a loan of less than five million yuan made up 99.16%. (See Table 5.1 for operating data of the Bank of Taizhou). Over a span of 25 years, the Bank of Taizhou has extended more than one million loans, amounting to more than 450 billion yuan, to SMEs, which makes a best note to the Bank's insistence on serving SMEs (Table 5.2).

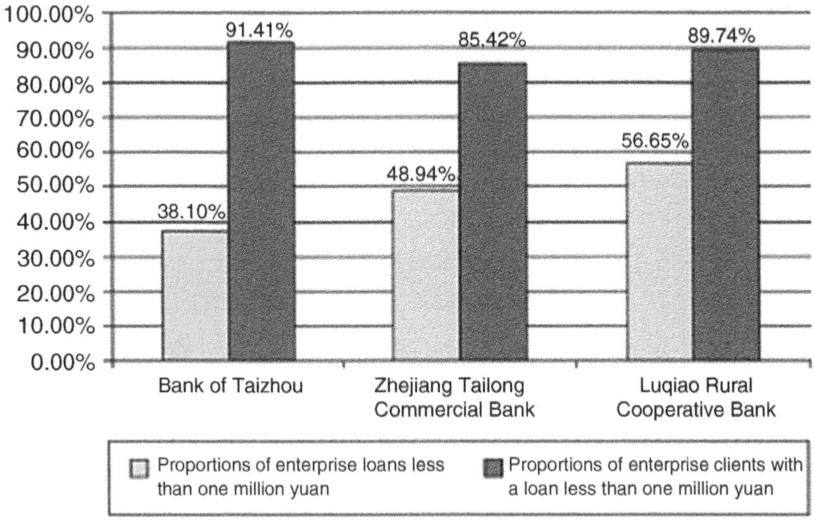

Fig. 5.1 Proportions of loans from Luqiao's three banks to SMEs

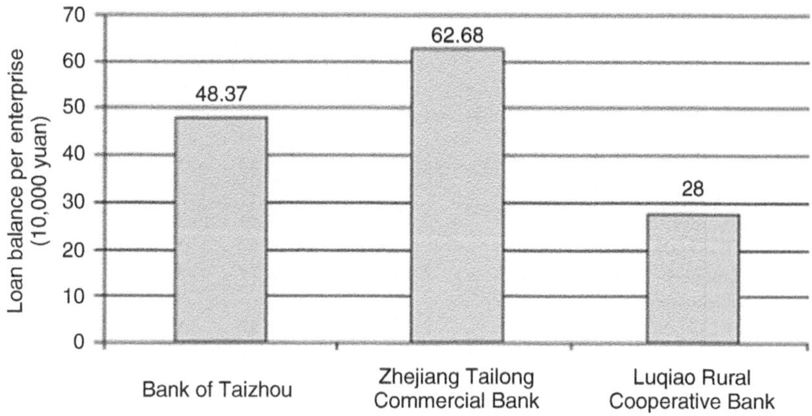

Fig. 5.2 Loan balances per enterprise from Luqiao's three banks to SMEs

Table 5.1 Operating data of the Banks of Taizhou

	2007	*2008*	*2009*	*2010*	*2011*	*2012*	*2013*
Deposit balance (100 million yuan)	164.60	221.46	301.90	420.37	435.60	502.18	607.21
Loan balance (100 million yuan)	115.39	148.55	208.11	274.25	322.13	366.62	417.42
Operating revenue (100 million yuan)	11.78	18.26	19.51	27.64	39.40	49.47	54.91
Interest income (100 million yuan)	11.03	17.03	17.81	24.47	35.35	44.88	48.36
Loan provision rate (%)	0.93	0.91	0.76	0.93	1.65	2.04	2.50

Characteristic services offered by the Bank of Taizhou mainly cover the following:

First, making itself "a convenience store" of financial services. It extends its outlets to communities and villages to better deliver financial services to support agriculture and SMEs. Upholding the model of a community bank, it makes friends with clients. The Bank keeps a clear strategy and well-proven practice as a model of community marketing. Its outlets have taken several innovative measures in community marketing—imparting financial knowledge to villagers, making charitable and voluntary efforts like sponsoring utility carts and providing assistance to festivals and

Table 5.2 Operating data of the Bank of Taizhou

	2010		*2011*		*2012*		*2013*	
Deposit balance (100 million yuan)	59.43	10.84	64.48	10.79	68.70	10.64	73.98	10.25
Loan balance (100 million yuan)	49.22	9.62	53.15	8.98	58.23	9.51	64.52	10.31
Operating revenue (100 million yuan)	3.32		3.31		3.34	49.47	3.53	
Interest income (100 million yuan)	2.59		3.18		3.77	44.88	3.89	
Net Profit	1.99		2.33		2.27	2.04	2.59	

celebratory activities, and improving the loyalty of their clients by making friends with them.

Second, innovating financial services to SMEs to meet special needs. The Small Business Loans innovatively launched by the Bank mainly serve low-income groups and business starters. The current balance is 5405 million yuan. Since its launch in 2006, a cumulative amount of 27,047 million yuan was offered, which has supported nearly 200,000 entrepreneurs in realizing their dreams of becoming rich through labor and has directly created more than 800,000 jobs. Its self-service loans and credit loans have given its quality clients the experience of obtaining loans as easily as depositing. The Green Energy-saving Loans serve the transformation and upgrading of SMEs. The Taihang Yinzuo Poverty Alleviation and Entrepreneurship Fund, free of interest, mortgage, guarantee, and service fee, is mainly dedicated to helping poverty-stricken business starters.

Third, providing efficient, convenient, and quick professional services. "Efficient" means that SMEs need only submit an identity card and their business license while other formalities are completed by an account manager of the Bank. "Convenient" refers to the fact that its outlets are open for business from 7:30 am to 7:30 pm, 365 days a year. By "Quick", its account managers know their clients well enough to make a loan immediately available to them or to have it transferred to the accounts of new clients within two days.

Fourth, reducing service fees and surrendering part of its profits to practically support the development of SMEs. Since March 2012, the Bank has actively assumed its social responsibility by reducing fees and surrendered part of its profits to cope with the economic downturn together with SMEs. It has made a public commitment that some of its "services are provided for free and more thoughtfully." Consequently, it has voluntarily taken 42 measures to reduce fees and surrender part of its profits, which has been highly commended by various sectors of the society and reported by such media as the Xinhua News Agency. In 2012, it reduced fees worth more than 26 million yuan for SMEs, clients of agriculture and rural areas, farmer clients, and citizens. In 2013, the Bank continued its policy of "free services".

Professional crediting techniques have also guaranteed a good quality of its credit assets. During the 14-year-long, from 1988 to 2002, history of Yinzuo (its predecessor), before the Bank of Taizhou was established, no bad debt was written off and the total amount of non-performing loans was only 3.01 million yuan. In 2002, the Bank of Taizhou was established and undertook the non-performing assets equivalent to 351 million yuan from credit cooperatives, thus the non-performing asset ratio soared to 13.1%. But, with hard efforts, it only took the Bank four years to make it lower than 1% in 2006. Up till now, the non-performing asset ratio at the Bank has always been kept below 1%.

Tailong Bank

Taizhou Tailong Bank has gradually lowered its loan limit and has built itself a community bank to ease the financing dilemma of SMEs in Taizhou. The Bank dedicates itself to financial services for small enterprises. Regarding its client composition, those with a loan limit below five million yuan accounted for 99.5%, and their loan balance accounted for 85%; those with a loan limit less than one million yuan made up 92%, their loan balance accounted for 52%; those with a loan limit less than 500,000 yuan 81%, their loan balance 51%. Meanwhile, the loan per borrower from the Bank decreased year by year—540,000 yuan, 510,000 yuan and 480,000 yuan in 2010, 2011 and 2012 respectively, which was closely related to the Bank's developmental policy—to lower thresholds for clients and to extend outlets in remoter areas. (See Table 5.3 for its operating data from 2008 to 2013.)

In Taizhou, the manufacturing industry is well-developed, and the real economy is dominated by SMEs. With the macroeconomic slowdown, the SMEs in Taizhou have been gradually exposed to financial difficulties. The Bank has accurately interpreted the situation and adjusted its developmental orientation by innovating its financial services to provide financing assistance to SMEs.

Table 5.3 Operating data of Tailong Bank

	2008	*2009*	*2010*	*2011*	*2012*	*2013*
Deposit balance (100 million yuan)	166.49	233.59	327.84	391.08	447.91	603.80
Loan balance (100 million yuan)	101.95	154.09	213.16	281.05	346.17	405.39
Operating revenue (100 million yuan)	6.79	9.99	19.75	26.43	26.24	36.16
Interest income (100 million yuan)	9.75	12.67	21.44	31.24	22.79	30.25
Profit (100 million yuan)	2.39	3.44	7.53	7.72	6.22	7.74
Total assets (100 million yuan)	180.96	262.49	367.23	478.31	582.63	769.69

First, setting up sub-branches in batches. To better serve SMEs and provide financial services to SMEs adjacently, the Bank built in batches special sub-branches of SMEs in towns, communities, and sub-districts to make itself a next-door neighbour to them. In 2012, it established 18 outlets for these special clients. Pingdu Sub-branch in Qingyuan County, one of its experimental pioneers of the move, achieved break-even and a win-win outcome of assuming social responsibility and reaping economic benefits in one year.

Second, granting batch loans to SMEs. To effectively reduce the high costs of financial services for SMEs, the Bank actively experimented in batch loan operation for SMEs. Many measures, including group audit and approval and standardized operation were taken to choose, analyze, develop, and market, in a centralized way, among clients with similar business model, operations, and risks. This practice targeted at clients with a financing demand of 500,000 yuan or below and followed a "develop in batch and audit case by case" principle. It encourages its lending personnel to offer small, short-term loans to SMEs through group operations in order to improve the efficiency of its service and to effectively reduce the service costs.

Third, innovating its credit products. The Bank gives priority to independent research and development, and continuously intensifies its efforts in researching and developing new products with an aim to optimize its products through innovations. To begin with, the guarantee mode was modified and the focus was shifted to launching Xinrongtong credit loans,

Yirongtong morality guaranteed loans, Dingrongtong deposit pledged loans, and Yamanrong mortgage combined loans. Then, the repayment mode was adjusted. Jielidai revolving loans, Zhengdai Linghuan instalment loans and SG Tairongyi medium-term loans were introduced to its clients. Furthermore, new channels were created. Traditional credit products were integrated into electronic banking Rong-e-Dai revolving loans were launched, making the borrow channels diverse, electronic, and convenient so that time and fund costs for clients were greatly reduced. A service of 3 minutes was cut short to 3 seconds.

Fourth, serving the real economy. To better serve the real economy and based on free provision of 63 services, including online banking and account opening, the Bank, with further efforts to benefit enterprises and to alleviate their burdens, reduced or canceled, to varying degrees, fees concerning 13 services, including bank acceptance and bank confirmation requests. As a result, services are basically provided free of charge and benefits were really surrendered to SMEs. Still, the internal evaluation performance levers were coordinated and evaluation was rationally arranged to prevent the grass-roots units from seeking quick success and instant benefits. They were guided to shift from scale increase to quality and efficiency improvement to ensure the Bank's orientation of serving SMEs. Finally, the Bank lifted its tolerance of non-performing loans by encouraging the offering of credit loans and morality guaranteed loans to earnestly serve the real economy and SMEs, by which it fulfills its social responsibility.

Luqiao Rural Cooperative Bank

Luqiao Rural Cooperative Bank was established on March 18, 2005. At present, it has 1 business department, 14 branches, 44 business outlets, and 698 employees. It is a bank with the largest number of business outlets and the greatest support for agriculture in Luqiao area. With an objective of "supporting agriculture and micro and small enterprises", the Bank has been developing an inclusive finance and making itself a highly reliable bank for local people. Till late August 2013, its deposit balance and loan balance were 15.4 billion yuan and 10.3 billion yuan respectively. It took the initiative to undertake more than 99% of the agricultural loans in Luqiao District and vigorously supported more than 50,000 rural households, and more than 3000 SMEs there. Its remarkable performance has won many accolades, including China Rural Financial Institutions with

Greatest Developmental Potential, China's Top 10 SMB Brands, Top 10 Rural Banks in Zhejiang Province, and Top 10 Banks for Supporting Agriculture, and Micro and Small Enterprises in Zhejiang Province.

The Bank has attached great importance to providing financial services for micro, small and medium-sized enterprises. As of late August 2013, its enterprise deposits amounted to 3412.06 million yuan, accounting for 22.17% of the total deposit balance, 739.06 million yuan up or an increase of 27.65% compared with the end of the previous year. The balance of enterprise loans was 2236.56 million yuan (excluding the loans used in enterprise operations in the name of individuals), accounting for 21.62% of its total loans, 333.39 million yuan up or an increase of 17.52% compared with the beginning of the year. The balance of loans for micro and small enterprises was 1749.06 million yuan, 366.55 million yuan up or an increase of 26.51% (higher than the 17.52% growth rate of loans) compared with the beginning of the year. The face balance of bank acceptance was 1714.02 million yuan, 253.55 million yuan up compared with the beginning of the year. The balance of trade financing was 6,115,300 USD. From January to August 2013, it offered a total of 2981 million yuan in corporate loans and issued 2293 million yuan in bank acceptances. Overall, the scale of credit loans for SMEs grew rapidly as compared with the beginning of the year.

First, optimizing the business process. To shorten the time for clients to obtain loans, the operational mode, under which the granting of a credit line and the utilization of that line are audited and approved thoroughly, was adopted for guaranteed SME loans equal to or below three million yuan, and mortgages or pledge SME loans equal to or below five million yuan. Paperless credit operations and an electronic credit audit and approval process were launched in an all-round way to shorten the credit business process and to ensure that enterprises could obtain credit fund support in the shortest time span. Meanwhile, green channels for micro and small enterprise credit services were opened, by which priority was given to audit and approval of loans to micro and small enterprises. The Bank offers time-bound service to loan application. For regular clients, loans are instantly available upon application; for new clients, the time generally does not exceed two working days. It may be three working days at most.

Second, innovating its credit products. The Bank has made product innovations to meet the financing needs of SMEs from different industries and different industrial cycles. It has launched Lvdaitong (green loans) and Nongdaitong (agricultural loans) to support micro and small enterprises and agricultural enterprises which operate in line with the national environmental protection policy. Regarding its innovative financing guarantees, this bank has launched a series of new-type guaranteed credit products, including Luyintong credit loans, accounts receivable pledge loans, and shop site use right pledge loans. What's more, it has engaged in bank guarantee cooperation with Zhejiang Fanglin Guarantee Co., Ltd. to overcome the guarantee difficulties of micro and small enterprises. With respect to its innovative repayment mode, it has provided some credit products under new types of repayment modes, including interest-paid revolving loans, seamless relay loans, emergency deferred loans, free installment loans, and special revolving loans to solve temporary fund turnover difficulty of enterprises, under the condition that risks are controllable. As of late August 2013, it, under these new types of repayment modes, granted a credit line of 163 million yuan to 54 enterprises, and had revolved 37 loans amounting to 51.60 million yuan.

Meanwhile, it launched micro and small quick loans for newly-established enterprises, and the enterprises transformed from individual businesses—it offered prompt loans to micro and small enterprises with small amounts of loans and low risk of debt after analyzing their indicators of water and electricity charges, tax payments, and import and export data. Since its launch this May, it has issued 32.09 million yuan in loans to 36 enterprises. It has introduced Taizhou businessmen convenience loans to businessmen who do business outside Taizhou. In that case, it issues Harvest Entrepreneurship Card to the qualified borrowers so that they can obtain, repay, and revolve their loans at any time after a one-time granting of a credit line. The borrowers can also enjoy the convenience of self-service borrowing and repayment through online banking.

Third, improving the professional level of the team. It has made great efforts to train teams, set up institutions, and tailor businesses, and has established a professional, specialized, and project-specific system for credit management. For one thing, it has set up a separate professional service team. The advantage that its outlets spread in urban and rural areas was given full play and identified 16 outlets according to their businesses as major service providers to micro and small enterprises. And it assigned on-the-job lending personnel with high professional quality and a strong sense of responsibility to serve micro and small enterprises. For another, the Bank has cooperated with Taiwan SMEGOLD with a view to drawing upon their mature microfinance service philosophy and rich experience so that it can set up well special service institutions, including service centers for small enterprise loans, and can run micro and small enterprise credit businesses professionally.

The Bank keeps risk under control through the following measures:

First, improving its incentive accountability mechanism. Regarding the evaluation of remuneration, it tilts toward service support to micro, small and medium-sized enterprises and encourages its lending officers to increase credit loans to such clients. Meanwhile, it adopted a responsibility exemption system based on due diligence for micro and small enterprise credit loan business so that responsibility exemption based on due diligence and bad debts can be properly dealt with. The responsibility of a loan loss incurred by non-subjective factors can be exempted as regulated.

Second, increasing tolerance of non-performing loans to micro and small enterprises. It has raised its tolerance of non-performing loan ratio for micro and small enterprises by a 0.5 percentage. With regard to a small or micro enterprise of high integrity but having incurred loan risks due to temporary operation difficulties, it adopts active disposition means, including renewal and reorganization of credit assets, to liquidize assets as much as possible and thus helps such enterprise survive their difficulties.

Third, regularizing management of credit risks. It strictly exercises payment management of micro and small enterprises, and keeps track of credit funds for such enterprises to prevent credit funds from being embezzled and entering fields other than the real economy. Still, it strengthens the collection of information on private financing and social risk events and frequently communicates with relevant government departments to form a mechanism for jointly dealing with risks. Meanwhile, it keeps dynamic monitoring over its employees to prevent their involving in private financing.

5.2 Path Explorations of SMBs Developing Microfinance

In Luqiao, Taizhou, private financing, especially SMBs, has achieved remarkable development. At present, there are three SMBs—the Bank of Taizhou, Tailong Bank, and Luqiao Rural Cooperative Bank in the district. These SMBs are dominated by private capital and mainly serve SMEs in the district during their development. They continually lower their thresholds for service recipients, simplify the process of loan application to SMEs, and have become growth partners of SMEs.

Exploration of Inclusive Credit Loan

To further develop the rural market and make finance more inclusive, Luqiao District has energetically introduced inclusive credit loan, vigorously advocated the concept of family credit, and effectively alleviated the guarantee difficulty that ordinary people encounter.

The inclusive credit loan was first launched by Luqiao Rural Cooperative Bank. It is mainly a small loan below 50,000 yuan, based on family credit, and can be provided on the following conditions: any family member with an independent capacity for civil conduct of the borrower, including his/her spouse, parents, and children, agrees to borrow and signs a letter of guarantee for jointly repaying the debt. No other guarantee is required. It eliminates the worries and difficulties arising from the past requirement that a borrower had to be supported by a guarantor. Meanwhile, in case bad records may result from issuing a loan by a lending officer, a principle of responsibility exemption based on due diligence is enforced at the time of evaluating the non-performing loan ratio, thus removing the worries of lending officers.

Till late March 2014, it had provided small credit loans to 2418 borrowers and the loan balance was 131 million yuan. It is expected that by the end of the year, with the promotion of inclusive credit loans, individual credit loan borrowers of the Bank will reach 4000 and the balance will exceed 200 million yuan.

Exploration of Advance Granting of Credit Lines to Rural Households

To further resolve the financing difficulties for rural households and to break away from the traditional mindset of giving credit lines only to large clients, advance granting of a credit line to rural households was carried out in Luqiao District. Applicants directly complete the formalities for obtaining a loan by filling an application card for advance granting of a credit line. This innovative measure overcomes difficulties for rural households to obtain loans and is highly commended in the society. For example, since Luqiao Rural Cooperative Bank commenced an advance granting policy, it has provided new personal credit lines worth 1343 million yuan to 7184 households in the first quarter of 2013. Currently, 40,638 households have obtained personal loans and the loan balance stands at 7796 million yuan.

The advance granting of a credit line is a new policy through which lending officers conduct in-depth surveys, pay visits, solicit opinions from various sources, including village cadres, and set a personal credit rating for rural households. Then they grant credit lines to villagers in advance, no matter whether they have a loan relationship with the bank. To establish a long-term mechanism for advance granting of a credit line, Luqiao Rural Cooperative Bank focuses on the following two priorities: First, improve their personnel arrangement. At outlets of a relatively large deposit scale, it separates loan service into small and large zones, different personnel serving targeted clients. Second, innovate its marketing mode. Account managers are required to establish an account manager marketing log and fill in the log relevant data. They need to contact and visit a preset list of advance granting candidates every day, every week, and every month, thus enforcing an active marketing. Meanwhile, pilot sub-branches of advance granting of credit lines are required to establish a bi-monthly meeting system for lending officers. Sub-branch management periodically conducts spot checks of the account manager log to ensure telephone contacts and visits are done as regulated.

In the exploration process of advance granting of credit lines, the Bank has put forward a five-step re-generation process: build teams and coordinate work; pay field visits and establish credit archives; conduct comprehensive analyses, evaluate, and determine credit lines; set up standing book and do solid audit; pay visit and issue advance granting card.

Comprehensive advance granting of credit lines among common people brings about a win-win outcome for banks and rural households. It solved the financial difficulties for rural households, laid foundation for banks' deep involvement in the rural market, and carved out a new way for rural households to obtain loans. In 2014, the business of advance granting of credit lines will be conducted in an all-round way in the whole district, consolidating the foundation and activating rural finance in Luqiao District.

Exploration of Repayment Innovations

To increase financial support for the real economy, to improve the financial services for micro and small enterprises and to turn Luqiao into the capital of micro financial services in China, Luqiao District has actively made innovations to credit mode and repayment mode, enabling a smooth connection between repayment and renewal of loans and reducing financial costs and ultimately, to help enhance the competitiveness of micro and small enterprises. The Bank of Taizhou has introduced a self-service loan, by which a client can, on a self-service basis, apply for a revolving loan, equal to or below a specified credit line, and obtain and repay it at any time within 1–2 years after the approval of his/her application. He can obtain his next loan, equal to or below a specified credit line, through a self-service mode before the expiry of the current loan, which really facilitates borrowing and repayment. Till late July 2013, the balance of self-service loans from the Bank of Taizhou was 838 million yuan, 125 million yuan up as compared with the beginning of the year. The cumulative amount of loans from the Bank was 3394 million yuan. All of the clients who successfully obtained loans were micro and small enterprises and individual businesses.

Zhejiang Tailong Commercial Bank officially launched Jielidai revolving loan in April 2012, under which a borrower can apply a second loan to repay his first one. As a result, it was welcomed by micro and small enterprises. Till late 2012, the Bank had offered 118 Jielidai revolving loans with a cumulative amount of 67.55 million yuan and the amount per loan being 572,500 yuan.

Luqiao Rural Cooperative Bank has promoted five products with an innovative repayment mode, including Interest-paid Revolving Loan and Seamless Relay Loan, which have produced good results. The Interest-paid Revolving Loan requires only interest payment at the time being, needing no principal repayment, and is available to excellent micro and small enterprises. When a loan is due to repay, if the borrower still needs the revolving loan, he/she needs only to pay the interest of the loan, re-sign a loan contract, and state that the loan is used for the "revolving" purpose, then he/she can obtain loan funds on a revolving basis many times without repaying the principal. The Seamless Relay Loan involves a method of repayment according to which the new loan can be promptly obtained after the old loan is repaid. When the loan is due, the borrower can first make a payment of the interest and the principal. When a new loan is sought, the borrow concerned can apply to renew the loan and the renewed loan funds can be put into his/her account on the repayment date so that the time the repaid funds are retained by the bank is nearly zero. The Emergency Deferred Loan—a renewable loan—is available for those enterprises which are under normal operation but are temporarily subject to a financial strain. If the enterprise files an application before the loan becomes due, after examination and approval, the loan term can be properly extended. The Free Installment Loan is a mode under which a loan is issued at one time and repaid by installments in line with the cash flow characteristics of the enterprise. Clients can determine the amount of each repayment and customize the repayment plan according to monthly (quarterly) equal-amount principal or equal-amount principal and interest. The Special Turnover Loan is managed under a list system with respect to some excellent micro and small enterprises, under which a special temporary revolving credit line is separately established for the enterprises on the list within the overall credit line. As of late July 2014, 54 enterprises had been provided a credit line under the new types of repayment modes, the credit line was 163 million yuan, 18 enterprises obtained loans, and the loan balance was 63.60 million yuan.

Exploration of Supply Chain Finance

With expanding of economic globalization, the competition among modern enterprises has changed from competition between enterprises to that between supply chains involving suppliers, manufacturers, and retailers. Luqiao is one of the areas with the most active private economy—the aggregate of private economy accounted for more than 90% of the economic aggregate of the whole district. Therefore, improving and strengthening financial support to supply chains for small and medium-sized private enterprises is not only the need of Luqiao's local economic development but also a strategic move for financial institutions. With this regard, Luqiao District has begun financial services to supply chains and is trying to provide integrated financial services to enterprises in industrial chains.

Citic Bank is one of the first commercial banks carrying out supply chain financial services in China. Given that there are many 4S auto shops in Luqiao, the Luqiao Sub-branch of Citic Bank gave priority to developing automobile financial business which was part of the supply chain financial business. It attached great importance to such development in two years since its launch. Till late July 2013, the Luqiao Sub-branch of Citic Bank had 13 automobile financial dealers with a total credit line of 420 million yuan. From January to July 2013, the cumulative volume of the automobile supply chain financial business concluded by the sub-branch reached 768.72 million yuan. It effectively addressed the financing needs of the automobile dealers in Luqiao District and achieved a win-win outcome for itself and the enterprises.

The Inclusive Finance Project Exploration

To go deeper into the rural market and make finance more inclusive, Luqiao District has launched inclusive credit loan and has vigorously advocated the concept of family credit. It is a livelihood project which benefits numerous families and also serves as an effective channel for providing both urban and rural areas with equal access to financial services.

The project was first initiated by Luqiao Rural Cooperative Bank. It has proactively optimized credit services, innovated its financial products, and expanded its service channels to shape a three-dimensional inclusive service mode integrating areas, outlets, and networks, which has produced a good effect. Cooperating with financial liaison personnel in villages, it has done surveys of 102,000 rural households with registered residence in Luqiao District and has set up personal credit archives. The leading body of sub-branches, account managers, members of villages' Party branch committees and villagers' committees, villagers' representatives, owners of micro and small enterprises with certain fame and influence form a credit line granting review group to evaluate and determine credit line on a household-by-household basis. Then they issue a credit advance granting notice to the doorstep of each household. A rural household can directly complete the formalities for obtaining a loan at an outlet on the strength of the notice. At present, loans have been delivered to 261 villages, 4.6 billion yuan of credit lines have been granted in advance, the credit line involving personal loans has been granted and utilized by 75,000 households, accounting for about 71.4% of all rural households in Luqiao District. To help rural households overcome guarantee difficulties, the Bank offers, being the first one to offer them an inclusive credit loan based on its family credit and under the condition that adults of the family are informed of the loan and make a written commitment to it. To help enterprises resolve their financing difficulties, it has broken the traditional practice of conducting a loan evaluation of micro and small enterprises by looking at their financial statements and launched a Fast Loan to Micro and Small Enterprises. It evaluates the operating status and debt risks of such enterprises by analyzing their water and electricity charges, tax payments, and their import and export data and then provides financial support, which has effectively met the financial demands of some micro and small enterprises. To address the financing difficulties of those businessmen who carry on business outside Taizhou, the Bank has introduced Taizhou Businessmen Convenience Loan with a Harvest Entrepreneurship

Card, ensuring that after a one-time granting of a credit line, the loan can be obtained, revolved, and repaid at any time. The borrowers can also enjoy the convenience of self-service through online banking. Transportation and other costs resulting from revolving loans can thus be reduced. Till late August 2013, the Inclusive Credit Loan had been offered to 1967 borrowers, the balance being 143 million yuan; 71 Fast Loan to Micro and Small Enterprises worth 60.49 million yuan granted; 104 Harvest Entrepreneurship Cards issued and 52.41 million yuan total credit line granted, with the loan balance being 23.57 million yuan.

Luqiao Rural Cooperative Bank has also deployed, in a unified way, some village-level financial service outlets at community service centers, agricultural POS, agricultural terminals, and other feature service channels, and has adopted such measures as setting up off-premise ATMs and self-service terminals to actively push forward the building up of micro banks. At present, it has set up 158 ATMs and cash recycling systems and 36 self-service terminals, with 4.9 self-service machines available for every 10,000 people. The financial institution has now laid out most self-service machines and boasts the widest service area and the largest client group in Luqiao District.

5.3 Cases of Luqiao SMBs Developing Microfinance

Moral Quality, Products, and Collateral; Water Meters, Electricity Meters, and Customs Forms Stressed by Tailong Bank

Information asymmetry, difficult guarantee, high benefit coverage risk are universal problems of micro and small enterprises financing. But after 20 years of exploration and practice, Tailong Bank has developed a micro and small enterprise financial service mechanism and a risk control mechanism which center on moral quality, products, and collateral, water meters, electricity meters, and customs forms. As a result, it has achieved healthy and sustainable development under the positive energy of Tailong culture.

To Overcome Information Asymmetry Through Moral Quality, Products, and Collateral; Water Meters, Electricity Meters, and Customs Forms

To overcome the problem of information asymmetry in small enterprises, Tailong Bank has built a highly self-disciplined a large team of account managers. They combine digital "hard information" with social "soft information" through effective communication and services to conduct qualitative analyses and quantitative evaluations to fully understand its clients.

Account managers of the Bank account for more than 50% of the employees at the Bank. They make great use of their geographical, interpersonal, and kinship advantages, carry out field surveys and observations, and face-to-face communication to gain back-to-back understanding of their clients' operation status, family property, and moral quality through multiple channels and sources. Specifically, the managers concentrate on whether a client has bad habits, whether he enjoys a good reputation among friends, and whether he keeps a harmonious conjugal relationship. They observe moral quality, products, and collateral of clients. Among moral quality, product, and collateral, moral quality is the first priority. Attention is paid to, first, the client's moral quality, focusing on his trustworthiness to examine his willingness to repay the loan; second, his products, emphasizing their marketability to examine the client's capability for repaying the loan; third, his collateral, stressing the client's reliability, to examine his guarantee for such a loan.

Tailong Bank does not mechanically check its clients' financial statements, in particular, financial statements of small enterprises engaging in production and foreign trade. Besides financial statements, it pays more attention to their water meters, electricity meters, and customs forms. First, water meters. Water consumption in productive enterprises often reflects changes of production and operations. Second, electricity meters. Electricity consumption in productive enterprises can also indicate the production and operation status and the changes therein. Third, customs forms. The customs forms of foreign trade enterprises are basically able to accurately reflect their operations. Water meters, electricity meters, and customs forms can reflect realities of enterprises, effectively validating and supplementing their financial statements, and truly represent their digital information.

To Resolve the Guarantee Difficulty Through Credit Guarantee

Given that small enterprises have no adequate collateral, Tailong Bank has experimented on and innovated its guarantee mode, putting guarantee credit in comprehensive practice and reducing reliance on a mortgage. Besides providing a guarantor(s), small enterprises need to make their legal representatives, shareholders, and actual controllers guarantors to turn limited liability of enterprises into unlimited liability of such individuals. Meanwhile, it has combined kinship and personal integrity into the Morality Guarantee Loan, by which relatives, friends, and benefactors provide guarantee to owners of small enterprise, which increases the moral costs of breach of contract and effectively guards against clients' moral risks. Till late 2012, credit guaranteed loans from Tailong Bank accounted for 95.87% of all loans, while mortgage (pledge) loans made up 4.13%. The threshold for small enterprises to obtain loans was effectively lowered.

To Cope with the Benefit Coverage Risk Through Three Low Costs
To face up to the challenge that the benefit of loans to small enterprises is not always sufficient to cover the risks, Tailong Bank has taken a differentiated, characteristic developmental path to achieve "three low costs" and has created a Tailong phenomenon. First, to obtain information at low costs in advance. It conducts field surveys, observations, and face-to-face communication, to gain back-to-back understanding of its potential clients. Then it examines their moral quality, products, and collateral, checks water meters, electricity meters, and customs forms, obtaining background information at low costs and to accurately evaluate client credit. Second, to exercise low-cost monitoring and management in the process. Tailong Bank has independently developed a cash flow evaluation mechanism according to deposit and repayment data and has built a flat management system characterized by full authorization and strict accountability to ensure that rights and benefits are commensurate with responsibilities. Meanwhile, Tailong Bank adopts the "three-three system" to handle business to ensure that loans can be obtained as conveniently as depositing money to meet the financing needs of small enterprises characterized by "short, small, quick, urgent, and frequent", which can effectively reduce monitoring costs and improve the service efficiency. Third, to impose penalties on breach of contract at low costs. Tailong Bank places great emphasis on management of employees and clients. On the one hand, clients are classified according to their industry, specialty, and level and the interest rate is differentiated according to account, loan, and transaction. On the other hand, measures are taken to strengthen management of employees to guard against their moral risks so that they "are unwilling to, unable to, need not or dare not misbehave".

Small Business Loans from the Bank of Taizhou

Small Business Loan is a characteristic product specially designed by the Bank of Taizhou for businesses starters. In 2006, Taizhou Commercial Bank (the predecessor of the Bank of Taizhou) cooperated with the China Development Bank in introducing microfinance from European Bank for Reconstruction and Development and localized it into a new product. Threshold of the loan is 2000 yuan and the conditions are very simple—as long as one has labor skills, is willing to work, and his business is in operation for three months, then he can apply for the loan from the Bank of Taizhou on the strength of their ID card. Then lending officers complete a field survey within 1–2 hours. Generally, the loan funds will be transferred to his account or a definite reply will be made to him within two days. Since its official launch in 2006, Small Business Loan has been well-received by its clients. Till late 2012, the balance of the loan from the Bank of Taizhou was 3401 million yuan. Since its launch in 2006, it has extended 161,600 small business loans of a total amount of 18,868 million yuan. Village banks mainly sponsored by the Bank of Taizhou offered 22,700 small business loans worth 2322 million yuan and supported 160,000 farmers, urban laid-off workers, immigrant population, and other low-income groups to start a business. More than 60% of the clients obtained bank loans for the first time. The Small Business Loan offered by the Bank of Taizhou (see Table 5.4 for basic information) is hailed by experts as the China Small Business Mode in the international field of microfinance, alleviating poverty.

Table 5.4 Basic information of the small business loan from the Bank of Taizhou

Lender: Bank of Taizhou	Institution type: micro-loan bank
Loan type: guaranteed loan	Repayment mode: installment repayment
Loan limit: 50,000–300,000 yuan	Suitable for: Taizhou City
Loan currency: RMB	Suitable for: enterprise legal persons, individual businesses
Loan interest rate: 0.60%–0.70%	Loan term: 1–36 months
Handling time: 5 days	Intended use of the loan: short-term revolving loan, operation loan for individual business
Other charges: no other charges	

The Bank of Taizhou has tried to provide a commercially sustainable micro enterprise credit, and dedicates Small Business Loan to micro and small enterprises in the forms of individual businesses and family workshops have been excluded from services of financial institutions. It subdivides the loan into small loans with an amount of 100,000 to 300,000 yuan for small enterprises and micro loans with an amount of 2000 to 100,000 yuan for micro enterprises, with micro loans below 100,000 yuan as the major targets. As is shown by the current operations, a loan limit (10,000–100,000 yuan) is set to each per borrower to make it consistent with the target groups and the coverage is continuously expanded. It is financially sound and highly sustainable. As Small Business Loans overcome the difficulty that micro enterprises encounter in obtaining credit loans, the key for a bank to making profits is that lending technique, internal organization structure, innovations in its incentive system, the arrangement of the mechanism for the market-based interest rate, and benign market competition are put into place to mitigate and/or remove the restrictions imposed by the above factors on micro enterprise credit loans.

As for the Small Business Loan, the Bank of Taizhou combined the IPC standard micro and small loan technique with the relational loan technique accumulated by itself in serving micro, small, and medium-sized enterprises and has developed an efficient, simple, quick, and standardized micro enterprise credit technique suitable for the district.

First, a loan decision-making entails collecting and processing of a potential borrower's information. At an early stage of loan marketing, microfinance lending officers widely publicize Small Business Loan through various channels, and such officers are rationally allocated in line with the market segmentation of Small Business Loan, geographical locations (villages or communities), industries, supply chains, associations, and other intermediary organizations. They professionally work in the business fields designated to them to keep a long-term, multi-dimensional contact with the enterprises, their owners, and the residents in the corresponding communities, industries, and supply chain. They can easily collect "soft information" about a borrower. This kind of information is qualitative. For example, the character, habits, and other aspects of a borrower are difficult to be quantified, confirmed, and communicated among bank personnel. In the Bank of Taizhou, account managers account for more than 1/3 of the employees. Each account manager manages 200 valid clients on average. They are localized and their social capital role is given a full play. In this way a social network with a certain coverage is built. They painstakingly maintain relationships with the clients, providing them, besides management and supervision, with extended services like keeping daily contact and adeptly serving as consultants (Ying Qianfan, et al. 2009; Shi Jinchuan, et al. 2010).

Second, given that borrowers of Small Business Loan generally lack properties for mortgage, hard and soft information about the borrowers is collected before lending as much as possible to select borrowers and control the risks. Moreover, because the credit line is relatively low, the opportunity cost of personal strategic default is higher than the income, thus the guarantee or mortgage for a Small Business Loan takes the primary repayment source of the borrower. He needs to present a guarantor while a mortgage is not mandatory. For a micro loan, it is not necessary to conduct an in-depth analysis of the guarantor's financial conditions, only the basic information including name, address, income, etc. is required.

Finally, the post-lending supervision mainly involves monitoring of the maturity of the repayment installments. Small Business Loans are repaid monthly in all cases. Interest must be paid each month, but the principal amount can be adjusted by lending officers in line with the actual situation. This installment repayment is currently the most common mode of repayment in microfinance. For one thing, in this mode an early warning system for loan risks has been established. Lending officers revisit the clients before the first repayment and subsequently contact and supervise by telephone or other means each time. This process provides the lending officers with access to the information on loan use and fund flow, helps identify any possible problem early on, makes it possible to have a quick response, and develops a stricter abnormal loan monitoring procedure. For another, with frequent engagement in installment repayment, it is easier to establish a personal relationship between a lending officer and a borrower. The costs for obtaining information can be reduced and the necessary information can also be gotten in a more opportune manner. Furthermore, this mode of repayment helps the bank choose its clients at relatively low risks. This is because the borrowers generally have multiple repayment sources, and it is impossible to fully rely on the returns from the loan project, since it is very difficult for the project to deliver corresponding returns within one month, thus some highly risky borrowers can be excluded (Aghion & Morduch, 2005). Still, this mode can stimulate and enhance the borrowers' awareness to save, reduce the sensitivity of micro enterprises to interest rate, ease their huge financial burden for one-time large-amount repayment, and improve their ability to repay loans.

The Baixiao Loan Project of Luqiao Rural Cooperative Bank

In recent years, Luqiao Rural Cooperative Bank in Taizhou, Zhejiang Province has attached great importance to micro and small financial services and has carried out the Inclusive Finance Project and built a diversified, multi-channel and multi-tier financial service and product system with an effort to gradually resolve the financial difficulties for micro and small enterprises, which has produced remarkable results. It focuses on Sunshine Credit and intensively works on Inclusive Finance. Baixiao Loan Project is a new brand for providing convenience to local people and promoting agricultural development. With the Baixiao Loan Project, the Bank conducts active door-to-door surveys and proactively offer loans and grant credit lines to rural households (residents) with registered residence at the villages in Luqiao District. Baixiao means expertise in Taizhou dialect. More than 100 account managers of the Bank have worked in rural areas for a long time, so they know well about the residents and happenings there. In carrying out the above three major projects, they visit households, learn about their needs, and dispel their worries. They deliver loans to villages, to households, and online so that the people in the district can enjoy the basic credit services.

First, publicize relevant information and deliver loans to villages. To remove the scruples and prejudice that many local people hold towards financial institutions where high thresholds for loan application are set and the loaning process takes long time, the Bank actively delivers loans to villages. The credit business flow chart is exhibited in all its outlets. The basic information of account managers is also exhibited on village bulletin boards, in financial knowledge publicity windows, in offices in industrial parks, and in densely populated areas in 312 villages and seven main industrial parks in September 2012. On the chart all of the steps, from loan application, interview, loan origination, and recovery are illustrated to ensure that villagers can directly contact account villagers to acquire financial knowledge and discuss loan applications without leaving their villages. Making financial knowledge easily available and rendering it known to all local people can provide convenience and keep a closer relationship with them.

Second, push forward sunshine granting of credit lines and deliver loans to households. Since 2010, the Bank has conducted an annual financial census to find solutions for offering credit support to agriculture and upgrading rural industries. After more than three years of efforts, it has obtained first-hand data about all rural households and villages in the district. To make this work play its due role, as from September 2013, it has carried out pilot advance granting of credit lines. With a village as a unit, it organized account managers to work with village financial liaison personnel to survey 102,000 rural households with registered residence in 312 villages in the district according to the household registration data, and has set up personal credit archives. 3 to 5 people chosen from members of the villages' Party branch committees and villagers committees, villager representatives, and owners of individual businesses or SMEs who enjoy high prestige among local people, have good character, know a lot about the community, and boast certain popularity and influence among local people form a panel for evaluating and determining, in a back-to-back way, credit line for those households having a borrower qualification according to legal provisions, having not established credit loan relations with the Bank, and having no severe bad credit records. Then advance granting notices were issued and presented door by door. Below the given credit line, a rural household can directly get to the audit and approval stage on the strength of the loaning notice. With time for survey and credit line granting saved, the time for completing loan formalities has been greatly reduced. In the first quarter of 2014, this practice was extended to all levels of the Bank.

Taizhou Rural Cooperative Bank has more than 40,000 credit clients, more than 95% of which are micro and small enterprise owners, individual businesses, and rural households. To serve grassroots people and micro and small enterprises well is of vital importance to sustainable development of the Bank. In this regard and based on financial censuses conducted and visits to villages and enterprises, the Bank drew on its promotion of the three major projects, especially the Sunshine Credit Project, and has identified its strategic positioning—with support to agriculture and small enterprises and inclusive finance as its focus, continuously increasing its popularity and share in the rural market. And now, the strategic transformation has produced preliminary effects.

The Baixiao Loan Project has brought transformation from active lending to active marketing, from single credit support to multifaceted financial services, and has made rural households and small enterprise owners fully enjoy convenient, quick, and secure financial services. In the past, when rural households sought loans for the first time, the shortest time for getting approval was 3–5 days; now with the help of the advance granting notice, loan funds below 300,000 yuan and 100,000 yuan can enter into the applicant's account within 1 day and 30–50 min, from acceptance of application till the approval of the loan, respectively.

In the process of pushing the Baixiao Loan Project ahead, account managers of this bank paid extensive visits to identify fund demands rural households and enterprises encountered in production or operation. A series of new products and new measures have been developed and introduced. Consequently, the financing difficulties of such clients were overcome.

As 698 employees and 410 financial liaison personnel of the Bank have been working in rural areas for a long time, they have built a natural bond with the local people for common growth and development. At present, it has 290,000 valid deposit clients, accounting for 66% of the total population of Luqiao District (440,000 people). It is the first bank to initiate Baixiao Loan Project, which granted credit lines to local rural households door to door in advance so that everyone in Luqiao District can enjoy the basic credit services. It is also the first bank to launch Inclusive Credit Loan, Micro and Small Quick Loan, Taizhou Businessmen's Convenience Loan, and "Family Credit" interest rate mode to tackle financing bottlenecks for rural households, and micro and small enterprises—it is difficult to raise funds and the financing cost is high. In 2013, the balance of agricultural loans was 8.7 billion yuan, a 12.4% up as compared with last year; the balance of loans for micro and small enterprises was 3.69 billion yuan, a 22.6% up as compared with the year before.

5.4 Summary

SMBs are the main force in the micro and small financial service market. According to a great deal of research, when the relations between credit loans for SMEs and bank scale and structure are concerned, small and medium-sized financial institutions enjoy information advantages in providing information services to SMEs. On the one hand, small and medium-sized financial institutions are unable to operate large loan projects due to their small scale. They have no choice but to serve SMEs. On the other hand, small and medium-sized financial institutions are local, conveniently available to SMEs. It is easy for them to understand the credit and operation status of SMEs, thus reducing the difficulty caused by information asymmetry and greatly mitigating loan risks. Small and medium-sized financial institutions are more willing to provide financing services to SMEs than large financial institutions are. Compared with large banks which are advantageous in financing large enterprises, SMBs are based in local markets, and understand the development and credit status and financial conditions of local SMEs. Likewise, SMEs enjoy more advantages in the local SME loan business. Therefore, all SMBs have devoted themselves to exploring local markets and serving SMEs. They reform their financial services and innovate their financial products, thus largely alleviating the financing dilemma for SMEs.

However, in the existing financial system of small and medium-sized financial institutions, including SMBs, there are a slew of problems which restrict their operations and obstruct their healthy development. Firstly, the market positioning of some small and medium-sized financial institutions is not accurate. Their operation patterns are identical and need upgrading. For example, the "integration" of some city commercial banks is only a pulling-together. Parts are in fact still in a state of disunity. Many branches and their operation management personnel do not actually carry out the overall strategy of the corporation. What they seek is to make use of the new conditions and make immediate benefits. Secondly, the property rights of small and medium-sized financial institutions are not clearly defined, and their corporate governance structure is unsound. Most small and medium-sized financial institutions have not yet given the strength of the shareholding system to full play. They have not yet developed a real scientific, efficient, complete, and effective internal control mechanism. Most of them follow passively the lead of the government. Their property rights structure is unclear. An internal incentive and restraint mechanism has not yet been established. An irregular governance structure results in an improper mechanism for operation management, and their awareness of external constraints is still weak. Thirdly, there exists prejudice in national policies. As a result, small and medium-sized financial institutions cannot achieve trans-regional development. Some national treatments towards large financial institutions and state-owned banks and small and medium-sized financial institutions are different. Such discriminatory treatments due to national policies become the most important external factor which restricts the development of small and medium-sized financial institutions. Government departments have excessive administrative intervention in small and medium-sized financial institutions. Fourthly, there are no relevant laws and regulations in this field, so the governance is problematic. China's financial regulation body consists of one bank and three commissions—the People's Bank of China, the China Securities Regulatory Commission, the China Banking Regulatory Commission, and the China Insurance Regulatory Commission. Small and medium-sized financial institutions emerged late and have been developing rapidly. There are many problems and loopholes waiting for resolution.

However, as proven by the practices of promoting small and microfinance development by SMBs in Luqiao District, Taizhou City, full competition among banks can effectively expand credit more channels for enterprises and enhance the competitiveness of banks. Firstly, fierce competition between SMBs in Luqiao District and the branches of large and medium-sized banks and rural credit cooperatives urges them to go downward to increase their market share and development space. For example, Small Business Loan developed by the Bank of Taizhou was designed to seek new profit sources. Secondly, the development of SMBs in Luqiao District and their intense competition can effectively promote a spillover effect of advanced credit techniques and institutional innovations which would expand throughout the district. For example, Small Business Loan created by the Bank of Taizhou has been, to a certain degree, imitated by Tailong Bank and Mintai Bank, which have designed similar micro-loan products. As is shown, this spillover effect can increase the level of credit supply of banks, dramatically reduce credit expenditure of enterprises, and control credit rate for local enterprises. Thirdly, the banks in Luqiao District can cooperate in business promotion. In particular, they can jointly build a credit reference system to share enterprise information to avoid reputation and dynamic incentive mechanism failure in their competition. Moreover, the information screening cost can be effectively reduced. Overall, under the current bank scale structure and property rights structure in Luqiao District, Taizhou City, such benign market competition effectively plays an important role in allocating micro and small financial resources.

According to the developmental experience of SMBs in Luqiao District, Taizhou City, to promote credit supply to enterprises, attention should be paid to the development of local small banks because it is easier for SMBs to realize product, technical, and internal structural innovations catering to the credit demands of micro and small enterprises. SMBs are more advantageous than traditional large banks in this regard. Their market positioning is different from that of traditional large banks. In addition, benign competition and cooperative relationship among SMBs can contribute to continuously expanding enterprise credit coverage, promote the diffusion effect of credit techniques and institutional innovations, widen the channels of fund supply to enterprise credit, reduce the transaction costs in financing, avoid monopolistic interest rates, and lower the interest cost for micro and small enterprises. Resultantly, cooperation among various types of banks and co-building and sharing loan information facilities, including personal credit reference systems, can be enhanced.

References

Modigliani, F. & Miller, M. The Cost of Capital, Corporate Finance and the Theory of Investment [J]. *American Economic Review*, 1958(48): 197–261.

Myers, S. C. & Majluf, N. Corporate Financing and Investment Decisions When Firms Have Information that Investors Do Not Have [J]. *Journal of Financial Economics*, 1984(13): 187–221.

Ang, J. S. Small Business Uniqueness and the Theory of Financial Management [J]. *Journal of Small Business Finance*, 1991(1): 1–13.

Jensen, M. & Mecking, W. Theory of the Firm: Managerial Behavior, Agency Costs and Ownership Structure [J]. *Journal of Financial Economics*, 1976(3): 305–360.

Horworth, C. A. Small Firms Demand for Finance: A Research Note [J]. *International Small Business Journal*, 2001, 19(4): 78–86.

Stiglitz, Joseph & Andrew Weiss. The American Economic Review [J]. *Credit Rationing in Markets with Imperfect Information*, 1981, 71(6): 393–410.

Zhang Ge, The Financing of Small and Medium-sized Enterprises and the Development of Small and Medium-sized Banks [J]. *Finance Forum*, 2009(9): 58–63.

Ling Xin, The Financing Dilemma for Small and Medium-sized Enterprises [J]. *Finance & Economy*, 2011(12): 16–18.

Chen Lei, An Analysis of the Financing Dilemma for Small and Medium-sized Enterprises from the Perspective of Information Asymmetry [J]. *Review of Investment Studies*, 2011(10): 56–65.

Wang Liming, Lu Shoubo, Wang Yuhua, An Analysis of the Financial Mode of Small and Medium-sized Enterprises from the Perspective of Industrial Cluster [J]. *Journal of Chengdu University of Technology (Social Science Edition)*, 2012, 20(1): 26–30.

Guo Bin, Liu Manlu, Private Finance and the Development of Small and Medium-sized Enterprises: An Empirical Analysis of Wenzhou [J]. *Economic Research Journal*, 2002(10): 40–46.

Lu Yajuan, Zhang Longyao, An Empirical Analysis of the Financing Demand from Small and Medium-sized Enterprises from the Perspective of Industrial Cluster [J]. *Shanghai Finance*, 2012(12): 95–98.

Wang Xianmeng, Zhou Faming, Yang Yimin, An Analysis of the Impact from Industrial Cluster on the Financing Behaviors of Small and Medium-sized Enterprises [J]. *Communication of Finance and Accounting*, 2011(9): 6–7.

Zhang Chenxi, An Exploration and Analysis of Innovations in the Trade Finance Strategy for Industrial Cluster [J]. *China Business & Trade*, 2012(22): 165–166.

Yuan Man, An Analysis of the Financing of Small and Medium-sized Enterprises within the Industrial Cluster [J]. *Journal of Southwest Agricultural University (Social Science Edition)*, 2012(7): 34–35.

Gui Binwei, Private Finance, Small and Medium-sized Financial Institutions and the Solutions for the Private Lending Crisis [J]. Modern Economic Information, 2012(14): 212–213.

Jiang Hai, A Study of the Financing Constraints for Small and Medium-sized Enterprises and the Development of the Small and Medium-sized Financial Institution System [J]. *Journal of Jinan University (Philosophy & Social Science Edition)*, 2002(2): 53–60.

Lei Wenwen, An Analysis of the Development of Small and Medium-sized Financial Institutions and the Financing of Small and Medium-sized Enterprises (D), Jiangxi Normal University, 2011.

Wang Suyan, The Financing Innovations in Small and Medium-sized Enterprises from the Perspective of Industrial Cluster-Take the Hohhot-Baotou-Ordos Economic Circle as an Example [J]. *Future and Development*, 2013(3): 100–101.

Yang Yun, Luo Shihua, Tao Ye, A Study of Innovations in the Financing Mode of Small and Medium-sized Enterprises from the Perspective of Industrial Cluster—Take Foshan City, Guangdong as an Example [J]. *Securities & Futures of China*, 2013(3): 183–184.

Wang Qingjuan, An Analysis of the Financing Dilemma for Small and Medium-sized Enterprises in Henan Province from the Perspective of Industrial Cluster [J]. *Economic Research Guide*, 2012(23): 124–126.

Lai Yongneng, The Innovations in the Financing Mode of Small and Medium-sized Enterprises from the Perspective of Industrial Cluster [J]. *Money China (Academic Edition)*, 2012(12): 91.

Guo Jianluan, The Financing of Small and Medium-sized Enterprises in the Growth Period and Industrial Cluster Community Banks [J]. *Review of Investment Studies*, 2011(1): 44–47.

Zeng Hongzhi, Huang Siming, A Study of Innovations in the Financing Mode of Small and Medium-sized Enterprises from the Perspective of Industrial Cluster [J]. *Enterprise Economy*, 2012(12): 86–88.

Xu Jing, An Exploration and Analysis of the Financing Issues Concerning Small and Medium-sized Enterprises from the Perspective of Industrial Cluster [J]. *Market Modernization*, 2012(9): 33–34.

CHAPTER 6

Non-bank Financial Institutions Promote Micro and Small Financial Innovation in Luqiao

Because of their credit creation function and great influence on the fluctuation of the financial and economic situation, banks are strictly controlled by the government and often become the main adjustment object when the central bank implements monetary policy. By contrast, the activities of non-bank financial institutions are less regulated by the government because they are not directly linked to the increase or decrease of the money supply. Under the current monetary tightening policy implemented by the Chinese government, the total amount of bank credit has become the main control object of the government while non-bank financial institutions have less loan constraints, we can change the structure of social funds through professional investment, and lead the idle funds to the SMEs with the most urgent demand for funds. This not only solves the problem of fund shortage of SMEs but also maximizes the income of investors; it does not violate the keynote of the current tight monetary policy. Therefore, under the condition of tight monetary policy, non-bank financial institutions can take on the responsibility of financing SMEs. The development of China's non-bank financial institutions is relatively backward, and it was not until 1979 that there was rapid development. According to the latest data released by the People's Bank of China, the loan market share of non-bank financial institutions in China is very low, accounting for less than 7% of the total loans. Non-bank financial institutions in China are still at a low level of development, and corporate loans are monopolized by banks.

W. Xiao et al., *Microfinance and China's Regional Development*,
https://doi.org/10.1007/978-981-99-1960-4_6

6.1 The Paths for Non-bank Financial Institutions in Promoting the Development of Micro and Small Finance

The development of non-bank financial institutions is a great supplement to the financing of SMEs. Due to the problems of SMEs such as imperfect financial information and lack of relevant collateral, bank loans often bring problems such as long approval time, limited loan funds and high loan interest, which means they fail to meet the internal financing needs of SMEs or cannot adapt to the "emergency needs" of SMEs. Therefore, the development of non-bank financial institutions is undoubtedly a timely assistance for SMEs. Non-bank financial institutions can be defined with the friction cost and information cost in investment and financing reduced. According to the definition, non-bank financial institutions cover securities, insurance, guarantee, pawn, credit rating, financial intermediation, financial services and other fields. Luqiao has developed private finance and a large number of non-bank financial institutions. At present, according to incomplete statistics, there are more than 20 branches of insurance companies including People's Property Insurance of China and China Life Insurance; several pawn companies represented by Taizhou Jinzuo Pawn Company and Huitong Pawn Company; several financing guarantee companies including Zhejiang Fanglin Guarantee Co., Ltd.

Pawn financing refers to a fast and convenient financing method for SMEs to obtain funds from pawnshops by means of pledge or mortgage by taking advantage of the emergency features of pawnshops in short-term capital needs. As a special financing institution authorized by the state to engage in lending business, compared with bank loans as the mainstream financing channel, the market positioning of pawn shops is as follows: to solve the short-term needs of SMEs and individuals and play a supporting role. As an ancient business, pawnshops have been increasingly favored by SMEs due to the convenience of obtaining funds. But as far as the Luqiao region is concerned, there are many pawnbrokers such as Jinzuo and Huitong. The biggest feature of these pawnbrokers is still to serve local SMEs as well as individual industrial and commercial households, and the loan funds are often urgently needed by SMEs, so the emergence of pawnbrokers has provided convenience for SMEs to acquire finance under emergency conditions. Moreover, these pawnbrokers are constantly innovating their own business models, sinking existing services and making contributions to the development of local micro finance.

Financing guarantee refers to the principal and interest repayment guarantee provided by the guarantor to the beneficiary for financing. Financing methods include: borrowing, issuing securities (excluding stocks), overdraft, deferred payment and credit line granted by the bank, etc. Due to the limitations of their own conditions, SMEs often need guarantors in the process of lending from banks, small loan companies, and other financial institutions. Based on the guarantee needs of SMEs, professional financing guarantee companies emerged. Before this, local governments often issued relevant support policies or directly guaranteed SMEs in order to solve the financing difficulties of SMEs. With deepened marketization, professional financing guarantee companies led by the government or initiated and established by private capital continue to rise, and have been quite effective as an irreplaceable part of small enterprises in their financing process. The rise of local financing guarantee companies not only promotes the innovation and development of local micro and small finance but also makes the local credit market continuously professionalized, market-oriented and streamlined, improves the credit market and reduces the problem of information asymmetry between banks and enterprises.

Auction financing means that the assets are mortgaged in the auction company. If the assets can be repaid within the specified period, the collateral can be redeemed. Otherwise, the collateral will be auctioned. Auction financing is an extension of pawn financing services, but at present, real estate, land, equipment, patents and other auctions have gradually become an important way for SMEs to finance. While auction financing provides SMEs with a new choice of financing, in the mortgage process, it also gives SMEs a certain period of time to repay the loan to redeem the collateral. Compared to bank loans, the biggest advantage of auction financing is that the approval period is short, and loans are made with intangible assets such as real estate as collateral. If a mortgage loan is made to a bank, it must go through a series of processes such as evaluation, notarization, and insurance. However, if a mortgage loan is made to an auction company, it only needs to go through evaluation and notarization, which greatly shortens the process and can meet the urgent needs of SMEs for funds.

As can be seen from the above paths, the development and service innovation of non-bank financial institutions have played an important role in the financing of local SMEs, which can meet the financing needs of SMEs when they encounter difficulties in bank lending and long cycles. At the same time, non-bank financial institutions are constantly improving themselves and innovating services to meet the financing needs of SMEs as far as possible and facilitate their loan applications, which means a great contribution to the innovation and development of local micro and small finance.

6.2 Innovative Practices in Micro and Small Finance Business of Non-bank Financial Institutions

The Development of Pawn Financing in Luqiao District

Pawnshops, as an important part of private finance, have greatly expanded in their functions and businesses in recent years. For example, with financing services mainly for SMEs, and businesses that banks are unwilling or unable to do, they make up for deficiencies in mainstream financing channels, hence their proper market positioning. As an emerging non-mainstream financing channel, pawn financing aims to serve SMEs that have strong demand for seasonal and emergency funds in production and operation, and these enterprises often have high requirements for the timeliness of funds when financing, but their own financing ability is quite limited. Pawn financing in Luqiao district has the following characteristics in solving the financing needs of local SMEs.

The Collateral of Pawn is Extensive, Making Full Use of Enterprise Resources

In terms of loan types, pawnshops are also institutions dealing in currency, especially in mortgage loans, which are similar to banks. But pawnshops accept a wider range of collateral. Banks generally only accept real estate as collateral, and only right mortgage with a single content, refusing chattel mortgage. Pawnshops accept chattel mortgage and right mortgage with abundant contents. In this way, enterprises can cash idle plant buildings, equipment and production materials at a price, turning real estate into working capital to meet their daily financing needs.

Pawn Loans Have Low Credit Requirements for Enterprises and Flexible Loan Limits

Compared with bank financing, pawn financing can be obtained more easily. Pawnshops have almost zero credit requirements for SMEs, and lend money in the form of pledge. Pawnbrokers only pay attention to whether the pawned goods are genuine, whether their source is legal, whether the ownership is clear. They recognize the goods but not the people, and are not picky about the loan recipients. Thus, SMEs can easily obtain loans from pawnshops. In contrast, it is difficult for SMEs to obtain loans from banks because banks generally prefer to finance large state-owned enterprises with good credit, while the credit conditions of SMEs are poor, and the banks' financial information about enterprises is seriously asymmetric toward state-owned enterprises (SOEs). Additionally, banks need guarantors to provide guarantees. Banks also need to assess the credit of enterprises and restrict the use of loans. But pawnshops do not ask about the purpose of the loan, and the money can be used freely, which can greatly improve the utilization rate of SMEs. The amount of a pawn loan is relatively flexible, and it can be as little as several hundred or several thousand yuan according to the items mortgaged. In conclusion, pawn loan is more suitable for financing of SMEs that do not need much capital but need it urgently.

The Term of Pawn Loan is Short and the Speed Fast

The bank's loan procedures are complex, the credit rating of the enterprise is required to be high, and it needs a complex and long investigation process, so it is difficult to deal with emergencies. Pawn financing, on the other hand, is easy and quick. The threshold of pawnshops is low, and the procedures are flexible and simple. Customers can raise relevant funds by relevant procedures in the way of mortgage or pledge with precious articles for civilian use, such as gold, silver and jewelry, or real estate, materials, motor vehicles, securities, etc., which they have the right to dispose of. There is no need to look for a third party guarantee and a series of approval procedures as in banks. Once the value of the pawn is verified, it can be cashed in proportion. It only takes half an hour to handle ordinary business on average, and the most cumbersome real estate pawn can be completed within 3 to 5 days. Therefore, pawn loan is the best choice for emergency microfinance.

Pawnshops are Highly Autonomous in Loan Term and Loan Limit

As the amount of bank loans is generally large, they are unwilling to provide daily sporadic small loans, while SMEs have a large demand for short-term small financing. For example, if an enterprise wants to borrow tens of thousands of yuan for one or two months, it is very difficult for the bank to oblige. However, in a pawnbroker, it is not only feasible, but

Table 6.1 Basic information of the first two pawnshops in Luqiao district

Companies	*Date of establishment*	*Scope of business*
Jinzuo Pawn Company	December 1999	Chattel pledge and pawn business; pledge and pawn of property rights; real estate mortgage and pawn business; the sale of dead pawn items within the limit; appraisal and consulting services; other businesses as approved by the Ministry of Commerce according to law.
Huitong Pawn Company	July 1995	Mainly engaged in chattel pawn, dead pawn chattel auction

the repayment date can be set within the specified period and settled immediately according to the wishes of the people. Customers only need to pay two fees, namely, service fee and loan interest, and can redeem the pawn items any time.

To sum up, it is not difficult to explain the financing difficulties of SMEs in theory, and the financing methods of enterprises will undergo a transformation from internal financing such as self-owned capital to informal finance and bank credit, and eventually mature and transparent enterprises will choose to finance in the capital market. However, at this stage, China's SMEs and financial markets are still in the development stage, so the services provided by pawnbrokers can alleviate the relevant financing difficulties to a certain extent. Under the government regulation and its own continuous improvement, the pawn business will have its broad prospects. Pawn enterprises in Zhejiang province are privately funded, 439 in all, accounting for 97.56% of the total number; the total registered capital is 7.106 billion yuan, or 94.13% of the total paid in capital of pawn enterprises in the province. Pawnbrokers in Luqiao district have developed rapidly, including four registered locally and many other pawnbrokers are operating in Luqiao district (Table 6.1).

Development of Guaranteed Financing in Luqiao District

There are six financing guarantee companies including Zhejiang Fanglin Guarantee and Win-Win Guarantee in Luqiao district. In order to prevent default risk in the financing process, banks and other financial institutions generally require SMEs to provide mortgage guarantee or third-party guarantee, and specify the liability for breach of guarantee in the financing contract. Although the development of credit guarantee agencies has shared part of the credit risks for banks, the credit guarantee agencies, while providing guarantees, also require SMEs to provide certain counter guarantees, which will cause default risk of SMEs. Therefore, how to improve the quality of guarantee and reduce the credit risk caused by inadequate guarantee is a common concern of banks and credit guarantee institutions. The main function of credit guarantee for SMEs is to guarantee the credit of the guaranteed or to upgrade the credit of the guaranteed, so that it plays a positive role in improving the availability and conditions of loans for SMEs.

Credit guarantee for credit financing is equivalent to the reduction of market interest rate. The reduction of interest rates caused by such financing guarantee has two effects: the lower market interest rates will induce those SMEs with high expected income and high loan repayment probability but no investment to invest, which may reduce potential borrowers with high expected income and high loan repayment probability and improve social welfare; more SMEs with low income and low repayment probability are attracted to the rank of investors. The former is beneficial to society, while the latter will reduce social welfare. If the first effect is greater than the second, the total effect of credit guarantee is positive. It is worth noting that moral hazard caused by information asymmetry has a restrictive effect on the efficiency of credit guarantee. Because of information asymmetry, SMEs have information advantages on their expected returns and loan repayment probability, which increases the supervision cost of banks over SMEs, otherwise, moral hazard in the credit market will occur. If the asymmetry of loan repayment information is considered, the adverse selection effect will reduce the allocation efficiency of the credit market. Because, on the one hand, SMEs have more information than banks, and borrowers with higher loan repayment probability have little demand for loans, while those with lower loan repayment probability are overly encouraged to invest, resulting in inefficient loans in the credit market. The government supported credit guarantee can not eliminate this information asymmetry. Besides, the credit financing guarantee is only a credit guarantee provided to supplement the credit shortage of SMEs. This guarantee ensures that the average income of bank loans to SMEs is equal to or even greater than the income of risk-free investment, which may lead to the failure of banks to prudently issue loans to borrowers, resulting in a reduction in the average loan repayment probability, so that the gap between the risk-free investment income of banks and the expected income of SMEs' lending is made up by the credit guarantee institutions funded by the government. If the money needs to be raised by the government through tax increase, the loss caused by tax increase constitutes the additional cost in the financing guarantee plan. Therefore, for a functional guarantee scheme, it is feasible only when the marginal income of the guarantee expenditure is lower than its marginal loss.

Development of Auction Innovation Business

The auction companies in Luqiao are also quite instrumental in the innovation of micro and small financial services. Taking Win-Win Auction as an example, we began to gradually explore a new mode of "auction + financing" in the field of SMEs and personal financing. It is reported that through the innovative integration of auction and financing, the financing channels of SMEs can be increased, and the financing mode can be more flexible and convenient, thus alleviating the financing difficulties of SMEs. The new mode of auction, with the network platform as the medium, builds a bridge between the client, auction institutions, financial institutions and the buyer for the integration of financial products and auction transaction methods, and facilitation of capital and asset turnover in frequency and speed.

To sum up, the three industries of guarantee, pawn and auction are beneficial supplements to financial financing in the market economy. Especially, in the case of financing difficulties for SMEs, these industries often extend a "hand of friendship" to help SMEs in their urgent needs. In recent years, the government of Luqiao has emphasized the construction of financing service platforms for SMEs. Enterprises like Win-Win Auction Company, Win-Win Guarantee Company and Jinzuo Pawn Company have exerted themselves to serve SMEs through business innovation and market development, thus broadening the financing channels for SMEs.

6.3 Cases of Non-bank Financial Institutions Promoting the Development of Micro and Small Finance

Jinzuo Pawn Company

Featuring fast, simple and flexible financing, pawnshops are popular with SMEs, the self-employed and the majority of natural persons. Pawnshops in the new era are essentially a financial service-oriented industry. It is no longer a consumer financing that simply solves the livelihood problems of natural persons. More importantly, it has become a productive and operational financing that widely develops the economy, supports production, enlivens circulation, and provides production-based and operational financing for SMEs and individual operators. The business scope of pawnbrokers is wide. The pawn items mainly include: real estate, motor vehicles, ships, securities (including bonds, bank acceptance bills, etc.), jewelry and jade, gold and silver jewelry, laptops, high-end watches, mobile phones, enterprise movable property, etc. Different enterprises or natural persons can quickly obtain pawn loans from pawnbrokers through mortgage (pledge) of the above items, thus solving the urgent problem of temporary shortage of funds. The main differences between pawn loan and bank loan are as follows: first, pawn loan procedures are simple, fast, time-saving and labor-saving; bank loan procedures are cumbersome, and the approval period is long, so it is difficult to deal with emergencies. Second, the objects of pawn loans are SMEs, individual operators and natural persons; the main targets of bank loans are large and medium-sized enterprises. Third, the pawn loan can be renewed several times when it is due; and the bank loans must be paid off when they are due.

Luqiao Jinzuo Pawn Company is a case in point. It has launched a number of special services to alleviate the short-term financing difficulties of SMEs. Taizhou Jinzuo Pawn Co., Ltd. was founded on December 18, 1999. It is the first legally operating non-bank financial institution approved by the People's Bank of China in Luqiao. The company is dedicated to serving the general public, individual industrialists and SMEs, providing a convenient financing platform to solve the urgent need of funds. On August 8, 2011, the company set up "Taizhou's first pawn branch" at No. 138, Sanxing Avenue, Wenling City. On May 11, 2012, the company was awarded "Taizhou's first three-star pawn enterprise" by the Department of Commerce of Zhejiang Province.

The business scope of the company includes chattel pledge and pawn business; pledge and pawn of property rights; real estate mortgage and pawn business; the sale of the dead pawn items within the limit; appraisal and consulting services; other business approved by the Ministry of Commerce according to law. The main business of the company is: real estate mortgage pawn, motor vehicles, securities, gold, famous watches, diamonds, high-end electrical appliances mortgage pawn. The businesses that can be handled include: automobile mortgage loan, civilian goods mortgage loan, real estate mortgage loan, appraisal and consultation.

The charging rate of the pawn shop is: the minimum term of pawn is 1 day, and the maximum is not more than 3 months. The pawn due can be renewed with the consent of the pawnshop. The charges are reasonable. For example, for pledge pawn of automobiles and civil goods they charge 0.84 to 1.00 yuan / day for every 1000 yuan, and for real estate mortgage pawn 6–8.4 yuan / day for every 10,000 yuan.

The company's ten features include: (1) Convenient and fast. It provides real time loan of civil goods pawn, loan for automobile pledge pawn within 30 minutes, loan of real estate mortgage pawn within 3–5 working days, and loan of stocks and other securities pawn within 1 working day. (2) High quality and high efficiency. It provides on-site pawn service for special customers (such as those handicapped); VIP customers can be picked up by special vehicles, and large-scale pawn businesses are escorted by cash wagons. (3) Preferential interest and fee. For the pawn of civilian goods, only the comprehensive pawn fee is charged, with pawn interest exempted; the interest rate standards of large amount pawn such as real estate, motor vehicles, and securities can be negotiated in person, and the relevant fees such as evaluation, notarization and registration are exempted. (4) Complete varieties. Pawn can be accepted as long as the source of the pawn is legal, liquidable or circulation is strong, the variety and the amount is not limited. (5) Term of pawn free. The pawn term is 5 days, 10 days, 15 days, 20 days, 1 month and 6 months respectively, with a maximum of 6 months; the term can also be renewed. (6) Remote renewal. At the expiration of the term, the client may entrust others to renew the pawn on his behalf, or may renew it remotely through bank transfer. (7) Simplified redemption. The pawner can entrust others to redeem the pawn on his behalf with his pawn ticket and password (registered by the pawner at the time of the handling the pawn). (8) Flexible repayment. No matter how much the pawn is, the pawner can choose to repay in installments according to needs and reduce the interest fee. (9) Green channel. It provides a green channel for short-term capital turnover loans of SMEs and individual industrial and commercial households with good credit conditions and good project investment benefits. (10) Safe and reliable. The pledged pawn shall be kept by special personnel and in special warehouse after being signed and sealed by the pawner, equipped with high-tech and all-weather anti-theft monitoring facilities, and relevant insurance shall be able to ensure the safety of the pawn.

The characteristics of the pawn industry make it an effective supplement to bank loans and other financing methods. Although Taizhou's banking system continues to reform and innovate and launch new products, there are still many gaps to be filled. What big banks are unwilling to do, Taizhou Bank is willing to do; what Taizhou Bank is unwilling to do, Yintai pawn is willing to do. It is precisely because of many non-bank financial institutions that provide short-term emergency loans for financing activities of SMEs, relatively flexible and fast pawn financing plays a role in filling the blank in the banking system to a certain extent, thus providing timely help for SMEs. Pawn financing not only meets the financing needs of the development of SMEs at the present stage, but also adds new projects to the construction of a modern service industry system, which is an important achievement in the innovation of financial service of Luqiao.

Win-Win Guarantee Company

Luqiao Win-Win Guarantee Company has managed to provide guarantee for SMEs in Luqiao, and promoted their development and prosperity in spite of the relevant risks. Tongyu Neighborhood is located in the west of Luqiao district, Taizhou city, Zhejiang Province. Its industrial and economic development has been lagging behind. In 2000, Tongyu government led dozens of enterprises to set up a plastic industrial park, with a total area of 230 Mu and more than 20 enterprises in the city. By 2001, there were 95 SMEs in the neighborhood, with an industrial output value of 1.16 billion yuan, accounting for 95.7% of the total industrial and agricultural output value of the district. SMEs made important contributions in driving the local economy. However, the main problem faced by SMEs is the difficulty in financing, which the local government has been working hard to solve. In order to ease the difficulty of loan operation for SMEs, the government of Tongyu took the lead in setting up Win-Win Guarantee Company on December 24, 2001 to provide guarantees for bank loans to SMEs, which helped solve the financing difficulties of local SMEs. However, in the process of operation, the company also found a series of problems.

Win-Win Guarantee is a closed limited liability company with a membership system. It has 10 shareholders, each of which has invested 50,000 yuan. The local enterprise management service provided a registered capital of 500,000 yuan, with a total registered capital of 1 million yuan. It has provided loan guarantees for 8 member enterprises in preferential loans of 3.1 million yuan from Tongyu Rural Credit

Cooperative. As of 30 June 2002, no loan was in arrears. By the end of June, these eight enterprises had realized an output value of 43.2 million yuan and a profit of 4.76 million yuan. At the same time, the company charges the guaranteed enterprise 1% to 10% of the guaranteed amount every month, and has earned 16,800 yuan in service fees. In this way, Win-Win Guarantee Company has achieved some initial results, not only solving the financing difficulties for SMEs, but also the problem of difficulty in providing loans for the financial sector.

More than 20 small enterprises in the Plastics Park of Tongyu Neighborhood have been troubled by financing difficulties for a long time. As members of Taizhou Win-Win Guarantee Service Co., Ltd., these enterprises no longer need to worry about getting loans. In order to solve the financing problems of SMEs, the loan limit of Win-Win Guarantee Service Co., Ltd. is enlarged by 5–10 times the registered capital of the company. For the loan guaranteed by the company, Tongyu sub-branch of Luqiao Agricultural Cooperative Bank of China will reduce the current interest rate by 15–20%.

Win-Win Guarantee will not use the registered capital deposited in Tongyu sub-branch in the form of one-year fixed term. The funds that can be guaranteed shall be enlarged by 5–10 times the company's registered capital upon consent of the Tongyu sub-branch. The bank and the guarantee company have separate rights and act independently. The guarantee company does not provide guarantees for enterprises other than members. Each guarantee shall be approved according to the amount authorized by the board of directors. Due to strict management and standardized operation procedures, only Taizhou Win-Win Guarantee Service Co., Ltd. is still in normal operation among a dozen non-profit guarantee institutions in 10 towns and townships (neighborhoods) of Luqiao district. Over the past seven years, it has handled loan guarantees for 20 enterprises, with a total guaranteed amount of more than 120 million yuan by the end of this October. It is known that the average annual profit and tax growth rate of the supported enterprises is more than 15%, providing employment of at least 2500 local people.

Due to such factors as unsound finance, low technological content of products, low self-possessed capital and poor solvency, it is difficult for SMEs to find guarantees. They often have a high threshold for loans from banks or credit cooperatives, with complicated procedures or no access to loans. In consideration of the security, liquidity and profitability of funds, the financial department requires enterprises to use effective assets as collateral or enterprises with financial strength as guarantee. Some enterprises have incomplete factory building certificates, and there are no invoices for market purchased or self-imitation equipment, so it is impossible for mortgage registration. It is difficult to provide loans to these enterprises that cannot handle mortgage guarantee. Therefore, the intervention of guarantee companies has also found a way out for the financial sector to lend. The guarantee company is small in scale, small in guarantee amount and narrow in scope, and only plays a small role. As far as enterprises are concerned, each of them can only enjoy the credit guarantee of 250,000 yuan if it invests 50,000 yuan of shares and get guaranteed at a ratio of 1:5. For example, a plastic products Co., Ltd. has borrowed 3 million yuan from the credit union, of which the guarantee company only guarantee 300,000 yuan, financing 10% for it. However, the coverage of the guarantee company is very narrow, accounting for only 10.5% of the number of SMEs in Tongyu. There is a guarantee risk. The guarantee company considers the loan guarantee amount based on the amount of the enterprise's shares, that is, on the basis of the 50,000 yuan, it enlarges the guarantee multiple by 5 times with appropriate increments. However, it does not analyze the overall assets, liabilities and capital operation of SMEs. Some SMEs seem to be behemoths, but they have already been insolvent, so without overall risk prediction, they have serious potential risks. Although the guarantee company only guarantees 300,000 yuan, that enterprise borrowed a large amount of loans from other financial institutions, which will also cause guarantee risks.

The guarantee company is on a small scale with small business, which will inevitably affect its survival and development. Since its establishment, the average monthly guaranteed loan of the Win-Win Guarantee Company has been between 2 million and 3 million yuan. The fee is charged on a monthly basis. Only 2000–3000 yuan of guarantee service fee can be charged every month, and only 16,800 yuan of actual income can be collected in half a year to pay the salaries of the company's staff and operating expenses. The guarantee company will undoubtedly incur losses, which severely hinders its development potential. Lack of effective preventive measures against guarantee risks. From the current operation situation, except for the equity capital, the loan guarantee of the 8 enterprises guaranteed can only be based on credit, and no counter guarantee is adopted to ensure the security of the guarantee. At the same time, there is no effective internal control system or system of separation between audit, guarantee and compensation. Direct government involvement affects the independent development of guarantee companies. Win-Win Guarantee Company was established under the direct support and participation of district and town government departments. The government sends personnel to serve as the manager of the guarantee company, which again reflects the government's act. In the business operations, if the government's behavior is not effectively restricted and regulated, the government will intervene in the activities of guarantee business as the investor, and various forms of instructed guarantee will appear. The guarantee company cannot do without the policy support of the government, especially financial support, and must rely on the government. All the above aspects have become the bottleneck of the development of guarantee companies, restricting guarantee companies in their financing functions and support of SMEs.

Win-Win Guarantee Company has accumulated some experience in guarantee business. It needs to overcome its existing difficulties, find the best point of penetration and combining point, and further improve itself. First, it is to expand shares and increase capital to improve its ability to fend off guarantee risks. The company shall, on the principle of voluntary participation in shares, absorb new enterprises, and the amount of capital should be based on the capital needs of local SMEs and calculated according to the guarantee multiple. It is estimated that local SMEs need about 20 million yuan of capital. Excluding mortgage, it is appropriate to increase the registered capital from 1 million yuan to 3 million yuan at a ratio of 1:5. The guarantee company will not have a chain reaction due to the breach of one guarantee, resulting in the inability to guarantee other enterprises. Second, it is to establish a guarantee risk fund. The amount of shares invested by enterprises is different from that of guaranteed risk funds. According to company law, the operation of the guarantee company should adhere to the principles of voluntary participation, independent operation, risk bearing, self-financing and independent accounting. Therefore, if an enterprise becomes a shareholder, it should enjoy the rights of shareholders, but there is no necessary connection whether the company guarantees loans for it or how much it guarantees. If the company guarantees an enterprise, the guaranteed enterprise shall pay a certain proportion of the risk fund to the company according to the guaranteed amount, so as to prepare for the risk. Thirdly, it is to establish counter guarantee measures and improve its internal control system. The company shall determine the amount and term of guarantee according to the operation status, balance sheet and the status of counter collateral or person of the guaranteed enterprise. In particular, the administrative role of the park administrative committee in land transfer and sale should be given full play, and the plants with incomplete certificates can be set up as counter guarantees. In case of risks, the government takes the initiative to purchase and dispose of them to ensure the safety of the guarantee. Finally, it is to play the intermediary role of the guarantee company. Establish and improve the social service system of SMEs, organically combine credit guarantee with comprehensive guidance, help enterprises collect market information and business management, improve the overall quality of SMEs, enhance market competitiveness and resist risks. In particular, once the enterprise has a risk, the guarantee company should respond quickly, carry out emergency disposal and preserve its assets. Through the above measures, we can promote the healthy and rapid development of guarantee companies, and give full play to the positive role of guarantee companies in helping SMEs to acquire finance and supporting the development of enterprises.

Win-Win Auction Company

Zhejiang Win-win Auction Co., Ltd. (formerly known as Taizhou Luqiao District Auction Center) was established in 1996. The company is located in Luqiao district, Taizhou city. Its legal representative is Liu Bing'e, and its registered capital 5 million yuan. In 1998, the company was approved by the Council of China Auction Industry Association as a member of China Auction Industry Association. In 2000, after comprehensive investigation by Taizhou Intermediate People's Court, the company was appointed as one of the four auction enterprises designated for entrusted auction. The company has a two-story office building with a floor space of more than 1200 square meters and an auction hall that can accommodate hundreds of people. It can also carry out business consulting, registration, payment, and various types of auctions. At present, the company has 16 employees, including 12 with junior college education or above, 2 registered auctioneers of the People's Republic of China, 9 certified auctioneers and 6 professional technicians, with an average age of 30.

Since its establishment, the company has strictly abode by *the Auction Law of the People's Republic of China*, adhered to the principle of openness, fairness and justice, standardized auction behavior, strove for survival by quality, and sought development by reputation. Under the leadership of the general manager and with the strong support of all sectors of the society, the company has continuously expanded the market and its business sources in the past six years. It has successively held more than 200 local influential auctions, with an auction turnover of more than 1 billion yuan, including more than 200 million yuan of auction turnover of state-owned land use rights. In 2003, the turnover of auction of mining rights in Luqiao reached more than 30 million yuan; the assets seized by the court, materials seized by the industry and commerce, customs and other departments and other auction transactions amounted to more than 100 million yuan. In 2004, the auction turnover of street shops in Luqiao Fushi Square reached more than 80 million yuan; in 2005, the auction turnover of Huangyan Dahuan Jiayuan residence, Dahuan Mingzhu single apartment, and Luqiao Ancient Street shops, etc. reached more than 200 million yuan; in 2006, the auction turnover of Huangyan Cedar, Shuangjiang, Dahuan, Lily Community, Jinqing "Jinyuan Square" commercial and residential building, Luqiao Yongyue Road, etc. reached more than 80 million yuan. In 2007, the auction turnover of Sanba Store and old coal yard of Jinqing Supply and Marketing Co., Ltd., the real estate of Zhejiang Sanxing Industrial Co., Ltd. and the real estate of Luqiao Jiexin Park reached more than 50 million yuan.

At present, the company has been involved in the auction of state-owned land use rights, mining rights, real estate and related materials seized by the court, the auction of goods confiscated by the customs offices, goods confiscated by the industrial and commercial departments, motor vehicles, and intangible assets. After a dozen years of struggle, the company has gradually matured. At present, the company is in a leading position among enterprises in the same industry in Taizhou in terms of size of its premises, staff level, service quality, corporate reputation, number of auctions, and transaction volumes. The company's auction varieties have been expanded to real estate, vehicles, intangible assets, materials, license plates, equipment and all other items with intrinsic value. The rich variety of auctions enables SMEs to quickly realize the temporarily idle machinery and equipment or other assets, and opens a new financing channel for SMEs.

6.4 Summary

In western developed countries, non-bank financial institutions play an important role in corporate financing. The development of foreign non-bank financial institutions has a history of several hundreds of years, generally including contractual savings institutions and investment financial intermediaries, the former being insurance companies, while the latter mutual funds and financial companies. The proportion of the total loans of American non-bank financial institutions in the market share has kept at about 30%, or a very important role in the American credit market. The development of China's non-bank financial institutions is relatively backward, and it began to develop rapidly only in 1979. According to the latest data released by the People's Bank of China, the loan market share of China's non-bank financial institutions is very low, accounting for less than 7% of the total. Non-bank financial institutions are still at a low level of development, and enterprise loans are mainly monopolized by banks. Therefore, under the current financial policy environment, banks prefer large enterprises and large projects, and SMEs lose their financing channels, while non-bank financial institutions are underdeveloped, resulting in the lack of alternatives for financing of SMEs.

In the current large financial environment in China, the total amount of bank credit has become the main control objects of the government, while the loan restriction of non-bank financial institutions is less. It can change the structure of social capital through professional investment, and lead the social idle funds to the SMEs with the most urgent capital demand, which not only solves the problem of capital shortage of SMEs, but also maximizes the income of investors; it does not violate the keynote of the current tight monetary policy. Therefore, under the condition of tight monetary policy, non-bank financial institutions can play the important role of financing for SMEs. To solve the financing difficulties of SMEs through the market, one of the ideas is to develop non-bank financial institutions and build a financing platform from individual investors to SMEs. The most essential difference between non-bank financial institutions and banks is that the former have no settlement business, so they do not have the function of credit creation. Generally speaking, a bank creates money in the process of lending, that is, when it transfers the right to use loans, it can increase the money supply and demand through its own deposit and loan mechanism, thus creating money. However, non-bank financial institutions only transfer funds under the condition that the money stock is established, and do not increase the total amount of money supply. Instead, they change the stock structure, affect the money turnover rate, and do not have the function of credit creation. Although the Chinese government has formulated relevant measures to try to provide SMEs with small guaranteed loans, for SMEs, the guaranteed loans are of narrow capital side and on a small scale, which fails to fundamentally solve the problem of fund shortage of SMEs.

From the practice of non-bank financial institutions in Luqiao district participating in the micro and small financial business, we should seize the opportunity to strengthen the development of China's non-bank financial institutions in dealing with the financing difficulties of SMEs, to promote the steady and rapid development of the economy. First, we will improve the institutional arrangements for the development of non-bank financial institutions and regularize the order of the financial market. The government must further improve the corresponding institutional arrangements, promote the innovation of financial institutions and promote the healthy and orderly development of non-bank financial institutions. Some quasi-financial institutions should be transformed into credit institutions to accelerate the construction of financing platforms for SMEs. Second, we should timely launch various preferential policies for the development of non-bank financial institutions to promote the rapid development of non-bank financial institutions. For example, on the basis of improving the system, we should supplement the capital of non-bank financial institutions through financial subsidies and other means, and implement differentiated tax policies for these enterprises to promote their rapid development and better achieve efficient capital allocation. Third, we should actively guide non-bank financial institutions to provide financial services to SMEs. We will further innovate financial instruments, establish a financing relationship between non-bank financial institutions and SMEs through the guarantee of financial funds, improve various types of loan guarantee institutions, and establish various types of guarantee companies to meet the flexible needs of small enterprises for mortgage loans. In addition, in order to promote the virtuous cycle of non-bank financial institutions providing financial support to SMEs, the government should actively build a financing platform between non-bank financial institutions and banks and other institutions, provide financial support to non-bank financial institutions, realize the diversification and stabilization of financial sources of non-financial institutions, promote the rapid development of non-bank financial institutions, and effectively solve the financing difficulties of SMEs.

References

Horworth, C.A. Small firms demand for finance: A research note [J]. *International Small Business Journal*, 2001, 19(4): 78–86.

Stiglitz Joseph and Andrew Weiss. The American economic review [J]. *Credit Rationing in Markets with Imperfect Information*, 1981, 71(6): 393–410.

Garmaise, M. Informed investors and the financing of entrepreneurial projects, *Stanford University Working Paper*, 1997.

Berger, A.N. & Udell, G.F. The economics of small business finance: The role of private equity and debt markets in the financial growth cycle [J]. *Journal of Banking and Finance*, 1998, 22: 613–673.

Li Yanhui. Research on financing of SMEs based on industrial clusters [J]. *Journal of Zhongzhou University*, 2012, 5.

Fu Wenping. Research on financing of SMEs from the perspective of industrial cluster development—Taking Sichuan Province as an example [D]. Graduate School of Sichuan Academy of Social Sciences, 2011, 4.

Li Jimei. Research on financing model innovation of SMEs based on cluster joint guarantee [D]. Yunnan University of Finance and Economics, 2011, 4.

Ma Changgang, Zhang Jinsong, Li Yanru. A review of SME financing research from the cluster perspective [J]. *Communication of Finance and Accounting*, 2011, 7.

Xu Lingfang, Chen Guohong. Financing analysis of SMEs in industrial clusters from signaling game [J]. *China Journal of Management Science*, 2012, 4.

Zhang Xin, Zhao Juli. Research on financing of small and medium-sized enterprises in Hohhot-Baotou-Hubei region of Inner Mongolia—From the perspective of industrial clusters [J]. *Inner Mongolia Science Technology and Economy*, 2012, 19.

Chang Jie. Discussion on risk management of commercial banks in developing industrial cluster financing for small and medium-sized enterprises [J]. *Modern Economic Information*, 2011, 4.

Xu Xianli. Analysis of financing characteristics of SMEs in industrial clusters [J]. *Modern Marketing (Xueyuan Edition)*, 2013, 1.

Cheng Shuqiang. Research on financing of SMEs in industrial clusters [J]. *Journal of Xi'an University of Finance and Economics*, 2012, 9.

Xu Lianghu, Liu Xiaofei. Optimization of financing mode of mutual fund for small and medium-sized enterprises from the perspective of industrial clusters—Based on the case study of financing of small and medium-sized enterprises in Huangjing town [J]. *Special Zone Economy*, 2012, 11.

Zhang Yanting. Research on financing mode of small and medium-sized enterprises in Quanzhou from the perspective of industrial clusters [D]. Huaqiao University, 2012, 3.

Zhang Xuan. Research on commercial banks' credit business for SMEs in industrial clusters [D]. Yanshan University, 2011, 12.

Wang Yajiong. Review on the source of financing theory of small and medium-sized enterprises, 198l–2011 [J], *Wuhan Finance Monthly*, 2012, 4.

Liu Ji'ce. Problems and suggestions in credit rating of small and medium-sized enterprises [J], *Credit Reference*, 2011, 1.

Zhang Ming. Research on credit rating of SMEs [J], *Wuhan Finance*, 2008, 2.

Deng Qiwei. Analysis on equity financing problems and countermeasures of small and medium-sized enterprises in China [J], *China Business and Trade*, 2011, 24.

Jin Dan, Zhang Guoliang. Thoughts on the development of collective bonds for small and medium-sized enterprises [J], *Academic Journal of Zhongzhou*, 2009, 3.

Lin Yifu, Sun Xifang. Information, informal finance and SME financing [J], *Economic Research Journal*, 2005, 7.

Li Zhiyun. Bank structure and SME financing [J], *Economic Research Journal*, 2002, 6.

Lin Yifu, Li Yongjun. Development of small and medium-sized financial institutions and financing of small and medium-sized enterprises [J], *Economic Research Journal*, 2001, 1.

Liu Lun, Tang Ruolan. Analysis on the innovation path of micro and small financial services to the real economy [J], *Beijing Jinrong Pinglun*, 2012, 10.

Qin Kai, Shen Guoru. Problems and solutions of financial services for micro and small enterprises [J], *Hebei Finance*, 2012, 12.

He Jiancong. Empirical analysis of financing problems of micro and small enterprises [J], Liaoning Economy, 2011, 9.

Gou Wenfeng, Liu Jie. Research on supply chain financing of small and medium-sized enterprises in China—Analysis from the perspective of industrial clusters [J], *China Business and Trade*, 2011, 2.

Liu Enhui. Research on building a multi-level financial support system for micro and small enterprises—Taking Zhejiang Province as an example [D], Zhejiang University of Technology, 2012, 12.

Chen Yuan. The development and countermeasures of micro and small finance in China's joint-stock commercial banks—Based on the case study of China CITIC Bank [D], Zhejiang University, 2013, 6.

Zhou Qin. Innovation and management of micro and small financial business of commercial banks—Research based on the life cycle of micro and small enterprises [D], Zhejiang University, 2013, 9.

Wu Jiangtao. Research on financial services for micro and small enterprises of commercial banks [D], Jiangxi University of Finance and Economics, 2012, 12.

Cui Jinging. Research on financing behavior of micro and small enterprises—Based on the survey of micro and small enterprises in Gansu Province [D], Lanzhou University, 2011, 4.

CHAPTER 7

Private Capital Activates the Innovative Development of Micro and Small Finance in Luqiao

Under the increasing pressure of declining asset quality and the formal implementation of the measures for *the Capital Management of Commercial Banks (for Trial Implementation)* of the CBRC, the banking industry will face a new round of capital replenishment pressure in the next five years, but the participation of private capital in restructuring will become one of the effective tools for small and medium-sized banks to replenish capital. At the policy level, the "new 36 articles" of the State Council, the local pilot financial reform, *the Implementation Opinions on Encouraging and Guiding Private Capital to Enter the Banking Industry* issued by the People's Bank of China and the China Banking Regulatory Commission, and *the Guiding Opinions on Financial Support for Economic Restructuring, Transformation and Upgrading* issued by the general office of the State Council on July 1, 2013 all clearly encourage private capital to invest in financial institutions and participate in the restructuring and transformation of financial institutions, support private capital to participate in the capital increase and share expansion of commercial banks by means of equity participation, participate in the restructuring of rural credit cooperatives and urban credit cooperatives, and will implement differentiated access management for different types of banking financial institutions in terms of business areas and business scope. The private capital in Luqiao district of Taizhou has taken the lead in this respect, and its contribution to micro and small finance is also rising, providing sufficient capital sources for financing of SMEs.

W. Xiao et al., *Microfinance and China's Regional Development*,
https://doi.org/10.1007/978-981-99-1960-4_7

7.1 Analysis on the Mechanism of Private Capital Activating the Development of Micro and Small Finance

The internal control of small, medium and micro enterprises is not standardized and imperfect, and their information is seriously opaque, which leads to the credit difficulties and problems of SMEs. The credit of SMEs is different from the standard mode provided by banks. They obtain loans through various geographical, blood and business relationships established in the past. In the future, in order to obtain reliable loans, how to establish and maintain the relationship between small enterprises and capital suppliers such as banks has attracted much attention in academic research. Greenbaum and Thakor (1993) argued that small enterprises would be faced with the problem of having no access to loans, especially when they could not obtain formal loan commitment or unconditional loan contracts from banks, they would often seek an alternative, resorting to market mechanisms. Small enterprises would establish closer relations with banks by purchasing invisible contracts containing commissions. Due to the existence of contracts, with the maintenance and expansion of the relationship between banks and enterprises, banks can better supervise enterprises. Nakamura (1993) stressed that banks are willing to maintain the credit relationships based on the original enterprise, under the conditions: first, banks have considerable advantages in information generation for some specific enterprises; second, these particular enterprises are small, unknown and only rely on the services of one bank. The relief of private capital to the financing of SMEs can be reflected in Table 7.1:

Specifically, private capital has the following four advantages:

Advantages in information resources. The convenience and transparency of information exchange will directly affect the transaction efficiency of both sides. In general, the borrowers and lenders of private capital (between citizens, between citizens and legal persons, and between citizens and other organizations) have relatively frequent contacts between the creditors and debitors due to factors such as contacts, regions, occupations, and blood ties. They have a good understanding of each other's income, financial strength, solvency, etc., and their access to information is convenient, so that adverse selection and moral hazard caused by information asymmetry can be avoided as far as possible. In addition, due to the relatively frequent contact between the borrower and the lender, the information advantage of private capital financing can make the lender

Table 7.1 Differences between private capital and regular finance

Financing characteristics of small and medium-sized enterprises	*Characteristics of private capital financing*	*Characteristics of regular finance*
Large financing demand, small amount, short term, strong timelines, short notice, high loan frequency, long credit approval time and high control cost.	There are many private loan transactions and oral agreements. The procedures are simple, the operation convenient, and the relevant factors can be flexibly adjusted according to the actual situation, and the borrowing cost is low.	It has high requirements on the scale of capital demand and capital strength of enterprises, many credit approval links, long time, high contract execution cost, and low cost of unit capital transaction.
It has a wide range of financing and a large amount, and is sporadic, diversified, flexible, seasonal and periodic.	There are various forms of private lending. Bond financing is completed directly between the supply and demand of funds or indirectly by private financial intermediaries. Most of them exist in the form of small-scale mutual assistance, individual, private and other enterprises' loans for production turnover, certificates of deposit, bonds, mortgage loans, and bill discounting.	Their role is positioned as a financial intermediary serving large enterprises and large projects. The financial products are standardized and the credit process unified. For the financing needs of enterprises with different growth stages, production scales or industry backgrounds, the product coverage cannot be fully realized.
With high risk premium compensation, interest rate pricing is higher than opportunity cost.	Its interest rate is determined by supply and demand relationship and the cost and income of the borrowing and lending entities. It is flexible, and the interest rate is flexible. It fluctuates according to different credit entities and credit scales, with regional differences.	On the basis of the benchmark interest rate, the loan interest rate of commercial banks to small and medium-sized enterprises has a high floating rate and over a large range, which is far higher than the interest rate differential level of international commercial banks, making the financial cost borne by enterprises high.

(*continued*)

Table 7.1 (continued)

Financing characteristics of small and medium-sized enterprises	*Characteristics of private capital financing*	*Characteristics of regular finance*
There is no standard information transaction and transmission mechanism.	They have a better understanding of the credit, income and repayment ability of the credit client, and the information production and transmission methods are authentic and hidden. With the increased frequency of contact between the supply and demand sides of private finance, the risk will also be reduced.	It is difficult to deal with the constantly changing and personalized information of small and medium-sized enterprises, asymmetric information in the regular financial market, and the cost of credit investigation is high.
There is great uncertainty in production and operation, with moral hazard and adverse selection, and the default rate is high.	The mutual trust and cooperation relationship of non-governmental financing established by long-term cooperation and multiple transactions has high efficiency in suppressing the moral hazard of both parties to the contract, has a demonstration effect on strengthening the binding force of the cooperation circle and improving the enforcement rate of cooperation, and further helps to promote the improvement of social capital credit relations and the establishment of credit relations.	In order to prevent behind-the-scene transactions and moral hazard, strict loan investigation and decision-making separation system should be implemented for small and medium-sized enterprises; When credit repayment difficulties occur, it will also put forward requirements for equity, which makes it difficult to extend the repayment period.

spend less energy in understanding the situation of the borrower in all aspects. It is not only convenient to supervise loans and timely understand the movements of funds, but also makes reasonable arrangement and utilization of resources according to the repayment order of loans.

Advantages in interest rate. At present, China has formed a dual-track interest rate system, which is represented by the dual interest rates of regulated deposit and loan interest rates and market-oriented repurchase interest rates, namely “restrict the lower limit of loan and the upper limit of deposit”. Banks play a role in focusing on scale: determining the scale of capital without determining the price of capital. Instead of adjusting interest rates and using market-oriented means to solve the financing difficulties of SMEs, banks tend to provide loans to large enterprises because they generally have larger capital needs. In addition, to a large extent, administrative intervention will play a considerable role in the loan behavior of China's commercial banks. The choice of loan interest rate can not fully reflect the scarcity of funds. The "visible hand" will replace the "invisible hand", and the interest rate will become the manifestation of the government's macro-control intention. If the financing mode dominated by private capital is allowed to adopt a flexible interest rate level, and the capital demander spontaneously forms financing with the capital supplier based on the capital needs for production and life, its capital transaction behavior can avoid administrative interference. Therefore, if the financing interest rate is formed on the basis of market game by both parties, it will be easier to realize the marketized interest rate, which fully reflects the supply and demand of market funds and the scarcity of funds, thus helping to improve the efficiency of fund allocation.

Advantages in guarantee. After private capital participates in the financing of SMEs, it can choose a flexible form of guarantee. Under the principle of "preferential" and "safe" guarantee, the guarantee assets do not need to be confined to those recognized by the state-owned commercial banks in the past, and the scope of collateral is further expanded to such commodities as land and real estate. In addition, the properties that were not used as collateral by regular financial institutions can also be used as collateral to form diversified guarantees in kind. At the same time, intangible and flexible social resources can be included in the scope of collateral, such as the credit relationship formed between the lender and the borrower, because the social relationship established due to geographical and business ties is an intangible and stable resource, which can bring both material and spiritual benefits to the lender and the borrower. The strict constraint of mortgage guarantee faced by SMEs can be alleviated to a certain extent through these flexible operations and intangible resources.

Advantage in transaction cost. The operation characteristics of SMEs make their financing small in scale, high in frequency and urgent in demand, which requires that main financial institutions provide services at low operating costs. The introduction of private capital lending just reduces its transaction costs. First of all, the private capital lenders have a low level of entry and a flat organizational structure, which inevitably requires simplifying the operation process, accelerating the financing process and reducing the transaction costs. Secondly, although there is no organization and operation that does not consume human and financial resources, the local characteristics of private capital lending are obvious, and the long-term cooperative relationship between them is bound to be beneficial to further reducing transaction costs. Thirdly, private lending has strong flexibility and can be adjusted and innovated. The interest rate, repayment period and other aspects are determined according to the actual situation, which can save transaction costs.

7.2 Analysis of Luqiao Private Capital Operation and Activation of Micro and Small Finance

Development Status of Small Loan Companies Nationwide

From 2004 to 2006, the No.1 CPC central document for three consecutive years focused on the issue of "agriculture, rural areas and farmers", and proposed to "cultivate micro credit organizations initiated by natural persons, enterprise legal persons or social organization". In October 2005, one county (district) of Shanxi, Sichuan, Guizhou, Shaanxi and Inner Mongolia was selected for the pilot small loan companies. By the end of 2006, four such companies had been established in Shanxi, Sichuan and Guizhou provinces. In 2008, the CBRC and the People's Bank of China jointly issued *the Guidelines on the Pilot Small Loan Companies*, and subsequently the piloting of small loan companies was extended to the whole country. In 2009, the CBRC issued *the Interim Provisions on the Restructuring of Small Loan Companies and the Establishment of Rural Banks*, which opened the institutional gate for small loan companies to move towards the banking industry. Inspired by good expectations, at the end of the year, the number of small loan companies in China rapidly increased to 1334, with a loan balance of 77.427 billion yuan and a paid-in capital of 81.72 billion yuan. The original intention of the establishment of small loan companies is to solve the financing service problem of "agriculture, rural areas and farmers". However, with the emergence of the financing difficulties of SMEs, the local government regarded the development of small loan companies as a way to solve the financing difficulties of SMEs. In addition, with the strong expectations of private capital for investment in the financial industry, all regard investment in small loan companies as the first step in the financial industry. Therefore, after

Table 7.2 Development of China's small loan companies from 2009 to 2012

	Institutional status		*Paid-in capital (100 million yuan)*		*Loan balance (100 million yuan)*		*Employees*	
	Number (No.)	*Growth rate (%)*	*Amount*	*Growth rate (%)*	*Amount*	*Growth rate (%)*	*No.*	*Growth rate (%)*
2009	1334	–	817	–	774	–	14500	–
2010	2614	96	1781	118	1975	155	27884	92
2011	4282	64	3319	86	3915	98	47088	69
2012	6080	42	5147	55	5921	51	70343	49

Source: *Statistical Table of Small Loan Companies by Regions* by the head office of the People's Bank of China

2009, domestic small loan companies developed rapidly (see Table 7.2). By 2013, the number of small loan companies in China had reached 7086, with a paid-in capital of 625.2 billion yuan, a loan balance of 704.3 billion yuan, and more than 80,000 employees. According to the current loan scale, the total scale of the small loan companies in the nation is equivalent to that of a medium-sized bank. It can be judged that small loan companies based on the operation principle of "small and sporadic" play an important role in solving the financing difficulties of SMEs and the financial service needs of "agriculture, rural areas and farmers".

Due to the remarkable features of small amount, short term and fast approval, small loan companies do not need assessment by third-party institutions, the loan term can be long or short, and the repayment method is flexible. They play an active role in helping SMEs and farmers solve the capital problems encountered in the production and operation process, and become a useful supplement to commercial banks when they carry out financial services for SMEs.

In terms of the number of institutions, the number of small loan companies owned by Jiangsu province ranks first in China, reaching 555. Liaoning province and Inner Mongolia ranked second and third with 508 and 473 respectively. From the perspective of loan balance indicators, the loan balance of small loan companies in Jiangsu province ranks first in China, reaching 112.756 billion yuan, accounting for almost one fifth in the country. Jiangsu province is also the only province in China where the loan balance of small loan companies exceeds 100 billion yuan (Figs. 7.1 and 7.2).

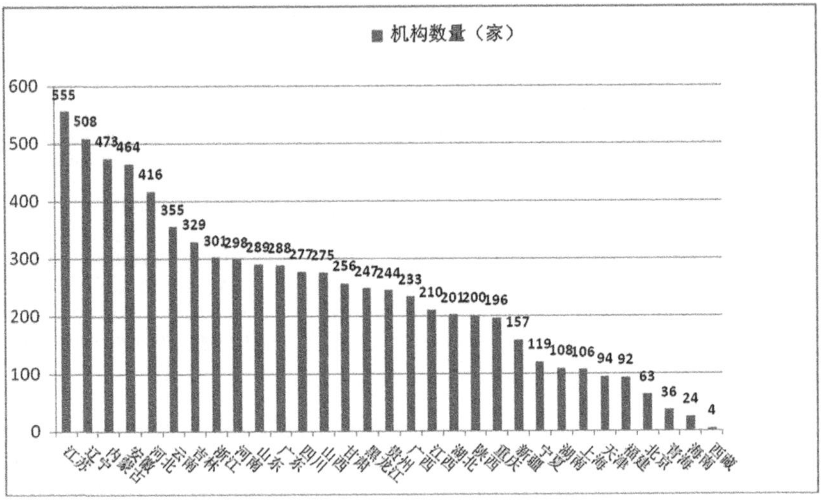

Fig. 7.1 Number of microfinance institutions in each province (Sept. 2013)

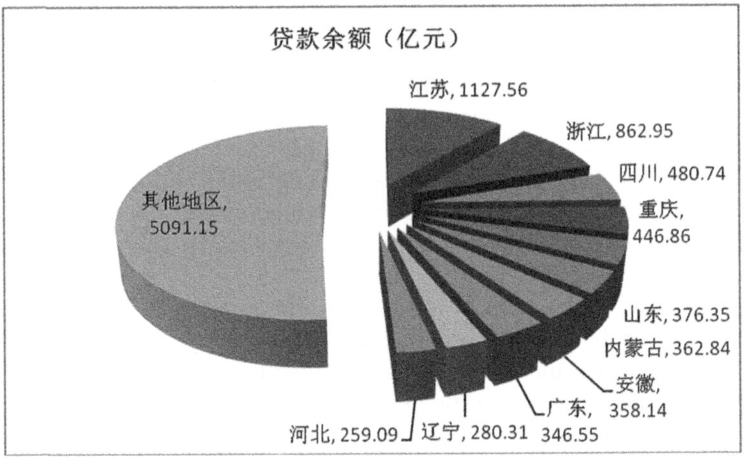

Fig. 7.2 Top ten provinces in terms of loan balance of small loan companies (Sept. 2013)

Development of Luqiao Small Loan Companies

Taizhou is a relatively developed area of private finance in Zhejiang Province. Small loan companies invested by private capital have provided great help to the financing of local SMEs in Taizhou. During the visit to Luqiao district, the project team learned that since 2009, Luqiao district had started the piloting of small loan companies to guide private capital to enter the real industry and promote the sunshine private financing. At present, there are four officially opened small loan companies in Luqiao district, with a total registered capital of 800 million yuan. The four companies can lend up to 790 million yuan, with a total loan of 5.34 billion yuan. In 2012 alone, the small loan companies of Luqiao granted 1516 loans throughout the year, with a total loan amount of 1.193 billion yuan, which solved some financing difficulties for local small businesses and "three rural" customers. The average comprehensive interest rate was 16.4%, lower than the private loan interest rate of Luqiao district during the same period. It had led the private loan interest rate to decline, making a certain contribution to the sound and rapid development of Luqiao's economy. By the end of 2012, the overdue rates of the three small loan companies were 0.67%, 0.001% and 0%, which were lower than the overdue rate of the local banking industry in the same period (0.93%) (Table 7.3).

Since the piloting, Luqiao district has actively developed and expanded the team of small loan companies, fully implemented various support

Table 7.3 Basic information of three small loan companies officially opened in Luqiao district (as of 2013)

Enterprises	*Date of establishment*	*Main initiator*	*Registered capital (million yuan)*	*Financing amount*
Yufeng Small Loan Company	March 2009	Zhejiang Yufeng Industrial Group Co., Ltd	150	75 million
Jiuding Small Loan Company	September 2009	Jiuding Construction Group Co., Ltd	150	90 million
Sanyou Jinlong Micro Loan Company	December 2012	Sanyou Holding Group Co., Ltd	200	Not yet financed
Wucun Small Loan Company	2013	Zhejiang Fanglin Group	300	Not yet financed

policies of Zhejiang, Taizhou and Luqiao governments, and constantly strengthened supervision to guide their compliance operation.

First, efforts for piloting quota and overall planning are made. In view of the developed market economy in Luqiao district, there are many SMEs, and the small loan market is broad. At the same time, there are abundant private capital and active private financing, and the development of small loan companies has good inborn advantages. Since the piloting, Luqiao district has actively applied to Taizhou Financial Office for the piloting quota, established the intention resource pool of small loan company initiators, and carefully selected the backbone enterprises with standardized management, honest management and strong strength as the main initiators of small loan companies. While actively striving for the piloting quota, Luqiao district adheres to the rational planning and layout, actively and steadily expand the coverage of the piloting on the premise of meeting the market demand, and gradually distribute to the central town. The third small loan company is located in Jinqing Town, a provincial-level central town, to avoid the phenomenon of small loan companies rushing into mass action, clustering together and excessive competition.

Second, active implementation of policies and vigorous support for the companies are maintained. In order to encourage the development of small loan companies, Luqiao district has actively implemented the relevant supporting policies issued by the provincial and municipal governments in tax relief, financial subsidies and small loan risk compensation. In 2010, the district finance subsidized the two companies with a tax of 1.819 million yuan and a small loan risk compensation of 550,000 yuan; in 2011, the subsidy tax was 1.943 million yuan, and the risk compensation of small loans was 7.029 million yuan (some small loan risk compensation in 2010 was subsidized in 2011). In 2012, the support funds of small loan companies reached more than 8 million yuan. Taizhou subsidized the small loan companies in Luqiao district in a ratio of 1:1 to the district level. At the same time, Luqiao district actively supported the addition, capital increase and share expansion of small loan companies and gives a one-time subsidy of 200,000 yuan to newly established small loan companies with a registered capital of 200 million yuan or more. For the existing small loan companies with additional capital and expanded loan scale, the district finance will give a one-time subsidy of 150,000 yuan to those whose registered capital reaches 300 million yuan or more after the increase. The implementation of the supporting policies has better stimulated the enthusiasm of the development of small loan companies, and further guided small loan companies to adhere to the positioning goals of "supporting agriculture" and "supporting small enterprises".

Third, improvement of the regulatory system and guidance of the compliance operation are sustained. Compliance operation is an important cornerstone for long-term and healthy development of small loan companies, which are engaged in high-risk businesses that financial institutions in the banking industry are "unwilling to do", and it is easy to form an impulse to "cover high risks with high returns" and ignore operational compliance. Therefore, since the piloting, Luqiao district has actively improved its regulatory and service measures, clarified the cooperative responsibilities of finance, industry and commerce, finance, audit and other departments, strove to establish a long-term regulatory mechanism, and strengthened business guidance for small loan companies on the basis of strictly controlling the entry threshold of small loan companies and comprehensively used on-site inspection, off-site inspection and other regulatory means and policy support to guide and standardize the business behaviors of small loan companies, improve their risk prevention and control awareness and operational level. At the same time, the Financial Office, the Industry and Commerce Department, the Finance Department, People's Bank of China and the Banking Regulatory Commission and other departments are regularly and irregularly organized to inspect and assess the small loan companies and guide their compliance operation. At the end of each year, the third-party audit institutions are required to conduct financial audit on the small loan companies. At present, the operation of the three existing small loan companies in Luqiao district is relatively good.

Intermediary Services Guided by Private Capital

Luqiao district has been listed as one of the first batch of pilot counties (cities and districts) of innovation in private financing management in Zhejiang. In order to further promote local financial innovation, strengthen the guidance and regulation of private financing, and give play to the positive role of private financing, next, while continuing to support the development of small loan companies, Luqiao district will do a good job in private financing management by making private financing transparent. In order to better regulate the management of private loans and fully guide private capital to meet the financing needs of SMEs, the government led the establishment of Luqiao private financing standard management service center, so as to open up the information channels between the supply and demand of private capital and regulate the flow of private capital.

Luqiao district is one of the first pilot areas for private financing management innovation. Luqiao Private Financing Standard Management Service Center is a management and service institution of the private financing market with the participation and unified supervision of the district government. It is a new platform for local private financing and financial management, which helps to realize the value maintenance, increment and optimize allocation of private funds, and to effectively make private capital serve local economic development. The Non-government Financing Standard Management Service Center was put into operation on March 21, 2014, always focused on business development, risk prevention and team building. At present, business development is focused on the customer group of "small amount and wide range". It has issued 160 loans worth a total of 70 million yuan, with an average of about 200,000 yuan per household. Since its establishment, more than 6000 loans have been registered every month, matching about 15 million yuan. The overall number of application volume and demand, it is about 50 million per month regularly, totaling 150 million in 360 transactions, which indicates that the demand for private capital is strong. In terms of risk prevention and control, the following three measures are mainly taken: household investigation, seeing is believing; double investigation, cross examination; overall credit risk prevention, focusing on moral hazard. Internal processes regulate the moral hazard of its own employees, so that each link is institutionalized and streamlined. In terms of team building, it implements team operation and introduces experienced management personnel from local banks and other industries. The following three products are introduced:

First, proactive products. Their main service object is the fund supplier who does not bear risks, who shall register in the Private Financing Service Center, who shall match with the fund demander, and sign the loan contract on his behalf, it shall bear the responsibility.

Second, progressive products. They are suitable for capital suppliers with certain risk bearing capacity, who shall register with the Private Financing Service Center, and the center and the fund supplier shall agree on an appropriate fund demander, sign a loan contract as an agent (or jointly), and bear the risks as agreed.

Third, aggressive products. They are suitable for capital suppliers with strong risk bearing capacity, who shall select the fund demander by itself, sign the loan contract by itself (or by the center on its behalf), and it shall bear all risks. The proceeds belong to the fund supplier, and the center only charges appropriate service fees from the fund demander.

Luqiao Private Capital Standardized Management Service Center not only provides a good intermediary platform for private capital guidance, but also makes the use of private capital more standardized and orderly, and brings the lending of private capital under "sunshine". Specifically, the Private Capital Standardized Management Service Center has the following three functions:

First, it provides an intermediary platform for private capital investment and opens up the information channels for both the supply and demand of funds. The private economy in Luqiao area is developed, the private capital has accumulated a large amount, and the investment demand of private capital is increasingly prominent; on the other hand, the expansion of SMEs needs a large amount of funds, and bank loans are restricted by approval and other factors, curbing the source of funds for SMEs. Therefore, the establishment of the Private Capital Standardized Management Service Center provides a bridge between the supply and demand of funds, breaking the original situation of asymmetric information between the two, and putting private capital investment under "sunshine".

Second, the Private Capital Standardized Management Service Center is not only an intermediary, but also a guide for the rational use of private capital. The role of Luqiao Private Capital Standardized Management Service Center is not only to match the supply and demand of funds, but also to establish a perfect registration and filing system, so that private capital lending can be more standardized and there can be evidence to rely on in case of disputes. This innovative management mode is better and more rational than the ordinary private capital intermediary services, so that private capital can match the capital demanding enterprises, but it also enables investors to feel easy in carrying out private lending activities.

Third, the Private Capital Standardized Management Service Center has improved the service and development of Luqiao micro and small finance. The development of micro and small finance is not only the development of urban commercial banks and the government's introduction of relevant policies to ensure the financing of MSEs, but also the innovation of relevant financial service models to makes it easier for MSEs to obtain financial support. The establishment of the Private Capital Standardized Management Service Center in Luqiao makes it easier for MSEs to borrow funds from the private financial market, and at the same time, the capital owners can also lend with confidence through this platform. It can be said that the Private Capital Standardized Management Service Center in Luqiao is the icing on the cake for the innovation and development of micro and small finance in Luqiao district.

7.3 The Cases of Luqiao Private Capital Activating the Development of Micro and Small Finance

Yufeng Small Loan Company

Taizhou Luqiao Yufeng Micro Loan Co., Ltd. was established in March 2009 by Zhejiang Yufeng Industrial Group in conjunction with seven strong local legal entities and three natural persons in Luqiao, with a registered capital of 150 million yuan. At present, there are 12 employees, including 4 with banking experience. So far, 4218 loans have been issued, with a total of 2.81 billion yuan. The accumulated net profit was 98.12 million yuan, and the taxes paid were 51.02 million yuan (an annual average of more than 10 million yuan). In the annual assessments, it has been rated as "Zhejiang A+ Class Excellent Small Loan Company" for four consecutive years (only 7 in the province). At present, Yufeng is an executive director unit of China Federation of Microfinance Institutions and has been awarded the "2010 Top 100 Competitive Small Loan Companies in China" and the "2011 China's Best Innovation Contribution Award" by the People's Bank of China. Specifically, the service innovation of Yufeng Microloan Company has the following three points:

First, the loans are small and sporadic, and offer support for farmers and small businesses for practical results. Yufeng always adheres to the principle of "small amount, low interest rate, more involvement in agriculture and more guarantees" in its operation, and does business that banks are unwilling or unable to do, which plays a role in picking up the missing parts of the banking industry. At present, the average loan balance of a single household is 540,000 yuan, and its proposed goal is to bring it down to less than 300,000 yuan. The average monthly interest rate is 13.6‰, which is basically the same as the interest rate of unsecured and non-accumulative loans of small banks. Among the balance, agriculture-related loans were 167 million yuan, accounting for 68%, and non-agricultural loans were 77 million yuan, accounting for 32%. Only 1% of the loans are mortgage guaranteed loans, and all the others are guaranteed loans, which solves the problem of borrowers (mainly farmers, individual industrial and commercial households and SME operators) having difficulty in guaranteeing.

The second is to think in a different position and strengthen services to improve efficiency. In the operations, Yufeng implements "three NOs" for customers: no deposit points; no pledge in kind; no financial statements; "four HELPs": as long as poor women, landless farmers, disabled people, poor college students and other vulnerable groups willing to work are willing to borrow money, Yufeng will promptly give them low-interest loans for entrepreneurship, employment assistance and interest-free student loans, as well as give them inspirational books. In order to improve service efficiency, Yufeng promised to the public that "new loans will be replied in three days, old loans will be replied the same day", so that all loans can be handled on-site, and necessary investigation can be carried out at the same time. SMS reminders will be carried out seven days and telephone reminders three days before the due date of loans in case the customer fails to repay on time due to negligence.

Third, both internal and external efforts are made to strictly manage and control risks. On the one hand, Yufeng actively cooperated with financial offices of the provincial, municipal and district governments in the strict management of small loan companies, and always achieved "no illegal absorption of public deposits, no usury, no violent urge to repay loans, and no off-book operation". On the other hand, on the basis of various rules and regulations, Yufeng has achieved the following "Four Say-No Loans": say no to production-and-business-less activities, say no to gambling and drug abuse, say no to court enforcement cases and say no to overdue loan balances; "Four No-guarantees" are implemented from the guarantor: no guarantee from family members, no guarantee from upstream enterprises, no guarantee from business partners and no guarantee from original customers; before each loan is granted, it checks the "five networks": court hearing announcement network, court execution information network, credit information network of the People's Bank of China; enterprise identity authentication network, and small loan city defense network. After each loan is signed by the guarantor, the guarantor shall be contacted separately before lending to further verify the guarantor's guarantee intention. In addition, in order to avoid the moral hazard of employees, a telephone bulletin board for employees to report corruption was set up in the business hall. If the report is true, the informer will be awarded 2000 yuan in cash.

Jiuding Small Loan Company

Jiuding Small Loan Co., Ltd. was established in September 2009, with China Yuding Group as the main sponsor and 16 shareholders contributing, with a registered capital of RMB 150 million yuan. In response to the call of the government of Luqiao, Jiuding Small Loan Company further adapted to the needs of rural economic development, updated and streamlined their mind on the focus of "agriculture, rural areas and farmers" and SMEs services. As of May 2014, Jiuding Small Loan Company issued 2668 loans, with a total amount of 3109.533 million yuan. There were 301 loans with balance, with a total amount of 345.066 million yuan. As to the loan objects, Jiuding Small Loan Company granted 259 loans to farmers, with a total of 286.806 million yuan; 40 loans were granted to individual industrial and commercial households, with a total of 48.26 million yuan; 2 loans were granted to enterprises, totaling 10 million yuan. In 2012, Jiuding won the title of "Zhejiang A+ Class Excellent Small Loan Company". Before that, the company had been awarded "Zhejiang A-class Small Loan Company" for two consecutive years.

The establishment of Jiuding Small loan Company has the following three meanings for the development of micro and small finance in Luqiao district: first, it played a supplementary role in alleviating the financing difficulties of local "three rural" and MSEs. It can independently determine a reasonable interest rate, alleviate the interest burden of "three rural" and MSEs to a certain extent, and enhance the financial needs of farmers. Second, Jiuding Small Loan Company meets the diversified requirements of farmers and MSEs in their loan demand structure. Jiuding has implemented a credit policy of "preferential interest rates and preferential loans" for its products such as "student loans ", "entrepreneurial loans for college students", "entrepreneurial loans for disabled people" and "entrepreneurial loans for land-lost farmers". Third, small loan companies have played a certain role in regulating and guiding private financing. The small loan companies' borrowing is simple and flexible, without mortgage guarantee and the term is flexible, meeting the characteristics of great speed, short term and strong seasonality of the capital needs of farmers and small business economic entities.

Sanyou Jinlong Micro Loan Company

Sanyou Jinlong Micro Loan Company was officially put into operation in November 2012, jointly funded by 4 legal persons and 11 natural persons, with a registered capital of 200 million yuan. As of May 2014, Sanyou Jinlong granted 1318 loans, totaling 743.42 million yuan, with a loan balance of 233.46 million yuan. A total of 1102 single household loans of less than 1 million yuan were issued, with the amount of 176.5 million yuan, accounting for 75.6%; a total of 65 loans to vulnerable groups were issued, with a total of 3.54 million yuan. Sanyou Jinlong issues loans according to the principle of "small and scattered", divided into loans for farmers, self-employed households and SMEs, and adheres to the market position of serving agriculture, rural areas, farmers and MSEs.

In terms of service innovation, Sanyu Jinlong Micro Loan Company put forward the business method of "looking at operation, stressing guarantee, checking four networks" ("People's Bank of China credit report", "local co-prevention", "court website", "industry and commerce website"), and preventing three evils (gambling, drug abuse and usury). Fully and effectively understanding the borrower's business conditions and loan risks, timely discovering potential risks, and taking corresponding measures to prevent them, Sanyou Jinlong actively helps vulnerable groups and fulfills its social responsibilities, with specially student loans for poor students as a highlight of assistance. Sanyou Jinlong Company also innovated the bank deduction of loan funds, and realized the whole non-cash settlement of issuing loans, collecting repayment and interest. They sign a three-party authorized deduction agreement with the customer and the bank according to the loan issuance demand, and then issue their loan according to the contract. Thus, it facilitates customers' loan reception, repayment and interest payment, reduces cash circulation and the workload of financial personnel, and improves efficiency. The small loan companies are an important supplement to the financing of local MSEs. Relying on local advantages, the above three small loan companies in Luqiao district have solved the problem of financial difficulties for farmers and small enterprises by serving local "three rural" and micro enterprises. At the same time, the three small loan companies continue to innovate services to facilitate loan customers, and signed a tripartite authorization agreement with the banks to strengthen the supervision of funds. It can be said that the development of small loan companies has enriched the innovative development mode of micro and small finance in Luqiao area and has made important contributions to micro and small finance in Luqiao.

7.4 Summary

In recent years, rural banks, small loan companies and other grass-roots financial institutions have developed rapidly. However, in general, there is a lack of local micro and small financial institutions with distinctive characteristics and a fully competitive financial system for MSEs has not yet been formed. Practice at home and abroad shows that the micro-finance supply model dominated by large banks can no longer meet the needs of MSEs, and it is necessary to vigorously develop micro-finance organizations that have symmetric advantages in information and transaction costs. For the financial system as a whole, the entry of private capital will undoubtedly play a great role in enriching the services of the financial market in the future. Using private capital to set up regional small financial institutions can help local enterprises solve their actual financing needs.

In the development of micro and small finance, private capital in Luqiao district of Taizhou has effectively solved the financing problem of farmers, self-employed households and SMEs through small loan companies and other channels. However, small loan companies are still in the piloting stage, and the number is still small. Compared with the number of SMEs, it is still a drop in the ocean, which is one of the reasons that make it difficult for private financial institutions to play a role. For example, small loan companies are still subject to some restrictions in the process of development. First, financing ability. Due to the restrictions of laws and regulations, the source of funds of small loan companies is limited. At present, they rely on the funds paid by shareholders of the company and the financing from no more than two banking institutions, which is the main reason that affects the development of small loan companies. Second, excessive taxes and fees. At present, the government classifies microfinance as a service industry. At the tax rate of the service industry, microfinance companies pay a lot more taxes than the financial industry, which affects the enthusiasm of microfinance development. Third, credit risk. The loan threshold of small loan companies is lower than that of banks, so most of the people who borrow from microfinance companies have some flaws in their credit, which increases the credit risk. Fourth, the problem of single business variety and sustainable development. According to the original policy, small loan companies can only engage in lending, consulting and other businesses, with a single type of business. Their operating income mainly comes from loan interest, and their profitability is limited.

Therefore, further liberalizing private capital and unblocking private financial channels have been regarded as the key to solving the financial dilemma of micro and small financing. Rural banks and small loan companies led by private capital are an important guarantee to unblock the financial "capillaries". To solve the financing problem, first of all, we need to unswervingly promote financial reform, break financial monopolies, and allow a large number of private capital to prepare for the establishment of small financial institutions serving SMEs and MSEs. At the same time, the marketization of interest rates will make financial institutions fully compete, guide and encourage more institutions to conduct private lending, and bring private capital into the standardized and legal channels. With the continuous development of private economy, private capital has been accumulating, and private credit has gradually become a new force to solve the financing difficulties of SMEs. Small and medium-sized financial institutions such as micro and small loan companies initiated and established by private capital play an important role in the process of relieving the financing difficulties of SMEs. However, due to the high risk and blindness of private capital, it is also an important task for the improvement of the private financial market to make good use of private capital. First, the government, with small loan companies as the carrier, actively guides private capital to enter. Small loan companies are the main channel for private capital to relieve the financing difficulties of SMEs, and also an important form of private capital utilization. However, due to the high risks of private capital and the problems in the management of small loan companies, the government needs to actively guide private capital to set up small loan companies. At the same time, financial regulatory authorities have strengthened supervision over small loan companies to reduce risks and crises. But this does not mean that the government can directly manage small loan companies, but that the government actively monitors risks to prevent risks from evolving into problems. Second, take the opening of private banks as an opportunity to explore the entry of private capital into the banking industry. With the continuous opening and improvement of the financial market, private capital has greater "activity", and with the opening of private capital and the establishment of private banks, private capital will play a greater role in relieving the financing difficulties of SMEs. Various localities should take this opportunity to explore the impact of private capital on the banking industry and how private capital can alleviate the financing difficulties of SMEs by entering the banking industry.

Anhui Province has begun to explore the establishment of private banks to solve the financing difficulties of SMEs, and various localities can start from "zero", allowing private capital to enter part of local small and medium-sized banks first, so as to test the feasibility of private capital entering the banking industry.

References

Berger, A.N. & Udell, G.F. Small Business Credit Available and Relationship Lending: The Importance of Bank Organizational Structure [J], *Economic Journal*, 2002, 112 (447): 32–54.

Harhoff, K Rung. Lending Relationships in Germany: Empirical Evidence from Survey Data [J], *Journal of Banking and Finance*, 22, 1998.

Peterson, M.A. & Rajan, R.G. The Benefits of Lending Relationships: Evidence from Small Business Data [J], *The Journal of Finance*, 1994, 49(1): 3–37.

Strahan, P. & Weaton, J. Small Business Lending and the Changing Structure of Banking Industry [J], *Journal of Banking and Finance*, 1998, 22: 821–845.

Charles B. Wendel & Matthew Harvey. SME Credit Scoring: Key Initiative, Oppportunities and Issues [J], *Access Finance*, 2006, (10): 35–41.

Modigliani, F & Miller, M. The Cost of Capital, Corporate Finance and the Theory of Investment [J], *American Economic Review*, 1958, (48): 197–261.

Myers, S.C. & Majluf, N. Corporate Financing and Investment Decisions When Firms Have Information That Investors Do Not Have [J], *Journal of Financial Economics*, 1984, (13): 187–221.

Liu Min, Ding Deke. Research on the Countermeasures of Innovating the Loan Model of SMEs in China [J]. *Management World*, 2010, (8): 1–6.

Yang Yun. Research on Market Process, Industrial Clusters and Financing Constraints of SMEs [D]. Suzhou University, 2012, 3.

Liu Yangyang. Research on Financing Mode of Mutual Fund for Small and Medium-sized Enterprises from the Perspective of Industrial Clusters [J]. Modern Business Trade Industry, 2013, 1.

Xu Shengdao, Liu Ting. SME Financing: Bottlenecks and Solutions—From the Perspective of Industrial Clusters [J]. *Journal of Shihezi University*, 2012, 6.

Wei Longbao, Chen Xuwei, Wu Junqian. Breakthroughs of Financing Dilemmas of SMEs—From the Perspective of Industrial Cluster Development [J]. *Zhejiang Social Sciences*, 2011, 12.

Li Lianheng, Wang Xu. Research on the Establishment of a Credit Reporting System for Small and Medium-sized Enterprises Centered on the Reporting and Verification Mechanism [J]. *Credit Reference*, 2011, 2.

Zhao Yuzhen. Building a Credit Reporting System for Small and Medium-sized Enterprises to Solve Financing Problems [J]. *Journal of Finance and Economics*, 2012, 7.

Huang Liu. Some Thoughts on the Direct Financing of SMEs in China [J]. *Review of Economic Research*, 2012, 17.

Zhang Jinsuo. Discussion on the Direct Financing of SMEs [J]. *Foreign Investment in China*, 2011, 14.

Wu Yankun, Dai Xiaoxue. The Key to Solving the Financing Dilemma of SMEs: Improving the Credit Reporting System of SMEs [J]. *Credit Reference*, 2013, 5.

Liu Yang. On How Commercial Banks Improve Financial Services for Small Enterprises under the New Situation [J]. *Money China (Academic Edition)*, 2013, 3.

Zhu Mengnan, Deng Wenxuan. A New Way to Solve the Financing Difficulties of Small and Medium-sized Enterprises—On the Integration of Financial Services of Small and Medium-sized Enterprises Led by Commercial Banks [J]. *Jiangxi Social Sciences*, 2013, 4.

Zhong Lei. On Building a Financial Service Platform to Solve Financing Problems [J]. *Science & Technology Information*, 2012, 12.

Wu Dongyan. Research on Financial Services for Small and Medium-sized Enterprises of Commercial Banks [J]. *Huabei Finance*, 2012, 6.

Dong Shaoguang. Improving Financial Service Capabilities to Solve the Financing Difficulties of SMEs [J]. *China National Conditions and Strength*, 2012, 6.

Jiang Yinhua. Improving the Financial Service System to Solve the Development Dilemma of SMEs [J]. *Modern Corporate Culture Magazine*, 2012, 12.

Tan Jing, Zhang Qifeng. Improving the Credit Guarantee System to Ease the Financing Difficulties of SMEs [J]. *Liaoning Economy*, 2011, 9.

Wang Xinglong. Factor Analysis of Financial Service Brand Difference and Satisfaction of Small and Medium-sized Enterprises in China's Commercial Banks—A Comparative Study Based on Questionnaires [J]. *Shanghai Finance*, 2012, 2.

Ma Juan, Wan Jieqiu, Shen Xiaoyan. Financing Innovation of SMEs Relying on Supply Chain Finance [J]. *Commercial Research*, 2013, 4.

CHAPTER 8

Luqiao Local Government Promoting the Innovative Development of Micro and Small Finance

The local government plays a leading role in the local financial market, because it not only finds it easy to break the financial repression caused by vertical regulation, but also has organizational and informational strengths, enabling it to play a synergistic role in guiding the development of local industries. When the government plays a leading role in local industrial planning and cultivation, it is bound to help foster local financial industry. Different regions have different economic bases and industrial environments, which inevitably require different financial environments and forms. The local government of Luqiao is more proactive in the innovative development of micro and small finance, thus creating a good ecological environment.

8.1 Positioning of Luqiao Government Policies to Help the Development of Micro and Small Finance

Based on the development of micro and small finance in Luqiao and the development of small and medium-sized financial institutions such as commercial banks in cities around the world, it can be clearly seen that the more diversified the financial players are, the greater the number of small and medium-sized financial institutions is, the more abundant the private

W. Xiao et al., *Microfinance and China's Regional Development*, https://doi.org/10.1007/978-981-99-1960-4_8

capital is, the larger the financing space for SMEs in the region is, then the more effective the relief of financing difficulties will be. In general, the government of Luqiao district helps boost the development of micro and small finance in three ways: first, it focuses on providing a good operational environment for financial institutions; second, it focuses on providing a good ecological environment for micro and small finance players; and third, it focuses on building an effective risks prevention and control mechanism.

Providing a Good Operational Environment for the Development of Micro and Small Financial Institutions

The government of Luqiao district focuses on opening up the local small and medium-sized financial market and setting up more competitive small and medium-sized financial institutions in keeping with local realities. The government allows competent private enterprises to establish small and medium-sized financial institutions, creates a good financial climate, and allows private small and medium-sized financial institutions to leverage their strengths and participate in fair competition in the regional financial market. At the same time, different measures were taken to loosen the restraints on small and medium-sized financial institutions and create a loose policy environment. As an indispensable part of the financial system, these financial institutions need more policy support from the government. At the same time, strengthening regulation and developing small and medium-sized financial institutions is conducive to promoting the regulated operation of small and medium-sized financial institutions, encouraging healthy competition in the financial market, eliminating those with poor performances, improving the stability of the financial system, and protecting the interests of SMEs.

Providing a Good Ecological Environment for the Development of Micro and Small Finance

The government of Luqiao district focuses on allocating limited financial resources to small and medium-sized enterprises undergoing upgrading by adopting business models such as "bank + government + guarantee + insurance + venture capital + brokerage". The financing difficulty of SMEs is a systemic problem and it lasts long. To continue to provide easier financing access, we need to pool the joint efforts of the government, businesses, financial institutions and all sectors of society to make overall planning and comprehensive management. On the one hand, the government of Luqiao district instructs financial institutions to change their business strategies, adjust the credit structure, increase credit supply to SMEs, and ensure that loans to SMEs grow faster than the average growth rate of all loans. At the same time, the government, banks, enterprises and intermediary institutions are encouraged to make bold innovations in financial products and in ways credit is issued, establish a positive incentive mechanism for the credit expansion for SMEs, innovate in financing models, and improve the development of a long-term credit mechanism for SMEs.

Focusing on Building an Effective Risks Prevention and Control Mechanism for the Development of Micro and Small Finance

The government of Luqiao district focuses on building an effective risks prevention and control mechanism for the development of micro and small finance. First of all, establish and improve the mechanism for preventing and defusing risks, and ensure the sound operation of regional finance, thus guarding against hidden dangers of regional financial security. To this end, Luqiao district has set up a special emergency loan fund of 20 million yuan to help growing enterprises increase turnover during repayment and enhance short-term security; in addition, an emergency loan risks fund of 20 million yuan has been put in place to help SMEs that encounter emergencies such as capital shortage during production and operation. Secondly, in local financial institutions, the risks control technology of Tailong Bank based on entrepreneurs' personality, products and collateral, as well as businesses' electricity meters, water meters and customs declaration, and the credit management system is improved to ensure quality. Strengthen the management of various financing intermediaries such as pawnbrokers, investment companies, guarantee agencies and so on. In order to step up risks prevention efforts, the approval and establishment of various financing intermediaries has been on halt recently, all kinds of operation rates and service fees have been kept within four times the benchmark interest rate of bank loans, and illegal financial activities have been put to an end. Thirdly, the government of Luqiao district addresses risks such as capital and guarantee breakdown for enterprises based on each business's case. For enterprises with good asset quality and product market that are affected by the guarantee chain, banks are required to refrain from recouping loans and from stopping issuing loans at all. For enterprises with unsalable products and insolvency, the government of Luqiao district protects the interests of creditors such as banks; the public security department is required to pay close attention to the business owners who tend to run away, and prevent evasion and abandonment of debts. In addition, the Luqiao district government, together with the court, industry and commerce, taxation and other relevant departments, cracks down on financial fraud and other illegal activities, and bans illegal private financial activities such as illegal fund-raising and loan sharks.

8.2 Guiding Approaches of Luqiao Government to Guarantee the Development of Micro and Small Finance

Specifically, the private economy in Luqiao district is well developed, and the financing demand of SMEs is strong. The government of Luqiao district makes efforts to promote the development of local micro and small finance, and solves the financing difficulties of SMEs through three major supporting policies.

Formulating Strategies, Strengthen Leadership, Solidifying Support, and Providing Good Government Services

First, scientifically formulate financial development strategies. Define the development goals of the financial industry. With the theme of "promoting local financial innovation and development and building micro and small financial service innovation demonstration zones", Luqiao district held the second plenary session of the fifth District CPC Committee to study financial innovation and development. The session proposed that Luqiao district should take the lead in terms of coverage of financial services for micro and small enterprises, satisfaction of financial services for micro and small enterprises, proportion of added value of micro and small financial services, the number and quality of local micro and small financial institutions, local micro and small financial service system and the credit environment, so as to establish the regional brand as China's capital in this regard. At present, all kinds of innovation is carried out in an orderly manner. Make a plan for the development of the financial industry. The 12th Five-Year Plan for the service industry in Luqiao district proposes to concentrate financial players on one street and one district. One street refers to Nangong Avenue and its surroundings where Taizhou Bank and Tailong Bank are located. One district means that Nangong Avenue extends northward, and the Luqiao financial headquarters cluster area will be planned and built around Taizhou Central Avenue, and other financial industries are introduced in this area.

Second, strengthen inter-departmental cooperation. The district party committee and government have always attached great importance to financial work. In 2010, Luqiao district established the financial work office of the district government at the section level, which is the earliest in Taizhou. This year, we also established a leading group of financial innovation and development in Luqiao district, led by the secretary of the District Party Committee and the district head, and deployed 15 key financial innovation tasks throughout the year. The whole region has created a good atmosphere of supporting the development of the financial industry, accelerating financial innovation and promoting the development of the real economy.

Third, formulate financial support policies. *Several Opinions on Supporting the Development of the Financial Industry (Trial)* was implemented. Since 2010, a yearly fund of 20 million yuan for the development of the financial industry has been in place, which is designated to support the development of the financial industry and reward financial institutions and individuals who have made outstanding contributions to local economic development. *Several Opinions on Supporting the Listing of Enterprises* were issued, and a yearly fund of 30 million yuan was set up for the listing of enterprises. In addition, the district-level finance will arrange a directive special fund of 2 million yuan for the subsidies of SMEs' energy-saving and efficiency projects (such as the introduction of the CLIMATE financing innovation loan project of UNEP by Taizhou Bank and the launch of green and energy-saving loan products).

Building Platforms, Focusing on Innovation, Serving Entities, and Making the Government Count

First, build a district-level financial development platform. *The Implementation Plan on Promoting the Innovation and Development of Local Finance* was implemented, and six district-level platforms were built, including demonstration platforms for micro and small finance, clustering platforms for financial institutions, innovation platforms for industrial finance, direct investment and financing transaction platforms, interactive platforms for micro and small finance and private capital, and R&D exchange platforms for micro and small finance. For example, in terms of the micro and small finance demonstration platform, through a series of policy support, the government focuses on enabling three local banks to become bigger, stronger, better and more specialized. In terms of financial gathering platform, land in the new town area was allocated, the shingles of the headquarters buildings of three corporate banks were hung at the beginning of this year, and other financial institutions also settled in this area. In terms of industrial financial innovation platform, the government plans to establish an auto finance company. In terms of the interaction platform between micro and small finance and private capital, the government is preparing to establish private sub-loan companies and private financing management centers, and creates a pilot area for private financing management in Zhejiang Province. In terms of micro and small finance R&D exchange platform, the government entrusted Zhejiang University to conduct research on the financial innovation and development of Luqiao district. The government hosted 2012 Cross-strait Seminar on Micro and Small Finance Development, which was recognized by Taiwan Affairs Office of the State Council and the provincial government, and continued to host it in 2013. The government organized financial institutions and relevant personnel to hold cross-strait financial advanced training courses in Taiwan. Now, the government is applying for the micro and small finance cooperation innovation pilot zone across the Taiwan Strait.

Second, promote financial institutions to innovate in products. The government encourages financial institutions to increase credit supply, innovate in financial products, and serve the real economy by assessing their performances in supporting economic development, allocating financial deposits, and organizing peer reviews. In 2012, new industrial loans in Luqiao district accounted for 45.4% of the total. Taizhou Bank introduced the Climate Finance Innovation Loan Project (CFIF) of the United Nations Environment Program, launched the green and energy saving loans, and encouraged SMEs to upgrade energy-saving equipment and improve production processes with preferential interest rates for the purpose of energy conservation and efficiency improvement. Zhejiang Tailong Commercial Bank launched the Sino-German financial micro and small enterprise loan project—known as SG Tailongyi, a medium and long-term fixed assets credit product, which helped micro and small enterprises speed up the structural adjustment of fixed assets by meeting their financing needs for equipment procurement and technical transformation. In order to further develop the rural market and increase financial inclusiveness, Luqiao Rural Cooperative Bank launched inclusive credit loans, upheld the concept of family credit, alleviating the guarantee difficulties of ordinary people.

Third, build a bank-enterprise cooperation platform. The purpose of supporting the financial industry is to enable the financial sector to serve the real economy. Luqiao district has continuously improved the bank-enterprise cooperation dialogue system, and held bank-enterprise meetings and dialogues between financial institutions and SMEs. The government has organized financial institutions to carry out activities, such as those that helped enterprises solve problems and promoted the development of the real economy, so that financial institutions could help address problems facing businesses. For example, Tailong Bank visited thousands of households and enterprises and thousands of households with thousands of people in one hundred days. It increased credit support for 186 enterprises in difficulties, implemented preferential interest rates, and supported SMEs to get out of difficulties.

Leveraging Strengths, Improving Mechanisms, Stabilizing Finance, and Providing Government Guidance

First, leverage strengths of private finance. Encourage and direct private capital to integrate into the existing financial system in an orderly manner. Guide the development of entrusted loans. Encourage cooperation between private capital and private finance, realize the connection between private capital and bank business, and ensure regulated private lending. Cultivate small loan companies. Guide and support small loan companies to absorb private capital to increase sources of capital, encourage them to issue targeted loans, and provide liquidity for loans. The government will speed up and guide the restructuring of Luqiao Rural Cooperative Bank. Introduce premium shareholders and strategic investors, encourage private capital to buy shares, and accelerate the reform of rural cooperative banks. Encourage the issuance of financial bonds. This is what Taizhou Bank and Tailong Bank have been doing.

Second, improve mechanisms. The government keeps improving the government-bank cooperation mechanism. The district finance authorities arrange a yearly fund of 3 million yuan to cooperate with Taizhou bank, China Construction Bank Luqiao sub-branch and other financial institutions. They set up micro and small enterprise energy-saving loans, electronic business e-commerce credit and others, and promoted local financial institutions to solve financing difficulties of small micro enterprises through financial interest discounts and a risk compensation mechanism. The government continues to improve the banking cooperation mechanism. Private financial institutions and state-owned commercial banks are encouraged to complement each other's strengths and share resources, and encourage funds in plenty from state-owned commercial banks to go to vulnerable SMEs through private financial institutions. Keep improving the win-win mechanism between banks and enterprises. In the face of the difficulties of SMEs, the district Party committee and the district government encouraged financial institutions to reduce fees and the burden on enterprises. Taizhou Bank built a "free bank", which meant a reduction to its annual returns by tens of millions.

Third, maintain financial stability. Establish a system to understand latest developments. *The Notice on Opinions on Preventing Financial Risks, Regulating Operation and Promoting Healthy Economic Development* was issued, and the leading group for preventing financial risks and regulating operation in Luqiao district and the leading group for combating illegal fund-raising in Luqiao district were established. The finance office, the Bureau of Economy and Information Technology, the Bureau of Industry and Commerce, the Bureau of Commerce, the Public Security Bureau, the court and other relevant departments were organized to get relevant information in a timely manner, and a monthly information reporting system was established, so that the government can keep tabs on the developments of enterprises with difficulties in the capital chain and illegal fund-raising cases. Precautions can be taken when risks emerge. A special government emergency loan fund of 20 million yuan was set up. For enterprises with temporary financial difficulties, relevant departments have been organized to use the funds to help them transfer loans, negotiate with financial institutions so as to refrain from not issuing loans, and help enterprises replace their assets in a timely manner. The Luqiao Court also set up a professional collegial panel for trials to foster the healthy development of the financial industry in the district.

8.3 Luqiao Government Ensuring Platform Building for the Development of Micro and Small Finance

Luqiao district focuses on building six major platforms in the development of micro and small finance.

Promoting the Development of Micro and Small Finance Demonstration Platform, and Further Developing the Core Brand of Micro and Small Finance

First, expand the three local banks. Taizhou Bank, Zhejiang Tailong Commercial Bank and Luqiao Rural Cooperative Bank are the three local banks in Luqiao, and models of micro and small financial institutions in China. The government promotes the construction of headquarters buildings of the three banks and develops financial headquarters economy. Accelerate the building of outlets of the banks, bring financial self-service machines to villages (residential quarters), aim to achieve full coverage of the outlets of two of the banks in all towns (communities), and full coverage of 100 financial self-service machines of the Agricultural Cooperative Bank of China in key villages (residential quarters) within three years. The government supports the three banks to expand their service networks based on Luqiao, and provides services in connection with local government in the process of carrying out cross regional business. Taizhou Bank and Zhejiang Tailong Commercial Bank are encouraged to exceed 100 billion yuan in asset scale in 3 years and 5 years respectively, and the number of branch outlets will exceed 100 in 3 years.

Second, strengthen the three local banks. Instruct Luqiao Rural Cooperative Bank to bring in strategic investors such as brand financial institutions and excellent private enterprises, optimize the equity and governance structure, carry out shareholding reform, and strive to transform into a rural commercial bank in 2 years. With the goal of establishing a modern banking system, the government will continue to push the three banks to deepen reforms and constantly innovate in their operating mechanisms, so as to become a featured bank with sufficient capital, strict internal control, safe operation, high-quality services, good efficiency, strong innovation capability and competitiveness, with focuses on serving SMEs. Support local banks to increase the supply of funds to serve SMEs by issuing special loans for SMEs, improving their ability to serve SMEs, and issuing more than 6 billion yuan of special financial bonds for SMEs throughout the region this year. Further deepen financial services provided by the three banks to SMEs in the region, encourage them to adopt preferential policies, and provide better financial services for SMEs in Luqiao.

Third, build a financial backstage service base. Support the three corporate banks, especially two city commercial banks, to build a computer center, a research and development center, a customer service center, a training center and other financial backstage service bases in Luqiao, and finish project site selection this year.

Promoting the Development of the Financial Institution Cluster Platform and Improving the Organization System of Micro and Small Finance

First, build a financial cluster. According to the zoning planning of Luqiao and the development of the financial industry, further sort out and improve the spatial layout of the financial industry, and focus on building a financial cluster. In preparation of the overall detailed plan and the annual land use plan, it ensures the availability of the land for building the financial cluster area, and ensures that the land bidding, auction and listing of the first-phase block will be completed in a year. Further study the characteristics of the development of the financial industry, make overall arrangements for the supporting construction of public utilities in the financial cluster area, ensure good electricity, communications, transportation, etc., and improve the service environment for office and commerce.

Second, accelerate the gathering of various financial institutions. According to the development plan for the financial industry, the government lays equal emphasis on bringing in and cultivating financial institutions, and accelerate the gathering of various financial institutions such as banks, securities, insurance, trust, financial leasing, equity investment, venture capital, small loan and financial companies. Support the development of finance-related intermediary institutions such as credit rating, asset evaluation, financing guarantee, investment consulting, accounting and auditing, and legal services, regulate the practices of intermediary service institutions, strengthen industry self-discipline, and improve the professional level and service capacity of intermediary service providers.

Third, promote the development of new financial organizations. Accelerate the development of new rural financial organizations, such as small loan companies, rural banks and rural financial cooperatives, which mainly serve micro and small enterprises and farmers, and have more than six small loan companies, one rural bank and one rural financial cooperative in the whole region by 2015.

Promoting the Development of Industrial Financial Innovation Platform and Better Serving SMEs

First, adopt innovative forms of industrial finance. Take innovative approaches to developing automobile finance, an automobile finance market, an automobile industry financial service chain covering all aspects of production, circulation, consumption, maintenance and recovery, and expand financing channels for the auto industry, such as supporting auto manufacturers to establish auto finance companies; encouraging banks to develop auto supply chain finance; develop automobile consumer credit; provide new credit products for SMEs in the automobile industry chain. Make innovative efforts to develop commercial finance, credit products and credit systems that meet the financing needs of businesses in professional markets, for example, support the financing of "market+businesses" through multi household co-guarantee by market and businesses or guarantee by market managers; develop logistics finance and supply chain financing products; strengthen the cooperation between banks and businesses to improve the efficiency of payment and settlement in the market circulation industry. Pursue innovative development of resources recycling finance, development of financing products able to meet large import volume, large logistics volume and extensive production mode by, for example, increasing the innovation of trade financing products, helping enterprises solve financing problems of import letter of credit and import payment in foreign exchange; promote the development of green credit and innovate in the financing of energy conservation and emissions reduction projects; adopt a new credit model to solve the problems related to large deposits and loans and logistics.

Second, adopt innovative financing guarantee. Work hard to expand new ways of financing guarantees for SMEs, encourage banking and financial institutions to issue pledge loans such as accounts receivable, trademark exclusive rights, intellectual property rights, automobile quality certificates, professional market stall use rights, warehouse receipts and equity, and promote supply chain financing and small loan guarantee and insurance. Keep improving the guarantee system, regulate the operation of financing guarantee companies, and encourage them to support the financing of SMEs.

Third, find new ways of repayment for SMEs working capital loans, support banks to launch revolving loans, seamless relay loans, emergency deferred loans, installment loans, special operating loans and other products, and encourage inter-bank cooperation to carry out bridge loans.

Promoting the Development of Direct Investment and Financing Trading Platform and Expanding Financing Channels for Micro and Small Enterprises

First, promote the tiered cultivation project of enterprise listing. Raise the proportion of direct financing, and publicize the functions of the capital market. Enterprises are encouraged to obtain direct financing through listing on the domestic main board, the small and medium-sized board, the growth enterprise market and the overseas capital market. Take the initiative to connect with Zhejiang Equity Trading Center, encourage enterprises to list on the center, realize share circulation, and create conditions for listing and financing.

Second, find new and diversified channels for direct financing. Support eligible enterprises to issue corporate collective bonds, collective bills and collective trust products, encourage SMEs to issue private placement bonds, and use the bond market to expand the scale of direct financing. Cooperate with securities companies to establish a convenient and quick bond issuance service platform and channel for enterprises, and create an optimal service environment for enterprises in bond financing. Establish equity investment funds. Accelerate the establishment of industrial and venture capital steering funds supported by district finance bureau, cooperate with well-known private equity institutions in and out of the province, and steer private capital to support industrial transformation and upgrading and enterprise development by means of limited partnership. Promote the return of Luqiao capital outside the region in the form of private equity and venture capital, and encourage private forces to independently establish private equity institutions and funds to invest in local enterprises.

Promoting the Development of Interactive Platforms Between Micro and Small Finance and Private Capital and Promoting the Conversion of Private Capital into Industrial Capital

First, explore effective ways of matching private capital with projects. The district government will try to take the lead in building a matchmaking platform for private capital, collect information on the supply and demand of private capital, form a pool of incremental customers and projects in banking business, and realize the docking through the products developed by three local banks, or provide channels for private capital and projects to connect with each other. Try to set up Luqiao Micro and Small Finance and Private Capital Mutual Assistance Service Center in one or more corporate banks, through which information on private capital supply and demand can be collected, and on this basis, micro and small loans, entrusted loans, private capital custody, private capital docking and other business can be made possible. Develop new financial business of banks—private capital matchmaking products, support corporate banks to research and develop them, and package scattered private capital and micro and small enterprise investment projects separately, and invest and finance through banks from package to package. Promote the reform of the government investment and financing system, improve the government project investment and financing platform, and guide all kinds of capital to invest in public welfare and basic projects.

Second, find a variety of private financing approaches to promote the sustainable development of small loan companies. Strengthen cooperation with specialized private equity institutions, establish small loan funds invested by private capital, and invest in the equity of small loan companies in a targeted way. After increasing capital and shares, small loan companies are encouraged to borrow from major legal person shareholders in order to increase the financing proportion of small loan companies, provide sufficient capital and raise financing leverage of small loan companies, and make small loan companies in our district bigger and stronger. Encourage leading enterprises in industrial clusters and professional market organizers to initiate the establishment of small loan companies, focus on serving SMEs and businesses in industrial clusters and professional markets, so as to form a new small loan service model that enables large, strong companies help their smaller counterparts.

Third, encourage private capital to connect with micro and small finance. Strive for and make full use of relevant policies, steer all kinds of private capital to participate in the establishment and development of micro and small financial institutions, encourage private capital to participate in the capital increase and share expansion of local banks, small loan companies and other financial institutions, and support private capital to participate in the establishment of micro and small financial service institutions such as rural banks (community banks), rural capital mutual aid cooperatives, financing guarantee companies, and private capital management companies.

Promoting the Development of Micro and Small Finance R&D and Exchange Platform and Enhancing the Sustainable Innovation Capability of Financial Institutions

First, establish micro and small finance research institutions. Increase support for micro and small financial innovation, encourage qualified financial institutions to set up and strengthen specialized research departments, improve the financial innovation mechanism oriented by market demand and dominated by financial markets and financial enterprises, and innovate in financial products, technologies, services, management, organizational forms, etc. Improve the protection mechanism for micro and small finance innovation, and strengthen the protection of intellectual property rights such as trademark rights, patent rights, copyright and trade secrets of micro and small financial innovation achievements. Develop incentive measures for micro and small finance innovation, and reward the R&D and promotion teams of outstanding innovation projects.

Second, establish a micro and small finance communication platform. Work with typical micro and small finance research institutions in the Chinese mainland and Taiwan to establish a cross-strait micro and small finance development forum and make it the most influential professional annual exchange platform. Hold the first cross-strait Micro and Small Finance Development Forum in the second half of this year, and invite micro and small finance experts and scholars from Taiwan and the Chinese mainland to conduct exchanges with financial institutions in Luqiao, so as to draw on Taiwan's good practices in micro and small financial services for the benefit of micro and small finance in Luqiao. Establish Luqiao district Financial Industry Federation, integrate banks, insurance, securities, guarantee companies, pawnshops, various investment and financing (consulting) companies and other institutions under the jurisdiction of

Luqiao district, and take this as a communication platform to give full play to the financial industry.

Third, establish a micro and small finance training base. Step up the training of micro and small financial talents, and support Ginza University and Tailong University in training more micro and small financial professionals. Encourage them to obtain social training licenses, and establish an open and professional training institution in Luqiao. Encourage private capital to provide micro and small financial talent training. Strive to become a typical micro and small financial talent training institution in China (Table 8.1).

Summary Based on the experience of Luqiao district, local government plays a great role in assisting the development of micro and small finance. In view of the problems in the innovation and development of enterprise financing organization system, the government of Luqiao district is positioned to speed up the vigorous development of various financial activities and strengthen policy support, especially the small and medium-sized financial institutions, while improving the legal environment, with the improvement of financial activities as the core, to play an effective role in alleviating the financing difficulties of SMEs. The local government plays a leading role in the local financial market. In addition to breaking the financial repression caused by vertical regulation, the local government also plays a synergistic role in guiding the development of local industries because of its strengths in organization and information. When the government plays a leading role in local industrial planning and cultivation, it is bound to help foster local financial industry. Different regions have different economic bases and industrial environments, which inevitably require different supporting financial environments and financial industry activities.

Local governments can rely on their own policy, strengths in credit, resources and platform to guide and support financial innovation in accordance with the requirements of industrial development, and cultivate diversified regional financial activities. Additionally, in the innovative practice of alleviating the financing difficulties of SMEs, local governments can also expand the financing channels for regional equity and debt transactions, and build a regional financing platform in line with the local economic situations. Besides, as the leader and participant in the construction of the regional financial ecological environment, local governments have

Table 8.1 List of key projects implemented by Luqiao to promote local financial innovation and development

Project Category	*Number*	*Projects and Requirements*	*Lead Department*
1. Micro and small finance demonstration platform construction project	1	Project: accelerate the construction of three corporate bank outlets Requirements: strive to achieve full coverage of outlets of two urban commercial banks in towns (communities) of Luqiao by the end of 2015, and 100 sets of financial self-service machines of Luqiao Rural Cooperative Bank will be fully covered in key villages (residential quarters) of Luqiao	District Finance Office
	2	Project: support the cross regional development of three corporate banks Requirements: In the process of cross regional development, the Luqiao government and relevant departments should provide assistance in connection with the local government. Through cross regional development, the Taizhou Bank and Zhejiang Tailong Commercial Bank have increased the financial influence of micro and small businesses on Luqiao. The asset scale of the Taizhou Bank and Zhejiang Tailong Commercial Bank has been striving to achieve an asset size of 100 billion yuan in three years and five years respectively, and the number of outlets exceeds 100 in three years.	District Finance Office
	3	Project: Luqiao Rural Cooperative Bank transformed into a rural commercial bank Requirements: bring in strategic investors, optimize equity and governance structure, and strive to transform into a rural commercial bank in 2014.	District Finance Office
	4	Project: issuing special financial bonds for micro and small enterprises Requirements: strive to issue more than 6 billion yuan of special financial bonds for micro and small enterprises throughout the region in the year, and increase the fund supply for micro and small enterprises.	District Finance Office
	5	Project: construction of financial backstage service base Requirements: support the two urban commercial banks to build computer center, R&D center, customer service center, training center and other financial background service bases in Luqiao, and complete project site selection within the year.	District Finance Office

(*continued*)

Table 8.1 (continued)

Project Category	*Number*	*Projects and Requirements*	*Lead Department*
2. Financial institution cluster platform construction project	6	Project: construction of financial cluster Requirements: study the development of the financial industry, make overall arrangements for the supporting construction of municipal public infrastructure in the financial cluster area and the guarantee of power, communication, transportation and other services, and improve the service environment for office and commerce. When preparing the regulatory detailed planning and annual land use plan, ensure the construction land of the financial cluster area, and ensure the completion of land bidding, auction, listing and building scheme design within the year of Phase I block.	District Finance Office
	7	Project: accelerating the cluster development of various financial institutions Requirements: lay equal emphasis on investment promotion and cultivation, steer financial institutions and financial intermediary service institutions to develop in the financial cluster area and around Nanguan Avenue, and basically form a financial cluster development of "one district and one community" by 2015.	District Finance Office
	8	Project: promote the development of new financial organizations Requirements: accelerate the development of new rural financial organizations focusing on serving micro and small enterprises and "agriculture, rural areas and farmers", and strive to reach more than 6 small loan companies in the region by 2015, including 1 village bank and 1 rural mutual fund cooperative.	District Finance Office

(*continued*)

Table 8.1 (continued)

Project Category	*Number*	*Projects and Requirements*	*Lead Department*
3. Industrial financial innovation platform construction project	9	Project: innovative development of auto finance Requirements: develop the automobile financial market, build the automobile industry financial service chain covering production, circulation, consumption, maintenance and recovery, and expand the financing channels for automobile industry development in many ways. Competent departments of the automobile industry shall, together with relevant financial institutions, formulate an implementation plan within the year to strive for achievements in automobile financial innovation.	District Economic and Information Bureau
	10	Project: innovative development of commercial finance Requirements: develop credit products and systems that meet the financing needs of professional market operators. The competent department of the trade industry will work with relevant financial institutions to formulate an implementation plan within the year, so as to strive for achievements in trade and financial innovation.	District Modern Service Industry Office District Commerce Bureau
	11	Project: innovative development of renewable resources finance Requirements: develop financing products that adapt to large imports, large logistics and extensive production of metal resource recycling industry. The Management Committee of the Metal Resources Recycling Industry Base and the competent department of the industry work together with relevant financial institutions to formulate a plan within the year, so as to strive for achievements in financial innovation of resource recycling.	Economic and Information Bureau of the Management Committee of Metal Resources Recycling Industry Base
	12	Project: guarantee system improvement Requirements: guide financing guarantee companies to support financing of micro and small enterprises; strengthen the regulation and assessment of guarantee companies. The assessment methods for guarantee companies shall be formulated during the year, focusing on the assessment of the guarantee business volume for enterprise financing.	District Economic and Information Bureau

(*continued*)

Table 8.1 (continued)

Project Category	*Number*	*Projects and Requirements*	*Lead Department*
4. Enterprise direct investment and financing trading platform construction project	13	Project: promote tiered cultivation project of enterprise listing Requirements: encourage enterprises to go listing to domestic and overseas platforms; Encourage enterprises to list in the equity trading center. The goal is 5 (domestic and foreign) listed enterprises in the region and 3 listed enterprises in the provincial equity trading center by 2015.	District Finance Office
	14	Project: innovate in diversified direct investment and financing channels Requirements: support eligible enterprises to issue corporate collective bonds, collective bills and collective trust products, encourage small and medium-sized enterprises to issue private bonds, and use the bond market to expand the scale of direct financing. It is expected that more than three enterprises will issue various bonds by 2015.	District Finance Office
	15	Project: establishment of equity investment fund Requirements: In the first half of 2013, set up the district financial steering fund, determine the partner of private equity investment institutions, and complete the first fund raising by the end of 2013.	District Finance Bureau

(*continued*)

Table 8.1 (continued)

Project Category	*Number*	*Projects and Requirements*	*Lead Department*
5. Micro and small finance and private capital interactive platform construction project	16	Project: explore the building of a private capital matching network platform led by the government Requirements: collect information on private fund supply and demand through this network platform for relevant parties to connect. Try to complete the feasibility study report of the project in the first half of next year, and start relevant work in the second half of next year.	District Finance Office
	17	Project: explore the establishment of "Luqiao Micro and Small Finance and Private Capital Mutual Assistance Service Center" Requirements: set up the center in one or more corporate banks, collect the supply and demand information of private funds through the center, and carry out micro and small loans, entrusted loans, private capital trusteeship, private capital docking and other businesses on this basis. Try to complete the feasibility study report of the project in the first half of next year, and start relevant work in the second half of next year.	District Finance Office
	18	Project: develop new financial products—"private capital matchmaking products" Requirements: the government supports corporate banks to research and develop "private capital matchmaking products", package decentralized private capital and micro and small enterprise investment projects separately, and conduct investment and financing in the form of package to package through banks. Try to complete the feasibility study report of the project in the first half of next year, and start relevant work in the second half of next year.	District Finance Office

(*continued*)

Table 8.1 (continued)

Project Category	*Number*	*Projects and Requirements*	*Lead Department*
6. Micro and small finance R&D exchange platform construction project	19	Project: establishment of cross-strait micro and small financial development forum Requirements: work with typical micro and small financial research institutions in the Chinese mainland and Taiwan to build the most influential professional annual exchange platform. Hold the first cross-strait micro and small financial development forum in the second half of this year.	District Taiwan Affairs Office &District Finance Office
	20	Project: establish Luqiao district Financial Industry Federation Requirements: combine the banking, insurance, securities and various institutions related to investment and financing, take this as a communication platform, give full play to the role of market players, and strive to establish within the year.	District Finance Office
	21	Project: establish micro and small finance training base Requirements: Ginza College and Tailong College are encouraged to establish open and professional training institutions in Luqiao in due time. Encourage social forces to carry out micro and small financial talent training. Strive to have one typical micro and small financial talent training institution in China by the end of 2015.	District Education Bureau &District Finance Office

(continued)

Table 8.1 (continued)

Project Category	*Number*	*Projects and Requirements*	*Lead Department*
5. Safeguard measures	22	Project: improve the use of "special funds for financial industry development in Luqiao district" Requirements: modify and improve the use of "special funds for financial industry development in Luqiao district" within the year.	District Finance Office
	23	Project: accelerate the training and introduction of financial senior management talents Requirements: focus on training financial operation and management leaders and senior management talents, formulate financial talent gathering, development planning and training, introduce plan and policies related to financial talents within the year.	Talent Office of District Party Committee &District Finance Office
	24	Project: credit platform construction Requirements: improve the three credit platforms of bank credit, small and medium-sized enterprises and social credit, strengthen the collection and management of non-bank credit information of relevant departments, take the lead in building a unified platform for information collection and sharing that matches the financial services of micro and small enterprises in Taizhou and even the whole province, and create a good social credit system. We will work out a construction plan within the year and start construction next year.	District Development and Reform Bureau

also played an important role in strengthening the construction of the credit environment and establishing a regional credit reporting system, such as building a government joint credit reporting system database and credit service database, building a government joint supervision system, an internet credit information release system, and developing government regulation and market-oriented services.

Therefore, local government can help alleviate the financing difficulties of SMEs in a variety of ways. First, bring out the enthusiasm of local governments, rely on their strengths on policy, credit, resources and platform, guide and support finance to innovate in accordance with the requirements of industrial development, and cultivate diversified regional financial activities. Attach importance to the creation of a sound financial ecological environment, such as policy, legal, talent, and credit environments. Formulate financial development plans suitable for regional economic and social development, establish and improve financial laws and regulations, etc. Second, in innovatively alleviating the financing difficulties of SMEs, build regional financing platforms in line with local economic realities. From the practice of six platforms in Luqiao district, building a sound regional enterprise financing platform provides good financing channels for local SMEs, and is also conducive to curbing financing risks and building an excellent regional ecological environment. Thirdly, as the leader and participant of regional financial ecological environment development, the local government focuses on strengthening the credit environment, and cooperates with credit departments to establish a regional credit system. Establish an information exchange and sharing platform, build a government joint credit reporting system database and a credit service database, build a government joint regulation system and an Internet credit information release system, and develop government supervision services and market-oriented services.

References

William D. Bradford & Chao Chen. Creating Government Ffinancing Programs for Small and Medium-sized Enterprises in China: Theory and Practice [J], *China & World Economy*, 2004, 145–153.

Ottati, G.D. Social Concentration and Local Development: the Case of Industrial Districts [J]. *European Planning Studies*, 2002, 10,(4): 613–673.

Ruan Jianqin & Zhang Xiaobo. Finance and Cluster-based Industrial Development in China [J]. *Economic Development and Cultural Change*, 2009, 58,(1).

Ang, J. Small Business Uniqueness and the Theory of Financial Management [J], *Journal of Small Business Finance*, 1991,(1): 1–13.

Luo Zhengying. SME Cluster Credit Financing: Advantages, Conditions and Countermeasures [J]. *Finance and Trade Economics*, 2010(2): 31–36.

Li Zhong, Liu Weibo. Countermeasures and Ideas for Financing Difficulties of SMEs—Based on the Perspective of Private Financing System Construction [J]. *Finance and Finance*, 2012(3): 16–20.

Xing Lecheng, Liang Yonggui. Difficulties and Solutions of Financing for Small and Medium-sized Enterprises [J]. *Journal of Jinan University (Social Science Edition)*, 2013(2): 1–7.

Zhang Li. Analysis on the Lack of Financing System and Countermeasures for SMEs in China [J]. *Statistics and Management*, 2012(1): 60–61.

Wang Xiaolu. Construction of Direct Financing System for Small and Medium-sized Enterprises in China [J]. *Modern Business*, 2011(24): 206–207.
Zhang Junjie. Institutional Factors Causing Financing Difficulties of SMEs and Corresponding Countermeasures [J]. *Management*, 2012(17): 185.
Zhu Weiwei. Interpretation of the Financing Bottleneck of SMEs in Zhejiang from the Perspective of Financial Services [J]. *Zhejiang Finance*, 2012(4): 77–79.
Yin Qiyue. Research on Financing Difficulties of SMEs [D]. Southwest University of Finance and Economics, 2012.
Miao Bin. Research on the Construction of Financing Credit Reporting Service Platform for SMEs [J]. *Credit Reporting*, 2012(3): 22–24.
Project Team of Zibo Central Sub-branch of the People's Bank of China. Innovative Modes of Direct Financing for Small and Medium-sized Enterprises: the Case of Zibo Qilu Equity Custody Center [J]. *Financial Development Research*, 2012(6): 33–36.
Wei Hong. Research on Direct Financing of SMEs [J]. *Property Rights Guide*, 2011(3): 46–48.
Cao Lianjuan. Institutional Analysis and Policy Suggestions on Financing Difficulties of SMEs [J]. *Wuhan Finance*, 2012(1): 66–67.
Chen Xiaoling, Zhou Baosheng. Accelerating the Development of Small and Medium-sized Financial Institutions and Expanding the Financing of Small and Medium-sized Enterprises [J]. *Modern Management Science*, 2005(8): 105–106.
Chen Ying. Solving the Financing Problems of Small and Medium-sized Enterprises from the Perspective of System and Technology—Taking X Province as An Example [J]. *Management Engineer*, 2013(3): 26–29.
Dai Lixia. Analysis on the Role of Small and Medium-sized Banks in Financing of Small and Medium-sized Enterprises [D]. Zhejiang Industrial and Commercial University, 2012.
Gao Minghua. On the Development of Small and Medium-sized Financial Institutions and the Financing of Small and Medium-sized Enterprises [J]. *Financial Theory and Practice*, 2008(4): 57–60.
Lin Yifu. Four Paths to Solving the Financing Difficulties of SMEs [J]. *Contemporary Economy*, 2006(6): 1.
Lin Yifu. Financial System, Credit and SME Financing [J]. *Zhejiang Social Sciences*, 2001(6): 9–11.
Lin Yifu, Li Yongjun. What Is the Fundamental Way out for SME Financing [J]. *Science and Technology Entrepreneurship*, 2003(3): 20.
Gu Haifeng. Research on Institutional Financial Innovation and the Development of China's SME Financing Guarantee System [J]. *Southern Finance*, 2012(3): 18–22.
Nie Congcong. Research on Credit Relationship between Small and Medium-sized Enterprises and Small and Medium-sized Financial Institutions [D]. Party School of Shanghai Municipal Committee of the Communist Party of China, 2011.

Peng Jiangang, Li Jinjie, Zhou Hongwei. Financial Needs of Small and Medium-sized Enterprises and Business Positioning of Small and Medium-sized Financial Institutions [J]. *Journal of Guangzhou University (Social Science Edition)*, 2005(1): 53–58.

Sheng Tao. On the Sustainability of the Development of the Credit Center for Small and Medium-sized Enterprises of State-owned Commercial Banks—Analysis Based on the Advantages of Small and Medium-sized Financial Institutions and State-owned Commercial Banks in the Credit Market for Small and Medium-sized Enterprises [J]. *Economic Outlook around the Bohai Sea*, 2012(6): 18–20.

Suo Hong. Countermeasure Analysis Based on the Development Status of China's SME Financing System [J]. *China Business*, 2012(8):127–128.

CHAPTER 9

Luqiao's Innovative Approach to Cross-strait Cooperation on Micro and Small Finance

In 2013, Luqiao district became a pilot area for micro and small financial innovation cooperation across the Taiwan Strait in Zhejiang Province. Taking the opportunity of the Cross-strait Micro and Small Finance Development Forum, the Luqiao district government worked with typical micro and small finance research institutions in the Chinese mainland and Taiwan, promoted the cooperation and exchange of financial services between micro and small enterprises across the Strait, studied and promoted the mutual establishment of banking financial institutions across the Strait, initiated investment and business cooperation, and timely promoted Luqiao enterprises to enter the Taiwan capital market. It introduced the best practices of Taiwan's micro and small financial services in the innovative development of Luqiao micro and small financial services. In addition, by building a micro and small finance cluster in Luqiao district, the government encourages local micro and small finance to cooperate with each other, and achieve cross-regional services based on Luqiao to make micro and small finance bigger and stronger.

9.1 Innovation Models of Micro and Small Financial Cooperation between Luqiao and Taiwan

Both sides share the same cultural background, and the experience of financial development that fits Chinese culture in Taiwan is more relevant to the financial industry of the Chinese mainland. Specifically, the

W. Xiao et al., *Microfinance and China's Regional Development*, https://doi.org/10.1007/978-981-99-1960-4_9

cross-strait banking industry can conduct micro and small financial cooperation from three aspects: technical cooperation, business cooperation and equity cooperation.

Technical Cooperation, Leading the Direction of Innovation for Trade Financing in the Chinese Mainland

With a high degree of market-oriented development, Taiwan's banking industry has rich experience in risk innovation, and small business financial services, among others. It has established credit rating models that conform to the realities of micro and small enterprises. Micro and small enterprises can access diversified financing services from banks, such as working revolving financing, trade financing and guarantee business, according to their needs. Taiwan's trade financing business is highly developed. Trade finance represents the financial instruments and products that are used by companies to facilitate international trade and commerce, including financing for inventory, payables, receivables and other assets in transactions. Banks not only use property as collateral, but also accept loans from enterprises using quasi-assets such as accounts receivable, order contract or cash flows. As the global market competition shifts from the sellers' market to the buyers', credit sales are becoming the main way of trade settlement. SMEs face more serious financing difficulties because they are forced to change the way payment is made. In order to adapt to the changes in settlement, trade financing such as factoring has become the main financing approach. Customers, especially micro and small enterprise customers, will continue to increase their demand for financing receivables such as collection, cash on delivery, and credit sales. The Chinese mainland banking industry should seize this opportunity to strengthen technical cooperation with Taiwan's banking industry, innovate in financial products, optimize processes, increase service channels, and steer the direction of technological innovation in trade financing.

At present, banks in the mainland still mostly adopt traditional ways of trade finance business, with limited emerging businesses such as factoring and forfaiting. Taiwan has greater development experience in small business financing, factoring, supply chain financing, etc. Different from western practices, factoring or supply chain financing in the Chinese mainland and Taiwan are dominated by banks. Taiwan's factoring business is quite developed, and many of the top banks in the factoring business are small and medium-sized private commercial banks. In the mainland, many banks doing factoring business aim for quick success and instant benefits without adequate preparation, especially small and medium-sized city commercial banks. In 2012, several large bad debt factoring cases occurred, with Shanghai and Zhejiang being the most intensive.

Syndicated Business Cooperation, Reducing Loan Risks of Small and Medium-sized Banks across the Strait

A syndicated loan is financing offered by a group of lenders—called a syndicate—who work together to provide funds for a borrower at an agreed time and proportion based on the same loan conditions. Members of the syndicated loan independently determine their own credit granting in accordance with the principle of information sharing, independent approval, independent decision-making and risk bearing. Syndicated loans are meant for mostly large and medium-sized enterprises and enterprise groups with huge capital needs. Compared with local SMEs, Taiwan-funded SMEs in the mainland and mainland-funded SMEs in Taiwan will bring more serious credit problems to the banking industry on both sides of the Taiwan Strait. For commercial banks, their credit risks are even much higher than those of local SMEs. In this case, a syndicated loan is the best option to reduce bank credit risks. Small and medium-sized commercial banks on both sides of the Strait can form a syndicate to jointly extend credit to Taiwan-funded SMEs in the mainland and mainland-invested SMEs in Taiwan. Through peer collaboration, they can adjust and optimize the credit structure, and prevent and mitigate risks.

Banks have a good knowledge of local enterprises. With closeness and familiarity of both parties, they can better address information asymmetry. However, once an enterprise invests abroad, the bank will have difficulty in making credit investigation, unless the bank sends staff to check on the business operation; or set up an office; or establish a business base through branches, subsidiaries or equity participation, otherwise it is difficult to solve credit problems. Taiwan-funded small and medium-sized commercial banks are often unable to compete with large commercial banks in providing financing services for Taiwan-funded enterprises in the mainland because they are not eligible to start businesses in the mainland. Like Taiwan-funded small and medium-sized commercial banks, small and medium-sized commercial banks in the mainland are unable to provide financing services for their customers who invest in micro and small businesses in Taiwan. Investment from the mainland in micro and small enterprises in Taiwan also faces financing difficulties. Small and medium-sized commercial banks in Taiwan and the mainland form a syndicate to jointly extend credit to micro and small enterprises, which can not only reduce banks' credit risks, and solve the financing difficulties of SMEs, but also enhance the competitiveness of small and medium-sized commercial banks in both sides. In particular, small and medium-sized banks in Zhejiang, private in nature, provide a good institutional basis for cooperation with Taiwan-funded small and medium-sized commercial banks. Therefore, Zhejiang and Taiwan shall focus on developing business cooperation between small and medium-sized private banks. Small and medium-sized commercial banks in Zhejiang and Taiwan first serve Taiwan-funded SMEs in the Yangtze River Delta, especially those that are themselves clients of Taiwan-funded small and medium-sized commercial banks and have not been financially served in the supply chain. After a good cooperation mechanism takes shape, small and medium-sized banks in Zhejiang and Taiwan can expand their service targets to Taiwan-funded SMEs in other regions of the mainland. Small and medium-sized commercial banks in Zhejiang and Taiwan will take the lead to attract the banks in the places where Taiwan-funded SMEs are located to form a syndicate, and the banks in the places where the investment is located act as the agencies.

Equity Cooperation, Promoting Taiwan-Funded Banks to Invest in Banks in the Chinese Mainland

Vastly different interest rates for the deposits and loans of banks across the Taiwan Strait have provided impetus for Taiwan-funded banks to enter the mainland. Buying and holding shares of mainland banks has become an important choice for Taiwan-funded banks to enter the mainland financial market. Taiwan's Fubon Financial Holding acquired 19.99% of the equity of Xiamen Commercial Bank through its Hong Kong subsidiary in 2008, making it the first case for Taiwan financial institutions to invest in mainland commercial banks via a third place. In 2012, Taipei Fubon Bank and Fubon Financial Holding acquired 80% of the equity of Huayi Bank, becoming the first case of Taiwan's acquisition of mainland banks. The upper limit for the mainland to allow Taiwan banks to participate in shares is 20%, the same as that for foreign capital. In April 2013, Taiwan raised the upper limit for mainland banks to invest in Taiwan, with a single mainland bank investing in Taiwan banks holding up to 20% of shares, and planned to cancel the OECD conditions for mainland banks to set up branches in Taiwan and participate in investment as soon as possible.

The CBRC clearly points out that the bounden duty of city commercial banks is to serve SMEs. They should leverage their strengths in support of the development of SMEs in line with national industrial policies and of promising prospects. City commercial banks are more suitable for providing financing services for micro and small enterprises, because their loan approval procedures are often simpler than those of large banks regardless of their size; moreover, the information on micro and small enterprises is mostly soft. When making moral assessment of micro and small entrepreneurs, city commercial banks have greater advantages than large banks as they know people and the city better. The best choice for Taiwan-funded banks, especially small and medium-sized commercial banks, to invest in the mainland market should be city commercial banks, because most of the 100-plus city commercial banks in the mainland are established in accordance with the principle of shareholding system, which has the possibility and equity framework for foreign investment.

At this stage, Luqiao should leverage the building of cross-strait micro and small finance cooperation and innovation experimental zone on the basis of Cross-strait Micro and Small Finance Development Forum at this stage, and strengthen cooperation with micro and small finance in Taiwan at greater depth and scope. Specifically, cooperation can be expanded from the following five aspects:

First, increase efforts to promote exchanges and cooperation on micro and small financial services across the Strait, and try to draw on best practices of micro and small financial development in Taiwan. Continue to hold the Cross-strait Micro and Small Finance Cooperation Forum, diversify forms and content of the forum, and build the forum into a cultural brand of micro and small finance in Luqiao. At the same time, organize high-level exchanges between the financial communities across the strait, especially micro and small finance or city commercial banks, to open up a bridge for talent exchanges. Draw on experience of Luqiao Rural Cooperative Bank in bringing in Taiwan's micro and small finance, encourage the banks in Luqiao to introduce advanced concepts, high-end talents and core technologies of micro and small finance of Taiwan, and enhance the core competitiveness of micro and small finance in Luqiao. Taking into account the combination of bringing in and going out, the government regularly sends local banking staff, sales talents and other practitioners to Taiwan for training and visits, and invite Taiwan financial executives, graduate students and other professionals to visit the three local corporate banks in Luqiao for talent exchanges.

Second, find a feasible path for banking institutions to mutually establish offices across the strait. With the development of the three banks in the Luqiao area, the demand for capital by the three banks is increasing. Bringing in strategic investors can improve banks' capital structure and governance structure. Therefore, this will help improve the overall development and competitive edge. We can explore the possibility of cross-strait banks mutually setting up offices when necessary. On the one hand, the three banks in Luqiao are encouraged to open up branches in Taiwan, so as to expand their business presence, strengthen cooperation and exchanges between the two sides, and also learn good experience from Taiwan. On the other hand, the government works to make banking institutions in Taiwan set up franchisers and other branches for micro and small enterprise services in Luqiao. On this basis, cross-strait cooperation should constantly reinvent the existing financial model, expand cooperation between branches and agencies of the cross-strait banking industry, and start with non-credit businesses such as remittance, letter of credit notice, document collection, etc.

Third, promote the interaction and cooperation between non-banking financial institutions (intermediaries) across the strait. Support Taiwan-funded institutions to set up wholly-owned or joint-venture intermediaries, including accountants, lawyers and asset appraisal firms, etc. Promote cooperation with Taiwan's commercial credit agencies, encourage Taiwan's commercial credit agencies to set up branches in Luqiao, give full play to their credit management experience, produce technology spillover effects, and provide consultation to local commercial banks, government departments, enterprises, and other credit intermediaries. At the same time, encourage and support Taiwan's financial institutions to set up or join joint ventures with various financial institutions, such as small loan companies in Luqiao. Given that Taiwan is similar to Luqiao in terms of development experience, and private capital in Taiwan is more easily accessible, Taiwan investment companies can be encouraged to set up micro loan companies in Luqiao, so as to draw on best practices in the management and operation of micro loan companies.

Fourth, establish a financing guarantee system and a financing guiding system for micro and small enterprises. First, participate in the development of the credit guarantee fund for micro and small enterprises, provide guarantee for loans by micro and small enterprises, and alleviate their financing difficulties. Learn from the credit fund model of SMEs in Taiwan, bring together local financial institutions, private enterprises and social capital to jointly invest for the establishment of a credit guarantee fund for micro and small enterprises in Luqiao, and the fund is run by the government, with a focus on public welfare and non-profit. The fund works with banks to establish a risks-sharing mechanism to help micro and small enterprises access financing from financial institutions by providing credit guarantee for micro and small enterprises, regardless of insufficient collateral when SMEs apply for financing. At the same time, learn from the model of the Taiwan SMEs Joint Guiding Foundation, establish a financing guiding center for micro and small enterprises in Luqiao to provide comprehensive and targeted direction for talents of micro and small enterprises, and strengthen the micro and small enterprises management system, thus making financing for micro and small enterprises more accessible.

Fifth, steer Luqiao enterprises to enter Taiwan's capital market. Learn from their transfer and docking mechanisms with the main board market established within the three trading platforms of OTC listing, emerging markets and property rights in Taiwan, timely bring in Taiwan's industrial forces to cooperate with Zhejiang Equity Trading Center in its operation and platform, and set up equities trading platforms at Luqiao to make possible transfer of equity or property rights, mortgage and other business for SMEs, improve equity or property rights financing channels for SMEs, and build a multi-level capital market. At the same time, strengthen cooperation and exchanges with the Taiwan OTC Trading Center, and help high-quality Luqiao enterprises enter Taiwan's capital market and become OTC listed in Taiwan.

9.2 Typical Cases of Innovative Cooperation on Micro and Small Finance between Luqiao and Taiwan

Micro Loan Technology of Rural Cooperative Banks

In June 2013, Luqiao Rural Cooperative Bank established a micro credit center in cooperation with Small and Medium-sized Auxiliary Financing Software (Shanghai) Co., Ltd., a subsidiary of Taiwan Small and Medium Financial Flow Co., Ltd. According to the *Micro and Small Loan Financing*

Advisory Service Contract that they signed, the bank borrowed the company's practices such as score card and post-loan early warning system, and developed micro-loan products for Luqiao Rural Cooperative Bank for various specialized markets (such as Fanglin second-hand car market, Luqiao hardware city, Luqiao electronic market) and the emerging e-commerce industry in Luqiao, and engaged in recruitment and training of personnel.

As a local financial institution, Luqiao Rural Cooperative Bank has directed loans at local small, medium-sized and micro businesses that it is familiar with. Such loans are convenient for small, micro and individual businesses, as they are issued in the quickest possible way, thus contributing to local economic development. Credit officers in the region can obtain more comprehensive information by relying on local credit. However, as urbanization gathers pace thanks to rapid economic development, a large number of rural population has moved to cities and towns, and that means they live in cities but are registered in rural areas. As a result, collecting a person's credit information by asking other people that are familiar with him\her is no longer viable in cities. At the same time, micro and small enterprises have increasingly prominent problems such as poor financial information disclosure, which makes information asymmetry between enterprises and banks increasingly obvious. Therefore, the traditional credit model is increasingly challenged, forcing Luqiao Rural Cooperative Bank to use Taiwan's micro loan technology. Different from the traditional one, the small loan model introduces micro credit products into the consumer market to understand the capital flow and business model of enterprises, and build a retail business service platform. At the same time, products are designed for different customer groups and industries, and service terminals are set up to maintain the financial needs of loan customers. Especially in product design, marketing survey, risks review and cost control and other links, the small loan model shows vitality.

In order to adapt to the new way of small loans issuance, Luqiao Rural Cooperative Bank worked on building a team with knowledge, creativity, capability and resilience. People from Small and Medium-sized Auxiliary Financing Software Company did the recruitment for the micro credit center, and provided them with training programs. First, internal competition. The bank selected outstanding young people to serve as the manager of the micro and small loan center and director of the business department. Second, recruitment from the society. Taiwan's personality testing tools were adopted, combined with test and interview results, to select good candidates. With the recruitment completed, the person in charge would lead the team to make detailed training plans, with a focus on practical training, so that this team could quickly take up their roles and find customers in unfamiliar areas and markets without foundation. In terms of business operation, the micro loan center adopted a system jointly developed by the provincial credit cooperatives and the Taiwan company as the application system, then introduced the loan review committee consisting of a Taiwan resident consultant, a person in charge of the micro loan center and 3 team leaders, and implemented the one vote veto system. Since September 2013, the micro-loan center has arranged visits to more than 6000 customers and initially reached initial agreement with more than 3300 customers. Among them, 247 households were granted loans, amounting to 64.36 million yuan, including 140 credit loans of 17.815 million yuan, 97 guaranteed loans of 27.12 million yuan, and 37 mortgages of 19.43 million yuan.

The establishment of the micro credit center is an adjustment of the system made by Luqiao Rural Cooperative Bank to meet the needs of the market and customers, a manifestation of the bank's efforts to expand the presence of its financial services, and an innovative attempt to provide easier access to the most basic financial services. In the future, Luqiao Rural Cooperative Bank will optimize and upgrade the micro loan system where necessary in line with local realities. Thanks to a sound credit environment in Taiwan, customer information can be collected through computers, but Luqiao area does not have such a credit environment. So, the rural credit cooperative bank reduced the amount of customer information that needed to be collected from the original six categories of basic information, family information, financial information, business information, asset information, and others to only three categories of basic information, financial information and asset information, and simplify the customer information, financial information and non-quantitative information. The amount of information collected fell from more than 300 to 180, so as to improve loan efficiency.

Cross-strait Micro and Small Finance Development Forum

On November 29, 2013, the Cross-strait Micro and Small Finance Development Forum was held in Luqiao of Taizhou. At the same time, Luqiao has become a pilot area for micro and small financial innovation and cooperation across the Taiwan Strait. With fierce competition in the banking industry in Taizhou, major financial institutions have turned their attention to SMEs. Taiwan's financial institutions are experienced in serving SMEs, which provides much food for thought for those in the mainland. According to the requirements for Taiwan-funded banks that want to set up branches and offices in the mainland, most small and medium-sized private commercial banks with a small asset size are not conditioned to set up branches or offices in the mainland. But they are unwilling to give up on the mainland market, making business cooperation with small and medium-sized commercial banks in the mainland an inevitable choice. Luqiao has established a micro and small financial service pilot zone on both sides of the strait, which is bound to help Luqiao further develop micro and small finance and serve the financing of SMEs. Specifically, since Taizhou Bank and Tailong Bank are similar to small and medium-sized banks of Taiwan, they mainly target micro and small enterprises, and Luqiao has long conducted economic and exchanges trade with Taiwan, so Taizhou Bank and Tailong Bank has the first mover advantage in their cooperation with Bank of Taiwan on people, business and capital.

First, increase mutual visits of talents. Banks in Taiwan are mainly small and medium-sized and the banking industry is in full competition. Compared with Taizhou Bank and Tailong Bank in Luqiao, banks of Taiwan have better management. So Taizhou Bank and Tailong Bank can learn from their experience through talent exchanges and other ways to improve their own management, in an effort to boost bank development through talents. To be specific, talent exchanges can be done in the following three ways: first, Taizhou Bank and Tailong Bank can invite business personnel of Taiwan's banks to visit Luqiao. Through communication with them, the government can fully understand how their financial services are provided. Furthermore, some staff of Taiwan banks can be invited to temporarily work for Taizhou Bank and Tailong Bank to conduct business training for employees, so as to improve their overall quality and business efficiency. Second, Taizhou Bank and Tailong Bank can send staff to Taiwan so that they can feel the working environment, learn how people manage the assigned tasks, and have a more comprehensive understanding of how to deal with micro and small financial businesses. Also, Taizhou Bank and Tailong Bank can send employees to Taiwan for short-term internships, with a view to improving their professionalism. Third, Taizhou Bank and Tailong Bank can jointly establish a training camp for talents. On the one hand, they can invite famous bankers in Taiwan to train them; and on the other hand, they can arrange staff to visit Taiwan to learn Taiwan's banking business.

Second, strengthen business exchanges. Taizhou Bank and Tailong Bank have always worked on becoming partners for micro and small enterprises, with micro and small enterprises and individual merchants as the main clients. For micro and small Taiwan enterprises investing in the mainland and the other way around, financing difficulties often arise due to various restrictions. Therefore, Taizhou Bank and Tailong Bank can cooperate with Taiwan's banks to ease their financing difficulties across the Taiwan straits. These enterprises tend to gather in investment parks, so banks can make full use of industrial clusters in parks, carry out micro and small financial products through financial cooperation, and facilitate the financing of micro and small enterprises on both sides of the strait. Specifically, Taizhou Bank and Tailong Bank can seek partners in Taiwan's banking industry, establish strategic alliances, and set up cooperative funds to solve the financing problems. For micro and small Taiwan enterprises investing in Taizhou, Bank of Taiwan can entrust Taizhou Bank and Tailong Bank to conduct business and provide financial support. For mainland enterprises investing in Taiwan, Tailong bank and Taizhou Bank can entrust their cooperative banks in Taiwan to provide them with financing credit. However, for the risks bearing, banks across the strait can set up a risk compensation fund based on the financing proportion of micro and small enterprises to share risks. Through business cooperation, the cross-strait banking industry can not only solve capital shortage of investment enterprises, but also expand the scope of business to achieve interoperability and mutually beneficial cooperation of the cross-strait banking industry.

Third, strengthen financial interaction. Due to fierce competition in Taiwan's banking industry, banks seek to expand their business presence outside Taiwan, and investing in the mainland is a must. However, due to policy restrictions and others, Taiwan's banks meet headwinds in investment in the mainland. However, these problems can be avoided through capital interaction. Taizhou Bank and Tailong Bank are opening branches in remote areas in order to build a community bank. Banks in Taiwan are the pioneer of community bank, which serves micro and small enterprises. Therefore, it is necessary for Taizhou Bank and Tailong Bank to carry out micro and small financial cooperation with banks of Taiwan. On the one hand, banks of Taiwan investing in Taizhou Bank and Tailong Bank can expand their business scope, increase profits and avoid fierce competition in Taiwan; on the other hand, Taizhou Bank and Tailong Bank attract funds from Taiwan's banks, which is conducive to their own growth and improvement of financial structure. It also benefits banks of Taiwan as they improved their own management. Therefore, Taizhou Bank and Tailong Bank have carried out micro and small financial cooperation with banks of Taiwan by attracting capital from Taiwan, which is of strategic significance to cross-strait banking cooperation.

Micro and small finance of Taiwan is developing well. Due to fierce market competition, Taiwan's banks have tilted their services to SMEs, so Taiwan's experience is worth learning for the mainland. With closer cross-strait economic cooperation and trade, it is of great significance to strengthen micro and small financial cooperation. Luqiao has established a cross-strait micro and small financial cooperation and innovation pilot zone, which not only provides a good platform for the local government, but also provides opportunities for other regions to carry out cooperation with Taiwan. The mainland should take this opportunity to learn from the advanced system of SMEs financing explored by banks and other financial institutions in Taiwan, and pilot and implement it locally according to the local situation.

9.3 Prospects of Cross-strait Micro and Small Financial Cooperation and Innovation Pilot Zone

Tasks

The tasks of Luqiao Micro and Small Finance Cooperation and Innovation Pilot Zone include building five innovation systems and four platform construction.

(1) Adopt an innovative multi-level financial service system for micro and small enterprises. Through cooperation with micro and small financial institutions in Taiwan, the government can learn from Taiwan's good practices in developing micro and small finance, especially in the service system of micro and small enterprises. For example, a good guarantee system for micro and small enterprises provides a strong guarantee for loans taken out by micro and small enterprises and address information asymmetry between banks and enterprises.

(2) Adopt an innovative support system of private city commercial banks. With the development of private economy, the three banks in Luqiao have played an important role in relieving the financing difficulties of micro and small enterprises in Luqiao. Moreover, the proportion of

private capital in the three major banks has occupied a vast majority. How to further develop such banks and innovate in their products and services is a priority.

(3) Adopt a system that encourages innovation on micro and small financial products and services. Products of micro and small finance are diverse under different names. However, financial products and systems launched by major banks are homogeneous. How to launch truly innovative banking products is an urgent need for major banks.

(4) Adopt a new system of multi-channel financing for micro and small enterprises. The vast majority of such financing comes from bank loans, and more and more loans are obtained from private financial institutions. However, the existing financial system has not really lowered the threshold for direct financing. How to innovate in the existing financial model and realize the direct financing of micro and small enterprises in a real sense is very important for providing accessible loans.

(5) Adopt an innovative risk-sharing system for micro and small enterprises. The main problem of indirect financing of micro and small enterprises is that the credit risk is too high, and information asymmetry between banks and enterprises is serious. How to learn from Taiwan's experience and establish a corresponding credit guarantee system is crucial for the government of Luqiao. Moreover, the risk-sharing system can also rely on innovative platforms such as industrial clusters.

(6) Build a credit information sharing and services platform. Information sharing is important for SMEs and small and medium-sized banks. How to establish a platform to enable information exchanges between banks and enterprises, so that financing demand and supply can be truly matched. Moreover, the establishment of a large sample of SMEs credit information database is also an important way to reduce the information asymmetry between banks and enterprises.

(7) Build a policy support platform for micro and small financial services. At this stage, the policy support for micro and small enterprises in Luqiao keeps improving, but these policies are excessively focused on the guarantee system, which cannot fundamentally address the financing difficulties of micro and small enterprises. The government can learn from Taiwan's experience and further delegate certain policy-making power to ease the problem from the source.

(8) Build a micro and small financial development cooperation and exchange platform. Strengthen the introduction and cultivation of financial talents. Incentives for attracting high-end financial talents should be

introduced, like increasing investment in financial vocational training and strengthening cross-strait micro and small financial cooperation and exchanges. The Cross-strait Micro and Small Finance Development Forum will be held regularly. Bring home Taiwan's practice of financial education and training institutions. Bring in Taiwan's financial intermediaries, and small loans, credit and risk prevention technologies.

(9) Build a platform for local financial ecological development. Based on the existing micro and small finance culture of Luqiao, efforts shall be made to strengthen policy support, step up benign cooperation with Taiwan, and create a local culture for the development of micro and small finance in Luqiao.

Missions

The development of micro and small finance in Luqiao has the following four missions:

First, be a front-runner in breaking through obstacles and problems. Through pilot projects, efforts shall be made to increase policy support, break through existing obstacles, and ease the financing difficulties of SMEs. At the same time, seize the opportunity of a new round of streamlining administration and delegating power, combine the development characteristics of local micro and small finance, undertake the government's streamlining administration and delegating power, and promote the market-oriented financial development by simplifying administrative approval.

Second, put in place a market-based mechanism. Based on the market, make full use of the market-oriented reform of interest rates, and give full play to the role of the market in leading the development of micro and small finance. Through cooperation and exchanges with Taiwan, the government will improve the market-oriented development of micro and small finance in Luqiao.

Third, pursue sustainable development in a scientific, orderly fashion. For high-risk financial activities conducted by micro and small financial institutions and private capital utilization and other high-risk financial activities in Luqiao, unified planning, layout and control are required. We can't eliminate them all because of the high risks, nor should we set up financial institutions blindly because of the existing large amount of private capital. It is necessary to plan the layout reasonably, but it is also not appropriate to regulate them too strictly, which would otherwise undermine market self-regulation.

Fourth, lead in demonstrating cross-strait cooperation and win-win sharing. Through cooperation and exchanges with Taiwan's micro and small finance, and drawing on Taiwan's cash experience, so as to promote the in-depth cooperation in cross-strait economic cooperation and trade. The development of micro and small finance in Taiwan has a long history and a large scale, and Luqiao experiences are worth learning.

9.4 Summary

Micro and small enterprises are important while financial support is lackluster. It is an important subject to addressing such problems. Taiwan's micro and small finance is developing in good momentum. Due to fierce market competition, Taiwan's banks have tilted their services to SMEs, so Taiwan's experience is worth learning from for the mainland. Cooperation on micro and small finance between Taizhou, Wenzhou and other places in Zhejiang province and Taiwan has already been there, especially Taizhou, which has the most developed micro and small finance in China. The cross-strait micro and small finance cooperation and innovation pilot zone established in Luqiao not only provided a good platform for local banks, but also for other regions in terms of cooperation with Taiwan.

Taiwan has been having better financial management than the mainland for many years. The two sides should make use of the opportunity of financial reform in Wenzhou for cooperation and win-win results, promote Taiwan's financial industry to set up branches in Wenzhou and bring with them capital and management experience. Promote financing innovation cooperation between enterprises, especially micro and small financial innovation cooperation, strengthen the seamless connection between Taiwan-funded financial institutions and regional financial markets in the mainland, so as to help realize deep financial cooperation between the two. First of all, financial institutions of Taiwan have rich experience in the fields of credit card, SMEs financing, corporate governance and consumer finance, which means useful reference for financial development in the mainland. In particular, a deepening financial reform in Wenzhou has expanded the scope for cooperation. Taiwan's financing in trade is especially developed, and it has rich experience in risks innovation, financial services for small enterprises, etc., and has established credit rating models that conform to the characteristics of micro and small enterprises. Clients, especially micro and small enterprises, continue to increase their demand for financing receivables, such as collection, cash on delivery, and credit sales. The mainland banking industry should seize this opportunity to strengthen technical cooperation with Taiwan's banking industry, by developing innovative financial products, optimizing processes, increasing service channels, and directing the technological innovation of financing in trade. Second, vastly different interest rates for deposits and loans of banks across the Taiwan Strait have provided impetus for Taiwan-funded banks to enter the mainland. City commercial banks are more suitable for providing financing services for micro and small enterprises, because their loan approval procedures are often simpler than those of large banks regardless of their size; moreover, information on micro and small enterprises is mostly soft. When making moral assessment of micro and small entrepreneurs, city commercial banks have greater advantages than large banks as they know people and the city better.

The mainland should take this opportunity to adopt an advanced system of the SMEs financing explored by banks and other financial institutions in Taiwan, and pilot and implement it according to local situations. First, step up financial cooperation for the sound development of cross-strait economic relations. Combined with the new transformation of the symbiotic mechanism following the financial crisis, the cooperation mode of the cross-strait banking industry is selected to help promote the normalization of cross-strait financial relations and ultimately the comprehensive and healthy development of cross-strait economic relations. Second, learn from the experience of Taiwan's micro and small finance to promote the efficiency of the mainland's banking industry. At present, the banking industry of the mainland is in a critical period of transformation and development. In terms of financial services for micro and small enterprises, Taiwan has unique practices, mature models and distinct characteristics. The government can learn from good practices of financial services for SMEs in Taiwan, improve the financial service system and financial services for micro and small enterprises, and promote better development of the banking industry. Third, strengthen micro and small financial cooperation between banks across the strait to ease the financing difficulties of micro and small enterprises. Stronger cross-strait banking cooperation in financing micro and small enterprises not only conforms to needs of both sides of the strait to jointly seek solutions to difficult problems, but also gives full play to the strength of Taiwan's financial industry in serving the financing of micro and small enterprises, and promotes the rapid development of innovative mainland banks to serve SMEs and drive deeper economic reform.

References

Stiglitz, J.E. & Weiss, A. Credit Rationing in Markets with Imperfect Information [J]. *American Economy Review*, 1981 (3): 393–410.

Xing Lecheng, Liang Yongxian. Difficulties and Solutions of Financing for Small and Medium-sized Enterprises [J]. *Journal of Jinan University (Social Science Edition)*, 2013 (2): 1–7.

Liu Bin. A Theoretical Review of Financing Research of Micro and Small Enterprises [J]. *Nankai Economic Research*, 2005 (1): 109–112.

Guo Na. Government? Market? Who Is More Effective—Research on the Effectiveness of the Mechanism for Solving the Financing Difficulties of Micro and Small Enterprises [J]. *Financial Research*, 2013 (3): 194–206.

Ye Yaoming, Qu Weiwei. ECFA and New Changes in Cross-strait Financial Cooperation [J]. *Shanghai Finance*, 2011 (6): 28–32.

Wang Tingting, Lu Minfeng. Research on Solving the Financing Problems of Micro and Small Enterprises Based on Mainland and Taiwan Commercial Banks [J]. *Financial Theory and Practice*, 2011 (11): 27–32.

Shan Yuli. Financing Modes, Bottlenecks and Countermeasures of Taiwan Funded Micro and Small Enterprises in the Mainland [J]. *Fujian Forum (Humanities and Social Sciences Edition)*, 2012 (11): 130–134.

Zheng Ming, Xiao Jian, Huang Guangxiao. Research on the Pilot Policy for the Development of Cross-strait Financial Cooperation under the New Situation [M]. *Xiamen University Press*, 2010.

Xiao Wen, Liu Liyun, Pan Jiadong. Discussion on Micro and Small Finance Cooperation Mode of Cross-strait Banking Industry—Case Analysis Based on Luqiao [J]. *Taiwan Studies*, 2014 (2): 16–20.

Yan Siping. Trade Credit—An Effective Financing Method for Small and Medium-sized Taiwan Funded Enterprises [J]. *Fujian Forum (Humanities and Social Sciences Edition)*, 2010: 67–69.

Wang Xiao, Zhang Jie. Bank Credit Rationing and SME Loans—A Theoretical Model of Endogenous Collateral and Enterprise Scale [J]. *Economic Research*, 2003 (7): 68–75.

Research Group of the International Department of the Shanghai Headquarters of the People's Bank of China. Financing Experience and Enlightenment of Taiwan's Micro and Small Enterprises [J]. *Shanghai Finance*, 2009 (1): 80–83.

Deng Lijuan. Possible Ways to Accelerate the Process of Cross-strait Financial Cooperation at the Present Stage [J]. *Taiwan Studies*, 2010 (1): 12–17.

Zhang Hejie, Yao Shuliang, Ye Yuan. Comparative Analysis of Cross-strait Financial Support for Micro and Small Enterprises [J]. *Taiwan Research*, 2012 (5): 11–16.

PART IV

Countermeasures

Zhejiang leads in private economy and Luqiao in micro and small finance.
—The author

CHAPTER 10

Experience and Enlightenment of Luqiao Micro and Small Finance Innovation

"Small is Beautiful". With the title of a book, the author, British economist Michael Schumacher vividly expounds such a truth: small work units and small-scale economies, with low access threshold and fast establishment speed, are like "ant soldiers" in economic development. In the international scope, many well-known multinational companies and large groups start from micro and small enterprises (MSEs) and gradually grow bigger and stronger. Data in China shows that micro, small and medium-sized enterprises have become the main driving force of China's economic development. In the current economic situation, micro and small economies are rising as a new force and gradually become significant in China's national economy. Speaking of the development of micro and small finance, Zhejiang may play as the leader nationwide, and Taizhou as the leader in Zhejiang. After decades of growth and development, Taizhou's private economy has achieved a double leap in quantity and quality from "picking up for the leftovers" in the 1980s to "more than 90% of the world" today. In Taizhou, the development of micro and small finance in Luqiao appears unique. It not only shows the general characteristics of the development of micro and small finance in Taizhou, but also shows the particular characteristics of Luqiao in some parts. In this chapter, the author will summarize the innovation experience of micro and small finance in Luqiao, obtain the "secret key" for its success, outline the main problems, explore the "source" of these problems, and finally condense these into a "unique strategy" that can be adopted for reference by other regions.

W. Xiao et al., *Microfinance and China's Regional Development*, https://doi.org/10.1007/978-981-99-1960-4_10

10.1 "Luqiao Secrets" of Innovative Development of Micro and Small Finance

Secret 1: Find the Right Market Position—Specialize in "Small Businesses"

The reason why the micro and small finance in Luqiao has become the focus nationwide is inseparable from its accurate market positioning and emphasis on long-term service. In Taizhou, three commercial banks have focused on serving MSEs for nearly 20 years, and this concept was put forward 20 years earlier than the slogan of serving MSEs proposed by the central government. At the moment when MSEs' development encountered a "breakpoint" in the capital chain, the local corporate bank in Luqiao was growing and becoming a model of service in the same industry with the strategy of serving MSEs, relying on "small business" and "small orders".

Different from the development path of state-owned banks, micro and small financial institutions in Luqiao have taken a complementary path of dislocation with state-owned banks—specializing in small orders, as well as small loans that big banks disdain to make and insist on "doing small business" to overcome various difficulties and keep moving forward. There is a vivid metaphor that in the market divided by industries, the state-owned banks and other large commercial banks focus on the "big meat", while the micro and small financial institutions in Taizhou choose "meat on the bone". It has been proven that even in such a niche market, focusing on "meat on the bone" can still achieve rapid growth, and gradually become the industry leader. Following the principle of "doing small business" without ignoring risk control, the non-performing loan rate of micro and small financial institutions is far lower than that of state-owned banks. As Wang Jun, chairman of Tailong Bank, said, "Others lend to those who wear leather shoes, while we lend exclusively to those who wear straw shoes". It fully reflects the unique and precise market position of micro and small financial institutions in Luqiao.

Secret 2: Accelerate Product Updating—Research and Develop Featured Financial Products

As is said, quietness leads to thinking, thinking leads to change, change leads to communication and communication leads to prosperity. Unremitting innovation is another magic for the success of Luqiao micro and small financial institutions. Small businesses are easy to turn around. Compared with large state-owned banks, local corporate banks have stronger market adaptability, gather enthusiasm for product development, and stronger pertinence in serving MSEs. As is known to all, financial products are the foundation of financial institutions. Therefore, Luqiao micro and small financial institutions are actively working on the research and development of featured products to create many featured high-quality financial products. These financial products have made important contributions to the local entrepreneurial environment, transformation of SMEs, and upgrading of industrial structure and sustainable development. For example, the "Chuangye Tong" loan launched by Talon Bank is dedicated to serving customers who are in lack of entrepreneurship funds or short-term liquidity at the start-up or development stage, which has activated the local entrepreneurial environment. In 2011, Tailong Bank launched the "SG Talon Easy" medium and long-term fixed asset loan product to help SMEs transform and upgrade. In addition, local corporate banks lost no time in launching financial products such as "Green Credit" and "Agricultural Credit", which not only supported local MSEs, but also injected vitality into the upgrading of local industrial structure. The R&D of financial products by micro and small financial institutions of Luqiao has also been supported and subsidized by the local government. In 2011, Taizhou Bank and the local government jointly launched a green financial loan, which is close to the pulse of the times, using economic leverage to guide environmental protection, so that enterprises can internalize pollution costs, so as to achieve management in advance, which is conducive to the long-term sustainable development of the local economy and has pioneering significance in Zhejiang province.

For the historic problem of MSEs' financing, the three urban commercial banks in Luqiao area have launched financial products with their own characteristics one after another and gradually explored methods suitable for MSEs' development. The three urban commercial banks give full play to their own strengths in innovation, among which Tailong Bank is in the forefront of financial product research and development.

Tailong Bank focuses on "combination fist" of micro and small credit. To meet the needs of financial services for the real economy and broaden the financing channels of the real economy, Tailong Bank has achieved a remarkable speed of financial innovation in loan products. In a short time, it has continuously launched a series of featured loan products, such as "credit financing", "justice financing", "fixed financing", "financing e-loan", "relay loan", "mortgage full financing", and "extension loan", which are applicable to the financial services for MSEs. Among them, it is worth mentioning that "Rong e-Loan", a featured product, has the characteristics of "one-time credit, recycling, borrowing and repaying on demand". Compared with other similar products, it is more flexible with a loan completed in a few minutes by moving your finger. While saving time, it can also minimize the inconvenience of customers' operation and simplify complexity. In addition, this financial product has also achieved the leap from the human brain to the computer chip for loan approvers, as well as from manual to automatic for loan disbursements, which is a new revolution for traditional credit.

In addition, Tailong Bank's financial product research and development focuses on entrepreneurs. In the initial stage of entrepreneurship, entrepreneurs have a large demand for capital and their assets available for mortgage are limited. In response to this situation, Tailong Bank has developed and designed the "Chuangye Tong" credit service, which is characterized by "convenience, no need for collateral, and flexible guarantee". It is suitable for early entrepreneurs facing financial difficulties to quickly deal with financing problems, thus effectively solving the difficult situation that unsecured loans are hard to acquire, which is encountered by self-employed households and small enterprises.

In the "entering villages and households" service activities of Tailong Bank, such a problem is generally found that farmers hope to expand their business volume by expanding production scale, improving technology, etc., but the shortage of capital has become the primary problem against these farmers. Therefore, for customers engaged in agricultural production activities, Tailong Bank has launched the "easy agricultural loan", a short-term and small-amount loan granted by Tailong Bank to eligible farmers for production and management. The financial support is for farmers whose production places, management places and residence are all in rural villages with demand for production and management funds. These farmers can enjoy preferential policies on interest rates and all guarantee methods approved by Tailong Bank; also, the formalities are applicable to farmers.

From the "combination" approach in financial product research and development, it is not difficult to see that Tailong Bank focuses on all potential MSEs and agricultural production customers, and launches special financial products suitable for them, with the characteristics of definite objects, easy and convenient handling, no harsh mortgage terms.

Great efforts are also made by Luqiao Rural Cooperative Bank to customize a variety of financial products according to the different characteristics of various financing entities, especially the "short, small, frequent and urgent" characteristics of MSEs, focusing on the launch of "Road Bank" brand series products, gradually making the brand well-known, so that credit support covers all aspects of enterprise production. Featured financial products such as flagship "Road Bank", small business loans, pledge loans for receivables, pledge loans for agricultural machinery, micro and small enterprise credit loans, etc., have created a path of "coexistence of flagship products and other complementary products, diversified guarantee methods, and integrated loan repayment methods", which fundamentally boosts the development and growth of partners.

Taizhou Bank also made fundamental innovation in concept. Instead of sticking to the old rules of traditional credit, it launched a special financial product—The Green Energy-saving Loan, which is specific to the actual situation of enterprises, to support enterprises' transformation and development through energy-saving reform. Originally, the knowledge of enterprises was limited to such data as balance sheet or income statement; now, Taizhou Bank has gone deep into enterprises, and explored their unique needs. In this way, Taizhou Bank has created an innovative path of "focusing on individualized financial products", which has enabled more MSEs to get support in credit.

Secret 3: Optimize Financial Services—"Go to Visit Thousands of Households and Grow Together"

As is known to all, the competition between banks lies in not only products, but also services. Therefore, the optimization of financial services has become the main foothold for micro and small financial institutions of Luqiao. At present, local corporate banks of Luqiao have basically cancelled the threshold for loans; at the same time, however, many enterprises do not need loans. Therefore, what the banks need to solve the most is how to lend out money. The service optimization of micro and small financial institutions in Luqiao releases a positive signal of serving MSEs and striving for market share.

Nowadays, individualized service is an emerging type of service industry. In Luqiao the micro and small financial institutions explored "door-to-door service". Entering villages and enterprises, and delivering services to fields and factories is a major measure taken by Luqiao Rural Cooperative Bank to optimize services and expand the market. Such services fully reflects the tenet of "customer first". In addition, Luqiao small financial institutions also consider the individualized needs of customers, give preferential interest rates, reduce unnecessary intermediate procedures, adopt a flexible guarantee policy, and thus effectively solve the problem of financial guarantee for local micro and small enterprise.

In addition to face-to-face or door-to-door service, Luqiao Rural Cooperative Bank launched the activity of "going to thousands of households, and growing together" just in the hardest period for MSEs' development. In the "Month of Financial Service for MSEs", it was made clear that the new loans would focus on micro and small enterprises with a credit line of less than 5 million yuan, used for entities with practical production and management, which won support from the majority of MSEs.

Big banks like to keep an eye on big customers, while micro and small financial institutions in Luqiao have a down-to-earth vision. They focus on the marketplaces, plant areas, communities, villages and towns to explore potential customers' needs instead of passively waiting for customers to come, so that MSEs can receive one-to-one services in the way of big banks for big customers. Therefore, unlike big banks, which tend to choose the "prime location" in the city center, the business departments of micro and small financial institutions are more "down-to-earth" in the location, and tend to settle in the suburban junction, that is, the gathering place of target customers, MSEs and farmers.

"Free Bank" is another boutique service created by micro and small financial institutions of Luqiao. Since March 20, 2012, Taizhou citizens can handle 42 services such as inter-bank remittance or ATM inter-bank withdrawal at Taizhou Bank without service charge.

Due to the particularity of the clients, the service of micro and small financial institutions of Luqiao is more considerate and ambitious than that of other large commercial banks. It is precisely because of such high-quality features, individualized customization, and low price service that the micro and small financial institutions of Luqiao have won the support from the majority of micro and small entrepreneurs, thus remain invincible in the intense market competition.

Secret 4: Developing Strategy in Different Places—Four "Persistence"

In the process of growth and expansion, local urban commercial banks will undoubtedly face the temptation and confusion of "going out", and the micro and small financial institutions in Luqiao are no exception. The success of urban commercial banks in Luqiao seems to be inseparable from the local regional particularity of Luqiao, because of the enterprise characteristics of "valuing trust" and "keeping promises" as well as the business form of small enterprises clustering. Whether such experience can be successfully replicated in other regions is doubtful in the eyes of many people. However, the facts once again proved that the successful experience in Zhejiang province and even in the Yangtze River Delta region is "one size fits all". Micro and small finance institutions of Luqiao have been established in Hangzhou, Shanghai, Suzhou and other places. After several years of cross-regional development, the business indicators of the two commercial banks, Tailong Bank and Taizhou Bank, have also been greatly improved.

The secret to the success of Luqiao's micro and small financial institutions in different places lies in four adherences: the positioning of self, the investment of human capital, the localization of personnel, and the improvement of the internal control system.

When setting up branches, micro and small financial institutions of Luqiao primarily adhere to serving MSEs, which is also the key to their success in cross-regional development. When it comes to the off-site location of branches, Tailong Bank and Taizhou Bank choose the road section where MSEs in various industries are concentrated. Also, they extend the business hours of branches to cater to enterprises.

Secondly, the micro and small financial institutions of Luqiao spare no effort to invest human capital and pay attention to close inspection within "zero distance" in the process of cross regional operation. The survey found that client managers played an important role in Tailong Bank and Taizhou Bank, and the non-local branches of the two banks, without exception, have a large number of client managers. The facts show that "soft information" with authenticity and comprehensiveness is the key of the two banks to control the rate of non-performing loans. The proportion of account managers in Tailong Bank reaches 50% of the total number. On the surface, this will increase the cost of personnel operation, but according to the fact that the account managers track more than 200 customers every month, behind each account manager is a strong customer network, which is very important for banks to know about customers' soft information. Not only will the group band effect bring more customers, but the soft information collected through this channel will be more real and comprehensive.

In addition to investment of human capital, adhering to localization of personnel is also one of the experiences of successful development of micro and small financial institutions in different places. At the time branches are set up in other places, these institutions, with no exception, choose to recruit local staff. The advantage of personnel localization is obvious, which is conducive to the branch's rapid intervention in the local market as well as adaptation to the local economic and financial environment in short time. This is similar to the strategy of many multinational companies, which, however, also brings about the problem of huge differences in corporate culture. Therefore, Ginza Finance College of Taizhou Bank and Tailong College of Tailong Bank have been set up to train the employees of branches and integrate them into the corporate culture of the Head Offices as soon as possible.

For development in different places, risk management is facing new challenges. In the face of risk control, micro and small financial institutions of Luqiao always adhere to improving the internal control system, establishing a risk control mechanism and an internal audit mechanism matching with cross regions. Internal audit is not a "formalism", but requires high frequency, high quality, and ultimately a complete and comprehensive audit report. In addition, it also emphasizes the strengthening of supervision linkage with regulatory authorities in other places.

Secret 5: "Catfish Effect" of Finance—Taking a Standardized Development Path

The rise of micro and small finance in Luqiao cannot be separated from three of them—Taizhou Bank, Tailong Bank and Luqiao Rural Cooperative Bank. The three banks were founded in the 1990s under the stimulation of the private economy development of Luqiao led by the professional market, and then continued to expand and grow. These banks have formed an effective market-oriented operation and management mode in their long-term service for small and medium-sized private enterprises, thus becoming the benchmark of local and even national micro and small financial services. It is precisely because of the stimulation of these three "financial catfish" that the environment of micro and small finance in Luqaio has been unprecedentedly prosperous. The "catfish effect" not only guides the development of Luqiao's financial industry, but also activates Luqiao's financial industry, which is transformed from decentralized to centralized, and embarks on a "regularized path of common development with the guidance of three giants, the support of local government, and the gathering of many financial institutions.

In addition, local microfinance companies have also played their "catfish effect" in reasonably guiding private capital and building a platform for private financial cooperation. In the first half of 2012, the weighted average loan interest rates of the two small loan companies—Jiuding and Yufeng—in Luqiao reached 15.64% and 13.3%, which were 2.61 and 2.22 times of the benchmark annual loan interest rates of the People's Bank of China in the same period. These small loan companies, as "catfish", have effectively ensured that interest rates of most private lending can be controlled within 4 times of the benchmark bank loan interest rate in the same period, thus have effectively reduced the interest rate of private lending, standardized the capital market, guided private capital and reduced financing costs of enterprises. Different from the Wenzhou model, this "regularized" road is standardized and efficient, taken by virtue of Luqiao itself.

Secret 6: Micro and Small Finance Cluster—Forming "Ecological Community"

Financial cluster promotes the growth of substantial economy through financial agglomeration benefits, financial diffusion effects, financial spillover effects and financial functions. Among them, financial agglomeration benefits are the additional benefits formed by financial agglomeration factors, which can affect the substantial economy through external economical benefits of scale, network benefits, innovation benefits, technological progress benefits and self-strengthening mechanism benefits; at the same time, the driving force of regional growth comes from the financial agglomeration effect within the internal growth point. Through cluster technology learning brought by the clustering of financial enterprises, knowledge spillover can be accelerated, then promote the learning of cluster technology in turn, so as to promote the clustering of financial enterprises and give full play to its financial spillover effect.

Luqiao creates a micro and small finance cluster. First, Luqiao encourages financial institutions to settle down. For the corporate headquarters of financial institutions such as banks, securities and insurance institutions approved by financial regulatory authorities and newly established, a one-time support subsidy of 5 million yuan will be given in the current year; for the newly established financial institutions with the headquarters in Taizhou, as well as village bank headquarters, a one-time support subsidy of 1 million yuan will be given that year. Second, Luqiao encourages innovation of financial products, with support to financial institutions to innovate featured financing products, financing guarantee methods and financing repayment methods, as well as M&A loans, syndicated loans, bridge loans, etc. There are awards for financial innovation every year, and the outstanding contributors will receive financial subsidies. Third, Luqiao encourages the economic development of headquarters. 1% subsidies of the district-level income formed by the annual business tax and enterprise income tax are given to financial institutions headquartered in Luqiao; 70% and 50% of the subsidies are given to the head office and middle level personnel respectively who pay the individual income tax in the current year; the branches outside the district who pay the enterprise income tax are subsidized at a rate of 5% for the portion of year-on-year growth. Fourth, Luqiao encourages the construction of an investment and financing market system. A credit guarantee fund for SMEs is established to assist enterprises in obtaining financing from financial institutions; Luqiao also supports non-banking financing of non-financial enterprises (excluding real estate), and gives a subsidy of 100,000 yuan to intermediaries that successfully issue corporate collective bonds, collective bills and other products and have raised more than 50 million yuan, listed in the provincial equity trading center and have outstanding private financing management pilot projects.

On both sides of Taizhou Shifu Avenue, there are more than 100 financial institutions and their branches, so the road is also nicknamed "Taizhou Wall Street" by local residents. In addition to the five major state-owned commercial banks, there are also ten joint-stock banks, Postal Savings Bank, Agricultural Development Bank, three private urban commercial banks, nine branches of Rural Credit Cooperative, five rural banks, two mutual fund cooperatives and other small corporate financial institutions with a wide range of locations. In particular, it is rare for three urban commercial banks to gather in the same area nationwide.

Secret 7: Appropriate Cooperation Between Government And Banks—Economic Support, Administrative Non-intervention

The successful development of micro and small finance in Luqiao is inseparable from the close support and reasonable planning of the local government. The government advocates financial institutions to follow market-oriented operation as the main body in private capital with no shareholding, which greatly promotes the local micro and small financial institutions to maintain strong independence in the decision-making process, making them less restricted. In addition, to not intervening in the internal operation and management of the institutions, the government also actively gives the institutions financial supports, which makes the cooperation between local government and banks present a benign and common prosperity. Specifically, Luqiao government explores the industrialization service system of micro and small finance, and effectively promotes the integration of micro and small finance and substantial economy. The government also promotes MSEs' development by setting up innovation incentive mechanisms and achieving direct government-bank-enterprise cooperation. "Micro and Small Financial Innovation Award" has been set up to encourage financial institutions to develop products and services, such as micro loans, green credit, letter of credit financing, science and technology finance, in response to MSEs' needs in Luqiao. The government of Luqiao has also actively established a non-governmental financing standardization center under unified supervision of the government, focusing on the formation of a win-win situation, with the voluntary registration of fund lenders, the sustainable commercial development of the non-governmental financing standardization center, and the increase of financing channels for MSEs. On this basis, the government of Luqiao has continuously strengthened financial credit risk control to create a healthy financial credit environment.

With the awareness that financing is the pillar industry of Luqiao, the government of Luqiao further has clarified the direction of support for the three local corporate banks, encouraged the transformation and development of private financial institutions, and actively promoted Taizhou Bank and Tailong Bank to implement the "going out" strategy, and carry out cross-regional operation, so as to expand broader space for development.

Secret 8: Attempts at Cross-strait Cooperation—The Introduction of Taiwan's Advanced Experience

If we are without regard of external circumstances and act blindly, we will lack communication with the outside world, and the pace of innovation may slow down. Therefore, learning from the advanced management experience in Taiwan will be conducive to the common development of micro and small finance across the Strait.

In recent years, cross-strait financial interaction has been frequent and cooperation has developed rapidly. On April 26, 2009, the Association for Cross Strait Relations (ARATS) and the Taiwan Straits Exchange Foundation (SEF) signed the Cross-strait Financial Cooperation Agreement, reaching consensus on cross-strait financial supervision and monetary management cooperation. On November 16, 2009, the two sides signed a memorandum of cooperation on banking supervision. On March 16, 2010, the two sides revised and issued the management measures for financial, securities and insurance business transactions and investment licensing, thus allowed mutual investment between financial institutions and joint stock investment, and also established a cross-strait financial interaction management mechanism. On April 25, 2011, the first meeting of Cross-strait Bank Supervision Cooperation Platform was held, in which the supervision cooperation mechanism for cross-strait banks was formally established. On July 21, 2011, the Taiwan Monetary Authority and the People's Bank of China jointly issued *the Provisions on Banks in Taiwan to Handle RMB Business*, which launched RMB business for OBU (Offshore Banking Unit) and overseas branches. On November 23, 2011, the Cross-strait Banking Supervision Cooperation Platform held the second meeting, in which the implementation of ECFA early receipt list was accelerated. On November 24, 2011, Taiwan amended and issued *the Regulations on Types and Limits of Securities Invested by Commercial Banks*, allowing banks' overseas branches and OBUs to invest and issue securities in the mainland. On January 2, 2012, BOCL's regulations on equity participation in Taiwan officially came into force. On April 25, 2012, the executive level meeting of the cross-strait bank supervision cooperation platform was held. On August 31, 2012, *the Memorandum of Cooperation on Cross-strait Currency Clearing* was issued, which established the main mechanism framework of cross-strait currency clearing. On September 18, 2012, the Shanghai branch of Bank of Taiwan was designated as the New Taiwan Dollar clearing bank in the mainland. The frequent financial interaction between the two sides provides an opportunity for micro and small financial cooperation across the Strait, and the establishment of cross-strait monetary clearing mechanism lays a solid foundation for cross-strait micro and small financial cooperation.

In 2013, the Cross-strait Micro and Small Finance Development Forum was held in Luqiao, with the theme "serving MSEs, and innovating development". At the forum, Luqiao was announced as an experimental area in Zhejiang province for micro and small finance innovation and cooperation across the strait, which launched the brand of "Taizhou mode of micro and small finance". This is a great recognition of the development of micro and small finance in Taizhou. Taking the opportunity of the Cross Strait Micro and Small Finance Development Forum, the Luqiao government explored how to promote the cooperation and communication of representative micro and small finance research institutions between mainland and Taiwan and the exchange of financial services as well as mutual establishment of banking financial institutions across the Strait, introduction of investment and business cooperation. It is also taken into consideration that Luqiao enterprises may enter into the capital market of Taiwan at appropriate time. If the successful experience of micro and small finance services in Taiwan can be effectively "localized" into the innovation process, it will play a strong role in promoting the development of micro and small finance services in Luqiao.

10.2 "Luqiao Problems" in the Innovation and Development of Micro and Small Finance

Problem 1: Common Financing Problems of MSEs—Difficult, Expensive, Disorderly and Risky

Like those in other areas, MSEs in Luqiao also encounter common problems in development, which can be summarized in four words: difficult, expensive, disorderly and dangerous.

"Difficult" refers to "difficult financing". At this stage, small micro enterprises of Luqiao are still weak in strength, poor in operating efficiency, high in debt ratio, with problems such as nonstandard corporate finance, scattered distribution, and large number, which are difficult to be favored by financial institutions, especially state-owned banks and other large commercial banks, and are thus unable to get their support in loans.

Especially in the period when the nation tightened the monetary policy, MSEs were the first to get trapped in a currency run.

"Expensive" refers to "expensive financing". It is well known that, for the sake of profit maximization, financial institutions tend to favor larger enterprises. That is to say, larger enterprises are easier to obtain loans from financial institutions; in contrast, MSEs are difficult to obtain bank loans. In this case, many MSEs have to turn to short-term funds through private lending to survive and develop. However, due to the high interest rate, the high borrowing cost will inevitably affect MSEs' survival and development in a negative way.

"Disorderly" refers to "disorderly financing". MSEs often finance in an irregular way, mainly through personal savings of entrepreneurs, loans from relatives and friends, internal fund-raising of enterprise employees, even illegal fund-raising. In this way, personal funds flow into the usurious loan market and the funds of some listed companies and even some banks participate in the private loan of usury, which makes the chaotic usury market more complicated.

"Risky" refers to "high risk". MSEs' operating profit is very low, and because of their single financing channel, poor financing environment, high financing costs, and participation in usurious lending, they bear a heavy debt burden, with certain financing risks. As is known, usury involves the risk of capital chain rupture. In that case, MSEs' survival will be threatened, even in face of bankruptcy.

MSEs' internal problems are the important source of their financing difficulties. First of all, their management level is seriously lagged. They are small in scale, low in technical level, weak in management, poor in operating efficiency, and are even heavily indebted. Most of them often lack projects that meet the loan conditions, and are not standardized in financial management, or even make false accounts. All these make it difficult for financial institutions to give their trust and provide credit. Secondly, SMEs are weak in bargaining with little or even no discursive power in the financing process. In cooperation with financial institutions, small micro enterprises are always in a completely inferior position due to the limitation of their own conditions. They have little or no right to argue. Therefore, they can only passively accept the interest rates, charging standards and other conditions determined by financial institutions, lacking the ability to bargain. In addition, Taizhou lacks private alliance organizations for MSEs to protect their rights and interests as well as enhance their bargaining voice.

Problem 2: Restriction on Financial Institutions—Shortage of Qualified Personnel and Fierce Homogenization Competition

The local corporate financial institutions of Luqiao started late, small in scale, with a narrow business scope. In addition, with the limitation of the economic system, national policies, historical reasons and other constraints, they were at a disadvantage in terms of overall financing capacity and level, such as limited number of credit scale, high concentration of short-term loans, etc., which has brought great uncertainty to the long-term development of enterprises and might easily lead to regional economic fluctuations. Local corporate financial institutions also have the characteristics of fierce competition with single homogenization. Their main business profits come from the net interest income of traditional deposits, which are highly sensitive to capital constraints and interest rate changes. Therefore, the subsequent growth of deposit business is weak. Furthermore, Luqiao is restricted by the shortage of financial personnel with high qualifications. Due to the insufficient development of Luqiao's urbanization and social public utilities such as higher education, high level financial administrators and high-quality financial professionals are in short supply, which is extremely unfavorable to the long-term development of local corporate financial institutions.

Problem 3: Deterioration of Financial Environment—Weak Credit Awareness and Poor Supervision

The development of local financial institutions is always closely related to the regional financial ecological environment. Although the financial ecological environment of Luqiao is among the best in Zhejiang province, the city is also faced with some practical difficulties and problems, such as the need to further improve social integrity, weak awareness of social credit, difficulties of non-bank credit information collection, etc. Some enterprises lend funds obtained from banks at higher interest rates through various ways, and some strong debtors are likely to make it difficult to enforce financial claims cases. In addition, the lack of financial intermediary services, the slow development of non-bank financial institutions, the small number and scale of trust companies and guarantee agencies, and the lack of standardized operation and management make it difficult to smoothly carry out the functions of local corporate financial institutions as well as micro and small enterprise in terms of financial services, financial consulting, enterprise transformation, etc. Also, the financial supervision mechanism needs to be improved without an established information sharing system. Besides, the vacuum and duplication of supervision still exist, with low coordination efficiency and the legal binding force is weak. All of these problems have strongly restricted the development of micro and small finance of Luqiao.

Problem 4: Ambiguous Positioning in the Future—Whether "Becoming Stronger" Must Be "Becoming Bigger"

As is known, the development of Wenzhou's micro and small finance follows an irregular path, gradually changing from "being small" to "being big". Although the development of Luqiao's micro and small finance is clearly positioned at this stage and follows the path of regular development, it is difficult to ensure that in the next few years, as micro and small financial institutions gradually become "stronger", the positioning may deviate from the original intention, and the ambiguity of the positioning may become a major obstacle to the future development of micro and small finance. The reason why the future positioning may deviate is, on the one hand, due to the possible industrial transformation and upgrading in the future, the demand for micro and small finance may be further reduced as MSEs themselves become larger; on the other hand, due to the large proportion of human capital investment in the operation of micro and small financial institutions, labor costs in the future will rise, which is likely to reduce the profits of micro and small financial institutions and slow down their development, prompting them to give up their focus on "small" and turn to "large" to seek "a share" in the new market. Thus how to consistently confirm the market positioning of micro and small finance, and develop better on the road of "becoming small and strong" has become a practical issue for micro and small financial institutions in Luqiao.

Problem 5: Cross-strait Financial Cooperation—Hidden Dangers

As is known to all, cross-strait cooperation is a new opportunity for the development of micro and small finance in Luqiao. However, how to introduce the advanced experience of Taiwan's micro and small finance without destroying the existing local financial environment is a new challenge for cross-strait financial cooperation. Although the original intention of the cross-strait financial cooperation is to further optimize the local financial ecological environment, once Taiwan's banking industry enters the mainland market, it may have a certain impact on the local financial industry in Taizhou. Especially for the relatively developed micro and small finance in Taiwan, the local corporate banks will suffer greater competition, which is detrimental to their further development. Therefore, while "Taiwan-Taizhou" cooperation has the positive significance of promoting financial development and deepening cross-strait cooperation, it also involves the hidden risk of damaging the local financial circumstance.

In addition, on June 21, 2013, the two sides of the Taiwan Strait signed the *Agreement on Cross-strait Service Trade*, which should have been another milestone in the normalization and liberalization of cross-strait economy and trade. However, due to the obstruction of the Taiwan Democratic Progressive Party, the agreement was not reviewed and passed. The failure of the agreement to take effect in time will have a negative impact on the deepening of cross-strait economic cooperation.

Once the cross-strait service trade agreement is implemented, it will help to accelerate the integration and complementarity of cross-strait service industries, and jointly enhance the international competitiveness of cross-strait service industries, including financial services. This is originally a good thing of "mutual benefit and win-win". The two sides will open their markets to each other. The mainland has vast market resources, and Taiwan has advanced service management.

However, because the extremist forces in Taiwan and the Democratic Progressive Party (DPP) "stigmatized" the service trade agreement with political purposes, falsely claimed that if Taiwan opened these markets, the relevant industries in the island would be annexed by the mainland industry, and that the mainland labors would snatch away the work opportunities of Taiwan people, which caused panic among Taiwan people, thus the opposition was growing. This will also affect the cross-strait cooperation in the field of micro and small finance to a certain extent. Whether the Taiwan authorities can properly deal with this issue in the future is crucial.

Problem 6: The Survival of Micro and Small Finance—Whether Taizhou's Private Economy Is Sustainable

Private economy is the soil for the development of micro and small finance. Therefore, whether the private economy in Taizhou is sustainable will be of vital significance to the survival of micro and small financial institutions in Luqiao.

At present, the survival and development of private enterprises in Taizhou is seriously squeezed, mainly due to the dual impact of domestic macroeconomic regulation and local economic internationalization. On the one hand, since the reform and opening up, the rapid growth and investment of Taizhou's private economy have brought about high consumption and high emissions. Resource factors, energy supply, ecological environment and infrastructure are seemingly difficult to support. There is a shortage of electricity, land, water, and migrant workers. In addition, the costs of environmental protection, raw materials and government services have increased dramatically, leading to a huge challenge for Taizhou's private enterprises dominated by traditional industries. On the other hand, the economic globalization has significantly put the competitive pressure on Taizhou enterprises.

In addition, the traditional family management mode of Taizhou private enterprises is difficult to meet the needs of sustainable development. The low level of industry, the difficulty of industrial upgrading as well as the lack of scientific and technological innovation have restricted the further development of Taizhou's private economy, making it "low, small and scattered". Once the development of Taizhou's private economy, the "engine", slows down or even stagnates, it will have a significant impact on the development of local micro and small finance, thereby squeezing the room for survival of micro and small finance.

10.3 "Luqiao Inspirations" of the Innovative Development of Micro and Small Finance

The problem of "financing difficulties" of SMEs in China has a long history. Luqiao district alleviates this problem through the "work along three lines" approach from government guarantee, bank innovation, and private introduction, and thus makes some achievements. On the one hand, the government of Luqiao plans the overall layout to relieve SMEs' financing distress through formulating strategies, building platforms, improving systems, stabilizing finance and other measures, coordinates the linkage effect between banks, enterprises and private capital, and provides solutions through multiple channels. On the other hand, by fully understanding the financing needs of SMEs, small and medium-sized commercial banks of Luqiao continuously innovate financial products and improve financial services to meet the differentiated needs of SMEs, thus build a "community bank", and strive to become a "growth partner" for the development of SMEs. At the same time, they rely on the industrial cluster platform to establish a "mutual fund" to relieve information asymmetry between the banks and enterprises so as to facilitate SMEs' loans. Besides, Luqiao has also actively guided and utilized private capital to establish relevant micro loan companies to provide new ways to solve the financing difficulties of small and medium-sized enterprises. Meanwhile, Luqiao has deepened cooperation with Taiwan's micro and small finance, established a cross-strait micro and small financial service pilot zone, and learned from Taiwan's advanced experience so as to build Luqiao into a micro and small financial services centre. Therefore, obtaining "unique secrets" from Luqiao experience will help to further attach importance to micro and small finance and promote the successful mode nationwide.

Inspiration 1: The Aggressive Overall Layout Is the Root of Success for Micro and Small Finance

Banks specializing in financial services for MSEs have been built. First, the government encourages local banks to expand their scale, vigorously promoting local corporate financial institutions with corporate to supplement capital through capital increase and share expansion, introduction of strategic capital, listing financing and other various means to enhance the supply capacity of credit services and further expand market share. In particular, the government encourages local corporate financial institutions to "go out", and steadily achieve cross regional development on the basis of development direction of serving MSEs, so as to further expand the influence of micro and small finance in Luqiao. Second, the government promotes the restructuring of rural cooperative banks, and further deepens the reform of rural cooperative financial institutions, exploring the establishment of joint-stock rural commercial banks, further increase capital and expand shares on the basis of clarifying existing property rights, and practically improving corporate governance institutions, so as to achieve the transformation to rural commercial banks within two years and promote the rural transformation of private capital. Third, the government vigorously promotes the construction of the financial cluster area. According to the urban planning of Luqiao, and the regional status quo of the development of financial institutions, the government gathers the headquarters of three corporate financial institutions into the cluster area, builds the headquarters and back office service center with high standards, and at the same time, focuses on introducing various financial branches, headquarters of listed companies, micro loan companies, investment companies and financial intermediary service institutions, gradually forming a cluster demonstration base for Luqiao financial services.

The financial service system for MSEs has been vigorously innovated. First, the government expands MSEs' credit business. According to the orientation and planning of Luqiao's industrial transformation and upgrading, the government strengthens the guidance of earmarked credits, and strives to take the lead in exploring the small loan mode based on industrial clusters and professional markets in Zhejiang province. The government also supports financial institutions to effectively develop industrial chain financial services targeted at leading industries such as auto and motorcycle manufacturing and metal recycling, deeply carry out commercial logistics and financial services, further innovate agricultural industrial chains and park financing modes such as "cooperatives+ farmers", "companies+ bases + farmers", so as to boost local industries to accelerate transformation and upgrading. Second, the government increases credit supply to MSEs, and encourages local small corporate financial institutions to increase credit supply through issuing financial bonds for MSEs, as well as improve their ability to serve MSEs. The government also gives full play to the leverage effect of financial funds and establishes a credit platform and compensation mechanism for medium and long-term loans to key MSEs, so as to strengthen the confidence of banks to issue medium and long-term loans, so that a sound working mechanism can be formed. At the same time, the government establishes and improves the credit personnel's due exemption mechanism, carries out risk compensation for loans to MSEs, and compensates for the banks' risk-taking with incremental loans to MSEs in proportion. Third, the government encourages the innovation of micro and small financial services, setting up an incentive mechanism, promoting local corporate financial institutions to develop and innovate green credit, credit financing, science and technology finance and other products in response to MSEs' needs, supporting various means of MSEs financing such as intellectual property pledge, warehouse bill pledge, shop operation right pledge, commercial credit insurance policy pledge, striving to expand MSEs' financing guarantee methods, thus to further enhance the advantages of financial services for MSEs. Fourth, the government strengthens the development of intermediary business, actively carrying out intermediary businesses in capital market, encouraging the innovation of financing management and investment products, promoting local corporate financial institutions to expand financing management business, even to develop private banking services in appropriate conditions, striving to change the traditional profit model based on the deposit-loan interest margin, to optimize the profit structure and improve service level.

A multi-level market system has been structured. First, the government encourages enterprises to speed up the pace of listing with the emphasis on the markets of small and medium-sized board and growth enterprise board the combination of short-term effects and long-term development targets, as well as implementing the five gradient cultivation work of training, restructuring, guidance, reporting for approval and listing according to the present conditions of different enterprises, so as to strive for more enterprises to realize direct financing in domestic and foreign capital markets. Second, the government accelerates the development of new type financial organizations, with encouragement and support for private funds to participate in the reform of local financial institutions, initiating the establishment of new financial organizations such as stock-sharing village and town banks, loan companies and rural mutual funds cooperatives in accordance with the law. In addition, the government accelerates the development of small loan companies, actively promoting the pilot project of small loan guarantee insurance, exploring the establishment of small loan funds which help to alleviate MSEs' insufficient mortgage guarantee as well as insufficient capital of small loan companies, encouraging qualified small loan companies to transform into rural banks. The government also accelerates the establishment of district-level industry and venture capital funds, introduces private equity institutions, guides various social capital investment in the upgrading of Luqiao industries and MSEs' development, and introduces financial leasing companies to broaden the financing channels in equipment investment. Third, the government develops the property-rights trading market, actively connecting with the Zhejiang unlisted company's stock trading center (OTC market). It also encourages enterprises to carry out property rights trading with the equity trading of unlisted companies and financial claims trading as the basic transaction varieties, promotes the reasonable circulation of equity and merger or reorganization between enterprises, and improves the efficiency of resource allocation. Fourth, the government guides enterprises to carry out bond financing, supporting eligible enterprises to issue short-term financing bonds and medium-term notes in the inter-bank bond market, exploring and backing up SMEs to raise funds through issuing collective bonds, collective bond funds and high-yield bonds, so as to diversify their financing. Fifth, the government builds an interactive platform between micro and small finance and private capital. The Luqiao Micro and Small Finance Mutual Assistance Service center was set up by the government to promote the connection between private capital and enterprise projects through the innovation of entrusted loans, private capital trusteeship and other business products developed by local corporate financial institutions, so as to achieve a win-win situation for banks, MSEs and private capital.

The financial ecological environment has been vigorously optimized. First, the government accelerates the improvement of the social credit system. With the market-oriented operation principle of "government guidance, government-bank cooperation", it fully integrates various kinds of credit information resources, establishes and improves the credit evaluation system for enterprises and individuals in Luqiao, actively promotes the construction of business integrity and social integrity, accelerates the collection of MSEs' archives as well as the electronic construction of farmers' credit recordings, so as to establish a good social credit environment. Second, the government accelerates the improvement of the intermediary service system, strengthening support for financing intermediaries, and standardizing the management of professional guarantee companies. The government also sets up special funds for government financing guarantee compensation, and explores the establishment of a MSEs re-guarantee system, so as to solve the obstacles of guarantee for MSEs in the process of financing. The government also introduces credit evaluation companies with good qualifications, establishes and improves the credit rating of loan enterprises, enhances the service for loan enterprises, vigorously cultivates a group of market-oriented law firms, accounting firms, evaluation agencies and other intermediary service agencies, so as to improve the level of professional services. Third, the government accelerates the improvement of the financial security guarantee system, strengthening and implementing the financial management responsibility of local governments, improving the comprehensive statistics and communication system of financial information, establishes and improves the regional financial security monitoring and early-warning as well as emergency response mechanism. In addition, the government severely strikes down on illegal financial activities such as illegal fund-raising and financial pyramid selling according to the law. With the achievement of monitoring in place, early warning and effective control, the government effectively holds the bottom line of no systematic and regional financial risks. Fourth, the government further strengthens the support system of talented financial personnel. With the Taizhou Bank Ginza Financial Training College, Tailong College and other specialized financial schools as the base, the government cooperates with colleges, universities and scientific research institutions to vigorously cultivate high-quality and versatile talents who can adapt to the current financial situation, and encourages the two colleges to open up to other financial institutions and society, so as to cultivate more financial talents, and form a nationally representative training base of qualified personnel for micro and small financial institutions.

Inspiration 2: The Construction of "Three Platforms" Is the Foundation of the Success for Micro and Small Finance in Luqiao

With the development of the national economy, SMEs are continuously increasing and gradually becoming the main force to promote the rapid growth of regional economy. Therefore, for local governments, relieving MSEs' financing difficulties should be gradually put on the agenda and become the focus of local governments. All levels of local governments should closely focus on the principal line of financial services for local economic development, firmly grasp the new opportunities of the transformation of economic development mode, and carry out their work in a solid, effective and innovative way from three aspects: "financing supply platform", "government credit enhancement platform" and "risk prevention platform".

Primarily, efforts should be made on the financing supply platform to enhance the financing security of the whole society. First, local governments should encourage local incorporate banks to continue to grow bigger and stronger, and provide all facilities to serve their development. Second, local governments should actively introduce more financial institutions, vigorously develop new financial organizations, introduce all kinds of banks, insurance and other financial institutions to set up local branches, and promote the establishment of local micro loan companies and other new local financial organizations to play the role of "financial ends". Third, local governments should promote the direct financing of enterprises, vigorously support MSEs' listing, and enhance the cultivation of backup enterprises.

Then, efforts should be made on the government credit information platform to effectively solve the problem of "two shortages" of enterprises. First, local governments should actively learn from advanced experience and participate in the construction of non-profit credit guarantee funds for SMEs invested by the government and participated by banks. Second, local governments should explore the establishment of a non-governmental financing standardization center under the unified supervision of the government, as well as the formation of a unified, orderly and standardized non-governmental financing platform within the local scope by establishing a non-governmental fund supply-and-demand registration and filing system, standardizing the transaction process, providing credit joint liability and authentication services. Third, local governments should explore the establishment of a local non-bank credit sharing system, which can collect the credit information of relevant enterprises from various local departments and provide to financial institutions for inquiry, so as to improve the information level of credit system construction in various regions.

In addition, efforts should be made on the risk prevention platform to practically maintain the stability of micro and small finance. First, local governments should explore the establishment of local SME financing guidance centers to eliminate such defects as no statements or accounting, thus guide SME financing toward standardization. Second, local governments should explore the establishment of non-governmental emergency on-lending, guiding private capital to set up service companies specially for the emergency turnover of matured loans for enterprises, so as to facilitate seamless renewal of matured loans for enterprises. Third, local governments should further strengthen the prevention and warning in advance against financial risks, by strengthening the dynamic monitoring of key industries, key areas and key enterprises, so as to prevent and resolve financial risks, promoting the analysis and judgment of emerging problems, striking illegal financial acts, with the focus on the prevention of systemic and regional financial risks.

Inspiration 3: Effective Use and Guidance of Private Capital Is the Pillar of Success for Micro and Small Finance

Considering the source of funds, with the continuous development and accumulation of private credit, it has gradually become a new force to solve the financing difficulties of SMEs. Small and medium-sized financial institutions, such as micro and small loan companies initiated by private capital, play an important role in the process of relieving the financing dilemma of SMEs. However, due to the high risk and blindness of private capital, making good use of private capital is also an important task for the improvement of private financial market. There are three points which can be learned from the experience of effective use of private capital by Luqiao.

First, the governments should guide private capital with micro loan companies as the carrier. Micro loan companies are primary means for private capital to relieve financing difficulties of SMEs, also an important form of private capital utilization. However, due to the high risks of private capital and the problems in the management of micro loan companies, it is necessary for the government to guide private capital to set up micro loan companies. At the same time, the financial supervision department should enhance supervision on small loan companies to reduce risks crises. But this does not mean the government can directly manage micro loan companies, instead, the government should consciously monitor risks to prevent them from evolving into problems.

Second, the governments should take the opening of private banks as an opportunity to explore private capital in the banking industry. With the continuous opening and improvement of the financial market, private capital has greater "vitality". Besides, with the opening of private capital and the establishment of private banks, private capital will play a greater role in relieving MSEs' financing difficulties. Therefore, local government should take this opportunity to actively explore the impact of private capital on the banking industry and how private capital can ease the financing difficulties of SMEs by entering the banking industry. Anhui province has begun to explore the establishment of private banks to deal with the financing difficulties of SMEs. So other local governments can also start from "the beginning", allowing private capital to enter some local small and medium-sized banks to test the feasibility of their entering the banking industry.

Third, the governments should take advantage of cross-strait economic and trade interaction to strengthen cross-strait micro financial cooperation. Micro and small finance is fully developed in Taiwan, and major banks have rich experience with it. With the increasingly frequent cross-strait economic and trade interaction, various regions can explore how to better engage in micro and small finance cooperation between the two sides, and learn from the cash practices of micro and small finance in Taiwan. Luqiao has taken advantage of local economic and trade interaction and established a cross-strait micro and small financial service cooperation pilot zone, making full use of Taiwan's effective resources. Other local governments can take this as a reference to explore opportunities for micro and small finance cooperation with Taiwan based on their local advantages.

Summary The experience of development in micro and small finance in Luqiao can be summarized as "Luqiao secrets, Luqiao problems and Luqiao inspirations". The "Luqiao secrets" involve positioning precise market, accelerating product innovation, optimizing financial services, developing strategies in different places, regularized development, concentrated development, political and banking cooperation, and cross-strait cooperation. The "Luqiao problems" are reflected in common financing problems, institutional constraints, poor environment, ambiguous positioning, hidden dangers of cross-strait cooperation and the sustainability of private economy. The "Luqiao inspirations" proposes that the overall layout of positive progress is the root of the success of micro and small finance; the construction of the three platforms is the foundation of the success of micro and small finance, and the effective use and guidance of private capital is the pillar of the success of micro and small finance.

From the Luqiao experience as well as the development of small and medium-sized financial institutions such as commercial banks in various cities, it can be clearly seen that the richer the financial formats, the greater the number of small and medium-sized financial institutions, the more abundant the private capital, the larger space of financing for SMEs in the region, and the more relieving for financing dilemmas. Therefore, in view of the problems existing in the innovation and development of China's enterprise financing organization system, the government should, while improving the legal environment, take the perfection of financial formats as the core, accelerate the vigorous development of various financial formats, and strengthen policy support. In particular, small and medium-sized financial institutions should play a central role in alleviating the financing difficulties of SMEs.

First, the market position should be clarified and the governance structure should be perfected. The government should extend the Luqiao model to ease the financing difficulties of SMEs, and, with precise positioning, vigorously promote the development of small and medium-sized financial institutions. In addition, small and medium-sized financial institutions also should highlight their own characteristics and define their own market positioning according to the flexibility of mechanisms as well as the newness of institutions. In terms of product positioning, small and medium-sized financial institutions should vigorously develop intermediary businesses with relatively low risk and stable income, such as agency, escrow, treasury bond trading, financing management and investment consulting, on the basis of primary traditional banking services.

Second, the access threshold should be lowered to attract private capital. Local governments should open up local financial markets for small and medium-sized enterprises, and set up more small and medium-sized financial institutions with capabilities of competition. The governments should also allow competent private enterprises to initiate the establishment of small and medium-sized financial institutions, create a good financial environment, and facilitate private small and medium-sized financial institutions with their own advantages to participate in fair play in the regional financial market.

Third, small and medium-sized financial institutions should be unshackled to create an environment with loose policies. As an indispensable part of the financial system, small and medium-sized financial institutions need more policy support from the government in the process of their development, including the establishment of a financial support system or the cancellation of some policies and regulations that are not conducive to the development of small and medium-sized financial institutions, such as removing the restrictions on small and medium-sized financial institutions to increase their business outlets, allowing them to freely participate in the national inter-bank lending market, etc.

Fourth, the legal system should be perfected and supervision should be strengthened. The governments should strengthen supervision over small and medium-sized financial institutions, and synchronously improve financial supervision and development of small and medium-sized financial institutions. A sound legal system and a strict regulatory system are conducive to promoting the standardized operation of small and medium-sized financial institutions, as well as healthy competition in the financial market, eliminating the fittest, improving the stability of the financial system and safeguarding MSEs' interests. According to its advantages, characteristics and actual conditions, the regulatory authorities should start to study how to standardize regulatory rules, unify regulatory standards, so as to create a transparent and fair competitive environment to support the development of small and medium-sized financial institutions.

As for the future development of micro and small finance in Luqiao, it is necessary to solve the existing problems, achieve the sustainable development of micro and small finance and further establish and improve the innovative model of "integrated system, leading technology, distinctive characteristics and superb circumstance". First, a sound financial service organization together with the support system for MSEs is essential. Services for MSEs can be improved, the financing threshold can be lowered, and the administrative procedures can be simplified, at the same time the risk of micro and small enterprise financing can be fully controlled. Second, an effective system of product technology and service innovation for micro and small financial enterprises is essential. It is due to micro and small finance combined with the demand of financing and innovation of financing characteristics that the financing products can get constant innovation with no homogenization. Third, a complete sharing system of financing risk for MSEs is essential. Establishment of the system can be based on such special platforms as industrial clusters and financing guarantee companies funded by the governments to get improvement. Fourth, a solid local financial environment system is essential. With financial exchanges and cooperation as the engine, the four distinguished industries (finance, auto and motorcycle parts, trade logistics and metal renewable resources) can get bonded so as to promote economic and trade cooperation with the development of modern service industry as the guidance. Fifth, an open development cooperation is essential. In accordance with the concept of sustainable development, the cooperation with Taiwan's financial industry, universities and research institutes can get strengthened, exchange and cooperation projects can get enriched and expanded, and the experimental zone can get jointly built. In addition, non-bank financial industries can get introduced more widely on the basis of deepening exchanges and cooperation across the strait.

References

Wang Zibin. Analysis of Advantages of Urban Commercial Banks in Financing of Small and Medium-sized Enterprises [J]. *Encyclopedia of Party History*, 2012, 8.

Wang Yuan. Thoughts on Effectively Guiding Private Capital to Ease the Financing Difficulties of Small and Medium-sized Enterprises [J]. *China Economic and Trade Guide*, 2011, 2.

Xie Ziyuan. Development of Private Financial Institutions and Financing Innovation of Small and Medium-sized Enterprises—Taking Taizhou Commercial Bank As an Example [J]. *Innovation*, 2011, 5.

Xu Wei. Analysis on the Development of Small and Medium-sized Financial Institutions [J]. *Legal System and Society*, 2013,11.

Xu Yan. Problems and Countermeasures of Small and Medium-sized Financial Institutions in China in Financing Small and Medium-sized Enterprises [J]. *Gansu Agriculture*, 2006, 6.

Ye Jiani. Research on Financing Difficulties and Countermeasures of Chinese MSEs [D]. *Shanghai Foreign Studies University*, 2013.

Zhao Xinjun. Research on the Synergy between Financing of Small and Medium-sized Enterprises and Private Lending—Taking Wenzhou As an Example [J]. *Journal of Southwest University for Nationalities (Humanities and Social Sciences Edition)*, 2012, 5.

Zhu Xiangwei. On the Development of Small and Medium-sized Financial Institutions and Financing of Small and Medium-sized Enterprises [J]. *Times Finance*, 2012, 5.

Focus on Luqiao Financial Innovation (I): How to Do "Small Business" for Banks [EB / OL]: http://jr.Luqiao.gov.cn/InfoPub/ArticleView.aspx?ID=53901.

Focus on Luqiao Financial Innovation (II): Going Global While Sticking to It [EB / OL]: http://jr.Luqiao.gov.cn/InfoPub/ArticleView.aspx?ID=53903.

Focus on Luqiao Financial Innovation (III): Keeping the Golden Name Card Shining [EB / OL]: http://jr.Luqiao.gov.cn/InfoPub/ArticleView.aspx?ID=53904.

Ye Tan. The Successful Experience of Talon Bank [EB / OL]: http://jr.Luqiao.gov.cn/InfoPub/ArticleView.aspx?ID=53913.

The Good Steward behind the Financial Legend—Summary of Financial Service Innovation in Luqiao District (Part I) [EB / OL]: http://jr.Luqiao.gov.cn/InfoPub/ArticleView.aspx?ID=53956.

Not the Most Powerful, But the Most Innovative—Summary of Financial Service Innovation in Luqiao District (Part II) [EB / OL]: http://jr.Luqiao.gov.cn/InfoPub/ArticleView.aspx?ID=53960.

People's Daily. The Cross-strait Talk about Micro and Small Finance to Promote the Interactive Development of Financial Institutions and MSEs [EB / OL]: http://jr.Luqiao.gov.cn/InfoPub/ArticleView.aspx?ID=53984.

Qiu Zhengxiong. Cross-strait Currency Clearing Mechanism and the New Direction of SMEs' Technological and Financial Innovation and Exchange [EB / OL]: http://jr.Luqiao.gov.cn/InfoPub/ArticleView.aspx?ID=53982.

Breaking the Homogeneity to Become a Brand—8-year Development Record of Luqiao Rural Cooperative Bank (Part I) [EB / OL]: http://jr.Luqiao.gov.cn/InfoPub/ArticleView.aspx?ID=53991.

Benefiting the People and Winning the Market—8-year Development Record of Luqiao Rural Cooperative Bank (Part II) [EB / OL]: http://jr.Luqiao.gov.cn/InfoPub/ArticleView.aspx?ID=53992.

Tailong Bank Launched a “Combination Fist” of Micro and Small Credit [EB / OL]: http://www.Taizhou.com.cn/news/2013-05/16/content_1140440.htm.
Xiao Longping. Solving MSEs’ Financing Problems [J]. *China Economy and Informatization*, 2012, 5.
Wu Teng. Reasons and Countermeasures for Financing Difficulties of Small and Medium-sized Enterprises in China [J]. *Financial Economy*, 2010, 12.
Tang Yueheng, Chen Yan. Analysis of MSEs’ Financing Difficulties and Countermeasures [J]. *Fortune Today*, 2011, 12.
Pan Jianhua. Investigation and Research on Local Corporate Financial Institutions Promoting the Development of Regional MSEs—Taking Luqiao District of Taizhou City As an Example [EB / OL]: http://www.tzzy.gov.cn/dwnews-Info.aspx/newsid=123.

PART V

Features

CHAPTER 11

A Chronicle of the Development of Small and Micro Finance in Luqiao

On June 6, 1988, The Ginza Financial Service Agency of Huangyan, Luqiao was co-founded by Chen Xiaojun and his business associates (the predecessor of Taizhou Commercial Bank). It is the first private financial institution in China since the reform and opening up.

In October 1992, the Luqiao Office of Bank of China was established under the management of Huangyan Sub-branch.

On June 28, 1993, The City Credit Cooperative of Tailong, Taizhou was established by Wang Jun and his business associates.

On May 10, 1995, Taizhou Luqiao district branch of Agricultural Bank of Tailong China was established.

In June 1995, Luqiao District Rural Credit Cooperatives Association was established, under the management of Agricultural Bank of Luqiao District.

On June 30, 1995, Luqiao District Branch of the People's Insurance Company of China was approved by People's Bank of Zhejiang Province.

On September 18, 1995, ICBC Luqiao District Sub branch was established.

In November 1995, Bank of China Taizhou Luqiao District Subbranch was approved under the management of Bank of China Taizhou Branch.

On November 18, 1995, Taizhou Luqiao District Sub branch of China Construction Bank Co., Ltd. was listed for business.

W. Xiao et al., *Microfinance and China's Regional Development*,
https://doi.org/10.1007/978-981-99-1960-4_11

In April 1996, the Luqiao District Insurance Company was divided into Luqiao Branch of Property Insurance Company and Luqiao Branch of Life Insurance Company.

In April 1996, Taizhou Luqiao Branch of China Insurance Life Insurance Co., Ltd was formally established.

In April 1996, Taizhou Luqiao Branch of PICC Property and Casualty Insurance Co., Ltd. was established.

In November 1998, Luqiao Ginza Financial Service Agency was renamed "Taizhou Ginza City Credit Cooperative".

In 2000, the Credit Group of Luqiao District, Taizhou City, Agricultural Development Bank of China was established.

On September 14, 2001, incidents of "collective withdrawal" happened in The City Credit Cooperative of Tailong as well as in Taizhou Ginza City Credit Cooperative, where a total of 790 million yuan was withdrawn in three days. It was finally settled with the attention from leaders of Luqiao District, Taizhou City, and Zhejiang Province.

In 2002, Luqiao Rural Cooperative Bank launched the "small amount credit letter". The loan limit is declared by the borrowers and approved by the bank. With the completion of procedures, borrowers can withdraw the loans at any time within one year.

In March 2002, Luqiao Ginza Urban Credit Cooperatives, jointly with eight other credit cooperatives, established the Taizhou Commercial Bank with stripping off non-performing assets and absorbing private SMEs as shareholders. The head office was set up in Luqiao, and 44 branches in the three districts as well as in Linhai, Wenling, Tiantai and Yuhuan.

In 2002, the construction of enterprises' credit project was implemented in Luqiao.

On June 26, 2003, the Branch of China United Property and Casualty Insurance Co., Ltd was officially opened in Luqiao, Taizhou. On July 27, 2003, the National Seminar on the Development of Local Commercial Banks and Private Economy was held in Luqiao. On December 13, 2003, the 2003 annual meeting of China Private Economic Research Association and the first China (Taizhou) Private Economic Development Forum was held in Luqiao. On March 18, 2005, Luqiao Rural Cooperative Bank was officially opened, as the first rural cooperative bank in Taizhou.

On December 9, 2005, the 2005 Annual Meeting of China Private Economy Research Association and the Second China Private Economic Development Forum was held in Taizhou International Convention and Exhibition Center.

In 2006, Luqiao Business Area of Taizhou Branch of Ping An Property Insurance Co., Ltd. was established.

On August 15, 2006, with the opening ceremony, Zhejiang Tailong Commercial Bank was established as another bank to serve small and micro financial enterprises controlled by private capital after the reform of shareholding.

In 2007, Taizhou Luqiao Branch of Shanghai Pudong Development Bank was established.

In 2007, Taizhou Luqiao Branch of Industrial Bank was established in 2007.

On March 31, 2007, Taizhou Commercial Bank was awarded the title of "China's 30 Most Competitive Financial Institutions" at the Third Annual Meeting of Chinese Financial Experts co-hosted by CCTV Economic Channel and China Financial Network. In April, it was awarded the title of "2006 National Advanced Unit of Banking Financial Institutions for Small Enterprise Loans" by China Banking Regulatory Commission.

On July 26, 2007, Luqiao Sub-branch of Bank of Communications was established. In August 2007, Luqiao Rural Cooperative Bank piloted a small business loan in Luoyang sub-branch, and set up a "small processing center for business loans" with branch units to build a framework for small business loans. On December 8, 2007, the Third China (Taizhou) Private Economic Development Forum and the 2007 Annual Conference of China National (Private) Economic Research Association was held in Taizhou International Convention and Exhibition Center. In 2007, Luqiao Rural Cooperative Bank took the lead in introducing the "Harvest Microloan Card" in Zhejiang province, and increased the credit extension to two years, giving full play to the advantages of harvest card of "one-time credit extension, loan upon use" to serve the people. In 2008, Tailong Commercial Bank launched the "Business Start-up Loan".

In 2008, the construction of social credit system was improved with the establishment of the leadership of credit construction in Luqiao and an information network of credit in Luqiao. In March 2009, Taizhou Luqiao Yufeng Small Loan Co., Ltd was established.

In August 2009, Taizhou Commercial Bank was awarded the title of "The Third Competitive Urban Commercial Bank in China" and "The Most Profitable Urban Commercial Bank".

In September 2009, Taizhou Luqiao Jiuding Micro Loan Co., Ltd was established.

In 2009, Tailong Commercial Bank launched the accumulative loan called Cunle Loan.

In August 2010, the Publicity Department of the Central Committee of the Communist Party of China took Tailong Bank as a model to transform the mode of economic development and serve small enterprises. Since then, Tailong Bank has been officially listed as a representative providing microfinance to SMEs.

In October 2010, Taizhou Luqiao Branch of Agricultural Development Bank of China was established.

In 2010, Luqiao district took the lead in setting up a financial work office in Taizhou.

In 2010, Luqiao district revised and issued Several Opinions on Supporting the Listing of Enterprises.

In 2010, Luqiao government issued Several Opinions on Supporting the Development of the Financial Industry (for Trial Implementation), with regulations that since 2010, the district government will set up special funds to support the development of the financial industry, with 20 million yuan earmarked each year to support the development of the financial industry and reward financial institutions and individuals who have made contributions to the local economy.

In 2011, Tailong Commercial Bank launched the joint guarantee loan of "Hand-in-Hand Loan".

In 2011, Tailong Commercial Bank launched the credit loan called "Credit Facility".

In 2011, Tailong Commercial Bank launched the industrial chain loan called "Chain Loan".

In 2011, Tailong Commercial Bank launched the revolving loan called "Relay Loan".

In 2011, Quzhou Branch of Zhejiang Tailong Bank set up Tailong Bank Red Cross Charity Relief Fund for public charities.

In 2011, Luqiao Rural Cooperative Bank launched the financial product called "Green Credit".

In 2011, Luqiao Rural Cooperative Bank launched the financial product called "Agricultural Credit".

In 2011, the government of Luqiao District issued the "12th Five-Year Plan for the Development of Service Industry".

In 2011, Luqiao Rural Cooperative Bank began to implement the "twelve-level interest rate pricing", providing loans with different interest rates for different SMEs to provide effective services.

In 2011, Taizhou Bank began to implement the service of "free banking", reducing and exempting 42 service fees, so as to effectively relieve the burden for SMEs that frequently use these services.

On January 10, 2011, Luqiao Sub-branch of Agricultural Bank of China vigorously implemented new policies to benefit farmers by means of micro loans with the "Benefiting Farmers Card" as an effective approach.

On January 18, 2011, Taizhou Insurance Industry Association, under the organization of PICC Property& Casualty Insurance Luqiao Branch, held the inaugural meeting of the self-regulatory coordination group for the insurance industry in Luqiao district. Leaders from the people's government of Luqiao district, Financial Office of Luqiao district, Wenzhou Branch of Zhejiang Insurance Regulatory Bureau, Taizhou Insurance Industry Association and other parties, as well as the principals of 23 property and life insurance institutions in Luqiao district, attended the meeting discussing and adopting the Working Rules of Self-Regulatory Coordination Group of the Insurance Industry in Luqiao district.

On May 18, 2011, Zhejiang Tailong Commercial Bank and China Construction Bank Zhejiang Branch signed a comprehensive cooperation agreement, with which the two sides will jointly provide customers with high-quality and efficient services through the dislocation division and cooperation.

On May 27, 2011, the Financial Symposium of Luqiao was held in the district government, where banks and small loan companies in the district communicate with each other about business operation as well as main problems. In addition, issues concerning innovation measures of financial institutions and the future development of small loan companies were also under discussion.

On July 27, 2011, the Luqiao Branch of Banking Association was established, which marked a new stage of financial development in Luqiao.

On August 17, 2011, Fengjiang Branch of Luqiao Rural Cooperative Bank began to provide entrepreneurial loans for farmers who lost their land.

On December 21, 2011, Luqiao government signed the Agreement on Credit Project of Energy Saving for Small-and-Medium-Sized Enterprises with Taizhou Bank, according to which Taizhou bank will provide financing channels for energy saving and efficiency enhancing preferential interest rates particularly for enterprises in Luqiao. At the same time, Luqiao will provide financial discount for SMEs that meet the requirements of "energy-saving credit" to jointly promote the development of Small-and-Medium-Sized enterprises based on energy saving.

On May 18, 2012, the loan for fixed assets called "SG Tairong Yi" was launched by Tailong Commercial Bank.

In 2012, Zhejiang Yilida Ventilator Co., Ltd. In Luqiao district successfully listed on Shenzhen Small-and-Medium-Sized Board with 270 million yuan finance.

In 2012, Taizhou Commercial Bank increased its capital and shares, officially renamed as Taizhou Bank.

In 2012, Luqiao Rural Cooperative Bank donated 10 million yuan to set up the "Charity Fund for Poor Farmers" so as to subsidize the life of indigent farmers and further promote the assistance to extremely poor farmers.

In 2012, the Luqiao District Party Committee and the government guided private capital by means of building reservoirs, digging channels and building water gates.

On November 9, 2012, the 2012 Cross-strait Seminar on Small and Micro Finance Development was held in Luqiao District.

In 2012, the People's Procuratorate of Luqiao District adopted 18 measures to guarantee the development of small and micro finance in Luqiao District.

In 2012, Luqiao Procuratorate issued the Opinions on Serving and Ensuring the Construction of "Innovation Demonstration Zone of Small and Micro Financial Service".

On February 27, 2012, Taizhou Bank and McKinsey & Company, the world's largest consulting company, officially launched the "Strategic Planning Project of Taizhou Bank".

On March 14, 2012, Tailong Bank officially signed an agreement with Tencent Holdings' online payment solution Tenpay to carry out cooperation with Tencent in terms of third-party payment business.

On August 13, 2012, the second plenary (enlarged) meeting of the fifth session of the District Committee and the plenary meeting of the District Government was held in the District Office Affairs Administration. Zheng Minqiang, the Secretary of the District Party Committee, on behalf of the District Standing Committee, made a report to the conference on Vigorously Promoting the Development of Local Financial Innovation and Creating a Demonstration Area of Service Innovation for Small and Micro Financials, followed with a special deployment on the issues.

On August 21, 2012, Taizhou Bank successfully issued special financial bonds for small enterprise loans, which was also the first in Taizhou.

On September 25, 2012, The Development Zone Sub Branch of Luqiao Rural Cooperative Bank was officially opened, which means that the bank officially launched cross-regional operations.

On October 31, 2012, the Department of Finance of Zhejiang Province issued 27.81 million yuan to financial institutions across Zhejiang province as the risk compensation for loans to small and micro enterprises in 2011. Among them, financial institutions in Luqiao received 800,000 yuan.

On November 29, 2012, Luqiao Sanyo Jinlong Microfinance Co., Ltd was officially opened.

In November 2012, Luqiao Yuehe Street Branch of CCB Women's Bank, as the first women's bank in Luqiao district, was officially established, which is a new attempt for the financial industry in Luqiao. At the same time, it is also the first basic business organization of CCB named after Women's Bank in Zhejiang province.

On November 29, 2013, the 2013 Cross-strait Microfinance Development Forum was held in Luqiao district.

In 2013, Luqiao district officially became the "Cross-strait (Taizhou Luqiao) Small and Micro Financial Cooperation and Innovation Experimental Zone in Zhejiang Province".

In 2013, the Luqiao District Government issued the Notice on Preventing Financial Risks, Standardizing Business Order and Promoting Healthy Economic Development, standardizing and assisting SMEs to prevent and control risks by means of fully understanding the importance of capital security, enhancing risk prevention awareness, standardizing guarantee to foreign enterprises, clarifying the bottom line of risk prevention and control, strengthening financial management, preventing investment deviating from entity economy to fictitious economy, innovating diversified financing approaches, increasing financing channels, reinforcing integrity culture and optimizing the environment for development of enterprises.

In April 2013, a professional collegial panel for financial trial was established in Luqiao. It can not only implement the major decision, made by the second plenary session of the fifth Luqiao District Party Committee, to launch the regional brand of "China's supreme city of service for small and micro financials", but also better practice active justice, extend services after trials, and guarantee the healthy development of the financial industry in Luqiao district.

In 2013, Rural Cooperative Bank of Luqiao District took the lead to launch the "Inclusive Credit Loan", mainly targeting small loans below

50,000 yuan based on family credit. In order to further specialize in the rural market and expand the scope of financial inclusion, Luqiao government promoted "Inclusive Credit Loan" and vigorously advocated "family credit" to effectively alleviate the inconvenience in guarantee of ordinary people.

In 2013, in order to further solve the financing difficulties of farmers and break the traditional concept of only granting credit to customers with large loans, Luqiao government began to implement the "pre-credit loan". Farmers with the pre-credit card can directly apply for loans, which effectively solves the problem of loans for farmers.

In 2013, Taizhou Luqiao Wucun Micro finance Co., Ltd was officially opened.

In 2013, Luqiao District became one of the first provincial-level pilot counties (urban areas) for innovation in private financing management.

In 2013, Luqiao District piloted the establishment of a private on-lending company—Taizhou Luqiao District Shifang Financial Service Outsourcing Co., Ltd., to provide service of capital turnover for various corporate enterprises or individual businesses with mature loans.

In 2014, Luqiao government set up the Luqiao Private Financing Standard Management Service Center on a pilot basis.

In 2015, Luqiao District promulgated the Administrative Measures for the Promotion and Application of Innovation Coupons in Luqiao District (for Trial Implementation), which issued electronic innovation coupons to technology-based SMEs in the whole district.

In 2015, Luqiao Rural Commercial Bank established China's first community platform for bank grid management.

In 2015, the construction of Luqiao microfinance cluster project was officially started, which was owned by Tailong Bank, Taizhou Bank and Luqiao Rural Cooperative Bank, with a total investment of 690 million yuan.

In 2015, Luqiao Government signed a financial strategic cooperation agreement with Luqiao Rural Cooperative Bank to support the bank to carry out financial businesses for science and technology. Xincheng Small and Micro Loan Center of Luqiao Rural Cooperative Bank became the first recognized science and technology branch in Luqiao.

In 2016, the district-level financial department granted 1:1 matching subsidies according to the provincial subsidy funds to small enterprises of financial institutions for the increased amount of loans.

In 2016, Luqiao government issued *The Implementation Opinions of Taizhou Luqiao District People's Government on Supporting Local Financial Development* as the policy support to small loan companies.

In 2016, the Luqiao government issued *The Notice on the Administrative Measures of Government Subsidies for Small and Micro Enterprises to Purchase Social Work Safety Services.*

In 2017, Luqiao government decided to increase subsidies for the construction of small and micro enterprise parks. The maximum amount of support for the same project was 3 million yuan.

In 2017, Luqiao government issued *Several Opinions of Taizhou Luqiao District People's Government Office on Accelerating the Construction of Small and Micro Enterprises Venture Park*, which required to provide small and micro enterprises with business sites, public facilities and supporting services to achieve the spatial agglomeration of small and micro enterprises.

In 2017, Luqiao government issued *The Notice of Taizhou Luqiao District People's Government Office on Printing and Distributing the Detailed Rules for the Implementation of Further Loosening the Restrictions for Registration of Enterprise Domicile (Business Place) in Luqiao District, Taizhou City*, stipulating that the commercial registration authority should establish and improve the credit information publicity mechanism of small and micro enterprises as well as the fair and standardized spot check system.

In 2018, Luqiao District carried out government-bank-enterprise cooperation on trademark pledge loans, and identified Tailong Bank as one of the first pilot banks to participate in deepening of the cooperation.

In 2018, according to Luqiao government, there were 258 enterprises transformed from self-employed individuals to enterprises in Luqiao in the whole year, including 252 corporate enterprises, accounting for 97.67%.

In 2018, the Luqiao government issued *The Implementation Plan of Luqiao District to Further Carry out Reform of the Commercial Registration System to Boost the Campaign of "One Visit Solve All"*, and comprehensively launched the commercial registration agency business in banking financial institutions so as to offer convenience for people.

In 2019, the Luqiao government issued *The Management Measures for "Enterprise Cloud" Special Funds in Luqiao District*, which granted 20% of the actual investment as subsidies to small and micro enterprises that met the requirements.

In 2019, Taizhou Bank launched promotion and application of the "smart and microenterprise" platform, which promoted the "two-hour" settlement system for enterprises' account opening to improve service efficiency.

In 2019, the Cross Strait Microfinance Development Forum was held in Taizhou. Now the Forum has become an important think-tank for the development of Taizhou's small and micro finance, as well as a business card for cross-strait economic and cultural exchanges and cooperation.

In 2020, the Luqiao government issued *The Opinions of the People's Government of Luqiao District, Taizhou City on Implementation of Promoting and Supporting the Development of Local Financial Industry.* The district government required actively developing the construction of basic small and micro franchise institutions as well as agricultural support outlets, and encouraged local financial institutions to set up outlets in professional markets and industrial clusters.

In 2020, the Luqiao government issued *Several Supporting Policies to Promote the High-level and Overall Well-offness of Low-income Farmers in Luqiao District*, providing low-income farmers with micro credit loans as poverty relief of less than 100,000 yuan for their production and operation, free of guarantee and mortgage, with 3% discount subsidy provided by Luqiao District Financial Bureau.

In 2020, Bank of Shaoxing, Taizhou Luqiao Small and Micro Enterprise Franchise Sub Branch was opened in Century Building of Luqiao District.

In 2020, the Luqiao government promulgated policies to subsidize the insurance premium of the guarantee fund serving small and micro enterprises, and explored the establishment of a risk sharing and compensation mechanism to provide guarantee services for loans to agricultural operation entities.

In 2020, the People's Government of Luqiao District promulgated *Several Opinions on the Pilot Work of Deepening the Financing Project and Promoting the Comprehensive Reform of Financial Services for Private Enterprises and Small and Micro Enterprises in Luqiao District* to guide financial institutions to increase credit extension to private enterprises and small and micro enterprises.

In 2020, the Luqiao government granted a cash reward of 100,000 yuan to the financing guarantee institutions for small and micro enterprises that made outstanding contributions.

In 2020, the agglomeration government promulgated *The Opinions of the People's Government of Luqiao District, Taizhou City on implementation of Promoting and Supporting the Development of Local Financial Industry* to reward local legal financial institutions for contributions to promoting the financial reform of small and micro financial institutions and approaching local unemployment.

In 2020, Taizhou Bank launched the Smart and Micro Enterprises Platform to improve service efficiency by actively promoting the "two-hour settlement" system for small and micro enterprises to open accounts.

In 2021, the Luqiao government approved *The Pilot Work Plan on Financial Services for Digital Enabling Technology Enterprises at the Initial Stage in Luqiao District*, and implemented new policies of assistance in the digital field for the financing of small and micro enterprises.

In 2021, the Luqiao government promulgated *Supporting Policies of the Measures for Loan Discount for Science and Technology Enterprises at the Initial Stage in Luqiao District (for Trial Implementation)* to motivate the development of science-and-technology-based small and micro enterprises at the initial stage.

In 2021, the Luqiao government required of the enhancement of the financing services provided by insurance institutions to small and micro enterprises, and provided risk compensation for qualified business of micro loan guarantee insurance at the rate of no more than 0.5% of the annual total financing insurance amount.

In 2021, the Luqiao government launched the innovative measures of "coupon" to reduce the cost of small and micro enterprises to help small and micro enterprises stabilize their posts.

CHAPTER 12

Collection of News Reports and Product Innovation Media Coverage

(1) February 20, 2004, Zhejiang Daily. Title: Luqiao Private Financial Institutions To Support SMEs.

Article excerpt: Nearly 45,000 self-employed businesses and small family workshops sprang up in Luqiao more than ten years ago. They, in desperate need of financial services with small amounts, short term and fast turnover, often have no access to loans. A business manager at Tailong Urban Credit Union recalled that when the state-owned commercial bank made a loan of 10,000 yuan and 100 million yuan, the transaction cost was roughly the same. The "short, smooth and fast" financial needs of SMEs, which were of little value for state-owned commercial banks, meant a huge market for private capital. In 1988 and 1993, with six or seven people and hundreds of thousands yuan, Ginza Credit Union and Tailong Credit Union were established successively. In order to "seize" the market, the two financial institutions had to provide efficient services, such as the "from 7a.m. to 7p.m."work time, only 5 minutes to transfer small loans to clients' accounts from 50,000 to 100,000 yuan, and half an hour to approve and transfer 500,000 yuan. The problem of credit and guarantee is the most troublesome for banks when granting loans to SMEs without a complete financial management system. To solve this problem, the local government took the initiative to "provide assistance" and the two private financial institutions also "explored effective measures". The Government of Luqiao District

W. Xiao et al., *Microfinance and China's Regional Development*,
https://doi.org/10.1007/978-981-99-1960-4_12

took the lead to set up a service center for SMEs, as well as policy-based guarantee companies in towns and communities to help or act on behalf of SMEs to handle procedures such as insurance, notarization and evaluation together with private commercial guarantee agencies, so as to shorten the period for loan granting. Each of the two private financial institutions has more than 100 account managers, accounting for one third of the total number of employees. Most of them are natives of Luqiao, and their assessment performance is directly linked to the loan qualification they are responsible for. Thus, they shuttle through the streets and alleys of Luqiao every day, initiatively go into enterprises, impartially evaluate credit risks, and actively explore opportunities for credit growth.

(2) June 28, 2004, Zhejiang Daily. Title: Private Capital Flows and Local Government's Actions

Article excerpt: Great development of regional economy is achieved in the large flow of private capital. In recent years, the great wave of capital outflow from Zhejiang, together with entrepreneurs from Zhejiang, is well-known nationwide. However, there has been an upsurge of return of capital and enterprises in Luqiao. Since the implementation of the return project in 2001, there have been more than 50 enterprises investing and setting up business in Luqiao, with a total investment amount of nearly 10 billion yuan, while private capital outflows from Luqiao around the year of 2000 reached an alarming level. According to incomplete statistics, more than 30 enterprises in the region invested more than 2 billion yuan in Shanghai, and more than 20 enterprises invested about 1 billion yuan in Jiangsu. From the large inflows and outflows of private capital in Luqiao, it is not difficult to find that in the process of the circulation and flow, the economy of Luqiao has shown a trend of spiral development. The scale and quality of private capital have changed a lot. The outflow is 3 billion yuan, the backflow is 10 billion yuan; the outflow is domestic capital, the backflow is domestic capital with foreign investment, the outflow is pure capital, the backflow is capital together with talents, information, technology and projects conducive to the promotion of the local industrial level. The smooth flow of private capital in Luqiao not only enables us to obtain resources, talents and profits, but also, more importantly, to find a shortcut to accumulate technology and experience. In this process, the entrepreneurs have updated their concepts, broadened world vision and strategic thinking, mastered the technical and market information of similar products, won the initiative in competition, understood and applied advanced management technology, and improved the management level. In addition, the enterprises have enhanced research, development and innovation capabilities, expanded the market and enhanced its comprehensive competitiveness.

(3) On May 22, 2009, Shanghai Financial News. Title: Tailong Bank explores the vitality "Password" of Luqiao private finance

Article excerpt: Luqiao District, Taizhou City, located in the middle of Zhejiang coast and the middle of China's gold coast, is one of the cradles of Chinese private economy. In Taizhou, it is an economic center, a financial sub-center, and a dynamic center of private finance. Zhejiang Tailong Commercial Bank, Taizhou Commercial Bank and Luqiao Rural Cooperative Bank almost "share the world". Why is private finance so strong? What "genes" constitute their vitality "password"? The vitality originates from the competition. Luqiao is a place of commerce, and the culture of "mercantilism prevails. Luqiao is a more competitive place. Zhejiang Tailong Commercial Bank and Taizhou Commercial Bank have become the "twin stars" of local private finance, while the four big banks, i.e. Industrial and Commercial Bank of China, Agricultural Bank of China, Bank of China, China Construction Bank, in big cities, "like a fish in water", are subjected to subordination here. It is often said that the market is like a battlefield where the competition is fierce. In my opinion, although monopoly can easily obtain huge profits, it is easy to slow down with complacency. Although the competition is cruel, it can stimulate the potential of enterprises and make progress. The reason why the Luqiao private finance is so active is largely due to "competition". Enterprises develop in competition and compete in development. The competition of Luqiao's financial industry is beneficial, and it is also what clients, competitors and local governments expect to see. Competition creates vitality, which has promoted the rapid, healthy and orderly development of Luqiao financial industry.

(4) July 23, 2010, Zhejiang Daily. Title: Financial Industry: The New Highlight of Luqiao Economy

Article excerpt: From January to May, the deposit income tax of two commercial banks and the rural credit cooperative bank in Luqiao has amounted to 282.75 million yuan, 60.33% up year on year, as a new engine of national tax revenue this year, also a new highlight of economic growth of Luqiao. Specifically speaking, the deposit income tax of Taizhou Commercial Bank has amounted to 93.7551 million yuan, with a growth rate of 57.07%; the deposit income tax of Zhejiang Tailong Commercial Bank has amounted to 71.2051 million yuan, with a growth rate of 85.43%; the profit of Luqiao Rural Cooperative Bank has amounted to 8.31 million yuan, with a growth rate of 30.99%.

It's a hard-earned success with the "three steps" approach. In the face of the demand of financial enterprises to solve the problem of uncollectible accounts, Luqiao District National Taxation Bureau cooperated with the municipal authorities to carry out specialized research work. In strict accordance with the relevant provisions of the Measures for the Administration of Pre-tax Deduction of Bad Debt Losses of Financial Enterprises promulgated by the State Administration of Taxation, and in combination with the practical development of private finance, the Bureau launched a specialized campaign to serve financial enterprises with the "three-step" approach, and put the problem of uncollectible accounts on the work schedule. Leaders of the Municipal Taxation Bureau and the Luqiao National Taxation Branch have personally visited the front line of financial enterprises many times, supporting the development and expansion of financial enterprises as an important breakthrough point to promote the increase of national tax and the development of local economy. They also managed to acquire information concerning operation of financial enterprises and the difficulties encountered in the operation, especially conducting a thorough investigation on the bad debts. In addition, face-to-face talks were organized between core members and directors together with financial staff of financial enterprises in attempt to approach problems, especially study new situations and problems existing in current financial enterprises. With the solution of non-collectable accounts as a breakthrough, the authority has implemented various tax policies of the central government on financial enterprises.

(5) November 11, 2010, Taizhou Daily. Title: Luqiao Gradually Moves Toward a "Financial City" with 60% Financial Enterprises

Article excerpt: Since this year, with the macroeconomic circumstance warming up, Luqiao enterprises have completely shaken off the subsequent impact of the international financial crisis, and all walks of life have shown a state of restoration and growth. SMEs have gradually made up for losses and entered the track of rapid development. The good operating performance of the enterprise has also been reflected in the financial field. By the end of October, the accumulated corporate income tax of Luqiao National Tax has amounted to 106.118 million yuan, a year-on-year increase of 463.08 million yuan, or 77.43%, among which, Taizhou Bank, Zhejiang Talilong Commercial Bank and Luqiao Rural Cooperative Bank have accumulated 641.28 million yuan, a year-on-year increase of 252.74 million yuan, or 65.04%, accounting for 60.43% of corporate income tax. In October alone, the three financial enterprises accumulated a total of 187.99 million yuan, accounting for 67.47% of the enterprise income tax in this month, especially, the income tax of Zhejiang Tailong Bank in October has increased by 100.84%.

(6) December 7, 2012, China Reform News. Title: Three Measures to "Purify" Small and Micro Finance in Luqiao District, Taizhou City, Zhejiang Province

Article excerpt: Luqiao district, Taizhou City, Zhejiang province, is full of abundant private capital and active private finance. According to statistics, in 2011, the region's per capita GDP exceeded 12,000 US dollars, with the per capita savings deposits more than 80,000 yuan, and the accumulated private lending more than 20 billion yuan. In order to prevent systemic regional financial risks, the Luqiao District Committee and Government guided private capital through three major measures: "building reservoirs", "digging channels" and "building gates". By the end of the second quarter of this year, the loan balance of Luqiao financial institutions amounted to 58.801 billion yuan, the non-performing loan balance 697 million yuan with the ratio of 1.14%. The guidance of local banks has been performed by "building reservoirs". According to Fu Zhouqing, director of the Luqiao District Financial Office, there are many forms of private finance in Luqiao, such as direct lending, social fund-raising, mutual financing and so on, forming a competitive coexistence with standardized credit funds. In this case, the government of Luqiao District, with financial resources of three local banks, namely Taizhou Bank, Zhejiang Tailong Commercial Bank (hereinafter referred to as Tailong Bank) and Luqiao Rural Cooperative Bank (hereinafter referred to as Rural Cooperative Bank), squeezed the space of private finance through the high fill rate of credit demand, thus effectively controlled the risks of private lending.

(7) On May 14, 2013, People's Court News. Title: Luqiao: Building a "Demonstration Area" for Financial Trial

Article excerpt: Luqiao District, Taizhou City, Zhejiang Province, is located on the southeast coast, with a developed market economy. There are two cross-regional private bank headquarters, 80 various markets, and over 10,000 private enterprises in the district. After the international financial crisis, many enterprises have suffered severe problems such as the rupture of capital chain, debt distress, and stagnation of production and development. In the face of this situation, the People's Court in Luqiao District has improved its judicial ability to serve finance, explored new measures to serve enterprises, and boosted regional economic development. A financial court has been set up to promote the specialization of trials. Due to rich private capital and active financing, financial cases account for about 60% of commercial cases accepted by the court, with the characteristics of large amount of subject matter, complexity of cases and difficulty for mediation. In 2012, the Luqiao District Court concluded a total of 2282 commercial cases, with the target amount of more than 961 million yuan. In August 2012, Luqiao District Committee made the decision of "building a demonstration area for financial service innovation". Then, the Luqiao Court has set up a professional collegial panel for financial trials, through which financial cases are dealt with in a centralized handling to improve the quality and efficiency of trials. In fact, with the establishment of the financial trial professional collegial panel, the financing cases and cases involving financial institutions have been centralized under the jurisdiction of the collegial panel, where simple cases are concluded quickly, complicated cases are examined intensively, and special cases are handled specially so as to promote specialization and intensification of trials. The functions of the professional collegial panel include providing better, faster and more powerful judicial guarantees for the development of private finance; preventing and defusing financial risks, especially centralized management of cases involving enterprises bankruptcy and the escape of enterprise owners, which is conducive to coordinating and defusing risks; carrying out bankruptcy and liquidation to promote the transformation and upgrading of enterprises; finding loopholes in the operation of financial institutions through trials, helping improve the management mechanism and promoting standardized development.

(8) August 8, 2013, Financial Times. Title: Zhejiang Luqiao Rural Cooperative Bank Building a new brand of Rural Financial Aid

Article excerpt: Luqiao is located in the southeast coast of Zhejiang province, with developed private economy and many private enterprises, among which small and micro enterprises, together with rural industry and commerce, accounting for half the businesses of local financial institutions, are recognized as the leading force of the local economy. In the promotion of the construction of "three major projects", Taizhou Luqiao Rural Cooperative Bank of Zhejiang Province, focusing on "sunshine credit" with the purpose of inclusive finance, strives to launch the "Baixiao Loan Delivery" project to create a new brand of convenience and assistance to farmers. By the end of May, the balance of all loans of the bank has amounted to 10.08 billion yuan, an increase of 1.59 billion over the same period of last year, with a growth rate of 18.72%, of which the balance of agricultural loans has amounted to8.35 billion yuan, an increase of 1.61 billion over the same period of last year, with a growth rate of 23.87%. From January to May, a total of 42,213 individual customers and 649 enterprise customers were provided with various credit loans, 1449 and 190 more than the same period last year respectively. The development of "Baixiao Loan Delivery" project has received continuous attention from the media, and the bank has also been rated as an outstanding unit of "Three Major Projects" by Zhejiang Rural Credit Union.

(9) May 27, 2016, Shanghai Financial News. Title: Small loan makes grass growers "turn grass into gold"

Article excerpt: Guo Guoyong, in his early 40s, is a native of Liuao Town in Sanmen County, who has been planting grass for many years. The wheat straw harvested has been purchased by a company in Xianju. Most tea products produced by the company are sold to Japan. The business of wheat straw has been stable, and the products are well-sold. Over the years, Guo Guoyong's "wheat straw territory" has become larger and larger. From 70 mu of land when he started to operate alone in 2011 to 1200 mu today, the scale has expanded over 10 times.

When Guo Guoyong started to independently contract land to grow wheat straw, there were troubles in capital turnover concerning land contract fee, fertilizer purchase and labor wage payment. As he felt worried, his friend introduced Small Loans to him. Soon, Guo Guoyong obtained a small loan of 100,000 yuan from Sanmen Yinzuo Liuao Sub-branch, which solved his urgent problem. It is reported that Small Loan is a special loan product launched by Taizhou Bank since 2006, which serves small and micro enterprises, individual businesses, family workshops and farmers. Over the past 10 years, small loans have been granted in total 71.6 billion yuan, supporting nearly 530,000 small and micro clients. Most of the loan officers come from the local area, who understand the situation of surrounding residents and farmers, make friends with customers, and provide considerate services.

(10) April 8, 2018, Zhejiang Daily. Title: the Legend of "turning around"—the development of small and micro finance with the rise of local urban commercial banks in Taizhou

Article excerpt: Huang Junmin, who has worked in Taizhou Bank, formerly known as Luqiao Ginza Financial Service Agency, since the 1990s, has experienced almost all major events on the founding of the bank. Huang is very proud of the transformation of Taizhou Bank from a private financial service agency to a modern commercial bank with clear property rights and private capital holding. Since the establishment of national-level reform and innovation pilot zone with financial service for small and micro enterprises in 2015, small and micro finance has made greater achievement and provided better services for small and micro enterprises. Thirty years ago, Luqiao was already a prosperous place with markets in every street, peddlers in every alley, businesses in every house. According to Wu Zhimin, the deputy director of Taizhou Banking Regulatory Branch, as a participant and witness of the development of Taizhou's small and micro finance, in the 1970s and 1980s, Taizhou's individual enterprises and joint-stock cooperative enterprises, though relatively remote, prospered unprecedentedly. "Grassroots economy" grew up vigorously in Taizhou, and a financial service agency specialized in financial assistance for private small and micro enterprises came into being.

(11) August 3, 2019, China News. Title: Cross Strait Microfinance Development Forum opened in Taizhou, Zhejiang

Article excerpt: After three successful sessions, the Cross Strait Microfinance Development Forum opened again in the fourth year. On August 3, more than 400 people from both sides of the Taiwan Straits gathered in Taizhou,

Zhejiang, to exchange and cooperate with each other and jointly promote the development of private economy. Since the first forum was held in 2012, the two sides have made many achievements through exchanges and cooperation in various fields with the forum as the platform. The data shows that the loan balance of small and micro enterprises in Taizhou accounts for 40.98% of the total, which is nearly 20 percentage points higher than that of the whole country. In addition, the loan application rate of small and micro enterprises reaches 94.39%.

According to Zhang Xiaoqiang, mayor and deputy secretary of Taizhou Municipal Party Committee, over the past seven years, the functional orientation, operation mechanism and development direction of the Forum have become increasingly clear, and the forum has become a brilliant card of cross-strait economic and cultural exchanges and cooperation, as well as an important think tank for the development of small and micro finance. Qiu Zhengxiong, honorary chairman of the Taiwan Financial Academic Union, believes that the opening of the mainland's financial market in the future will also be a great benefit to Taiwan-funded financial industry. "But in the face of numerous foreign competitors, the two sides should make good use of their common cultural and linguistic advantages to promote effective industrial and financial cooperation programs across the Straits and stand out." Gao Yi, deputy secretary general of Zhejiang Government, believes that this forum will further deepen cross-strait cooperation and exchanges in the field of small and micro finance and achieve more substantive results. At the same time, he also indicated that the Zhejiang Government would vigorously guide provincial financial institutions to participate in the construction of Taizhou Small and Micro Financial Reform Pilot Zone, and support the development of small and micro finance as always.

(12) June 6, 2022, Taizhou Daily, Title: Responsibility for common prosperity in finance. Taizhou Bank: To promote rural revitalization with power of finance

Article excerpt: Taizhou Bank, founded in 1988, formerly known as Luqiao Ginza Financial Service Agency, has focused on service market of small and micro finance for 34 years. Driven by the loan of Taizhou Bank, groups of entrepreneurs have become rich through labor, and countless innovative samples of common prosperity have emerged.

In terms of village service, the concept of focusing on serving small and micro businesses as well as "agriculture, rural areas and farmers" has been deeply imprinted in the minds of the employees of Taizhou Bank, as a spontaneous behavior of all employees, thus carry out inclusive financial support. Credit officer in red, village financial instructors and financial grid members are always seen running in the farmland. This is a financial team in a rural area willing to deal with micro enterprises and "agriculture, rural areas and farmers", able to bear hardships, good at communication and down to earth. In Shitang Town, in the past years, the fishery has been modernized with the update of fishing boats, which has also increased the cost of production tools for many fishermen. With the credit as a support of Small and Micro Enterprise Franchise Sub branch in Shitang, Taizhou Bank, the building of new fishing boats have been carried out as scheduled. This year, when fishermen applied for ship-building funds from Taizhou Bank, the sub-branch made rapid response, which ensured the 500,000 agriculture loan available in time. For fishermen, seizing the opportunity for shipbuilding during the fishing moratorium means a bumper harvest in full warehouse after the opening of the sea.

12.1 Product Innovation

(1) Product name: Changyi Loan.

Issuer: Taizhou Bank

Product description: "Changyi Loan" issued by Taizhou Bank is a loan product that repays the principal and interest of the loan by installment, mainly used to meet the needs of small and micro clients for medium and long-term financing due to the expansion of production and improvement of technology. The service target is small and micro clients with the needs of medium and long-term loans. The product advantages include: (1) long term, up to ten years; (2) repayment by installments with equal monthly principal. It is up to the clients to decide how much to repay each month; (3) low interest rate. The interest rate of short-term loans within one year is more favorable. Entry criteria: (1) individual clients should be aged between 20 and 60 years old; (2) the customers should have operated in the target market for more than 2 years (exclusive) in good business status.

(2) Product name: Business Guarantee Loan.

Issuer: Taizhou Bank

Product description: Business guarantee loan is a loan with financial discount granted by the local government especially for entrepreneurs who meet the qualification of public employment management service institutions. The product include such characteristics as low interest rate, high interest subsidy and convenient handling; the highest annual interest rate of the government is 7.35% (simple interest). The eligible clients, living up to the basic requirements of the Bank, should also meet the following standards with certificates issued by county (city, district) level public employment service institutions. (1) Urban and rural entrepreneurs start up business within 3 years, with monthly sales of more than 3000 yuan; (2) Entrepreneurial projects are industries supported and encouraged by policies, namely, industries except for construction industry, entertainment industry, real estate sales, transfer of land-use right, housing agency, sauna, massage, Internet cafes and oxygen bars; (3) The entrepreneurs should pay social insurance premiums according to law before the loan is granted, with the social insurance payment voucher presented.

(3) Product name: Small Loan

Issuer: Taizhou Bank

Product description: The choice for small business is Small Loan, which, with low threshold and fast granting, can meet the needs of farmers, self-employed households, entrepreneurs, small and micro enterprises for financing. Product features: (1) Large amount loan within 1 million yuan; (2) Light burden for repayment with the term of less than three years; (3) Various interest rates according to the numbers, terms, credit status, etc., of loans; (4) Flexibility of repayment with the pattern of installment.

(4) Product name: Small Loan

Issuer: Tailong Bank

Product description: Under the guidance of the credit policy of the People's Bank of China to support financial institutions to expand the loan issuance for small and micro enterprises, the products, with the refinancing fund of the People's Bank of China with credit access, are issued to qualified small and micro customers for conventional production and management. The characteristics include the following: (1) The maximum amount is 30 million yuan; (2) The maximum annual interest rate is limited to no more than 5.5%; (3) The credit guarantee approaches can be chosen flexibly; (4) The procedures are convenient.

(5) Product name: Credit Facility

Issuer: Tailong Bank

Product description: The loan is issued to qualified small and micro clients for conventional production and operation turnover, or consumption, after the bank conducts credit evaluation on the borrowers who meet the qualifications and submit applications for loans. The characteristics include: (1) Guarantee free. The product is a pure credit loan without any mortgage; (2) High efficiency. The loan can be approved the same day as is applied for at the earliest; (3) High quota, which can amount up to 5 million yuan; (4) Flexible repayment. The bank accepts various approaches such as installment, one-time repayment, pay-as-you-go, etc.; (5) Low interest rate. The annual interest rate can be as low as 4.2% (calculated as simple interest with no cost directly related to the loan); (6) Fees free.

(6) Product name: Yirongtong

Issuer: Tailong Bank

Product description: The loan is issued under the condition that the guarantee shall be provided by a third party who has a moral relationship with the borrower, such as kinship, love, friendship or kindness. The loan can be used for conventional production and operation turnover or consumption. Product features: (1) Free of mortgage and pledge. As long as the guarantee is provided by a third party who has a moral relationship with the borrower, such as kinship, friendship or love, the loan will be granted; (2) High efficiency with convenient procedures and complete data. The loan can be granted in 30 minutes at the earliest; (3) Low interest rate. The lowest annual interest rate can reach 4.2%; (4) Easy repayment. The repayment approaches can be customized according to clients' needs; (5) The maximum amount is 3 million yuan, meeting the financing needs of most small and micro clients; (6) Fees free. There are no intermediate fees, handling fees, commissions and other fees charged.

(7) Product name: Small Loan;

Issuer: Taizhou Bank.

Product features: Loan limit: 100,000–1,000,000 yuan (inclusive). Loan interest rate: depending on the number of loans and credit status. Repayment method: monthly installment payment as preferred, or customized according to the situation of the client's business. Term: up to three years. Loan objects: SMEs and entrepreneurs, self-employed workforce, family workshops and natural persons. Access to loans: bring ID card, business license, financial statements and other related credit certificates to the bank to apply; tell about business situation, financing plans, etc. Decisions will be made quickly with careful investigation and analysis, and loans will be granted after the signing a contract with the bank.

(8) Product name: Small Loan for Agriculture

Issuer: Taizhou Bank.

Product features. Loan limit: within 100,000 yuan (inclusive). Loan interest rate: preferential interest rate. Repayment method: Quarterly repayment of principal and interest, monthly equal installment or flexible repayment, etc., depending on actual production and management cycle as well as clients' demand for capital. Loan objects: Clients engaged in agriculture, forestry, grazing, fishing, etc., including planting, breeding, animal husbandry, and fishing.

(9) Product name: Small Micro Loan

Issuer: Taizhou Bank.

Product features: Loan limit: within 100,000 yuan (inclusive); Loan interest rate: depending on the number of loans and credit status; Repayment method: monthly installment payment as preferred, or customized according to the clients' business situation and repayment ability. Term: up to three years. Loan object: small enterprises, micro enterprises and entrepreneurs, self-employed workforce, family workshops and natural persons engaged in production and business activities, with employ ment for at least three months.

(10) Product name: Small Credit Loan

Issuer: Taizhou Bank.

Product features: Loan limit: within 1 million (including 1 million). Loan interest rate: depending on the number of loans and credit status. Repayment method: monthly installment payment as preferred, or customized according to the clients' business situation. Term: up to three years. Guarantee: On clients' credit only. Loan objects and conditions: honest clients with law-abiding operation, good credit standing, self-owned capital, good management, low debt, and at least one year of business.

(11) Product name: Small Joint Guaranteed Loan.

Issuer: Taizhou Bank.

Product description: Small Joint Guaranteed Loan refers to a small loan jointly guaranteed by other members of the team, jointly and severally liable. The principle of equality and voluntariness, risk sharing and joint liability shall be applied. Product features: members of the joint insurance team only need to sign a joint insurance agreement with our bank once, and the joint insurance quota can be recycled within the validity period. The term of the joint insurance agreement of small amount is between 3 months to 1 year (inclusive).

(12) Product name: Personal Self-service Loan.

Issuer: Taizhou Bank.

Product description: With Personal Self-service Loan the bank and the borrower sign a contract with the maximum amount for a self-service loan, verifying the maximum limit and term, then the borrower independently determines the amount, term and interest rate through the counter of business institutions, telephone banking system and online banking. Product features: one-time verification, recycling, loan upon use, coordinated loan and repayment. It can help borrowers to save loan interest expenses, allowing the client to borrow and repay through the bank's business outlets or e-banking, so as to improve the efficiency of loan processing, and obtain loans in time. Applicable object: The borrower of a self-service loan should be a natural person. In addition to complying with the relevant provisions of the bank, he must also provide a corresponding guarantee. Loan term and interest rate: the maximum term of the loan shall not exceed one year, and the maximum term of self-service real estate mortgage loan shall not exceed two years. The interest rate shall be based on the loan interest rate of the bank.

(13) Product name: Precious Metal Pledge Loan.

Issuer: Taizhou Bank.

Product description: Precious metal pledge and guarantee refers to the pledge and guarantee business under the tripartite agreement signed by the bank, the borrower and the pledgor, with the precious metal issued by the pledgor as the pledge collateral. Product features: preferential interest rates, with the advantages of clients' inventories engaged in precious metal business, no need to find a guarantor. Target clients: those with stable business and a certain amount of precious metal inventory. Handling process: accepting application—investigation—review and approval—signing pledge contract and pledge list of rights—loan issuance—debt settlement.

(14) Product name: Aquatic Product Warehouse Receipt Pledge Loan.

Issuer: Taizhou Bank.

Product description: Aquatic product warehouse receipt pledge refers to a pledge guarantee business conducted by the guarantor (which shall be the manufacturer and seller of aquatic products) to store the aquatic product goods in the storage company (hereinafter referred to as the "warehouse"), and the warehouse receipt issued by the warehouse as the inventory keeper is used as the pledge collateral of rights. Product features: preferential interest rate, with the advantages of bulk goods, no need for a guarantor. Target clients: those managing long-term aquatic products business, with a certain number of aquatic products in stock, stable in and out. Handling process: accepting application-investigation-review and approval-signing Warehouse Receipt Pledge Cooperation Agreement, Warehouse Receipt Pledge Guarantee Contract-loan issuance-debt settlement.

(15) Product name: Entrusted Loan.

Issuer: Taizhou Bank.

Product description: Entrusted Loan was funded by government departments, enterprises, institutions or individuals as trustors, then issued, supervised, and assisted to recover by the lender, with the bank as the trustee according to the loan object, purpose, amount, term, interest rate, etc. Appointed by the trustor. The bank provides financial services to the client while it does not bear any form of risk for loans. The amount of the entrusted loan is 50,000 yuan at least, and the specific loan amount shall be agreed by the borrower and the trustee. The term is generally no less than 1 year (inclusive), and no longer than 5 years (inclusive).

Joint guarantee business refers to the guarantee business in which the members of the group jointly provide guaranty for the loans of their members and bear liabilities jointly.

(16) Product name: Joint Guarantee Loan.

Issuer: Taizhou Bank.

Product description: Members of the co-guarantee group only need to sign a guarantee contract with our bank once, and they can use the joint insurance quota within the term of validity. Target clients: generally the regular clients of this bank with stable business. Handling process: accepting application-investigation-review and approval-signing joint insurance contract and loan contract-loan issuance-debt settlement.

(17) Product name: Warehouse receipt inventory pledge loan.

Issuer: Taizhou Bank.

Product description: Warehouse receipt inventory pledge loan involves a tripartite agreement among the bank, the warehousing party and the financing party, with the warehouse receipt issued by the warehousing company for the storage of inventory as the pledge collateral of rights. Inventories covered in this business include: precious metals, steel, iron, copper, aluminum, etc., some plastic or chemical raw materials, and other inventory recognized by the bank. Product features: preferential interest rate, convenient handling, with the advantages of bulk materials, no need for a guarantor. Target clients: those who can provide a permanent and standardized storage location with no mortgage and the storage companies that keep the inventory should be capable of inventory compensation, and willing to sign a tripartite cooperation agreement. Handling process: acceptance of application-investigation-review and approval-signing of Warehouse Receipt Pledge Cooperation Agreement-loan issuance-debt settlement and handover of pledged warehouse receipt.

(18) Product name: Shop Usufruct Mortgage Loan.

Issuer: Taizhou Bank.

Product description: To get Shop Usufruct Mortgage Loan, the client should apply to the bank with the shop usufruct purchased or rented from the market developer as mortgage, and repay the principal and interest either by one-time repayment of principal or by equal principal-and-interest installments within a specified time. The maximum mortgage rate of shops shall not exceed 50% of the assessed value of the collateral. For one-time repayment of principal, the loan term shall not exceed one year (inclusive); for equal principal and interest installments, the loan term is 1 to 3 years (inclusive). Product features: with the advantages of commercial assets, no need for a guarantor. Target clients: individually-owned businesses with shop usufruct. The following requirements should be met: the mortgagor must own the usufruct specified in the shop (booth) use certificate issued by the developer or the owner of usufruct specified on the lease agreement signed between the mortgagor and the developer; the mortgagor has paid the developer in full the shop lease fees up to the expiration date of the store (booth). Handling process: investigation of developers in the shop mortgage market-signing of cooperation agreement-loan application-loan investigation-contract signing-developer's mortgage signing-mortgage registration-loan issuance-post-loan inspection-registration of mortgage termination.

(19) Product name: Ship Mortgage Loan.

Issuer: Taizhou Bank.

Product description: Ship Mortgage Loan refers to the guarantee provided for the debtor's credit business in the bank with the ships owned by the client as the collateral. Product features: preferential interest rate, convenient handling, no need for the guarantor with the ships owned by the client as the collateral. Target clients: those with ownership of built ships. Handling process: acceptance of loan application-investigation-review and approval-sign Mortgage Contract and Mortgage (Ship) List-loan issuance-debt settlement.

(20) Product name: Village Juyi Loan.

Issuer: Taizhou Bank.

Product description: "Village Juyi Loan·Xingnong Card" refers to a debit card with financing function issued in bulk to villagers or members of agricultural cooperatives. In addition to the function of debit card, the borrower and the bank sign the loan contract of "Village Juyi Loan·Xingnong Card" to verify the maximum amount and term of the loan. Within the credit line, the borrower can recycle and self-repay through the counter of the bank's business institution, online banking and other ways.

Product features: Loan limit: the loan limit is less than 300,000 yuan (inclusive), of which 50,000 yuan (inclusive) can apply for a credit free loan. Loan term: no more than two years. Mode of use: recycling, loan upon use, coordinated loan and repayment; the interest is settled on a monthly basis on the 16th day of each month, made by paying off the principal together with interest. Loan object: the farmers in the village and agricultural cooperatives.

Handling process: 1. Application: the bank reaches an overall credit intention with the villages or cooperatives, and launches collective credit and batch card handling. Clients within the scope of business can apply on the spot at the "Village Juyi Loan ·Xingnong Card Recommendation Activity", or go to the sub branch for application. 2. Villages or cooperatives with the cooperation intention can also apply for "Village Juyi Loan ·Xingnong Card" in batches to each branch. 3. Information will be provided with visits. Loan officers will take the initiative to carry out the "one-stop" service door to door and handle in batches; 4. Upon the approval of the loan, the loan contract will be signed; 5. After credit granting, the clients can borrow and repay within the credit line as needed.

(21) Product name: Mutual Guarantee Fund.

Issuer: Taizhou Bank.

Product description: Mutual Guarantee Fund Loan is established by clients who meet the requirements of loan in the bank through appointed intermediate units to initiate and pay deposits. Each client as a member of the fund bears limited liability for the loans of all members with the payment into the fund, and can obtain loans or other credit lines more than five times the amount paid in our bank.

Business features: Credit loan will be granted when paying performance deposit in the fund. As a member of a specific mutual guarantee fund, the client only needs to pay part of the performance deposit to obtain credit loans with convenience in no need of any guarantee. The loan will be issued quickly on demand. The more fund members, the better the credit status, the lower the risk shared. The margin ratio depends on the situation. Membership is reviewed strictly while withdrawal is free. Newly established funds and new members shall be approved by all members with signing. Members shall be fully free to withdraw and the deposit will be returned according to the rules agreed in the articles of the mutual guarantee fund. The fund selects a standardized intermediate unit as the administrator, which is generally a legal corporate organization or legal enterprise (with legal corporate capacity, business license or account opening qualification, together with guarantee qualification) that has a certain influence on member units, such as the Federation of Industry and Commerce, the Economic Promotion Association, the Chamber of Commerce, industry associations, market administrators, government platform enterprises, village enterprises, and core enterprises of supply chain. The promotion will be ensured through self-discipline measures such as mutual supervision among members.

Target clients: Clients in industrial parks, development zones, science and technology parks, commodity trading market and shopping malls; members in chambers of commerce and industry associations; suppliers and other upstream clients and downstream clients of the supply chain recognized by the bank.

(22) Product name: Green Energy-saving Loan.

Issuer: Taizhou Bank.

Product description: Green Energy-saving Loan is issued specifically for industrial clients to save energy and reduce emission, improve energy utilization, update or eliminate outdated capacity. The loan persists in supporting small and micro enterprises to invest in the field of energy saving, efficiency enhancement, reduction of greenhouse gas emissions, promotion of economic transformation and upgrading of small and micro enterprises.

Business description: Loan limit: 50,000 to 5 million(inclusive); loan term: 3 months to 3 years. The loan is used as a special investment to reduce energy consumption in the production process of enterprises.

Repayment approaches can be selected according to the clients' production and operation cycle as well as capital demand, including equal installment, one-time repayment or flexible repayment.

Target clients: 1. Generally legal persons in enterprises, other economic organizations and individually-owned businesses engaged in production as well as management activities with total assets no more than 20 million yuan (inclusive), especially with assets of no more than 5 million yuan (inclusive); 2. New clients or clients with loan balances in the bank.

(23) Product name: Rong E-Loan.

Issuer: Tailong Bank.

Product description: Rong E-Loan follows the mode of "one-time credit, pay-as-you-go and recycling" with multiple channels. Loan issuance and repayment can be operated through electronic channels such as online banking, mobile banking, etc. Three secured loans, i.e. guarantee, mortgage, and pledge are available to flexibly meet the clients' needs. In addition, the clients only need to sign a contract with the bank in advance to complete one-time credit, thus enjoy the convenience of pay-as-you-go and recycling of the loan. Target clients: small enterprises, clients, etc. with frequent borrowing need, regular capital flow and good qualifications.

(24) Product name: Chuangye Tong.

Issuer: Tailong Bank.

Product description:"Chuangye Tong" is launched especially for small and micro business owners, as well as individually-owned businesses. It is a good assistant for business with low access threshold, no mortgage or pledge, fast processing, multiple repayment channels and handling for free. Product features: 1. Online revolving loan. With one-time credit, the clients can borrow and repay at any time online, seamlessly meeting business capital needs. 2. Flexible installment repayment can be customized depending on the state of businesses or capital flow. Target clients: small and micro entrepreneurs, individually-owned businesses and other real economy administrators with regular production and operation.

(25) Product name: Moral Guarantee Loan.

Issuer: Tailong Bank.

Moral Guarantee Loan is issued in condition of the guarantee provided by a third party with a moral relationship with the borrower and the borrower's legal representative. Target clients: SMEs or individuals who are in urgent need of financing without effective guarantees. Provided they or their principals are of good character and credit, together with feasible business projects, the financing can be approached through the primary source of repayment.

(26) Product name: The First Non-Accumulative Loan.

Issuer: Tailong Bank.

Product description: The First Non-Accumulative Loan, with the amount of less than 500,000 yuan and the term within one year, is granted to clients who have no business relationship with Tailong Bank but meet the qualifications. Procedures: 1. The client submits a written application together with relevant basic information to Tailong Bank; 2. Tailong Bank conducts investigation and review prior to approval in accordance with the Rules and Procedures for Loan Business of Zhejiang Tailong Commercial Bank and relevant regulations; 3. Tailong Bank signs the Guaranteed Loan Contract of Zhejiang Tailong Commercial Bank or the Loan Contract, and the Maximum Amount Guarantee or Mortgage (Pledge) Contract with the borrower, then goes through the loan granting procedures.

(27) Product name: Microcredit Loan.

Issuer: Tailong Bank.

Product description: Microcredit Loan, with a certain amount of quota in no need of guarantee, is granted for part of clients with good credit status. Handling procedure: 1. The customer submits a written application and relevant basic information to Tailong Bank; 2. Tailong Bank conducts investigation and review prior to approval in accordance with the Relevant Provisions of Rules and Procedures for Loan Business of Zhejiang Tailong Commercial Bank and the Administrative Measures for Personal Microcredit Loans of Zhejiang Tailong Commercial Bank; 3. Tailong Bank signs the Loan Contract with the borrower, then goes through the loan granting procedures. Target clients: small enterprises, individually-owned businesses or individuals with good credit standing.

(28) Product name: Personal Business Loan.

Issuer: Tailong Bank.

Product description: Personal Business Loan refers to the RMB loan business issued by Tailong Bank to qualified individual businesses, small private enterprise owners (or controlling shareholders, actual controllers) and other natural persons to support their production and operation as well as other reasonable investment needs. Handling procedure: 1. The customer submits a written application and relevant basic information to Tailong Bank; 2. Tailong Bank conducts investigation and review prior to approval in accordance with the Rules and Procedures for Loan Business of Zhejiang Tailong Commercial Bank and relevant regulations; 3. Tailong Bank signs the Guaranteed Loan Contract of Zhejiang Tailong Commercial Bank or Loan Contract, the Maximum Amount Guarantee or Mortgage (Pledge) Contract with the borrower, then goes through the loan granting procedures. Target clients: clients with regular production and management, frequent capital transactions, in occasional and seasonal capital demand, and a certain deposit accumulation.

(29) Product name: Pledged Loan with Fixed Deposit Certificate;

Issuer: Tailong Bank.

Product description: Pledged Loan with Fixed Deposit Certificate refers to the loan business pledged by the unexpired individual fixed deposit certificate and issued by the bank. Handling procedure: 1. The client submits a written application and relevant basic information to Tailong Bank; 2. Tailong Bank conducts investigation, review prior to approval in accordance with the Rules and Procedures for Loan Business of Zhejiang Tailong Commercial Bank and relevant regulations; 3. Tailong Bank signs the Loan Contract, as well as the Right Pledge Contract and the Maximum amount of Right Pledge Contract with the borrower, then goes through the loan granting procedures. Target clients: clients holding unexpired individual fixed deposit certificates issued by the bank and in need of financing.

(30) Product name: Working Capital Loan.

Issuer: Tailong Bank.

Product description: Working Capital Loan is a kind of loan business issued to meet enterprises' needs for short-term capital in the production as well as management so as to ensure the regular operation. The loan term is within one year.

According to different guarantee approaches, working capital guaranteed loan can be categorized as follows: (1) Guaranteed loan, which is granted under the precondition that enterprises, institutions or individuals with good credit standing and compensatory ability, at the request of the borrower, are willing to issue a written commitment to assume joint liability as agreed in case the borrower cannot repay the loan. (2) Mortgage loan, which is granted with the property of the borrower or a third party as collateral according to the mortgage pattern specified in the Guarantee Law of the People's Republic of China. (3) Pledged loan, which is granted with the current assets or rights of the borrower or a third party as the pledge in accordance with the pledge pattern stipulated in the Guarantee Law of the People's Republic of China. Target clients: small enterprises and individually-owned businesses with regular production and management, as well as frequent transactions, in obviously occasional or seasonal capital demands, and a certain deposit accumulation.

(31) Product name: Confirmer Wharf Finance.

Issuer: Tailong Bank

Product description: Confirmer Wharf Finance refers to the specific bill business service carried out by the bank with dealers and suppliers through the tripartite cooperation agreement referring to the warehouse preservation mode, that is, taking the real right control in trade, including goods supervision, repurchase guarantee, etc. as the measures for security. Target clients: commodity trading relationship or debtor-creditor relationship formed by the bulk supply of well-known brand product manufacturers (including their direct sales departments and sales companies) and their main downstream distributors.

Business application subject: the nominal seller in the shipbuilding (transaction) contract. Business content: Business amount: based on the provisions of the ship building (transaction) contract. Business applicants' qualifications: more than 3 years of shipbuilding experience, with disposable funds no less than 40% required for the construction project. Margin ratio: no less than 60%; Financing conditions: subsequent financing assured. Guarantee: provided by the major shareholders and spouse of the ship builder party. Soft guarantee: the use of exposure or subsequent financing funds shall be supervised by the bank; Insurance: the ship under construction shall be insured with Tailong Bank as the first beneficiary.

(32) Product name: Confirmer Wharf Finance.

Issuer: Tailong Bank

Product description: The business application subject should be the nominal seller in the ship building (transaction) contract. The main contents are as follows: the business amount is based on the provisions of the ship building (transaction) contract; the business applicant should have more than 3 years of ship building experience, with the disposable funds no less than 40% of the capital required for the construction project; the margin ratio shall not be less than 60%; the follow-up financing can be provided; Guarantee: provided by the major shareholders and spouse of the ship builder party; Soft guarantee: the use of exposure or subsequent financing funds shall be supervised by the bank; Insurance: the ship under construction shall be insured with Tailong Bank as the first beneficiary.

(33) Product name: Bid Bond.

Issuer: Tailong Bank

Product description: Business application subject is a construction enterprise or an organization combined with the construction enterprise that meets the construction qualification of the relevant bidding project; Business amount: based on the provisions in the bidding documents; Business content: the Bid Bond refers to the written guarantee bond issued by the bank to the tenderee at the request of the bidder (guarantee applicant) during the bidding of the project, to ensure that the bidder will not withdraw his/her bid before the opening of the bid, and will not refuse to sign the contract or pay the performance bond after winning the bid. Otherwise, the bank shall compensate for the loss of the tenderee or pay the specified amount to the tenderee within the scope of the guarantee bond. The margin ratio is 100%.

(34) Product name: Deposit-and-Loan points Linkage.

Issuer: Luqiao Rural Cooperative Bank.

Product description: The Deposit-and-Loan points Linkage refers to a loan mode in which the loan interest rate is determined according to the ratio of the customer's current deposit points accumulated in a certain period to the expected loan aggregate. Single or combined guarantee approaches can be adopted, such as credit, guarantee or mortgage (pledge). Product features: There are a variety of points offset for clients to choose. The more deposits, the more accumulated points, the more interest rate concessions they can enjoy. Applicable objects and target clients: generally legal persons in enterprises or public institutions as well as other economic organizations approved and registered by the administrative department for industry and commerce, and natural persons with full civil capacity, especially for those with long-term and stable cash flow. Loan limit: The corresponding loan limit shall be determined in accordance with demands on production and management as well as credit status of clients. Generally the maximum amount of loan shall not exceed 5 million yuan.

(35) Product name: Shop Leasehold Pledge Loan.

Issuer: Luqiao Rural Cooperative Bank

Product description: Shop Leasehold Pledge Loan refers to a mode in which the client should apply to the bank for a loan with the shop leasehold acquired from the market developer as pledge, and should repay the principal together with interest at one time or by installments within the specified time. Product features: No need for the guarantor with the efficiency of commercial assets; Applicable objects and target clients: individual businesses with the shop leasehold. The mortgagor shall meet the following conditions: the mortgagor must own the shop leasehold specified in the certificate issued by the developer or the lease agreement signed between the mortgagor and the developer; The mortgagor has paid the developer in full the shop leasehold fees up to the expiration date of the shops(booths). Loan limit: the starting point of a single loan is 50,000 yuan, up to 50% of the assessed value of the collateral; Loan term and interest rate: the loan term is generally within one year (inclusive) and shall not exceed half of the store lease term.

(36) Product name: Business Start-up Loan for Homecoming College Students

Issuer: Luqiao Rural Cooperative Bank

Product description: The working capital loan issued by the bank to college students who are registered in Luqiao or have a fixed residence in the service area of the bank, interested in starting a business in the local area, which is used to approach the difficulties in starting the business and financing for college students returning to their hometown for pioneering. Product features: one-time credit, distributed in batches, and recyclable. Applicable objects and target clients: fresh graduates or former graduates from junior schools as well as secondary specialized schools, or above, of full-time colleges, including adult universities and colleges, in the recent three years. Loan limit: generally less than 100,000 yuan, up to 300,000 yuan. Loan term and interest rate: the term of a single loan is generally no more than 1 year, and the longest is no more than 2 years. In accordance with the relevant provisions of the bank on interest rates, preferential interest rates can be applied to clients with good credit and excellent project recommended by the Youth League District Committee.

(37) Product name: Youth Entrepreneurship Loan.

Issuer: Luqiao Rural Cooperative Bank

Product description: Youth entrepreneurship loan refers to the working capital loan issued by the bank to urban and rural youth aged between 18 and 40, which is used to approach the difficulties in starting the business, financing and guarantee of entrepreneurial youth. Product features: one-time verification, loan upon use, simple procedures, preferential interest rate. Applicable objects and target clients: urban and rural young men and women who have fixed residence in the service area of the bank with practical and promising entrepreneurship projects. Loan limit: generally less than 200,000 yuan, up to 500,000 yuan. Loan term and interest rate: generally no more than 1 year, and the longest no more than 2 years. In accordance with the relevant provisions of the bank on interest rates, preferential interest rates can be applied to key projects recommended by the district committee of the Youth League as well as young entrepreneurs.

(38) Product name: Rural Housing Mortgage Loan.

Issuer: Luqiao Rural Cooperative Bank

Product description: Rural Housing Mortgage Loan refers to a short-term working capital loan for production, management or living consumption with the rural houses as mortgage which is legally owned by the borrower who applies to the branch of the bank. Product features: rural housing, the largest asset in the rural market, should be revitalized, to solve farmers' guarantee problem. Applicable objects and target clients: natural persons with two or more rural houses and full civil capacity within the service area of the bank. Loan limit: the maximum loan limit shall not exceed 60% of the assessed value of the collateral. Loan term and interest rate: the term of a single loan is generally less than one year. It shall be executed at the interest rate specified by the bank for rural housing mortgage loan.

(39) Product name: Small Loan for Entrepreneurship.

Issuer: Luqiao Rural Cooperative Bank
Product description: the working capital loan issued by the bank to the land-lost farmers and qualified "new Luqiao people" in the service area for the start-up and development period of entrepreneurship. Product features: low access threshold, few restrictions, no need for deposit points, simple and flexible procedures. Applicable objects and target clients: land-lost farmers and qualified "new Luqiao people" (non-Taizhou citizens who have lived in the service area of the bank for more than two years with residence certificates. Men should not be more than 65 years old and women should not be more than 60 years old. Loan limit: generally between 2000 yuan and 100,000 yuan, up to 300,000 yuan. Loan term and interest rate: the term of a single loan is generally within one year, and the longest term is no more than 3 years. The interest rate shall be subject to the bank's relevant provisions of interest rate pricing management.

(40) Product name: Small Credit Loan.

Issuer: Luqiao Rural Cooperative Bank
Product description: Small Credit Loan is granted by the bank to borrowers with good credit standing for production, management and consumption in no need of any guarantee. Product features: small amount, flexible term, no guarantee, simple procedures. Applicable objects and target clients: generally farmers and self-employed industrial and commercial businesses rated as users with good credit by the bank in its service area. Loan limit: determined according to the credit level, the maximum amount up to 100,000 yuan. Loan term and interest rate: determined comprehensively according to the clients' reasonable demand for capital, credit status, solvency and other conditions, generally no more than one year. The interest rate shall be subject to the bank's relevant interest rate pricing management measures.

(41) Product name: Merchant Hand-in-Hand Loan.

Issuer: Luqiao Rural Cooperative Bank

Product description: Merchant Hand-in-Hand Loan refers to the jointly guaranteed loan issued by the Bank to meet the needs of the specialized market operators for operating capital needs in the service area. Product features: the joint guarantee of five to six operators in the same specialized market. Applicable objects and target clients; operators as members of the joint guarantee team aged 20 to 65 with full civil capacity who have fixed premises in various specialized market in the service area. Target clients are those with potentials whose demands for capital are less than 1.5 million yuan. Loan limit: the loan limit of a single business operator is generally within 50% of the actual net assets, and the maximum is not more than 5 million yuan. Except for the first loan, the overall daily deposit-to-loan ratio of the joint guarantee group should reach beyond 0.2:1. Loan term and interest rate: the term of each loan shall be limited within one year, and the term of joint guarantee shall not exceed 2 years. The loan interest rate can be reduced by 10% within the range of the interest rate of guaranteed loan in the bank at the same level in the same period.

(42) Product name: Housing Loan.

Issuer: Luqiao Rural Cooperative Bank

Product description: Housing Loan refers to the consumer loan issued by the bank to meet the needs of the resettled households to purchase or decorate the resettlement houses. Product features: it can adopt the method of one-time repayment of principal and interest or installment repayment. Applicable objects and target clients: the resettled households aged no more than 65 years old with full civil capacity for the purpose of purchase and decoration whose originally self-built houses in the service area of the bank have been uniformly built by the government after the demolition. Loan limit: the maximum loan limit for the purchase of resettlement houses is generally 70% of the purchase amount, which can be extended to 80%. The loan limit for the decoration of resettlement houses can be up to 70% of the decoration amount. Loan term and interest rate: for the loan to purchase resettlement houses, the maximum loan term is up to 5 years. For the consumption loan to decorate resettlement houses, the maximum loan term is up to 3 years. The loan interest rate shall be subject to the bank's interest rate management measures.

(43) Product name: Loan for Non-local Members ofTaizhou Chamber of Commerce.

Issuer: Luqiao Rural Cooperative Bank

Product description: The Loan for Non-local Members of Taizhou Chamber of Commerce refers to the operational loan granted by Luqiao Cooperative Bank to the Taizhou entrepreneurs and business operators who are going out to run businesses and join the Taizhou Chamber of Commerce, or Luqiao Chamber of Commerce. This kind of loan is used to alleviate and approach the financing and guarantee difficulties of the non-local members of Taizhou Chamber of Commerce. Product features: both mortgage (pledge) and joint guarantee by members of the Chamber of Commerce can be adopted. Applicable objects and target customers: members of non-local members of Taizhou (Luqiao) Chamber of Commerce aged between 20 to 60 years old with full civil capacity, who are registered in Taizhuo or have fixed residence in Taizhou, while operate business outside Taizhou with fixed business premises. Loan limit: The loan limit of a single borrower is generally limited within 50% of the actual net assets, and the maximum limit within 5 million yuan. Loan term and interest rate: The term of a single loan shall not exceed 1 year (inclusive); The term of a jointly guaranteed loan shall not exceed 2 years (inclusive); The term of mortgage and pledge loans shall not exceed 3 years (inclusive). The interest rate shall be subject to the bank's relevant measures of interest rate pricing management.

(44) Product name: Agricultural machinery financial subsidy beneficiary right pledge loan.

Issuer: Luqiao Rural Cooperative Bank

Product description: Agricultural machinery financial subsidy beneficiary right pledge loan is granted by the bank to the borrower with the financial subsidy beneficiary right to purchase agricultural machinery or agricultural facilities and equipment as the pledge guarantee. Product features: the applicant must have the financial subsidy beneficiary right for purchasing agricultural machinery and facilities. Applicable objects and target clients: farmers, rural economic organizations and other agriculture-related organizations engaged in pure agricultural industries such as planting and breeding industry, agricultural machinery operation, etc. within the service area of the bank. Loan limit: the maximum amount of loan shall not exceed the total amount of financial subsidies for the borrower to purchase agricultural machinery or agricultural facilities and equipment. Loan term and interest rate: the loan term is determined according to the borrower's production and operation demand, financial subsidy cycle and other factors, generally one year. The interest rate shall be subject to the benchmark interest rate of the current RMB loan.

(45) Product name: Small Discount Loan for Rural Women's Entrepreneurship.

Issuer: Luqiao Rural Cooperative Bank

Product description: Small Discount loan for Rural Women's Entrepreneurship refers to the financial discount interest loan issued by Luqiao Rural Cooperative Bank to rural entrepreneurial women engaged in agricultural production and operation within the service area of the bank. Product features: implementation of benchmark interest rate with full financial discount interest. Applicable object and target clients: those recommended and confirmed by women's federations at all levels according to entrepreneurship and the capability of promoting surrounding rural women toward common prosperity. Loan limit: generally from 10,000 yuan to 20,000 yuan, those models with outstanding contributions to local women's common prosperity could be granted from 60,000 yuan to 80,000 yuan. Loan term and interest rate: the term of a single loan is generally within one year. The interest rate shall be subject to the benchmark interest rate of the current RMB loan, and the applicant shall apply to the District Women's Federation for the discount interest with the certificate of loan repayment or interest settlement.

(46) Product name: Letter of Guarantee Business.

Issuer: Luqiao Rural Cooperative Bank

Product description: Letter of Guarantee Business refers to the written commitment issued by the bank to the beneficiary of the letter at the request of the applicant to agree that the bank will bear a certain amount of financial liability as agreed when the applicant fails to perform its debts or specified obligations. Business objects and qualifications: The object of issuing the letter of guarantee must be the client who implements the loan credit (except for those with full amount of margin or valuable documents pledged in full amount), and opens basic accounts or general deposit accounts in in branches or departments of the bank.

(47) Product name: Taxi License Pledged Loan.

Issuer: Luqiao Rural Cooperative Bank
Product description: Taxi License Pledged Loan refers to the short-term loan granted by the bank with the borrower's unexpired taxi license as pledge issued by the Municipal Transport Management Division. Loan objects and qualifications: 1.The borrower shall meet the basic conditions specified in the Bank's Detailed Rules for the Management and Implementation of Working Capital Loans and Personal Loans; 2. The borrower shall own an unexpired taxi license issued by the Municipal Transport Management Division; 3. The loan term shall not be longer than the period of validity of taxi license.

(48) Product name: Pledge Loan for Commercial Space Leasehold.

Issuer: Luqiao Rural Cooperative Bank
Product description: Pledge Loan for Commercial Space Leasehold refers to the short-term loan granted by the bank with the borrower's paid leasehold of the market space as collateral. Loan objects and qualifications: 1. The borrower must be a legal person or a natural person to operate business in the market with the right to use the market position and conduct autonomous management; 2. The term of the borrower's leasehold at the time of loan shall be no less than one year; 3. The borrower shall meet the basic conditions specified in the bank's detailed rules for the management and implementation of working capital loans and personal loans.

(49) Product name: Pledge Loans of Accounts Receivable.

Issuer: Luqiao Rural Cooperative Bank
Product description: Pledged Loans of Accounts Receivable is issued by the bank to the borrower with accounts receivable acceptable to the bank as pledge. Accounts receivable refers to the creditor's right formed by an enterprise due to the sale of goods, export tax refund or permission for use of enterprise's assets. Loan object and qualifications: 1. The borrower must be a legal person of enterprise with independent qualification accordingly and able to bear civil liability independently; 2. The pledged accounts receivable have a real and legal trade background; 3. The purpose of the loan is limited to making up for the shortage of working capital; 4. A deposit of no less than 10% of the loan limit shall be paid.

(50) Product name: Guaranteed Loan.

Issuer: Luqiao Rural Cooperative Bank

Product description: Guaranteed Loan is granted by the Bank in the form of guarantee as stipulated in Guaranty Law of the People's Republic of China, which is committed by a third party to undertake joint guarantee liabilities as agreed when the borrower fails to repay the loan. Loan conditions: the clients should be enterprises and public institutions within the jurisdiction of Luqiao. The enterprises and public institutions approved and registered by the department of administration for industry and commerce shall complete the formalities of tax payment registration and annual inspection in accordance with regulations. The products shall have a place in the market, also the production and management are efficient, strictly abiding by the credit with no appropriation of credit funds. It shall have the ability to repay the principal and interest on schedule, which is verified according to the bank's corporate credit rating standards. In principle, the credit rating shall be A or above; The currency is RMB; The loan term shall be determined according to the purpose of the borrowing enterprise, which is generally a short-term working capital loan.

(51) Product name: Working Capital Loan.

Issuer: Luqiao Rural Cooperative Bank

Product description: Working Capital Loan refers to the domestic and foreign currency loan issued by the bank to enterprise, public institutions or other organizations that can act as borrowers as stipulated by the national government (hereinafter referred to as the borrower) for the borrower's daily production and operation turnover. According to different ways of guarantee, it can be divided as follows: Guaranteed loan, issued by enterprises, institutions or individuals with good credit and compensatory ability who, at the request of the borrower, issue a written commitment that if the borrower cannot repay the loan, they will assume joint liability as agreed; Mortgage loan, granted with the property of the borrower or a third party as collateral in accordance with the mortgage mode specified in the Guaranty Law of the People's Republic of China. Pledge loan, granted with the movable property or rights of the borrower or a third party as the pledge according to the pledge mode specified in the Guaranty Law of the People's Republic of China. Basic procedure of working capital loan: loan application-acceptance and investigation of the application-credit rating-credit granting-credit review-loan approval-contract signing-issuance and payment-post-loan management. Functions and characteristics: The loan term is flexible and can meet the temporary, short-term and medium-term liquidity needs of the borrower.

(52) Product name: Enterprise Credit Loan.

Issuer: Luqiao Rural Cooperative Bank

Product description: Enterprise Credit Loan refers to various on-balance-sheet financing businesses such as domestic and foreign currency loans granted by the bank to corporate enterprises or other economic organizations in the form of credit. Loan objects and qualifications: 1. The object shall be in line with the characteristics of small and micro enterprises specified in the Regulations on the Classification Standards of Small and Medium sized Enterprises issued by the Ministry of Industry and Information Technology and the National Development and Reform Commission; 2. The object shall open a basic deposit account with the bank, conducting settlement or credit business with the bank for more than 2 years (inclusive), and establishing a credit relationship with the bank for at least 1 year (inclusive). The reversion rate of operational and investment funds incurred by enterprises in the bank should be above 30% (inclusive); 3. The clients' credit rating shall reach the level of AA or above; 4. The number of financing guarantees for others shall be no more than 5 households, and the total liabilities shall be lower than the net assets. Functions and features: Enterprise Credit Loan can provide support with credit fund for clients' reasonable demand of capital arising from production and management activities. The loan is granted based on the borrower's reputation with no need of guarantee.

Afterword

This book is a tribute to the 20th anniversary of the establishment of Luqiao District, Taizhou City. It is also one of the follow-up achievements of the National Natural Science Foundation of China (NSFC) project "Research on the Strategy of Institutional Innovation to Relieve the Financing of Difficulties of SMEs" (No.: 71341011). This book studies the innovative development of SMEs in Luqiao from the perspectives of the development of small and medium-sized banks in the Luqiao area, the assistance of non-bank financial institutions, the activation of private capital, the ensurance of local governments, and the cross-strait micro finance cooperation, then proposes the "Luqiao Model". Among them, some research results of this book have been published in domestic first-class journals, which is undoubtedly a great recognition of the academic value and practical significance of this book.

In the process of writing the manuscript, we have received strong support and active cooperation from all walks of life. The author would like to thank the leaders of the Taiwan Affairs Office of the People's Government of Zhejiang Province, the Luqiao District Committee, the District Government and the District Financial Office for their care and support, which enabled the manuscript to be successfully completed. I would like to thank Mr. Lihua Ma, Director of the Taiwan Affairs Office of the People's Government of Zhejiang Province, for his valuable and pertinent comments to improve the manuscript. Thanks to Yuanyuan Yu, Deputy Director of the Financial Office of Luqiao District. The detailed

W. Xiao et al., *Microfinance and China's Regional Development*,
https://doi.org/10.1007/978-981-99-1960-4

information he provided and the thoughtful research he arranged have laid a solid foundation for the completion of the manuscript. Thanks to Liexun Yang, Director of the National Natural Science Foundation of China, and Debin Fang, Program Director of the National Natural Science Foundation of China, for their support to the National Natural Science Foundation of China project undertaken by the author; Thanks to Professor Shengju Gu, Vice Chairman of the Finance and Economic Commission of the National People's Congress, Shantong Li, Researcher of the Development Research Center of the State Council, Hanchuan Lin, Professor of the University of International Business and Economics, Professor Huifang Cheng, President of the Global Zhejiang Business Development Research Institute, Zengfu Xing, Chairman of the Bank of Wenzhou, and other experts and scholars. Their suggestions on the case part have laid a foundation for the early study of this book; Thanks to Taizhou Bank, Tailong Bank, Luqiao Rural Cooperative Bank, Luqiao Private Capital Management Center, Agricultural Bank of China Luqiao sub-branch and other institutions for their support and affirmation of the research results, which has brought more confidence and inspiration to the research team; I would like to thank postdoctoral researcher Bin Liu, Dr. Xiang Ma, Shenchao Han, Hao Chen, Lan Li and others from the School of Economics of Zhejiang University for their data collection and field research.

This book has comprehensively and deeply studied the historical background, stage characteristics, innovation mode, experience and enlightenment of the development of small and micro finance of Luqiao, then refined the "Luqiao Model" of the innovative development of small and micro finance, and enriched the existing research achievements of the academic community. However, at this stage, Luqiao has fully grasped the opportunity of national support for the development of small and micro enterprises to explore the "second innovation" of SMEs. For these new phenomena and new models, the book does not cover all of them. We sincerely invite colleagues from the academic and practical circles to put forward valuable suggestions so that we can further improve the study of "Luqiao Model".

What's worth mentioning is that the book was granted the 2020 National Social Science Foundation (Translation Project of the Chinese Humanities and Social Sciences Academic Boutique), and the project led by professor Liang Cai provides us an extra chance to update some data and materials in the 2014 version, including important events, news reports and product innovation. I would like to thank Professor Liang Cai at Ningbo Tech University and Professor Fei Long at Changshu Institute of Technology, together with team members in the translation project, Professor Xuyan Yu at China Academy of Art, Professor Xing Zhao at China Agricultural University, Lingling Wang at Hangzhou Institute of Technology, Xidian Univerisity and Lecturer Ying Ding, Dr. Bin Liu, Professor Xiangyang Xia at Ningbo Tech University in particular. In the past two years, they have mobilized all kinds of resources available to keep the endeavor going. I am grateful to professor Zhiguang Wang, Lecturer Jianmei Chen at Ningbo Tech University, and many scholars and experts who are willing to take their time to proof the English drafts and provide insightful suggestions. I am so grateful to Terence Needham and Dr. Zia Ullah for their meticulous proofreading and revision of the whole book. Without all this, the English version of the book would be impossible.

Wen Xiao
November 2022
Zhejiang University

Index

W. Xiao et al., *Microfinance and China's Regional Development*, https://doi.org/10.1007/978-981-99-1960-4

SPRINGER NATURE

GPSR Compliance

The European Union's (EU) General Product Safety Regulation (GPSR) is a set of rules that requires consumer products to be safe and our obligations to ensure this.

If you have any concerns about our products, you can contact us on ProductSafety@springernature.com

In case Publisher is established outside the EU, the EU authorized representative is:

Springer Nature Customer Service Center GmbH
Europaplatz 3
69115 Heidelberg, Germany

The manufacturer's authorised representative in the EU is Springer Nature Customer Service Centre GmbH, Europaplatz 3, 69115 Heidelberg, Germany. If you have any concerns regarding our products, please contact ProductSafety@springernature.com

Printed and bound by CPI Group (UK) Ltd, Croydon, CR0 4YY
30/09/2026
02225311-0015